Johanna Adriana Ader-Appels

HOUSE OF DEFIANCE:
One Family's Stand against the Holocaust

Translation by Andrew Healey

First Published in Great Britain 2017 by Mirador Publishing

Original 1st edition title: Een Groningen Pastorie in den Storm
Copyright © 1947 by J. Ader-Appels
Uitgeverij Kirchner, Amsterdam
Translation Copyright © 2017 Andrew Healey

First edition: 2017

This book was derived from the wartime diary entries of the author. References to places and war events are factual. Due to the sensitive nature of reporting at the time about real people who were linked in various ways with the Dutch Resistance, most given names and surnames are pseudonyms. Any offence caused by references in the historical narrative is completely unintentional.

A copy of this work is available through the British Library.

ISBN: 978-1-911473-76-3

Mirador Publishing
10 Greenbrook Terrace
Taunton
Somerset
TA1 1UT

Dedicated to Basjan and Erik

Preface

The book in front of you speaks for itself and tells a relevant and compelling story, even though it was written in 1945. All I can add comes from a present day perspective only. When my mother wrote the book she was not yet aware of the full extent of the rescue work organised by my father with the cooperation of the Resistance. The Holocaust museum 'Yad Vashem' in Jerusalem estimates that he managed, with the help of many, to rescue between two to three hundred Jewish compatriots. The full extent of his work will never be known, given its clandestine character. What is being told here is inspiring enough as it stands. Amongst many other things it is also a testimony of what an immense source of strength and joy their religious conviction was for my parents, as well as a moral imperative they could not possibly ignore.

My mother was committed to continue the work in their parish begun by my father, particularly in the outlying village of Drieborg that had not received a fair share of the attention of the church until they came to serve there. She did that as long as she was capable, well into her seventies. To safeguard this work for the future she created a fund, supplied by donations and the proceeds of her book in the Dutch, German and Finnish languages. Via the fund she managed to build a small church in the aforementioned village. The fund still makes a significant annual contribution to the work of the Protestant Church in the region. The proceeds of this translation will be used for the very same purpose.

Their eldest son, my brother, is the conceptual artist Basjan Ader, lost at sea in 1975. For the interpretation of his art more and more people turn to his youth and background, with good reason. This book is an invaluable source to that end.

The book enjoyed 13 reprints in Dutch over the years and was translated into German and Finnish.

We owe an enormous debt of gratitude to the translator Andrew Healey that this book is now also accessible to an English speaking audience. It was his initiative and he took it upon himself to translate it to the high standard you will find here. He did so literally pro deo, and also as a labour of love and dedication to my parents and what they stood for. We cannot be grateful enough.

Erik Ader
Chairman of the Reverend Ader Foundation.

Foreword

Finally this book is finished, a task which I commenced in 1943. During the war years it has been for the most part kept aside while certain parts of the narrative were being collected and added. When I started to write it, I never knew that its course would take it to what it has become. It is dedicated to my two boys, and to all who have known my husband and loved him and who recognise that he has fallen as a faithful son of his country.

In the end, its target is that great crowd of people, both inside and outside the Church, whom Domie always addressed, and for whom this book is to be a living testimony. But even writing such a book requires sacrifice. There are things which one would preferably like to keep to oneself. There are moments of weakness and doubt, which occur in everyone's life and that signifies a yielding of something precious; for all honest revelation there is a price to be paid.

But integrity demands this to be done, in that the story of genuine people is drawn from actual flesh and blood, with their very real and present temptations, their doubts, their struggles – and their faith as well. All linked together with their joys and sorrows. This account has been drawn from real human experiences, and to serve reality is its intention. That is the reality of God's Kingdom, whose strength is given to fill all our human weaknesses. In this province of our country there are many debts of the Church that remain unpaid. Some of her officials have irresponsibly neglected their duties and have rendered the Gospel powerless. They were not shepherds who gave up their lives for the sheep but just hirelings fleeing danger, and they left the good and right way, to create the difficulties that their ministry brought upon us, even in ordinary times.

There is still much work to be done; there is still unfinished business. There is the yet unfulfilled wish to found a church at Drieborg (the most populous part of our community) to which cause the proceeds from this book will be directed. His fidelity to the Church meant he did not wish to abandon her, for so much of her was to make good of what was corrupt. However, an entire lifetime of dedicated service would be needed to undo the damaged integrity of the Church here and transform its debit back into full credit. My two little boys are with me. They shall need to take up the flaming torch and carry it as a banner when they are full grown. Then I shall consider my working hours as over. And I can still be thankful for every single day given to me in order to accomplish the task I was handed.

Nieuw Beerta, end of May, 1945.
J. A. Ader-Appels

Chapter 1

The train steamed through the countryside. It was a royal holiday; in 1938 our Queen was celebrating her 40th Jubilee and I had time off, starting at noon. I could just do it; aboard the train by 1pm and by midnight I'd be back in Amsterdam. There were villages arrayed in festal decorations all along the line; flags and patriotic banners, here and there a single orange Chinese lantern. Our nation was a devoted people, whose culture expressed it in this way. The upbeat mood was reflected in lively conversations between people who were boarding and leaving the train. But I had to remain seated, because I was bound for a place even further than Groningen in the far north: right to the end of the Dutch railway line and the flat farmlands, beyond which lay the sea. Because there a lowland village awaited its new pastor and his wife... and I was that wife. An old *pastorie*[1] awaited us; our next home that had to be painted and brightened up before the arrival of its new occupants. *Could Mevrouw*[2] *just pay a visit? Then she might say how she would like to have it decorated.* Not so simple, though... the Director of the editorial office in Amsterdam where I then worked wasn't generous with granting leave. But on account of the 40th Jubilee celebrations he did give me the afternoon off. I jumped at the chance! The excellent train connections then made it possible for me to journey there and back in the 12 hours between noon and midnight. The train sped over the Veluwe... through

---

1   Residence of a Minister of the Reformed Protestant Church of the Netherlands, similar to a rectory or manse.

2   Mrs or Madam – a polite form of address, common in pre-war Dutch society, here referring to the author herself, but also used to address other married women, even among her associates and friends.

Overijssel and Drenthe... and everywhere en-route the villages were decorated; everywhere was caparisoned with banners and hanging orange lanterns. But the villages themselves were quiet and empty, for whoever could do so was today in the capital[3]. There the real party would be in full swing! And I would not be able to join in. Not today – not in the least! The previous evening I had already seen the beautifully illuminated canals and their buildings. Even the sombre edifice on the Keizersgracht where I worked was festooned and lit up. In the train I daydreamed again about the festival illuminations of Amsterdam, about the town squares with their banners and about the *pastorie* that had to be painted. The kitchen would have to be blue. *Ja[4]*, blue...

We had reached Assen. Now, just beyond came Groningen... and then the hinterland. I had seen it once before, that wide fertile hinterland, when I had gone there with my husband. At that time our predecessors still lived in the *pastorie*. And I had found it so lovely: fields of wheat with many large farms nestling between copses of taller trees. As soon as I'd stepped over the threshold of the *pastorie* I'd felt at home. It really was a fine old house with plenty of character. What would it look like now? It stood abandoned, the previous Minister's family having already departed for their new residence elsewhere. But it wouldn't be much longer before I caught a glimpse of the familiar farmsteads. The rail connections were very good in the days before the war. Once we reached Groningen I wouldn't have long to wait.

At Nieuweschans, the end of the line, I got an unexpected surprise. Someone came up to me and greeted me; a man serving on the Church Council with whom I had made acquaintance on my previous visit. He had been standing there waiting beside his car. So I shortly found myself sitting next to him in the front seat and we started off. Along the way he pointed out the various sights. See that big white house? That's where a

---

3   Although the seat of Dutch government is in The Hague, the capital city is Amsterdam.
4   "Yes" in Dutch, Flemish and German.

well-known member of parliament lived. And he himself lived over here, and another Church Council member there and then there yet another. And we had just joined a new road, that short-cut the old route by a fair bit. Consequently it was very much nicer now, since the old way had such awfully sharp bends. "*Ja*, and see... there's the church tower, and we're just about there..." because opposite the church stood the *pastorie*.

The car pulled up with a lurch and we stepped out, one from each side. *Ja*, there indeed stood the *pastorie*... and it looked even more friendly and familiar than I recalled, since the curtains were still gracing the windows, just as we had agreed. You should know that we would take over a house built according to the classic symmetrical design: a front door right in the middle with a *stoep*[5] and two very tall sash windows on both sides of it. Above on the upper floor were five smaller windows. Then a sloping roof, with, at opposite ends of the ridge, two symmetrical, sturdy chimneys, each with a four-sided pointed cap.

On the *stoep* I caught the odour wafting through the open door. The painter was busy. He was kneeling on the hallway floor, brushing the exposed wood on the edges, where the broad runner had been removed. Then a giant of a man with a welcoming friendly face appeared from one of the side rooms and approached me. He had a salt and pepper goatee and matching hair, neatly parted on one side. The clear blue eyes lay like deep pools in their sockets. This man looked like someone I'd seen before. All of a sudden I remembered! He looked like 'de lawd' (the Lord) from the 1936 film *The Green Pastures*. He proffered me his hand, and then from an empty room, where it reeked of fresh glue from the pasted strips of wallpaper, yet another member of the gang emerged. This one had a round and open face and he smiled a little shyly when he offered me his hand. "Welcome, *Mevrouw*," he said. He was introduced to me by the name Elderling. The one who had accompanied me there said something to the others in *Gronings*, the dialect of Groningen, which

---

5   An external platform or pavement at the threshold of a door, often with steps.

at the time I didn't yet understand, but what it amounted to was they could surely continue now without him. He took his leave and departed.

Now began a very systematic tour of the house: first up to the loft. "You know," said 'the Lord', who turned out to be one of our Churchwardens, "one of your predecessors really ruined the layout here; for over there they had a small room built, which doesn't belong in a loft." I was surprised, but kept silent. Why wouldn't it belong? To me it looked just fine. You could accommodate a guest there in summer when the house was packed to the rafters, however it appeared to be contrary to provincial customs, and so I said nothing. In the bedrooms, one floor below, evidently canvas tarpaulins or some other protective floor covering had been laid down everywhere, so nothing would damage the painted floors.

"Of course we'll also have these floors painted," said 'the Lord'.

"These floors? But there's nothing wrong with them!" I responded. "I'd much prefer to have the kitchen painted."

'The Lord' looked thoughtful. "You mean nothing needs to be done to the floors at all?"

"*Ja...* that's right. Absolutely. There's always something covering them anyway, and I'll put some rugs down as well," I said. "But the kitchen does look rather sombre and shabby. It would give me great pleasure if you had it painted blue."

The pronouncement was now made. The brown kitchen would become blue, and yet apparently my chosen colour was completely disharmonious. The good face of 'the Lord' displayed a look of reproach. He merely responded, "Blue?"

I sought and found support from the other Church Councillor. "If nothing needs doing to the bedroom floors, then perhaps there is no objection against it," he replied.

We came down the stairs. "Well no... but blue?" said 'the Lord'.

Opposite the staircase was the kitchen. 'The Lord' lifted the latch of the door and we went inside. The painter was called over. He was a small, old fellow with glasses, the very image of a philosopher.

The conversation now proceeded in the *Gronings* dialect and I stood there feeling rather out of it. The painter was apparently also fully set against my choice of blue, I could tell, but he simply responded, "As *Mevrouw* wishes..." He would prepare a small sample and then *Mevrouw* could see for herself.

And so he went to mix it. Rembrandt could not have done a superior job. When it was ready, he deftly brushed a small patch on the door frame.

"See now – *Mevrouw* must take a look."

It really gleamed rather nicely, I thought, but it rather resembled the garishly bright colour of laundry blue.

"Can't you make that a little darker?"

"I'll have to mix a bit of black through it."

More mixing then once again a deft brush stroke against the door frame.

"That's better."

"Very well then, we'll do the same on the walls."

"And the inside of the cupboards?" I asked, again with a hopeful glance at the Church Councillor. Once more he sprang to my aid.

"Since the floors upstairs won't be painted..." he began again.

"Alright then," said 'the Lord', stepping over all his previous objections. "That's how it will be. Would *Mevrouw* now like to choose a wallpaper?"

We all moved to the room that reeked of wallpaper paste. The painter was already busy pasting lining paper strips on the walls. Over the top of those I wanted to have a light-coloured design. He sought out a suitable one from a pattern book.

Then the tour continued throughout the house. In the scullery I got another surprise. It had just started to rain and inside the cistern there sounded the monotonous gurgling tone of running water.

"What's that?" I asked.

"That's the water supply that you will need to pump up... to wash with when you live here," stated 'the Lord'.

"And to cook food?"

"*Ja*, that as well. Outside there is a downpipe trap which removes the debris from the gutters, such as leaves and the like. You must remember to check that and make sure you keep it clear."

It suddenly seemed all very complicated – keeping house here without plumbing and gas.

"But you can cook with electricity," said the Councillor, as if he had discerned my thoughts.

"Is that expensive?" I carefully enquired.

"You'll need to ask my wife, when you visit her for a meal," he said. "She also cooks with electricity."

"I'd like to take a look at the leaf-trap filter," I said.

"It's out the back. Come with me."

The door-bolt was released and we went out and stood at the rear of the house. I saw an overgrown vegetable garden before me. 'The Lord' followed my gaze. He shook his head disconsolately and quoted a Dutch proverb: *Whoever neglects his cabbage patch for one year will be weeding it for seven.*

But to me this wilderness seemed a veritable paradise! Growing here and there amongst the weeds were flowers and even vegetables that in the city you'd pay a hefty price for. And it would all be ours! Perhaps it was already ours... a little anyway. All of a sudden it hit me how lovely it would have been each morning back in Amsterdam to place a pair of flowers on my bureau and what a happy surprise would have greeted my husband if he could have had freshly cooked cabbage on the table each day, picked that very morning from our small *pastorie* garden in the city. Overcoming my shyness, I coyly asked, "I'd really like to take some flowers with me to Amsterdam as well as a small cabbage from the garden. I suppose no-one else needs them?"

"No," said 'the Lord'. "As *Mevrouw* wishes... but really, they're nothing special at all."

They demonstrated the trap filter. Then we turned to go inside. I wandered slowly through the kitchen and passageways to the small room where the painter was going about his business. But where had my companions gone off to? Then suddenly out of nowhere, they re-appeared at my side. 'The Lord' had picked a sweetheart cabbage which he handed to me. And behind him stood the Councillor with a shy smile on his face, as in his hand he held – just as any man would, upright and stiff, as if it were another cabbage – a posy of flowers from the garden. At that very moment I lost my heart to this land and its folk. To the land because of the cabbage and the flowers, to the folk because of their reserved friendliness, which approached and embraced me on my first visit to my new home.

Chapter 2

Once again the train was passing through the changing countryside. It was now the end of September. I glanced out the window. The wheat that several weeks ago had stood in sheaves, had been brought in. The fields were decked with golden stubble. Here and there were patches of ploughed up land, open and black under the lowering clouds. A solitary crow flew in the direction of a copse of gold-tinted trees. In the air hung the stillness of autumn.

And home we go, and home we go, sang the wheels monotonously. But I was not yet freed from my old life, from my work and from the people whom I liked in the city I trusted... Amsterdam with her canals that lay there dreaming under this autumn day. I had to serve out my time in the office, through to the end of the month. Now everything was already gone from our canal house... we the occupants together with our furniture. It would be lovely to find everything again, installed at the now shipshape and spruced up *pastorie*. It would be good too to find my husband there, and in the middle of all the activity, to have a quiet moment with him, if necessary sitting together on an empty packing case. How far would they have got by now? And would our housemaid Greet, who had come with us from Amsterdam, like my blue kitchen, despite the prediction of my husband that she would find it perfectly dreadful due to the colour? Had I been too stubborn about it, to go against the advice of the Churchwardens, painter and other experts? After all that debate, I'd really just have to wait and see, which would not be long now, since the distant towers and windmills that gradually slipped into view, stood on Groningen land; the towers standing just apart from the churches and often topped with gable roofs.

I have to alight at the next stop. I am thinking that there will be no-one there to pick me up this time, as I am arriving rather earlier than I had notified by letter. How will I manage with my heavy case? I can't very well undertake an arduous three quarters of an hour walk carrying that. But it doesn't fall out too badly. There is a taxi there waiting on the station forecourt. The obliging driver opens the door when he sees me struggling through the ticket barrier with my heavy load. I cannot resist his inviting gesture and so get into the taxi and sit beside him. I have nothing to say.

"To the *pastorie*, j*a*?" he asks with a grin.

"*Ja.*"

Along the way we encounter typical Dutch sand-lorries for earth and road construction, standing here and there.

"What purpose do these serve?" I query, my interest aroused.

"Those get driven out on the roads every evening for constructing defences," the driver informs me. Then we find we must navigate through a roadblock and pass gun emplacements. I start to understand. This is a time of war and rumours of war and the month of September in the year of 1938 seems rather strange. The sand-lorries induce in me a frisson of awe. Not a single enemy takes all this defensive effort seriously. But will the gun nests nevertheless have to do their duty, perhaps even quite soon, while we are still living here? My husband has written me a letter this week; he asked if it still made any sense to unpack our furniture here... and if we were possibly standing on the eve of a frightful catastrophe. What to say? But in the words of Longfellow, I have written back:

Do thy duty, that is best,
Leave unto thy Lord the rest.

"Here we are." The voice of the taxi driver startles me out of my reverie. We sort out the fare and he carries my suitcase to the gate. I thank him and say that I can manage the rest of the way myself.

He drives off. Evidently no-one has heard the car stop, since no-one comes to open the front door. Light streams out from the ground floor windows of the living room. I walk up to them. I put down my suitcase under one windowsill and peek curiously inside, recognising all the items which stand there in their new surroundings. *Ja*, the dresser is along that wall, just as I had intended... and there is the piano. But the pastel drawing of the sheepfold hanging there isn't quite right; we shall have to find another place for it. The round table is not too big for this room and the chairs around it also are well suited. And that wrought iron lamp that we had made in Amsterdam especially for this room... isn't it hanging a bit too low? Slowly my eyes take ownership of these things. Slowly they become my possession once again.

Ah, look! On the windowsill there are flowers... autumn asters they are, together with goldenrod. These ones bloom right here in this garden. After all, I have already taken a posy with me to Amsterdam the last time I was here! Now a warm feeling of happiness streams inside, into my heart, because this... this room, this house, is now ours!

And surely somewhere about there must be an empty packing case! Because I'm not standing outside here a moment longer, just like a child full of yearning in front of a Christmas window display. I am going inside, and then I shall search throughout this large, untidy house, or in the stables, which are built against the *leerkamer*[6], until I have found my husband. And then we shall find that empty packing case upon which it will be so good to sit together!

During our first autumn in the *pastorie* we experienced many glorious days. Days when it was so still that with the wind from the west, you could hear the train in the far distance, gliding along its rails. That was always a very special sensation, as the train bound you to the

---

6   "Learning/training room." A general purpose room or annex for teaching
     catechism and church activities, holding men's, women's and youth meetings etc.
     Serves a similar purpose to a small church hall in the UK.

world that you had left behind. And up to the railway, as far as the eye could see, stretched huge tracts of arable land that were being ploughed. Heavy, glossy brown horses walked before the ploughshare. They trudged straight forward and cast clods of red earth about, on which hungry crows alighted. All around you, you could see far, far away, to where your eyes would rest on the point of a distant tower, or a mill, yet on every side stretched the breadth of this still land, and above the fields rippled the hazy blue sky.

In these days I thought often about the parable of the Sower. Figuratively, much of this land lay still fallow, which must first be thoroughly ploughed before the Word could be sown. And such ploughing was heavy work. We ourselves were the horses, figuratively speaking, who must be harnessed to the plough. The whole day we were harnessed, because everything had to be built from the ground up. And so it came to pass. First, the youth work. We initiated jigsaw activities, recitals, singing and learning to play the flute, handicrafts, and of course most important of all, Bible teaching (since each Protestant Association was obliged to teach catechism).

Soon enough a Women's Fellowship was started up. And soon enough the *leerkamer* became too small and had to be extended. The adjoining stables were put to good use. With the boys efforts, storage cabinets and a stage were built. My husband designed a ladder that could retract into the ceiling when not in use, in order to fetch fuel down from the *leerkamer* loft. *Ja*, as far as resourcefulness goes, Domie[7] was about as good an engineer as they get.

Patience, love, dedication, working and praying. In all these things we often fell well short, but that indeed was the daily program. Little by little something was won, something that carried the beautiful name of 'trusting'. Step by step the people started to let go of their reserved

---

7   In the northern provinces this is a term of endearment for a Dominee – a Minister of the Reformed Protestant Church.

attitude of *laten we de kat eens uit den boom kijken* (let's just wait and see). Time and time again there were things that made us rejoice... unexpected friendships, faithful words, timely help offered during a mouse infestation.

For that was our first inexperienced brush with the life of the flatlands, in that we hadn't reckoned on the mice!

Domie as a young man.

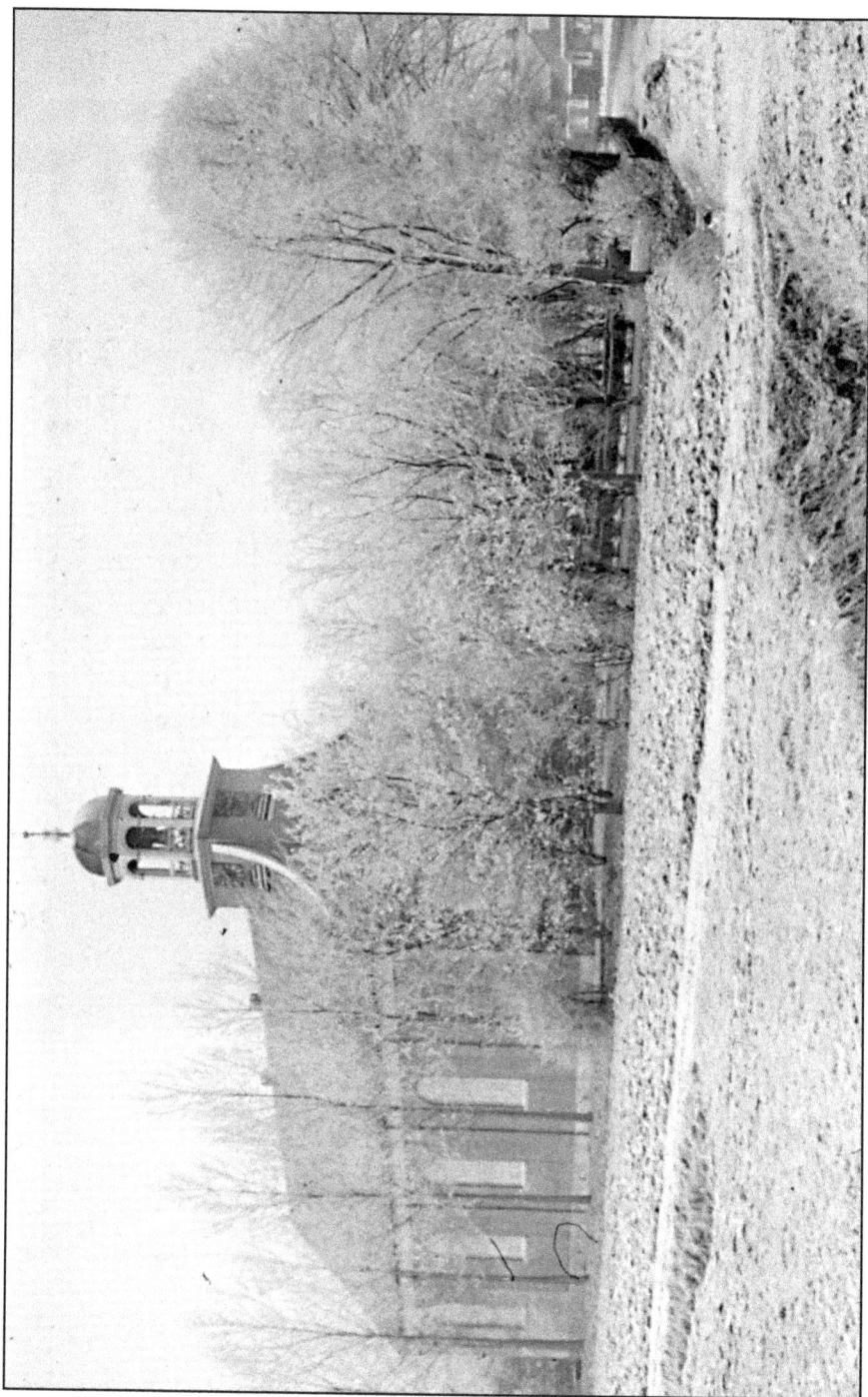

The church at Nieuw Beerta.

The Pastorie at Nieuw Beerta: Greet with the author on the front stoep. The leerkamer is the small extension on the right hand side of the house.

Chapter 3

During harvest, the threshing machine visits each farm here in turn. Among the wheat-sheaves around the large barns hide hundreds of mice that are now being startled out of their rest. But since not all of the grain is threshed at the one time, the mice are not all driven away immediately from their land of plenty. Most remain and scurry under the next stook. However, many of them find themselves without shelter as the wheat is progressively gathered from the fields and stored, and so seek better accommodation in the houses. One must be familiar with nature's laws of the land in order to know that, but at that point, we were completely raw and unsuspecting novices.

We had been away a couple of days and had left the cellar window open. The mice considered this an open invitation along the lines of "Come inside boys!" And when we returned on Saturday evening, we could see that the house during our absence had developed a well-lived in look through the actions of those little thieves. They had munched at the apples and relished the cheese. They also chewed a hole in the Brabant[8] cloth. At every turn we discovered further nasty surprises. Sadly, those creatures had wreaked absolute havoc. We had to lay down poisoned wheat grains here and there all around the house. On that particular Saturday evening after our homecoming we went to bed with a troubled heart. We heard the mice scuffling and squeaking behind the wallpaper, we heard them dancing on the tarpaulin under our bed, and

---

8   A decorative item, such as a wall hanging, made from quality woven woollen cloth manufactured in the southern province of Brabant.

whenever we switched on the light, we saw their instant flight to all corners of the room. We seemed to suffer no fewer mice than the Egyptians saw frogs during the second plague! What kind of defence could we muster against them? Nothing at all! It depended on their own courteous cooperation as to whether they would eat of the poisoned wheat or not. And they would almost certainly wise up and go for something better!

"A cat," I offered, cautiously.

"No, not a cat," said Domie, while by the light of the bedside lamp he checked if he had set the alarm to half-past six... because on Sunday mornings he was always up early. "With a cat you have even more trouble than with mice, and now let's try to forget about those wretched creatures, or by morning I'll have slept not even half the night." That was indeed so, and out of respect for his preaching I started no more nightly discussions on the pros and cons of a cat. When the light was switched off, I did my best to not hear the scuffling and the squeaking behind the wallpaper, nor the dancing on the tarpaulin that immediately began when it became dark in the room, and tried to fall asleep.

I don't know how it is in other pastorates, but in this one each Saturday night through to Sunday is always short. We often sit in the study until way past the midnight hour. Sometimes we talk over the sermon together and sometimes we have a chat that has little or no bearing on it at all. But while this is going on Domie is indeed working on it, as he terms it. Hence his subconscious mind is busy, I imagine, for I have no other explanation for the remarkable fact that he can discourse on many other topics and meanwhile the raw materials are all being brought together for constructing a sermon. Sometimes he also sits and reads, but I must not go to bed, even so. The atmosphere must not become silent and unsociable at home. I must stand by him, even if I already do all kinds of domestic chores, like bolting doors and tending to stoves and such trifles that always must be finished before nightfall. And therefore I managed to finally to drop off to sleep at 2am, putting all problematic thoughts of mice and cats out of my head. Has not each day enough of its own trouble and shall not the morning care for itself?

The morning came soon enough, as right at half-past six the alarm rattled in its leather case. My husband picked it up to switch it off. Then his fingers felt something strange. He opened his eyes wider and saw that our dear little friends had gnawed all round the leather casing during the night.

"And to think that this was my birthday present from you," he said gloomily.

"*Ja*, and do you think they really had that fact in mind? Those little vandals have scant respect for our most sublime feelings," I responded.

But my husband, with his violated trusty travel alarm in his hand, could not appreciate my humour so early in the morning, and so I turned over with my face away from the light, to weave myself a sequel and resolution to all my dreams.

But when I awoke from my fantasy I readily observed that the mice had not spared me their attentions either. There's an item of women's under-clothing we call a 'step-in'. Well then, when I stepped into it, it suddenly showered wheat grains upon the floor. And with that revelation manifested the horrible lack of respect that characterises the rodents; they had not foregone to exploit this intimate garment as their storehouse and during the night had kept busy with hoarding foodstuffs for themselves. Probably they had brought all these stuffed in their cheeks, mouth by mouth, up to the chair on which my clothes lay. How they then clambered up, time after time, they themselves would know best. Most likely by means of my slip draping over the edge, regarding it as a funicular. Or perhaps by sometimes clinging to each other's tails as a climbing rope.

Just imagine it... a mouse is sitting high up on the chair like a princess on the throne, and letting her tail hang down. From it hangs a second mouse, then on her tail a third, and so on, until they reach the ground. The uppermost empties her cheeks, which bulge with the deadly wheat grains, depositing them in my 'step-in'. Then number two arrives and does likewise. And so on and so forth along the whole chain. One must think of the coming winter, *ja*? And in the time of flooding, after the example set by Joseph, gathering grain for the seven lean years.

"Isn't this a good idea for the sermon for this morning?" I suggested.

"Now, you mustn't pull me out of my own world of thoughts with your little jokes," said Domie.

I just kept silent. He was right. On Sunday mornings he couldn't abide frivolity.

But we were hit hardest when the sexton turned up with the preacher's gown. Churches in Groningen don't have an assigned room for the Consistory[9] to meet. Instead we use the *leerkamer* attached to the *pastorie*. In the church itself there is only a small vestry in front, where the preacher puts on his gown; so the sexton dutifully brings over the case of vestments for us.

On this particular morning he need not have done that, because when I pulled the gown out of the case, it was completely spoiled!

The sharp little teeth of the mice had left their bite marks all over it. On top the velvet collar drooped its frayed ends, and there were marks right down to the hemline. We conferred together on the damaged vestment. This was so absolutely shocking, that the mice had not desisted to so thoroughly destroy it.

"No gown this morning," I said to the sexton. "The mice have chewed it to shreds."

So Domie preached that morning dressed in his normal suit jacket. It all went rather well actually, but I saw the congregation looking astonished when he entered the church. They were not accustomed to such attire.

---

9   In the Dutch Protestant Church, the Consistory is a governing body of elders appointed to administer the affairs and care for the assets of the Church, either locally over a congregation or regionally and nationally through higher level appointees.

As usual the members of the Church Council and Churchwardens remained behind after the service. But no-one remarked over the jacket or asked anything. Among the fine upstanding citizens of Groningen it just isn't done. They simply wait until you raise the matter yourself.

But then Domie launched into an explanation with a shy smile; it really was such a very strange story regarding those mice! "*Ja*, but now you're really up against it," said the 'brothers'. Inasmuch as they would not allow themselves to laugh, they were committed to our plight. And they all wanted to do something about it immediately. A lot more poisoned wheat was brought to us in boxes with a grinning death-head skull on top. I thought of the 'occupying hordes' and how their death wish had been granted. They had even put together from that poison a little stash before winter!

"We already have enough poisoned wheat," I said. "But haven't you something else more terminal, like a trap or something?"

Now 'the Lord' had the floor. "Well look," he said, "it's really and completely our fault; we should have warned you that it's like this every harvest time with the mice. Tomorrow the carpenter will pay you a visit and stop up tight any cracks and holes. The gown must be repaired at the cost of the Council. Where was it made?"

"At Jörgs in Utrecht," replied Domie.

"Then will you just send it off to him there and submit the bill to us."

That was a very fair outcome, we thought; to stand accountable for the damage.

Next came an elderly gentleman with a huge rat trap. This was set in the corridor. For your ultimate pleasure you should march right into it if you were a mouse (at least according to our logical way of thinking), but of course we caught nothing with it at all.

And a Deacon – I shall introduce him to you by the name De Lange, as later in the narrative you'll make your acquaintance with him – brought along a bag full of small spring-loaded mousetraps so by that time there were really no more rooms that didn't have an array of traps ready and set. And having convinced themselves that there remained no dark corner of the corridor or cellar without bait, the gentlemen departed. Now we had to carefully navigate through the house, because if the floor was stepped on too heavily, you were startled by the sudden sound of a nearby trap snapping shut.

Our neighbour made fun of all this – writing some verse for our village revue:

The Mice

Our Domie had to make a broadcast,
Preaching down in Amsterdam.
The family also travelled with him,
An outing's fun – and fit the plan!
The pastorie was left in silence,
Doors and windows shut up tight,
Except one tempting cellar window,
Trouble's looming out of sight!

Emboldened mice crept through that window
And explored the cellar space.
Undisturbed they ventured further,
What a house to make their base!
So they spread and took it over,
Nothing there could be a threat.
Zeal and greed did push them onward,
E'en more pleasures waited yet.

Rugs and carpets, tasty clothing,
Gnawed away in lusty bites,
Holes appeared in Domie's toga,
All to sate their appetites.
Chomping beasties did not spare
Voracious attacks on certain stuff,
So just the buttons were left over,
And tattered shreds and cotton fluff.

Frocks and robes and cloths and slippers,
Were not immune to teeth employed.
E'en the alarm clock's leather lining
On the casing was destroyed.
Domie came home from his journey,
What a cloud came o'er his face,
As the mice scrammed through the cracks and
Headed for their hiding place.

The entire village came to help then,
Donating traps and baits galore.
Snapping traps went off at random,
Whenever someone stomped the floor.
The outcome is extremely pleasing,
That those mice must die or flee.
Now you can sleep sweetly, soundly,
From the plague, for now, set free!

But in reality, all this effort was not sufficient. Temporarily freed from the scourge, it would only be resolved in our favour by the arrival of a small kitten.

Chapter 4

This story deals with farm folk and animals in a Groningen community centred around our *pastorie*. The animals play an almost equally important role as the people. The first one that we took in here was a small kitten; I might call her a vagabond. We named her Mieke[10]. Why? Well... because the name suited her to a tee. She was brought to our door by a couple of children, who had dared to rescue her out of the clutches of some adolescent boys. They assured me fervently that these lads had wanted to strangle it. And so I stood then with the scrawny, neglected kitty in my hands, who, courtesy of much hardship and mistreatment had become timid and so looked about anxiously. How would I cope with that little bundle? "By loving it, of course," said a tender voice inside me.

Ja, but hadn't Domie pronounced himself not in favour of expressing fondness for a cat? He came out of the room and saw me standing holding the small black kitten.

"Those boys wanted to strangle it," I said by way of explanation. "Why don't we then just put it here in the shed?"

At the sight of that small miracle my husband threw overboard all his previous objections against cats. He came to stand next to me and stroked its head.

"It's just how it's meant to be," he said.

And so Mieke came to win the contest for our hearts... all within a few minutes.

---

10 The name means a gangster's moll.

Provided with some hay and a small basket, Mieke was installed in the shed. For the time being, she did not emerge from her new abode. She was all worn out. And so she slept the whole day through, rolled up as a small, downy black ball. Then she stood up, arched her back, yawned so that her little rose tongue and her sharp teeth could be seen, drank her saucer of milk dry and began after that to wash herself ever so thoroughly. The tiny claws stroked behind her ears and over the nose and with her substantial Saturday spruce-up behind her, Mieke appeared to be as spiffy as a well-drawn black and white cat should be, with a pair of sharp, beady eyes.

The late autumn sun was shining inside, and Mieke wanted to step out for a stroll; to take a good look around in order to get to know her surroundings. She did that every now and then, but now she began to stay away really rather too long for her own good. Perhaps due to being a stray, or was it that vagabond blood running in her veins, so that she had no choice in the beginning but to run away time and time again? She was spotted once here, once there. But time and time again, the local children brought her back. Thenceforth she became known as Domie's kitty, since everything that belongs to the *pastorie* is regarded in the Groningen countryside as 'Domie's'... even *Mevrouw* Domie! Fine – I granted Domie the right to his kitty, for he was mad about her. He played with the tiny thing whenever he had time for it (and sometimes even when he didn't). Mieke then lay on her back grabbing out with both forepaws, like a pair of hands, toward Domie's hands, or she went to crouch on her hind legs like a little black footman and grabbed, while her sharp little twinkling eyes gleamed with pleasure. And when Sunday came and Domie preached in black and white, then it was apt that a very tall Domie and a very small Domie were at play together. For Mieke always turned out in black and white.

Mieke's tummy at first tolerated only a minimal amount of food.
"Its stomach is damaged," said our washerwoman.

But gradually things got better and after a couple more weeks she'd so recovered that Mieke no longer just ate, but devoured!

Was she now catching up with the other cats that were born at the same time as she was? Perhaps. At any rate, for the most part she succeeded, because when our washing lady returned after a fortnight and saw Mieke, she clapped her hands together. "It's a miracle, how much it's grown!" she exclaimed.

And who wouldn't have been worried? Not us though. Even in a pastor's life not everything is sweetness and light. But whatever concerns there might be regarding Mieke – the rotund yet sleek Mieke – we ourselves had none.

Ever since the second day after her arrival, Mieke, as you would naturally have expected, had no more need of her place in the shed. And even the basket with hay did not fully meet the demands that a kitten living an active life would make. For that reason she sought out on her own initiative the kitchen haybox. Regular use of a saucepan of food, still cooking but off the heat and insulated by the hay, had made the haybox nice and warm. In an unguarded moment, Mieke had nestled herself right in the opening, and henceforth considered this warm, soft nest as her own domain. What can a woman do about such a *fait d'accompli* which a cat presents to you? Do you then still place your cooking pans full of food in the haybox? For there are always concerns about hygiene in the kitchen.

Well, one fine day Mieke sat there, undisputed owner of the haybox, and looked out over the edge. But oh, did she look glum! I just had to laugh. "What's the matter, Mieke?" I asked. "Eaten too many mice again?"

As small as she was, Mieke was already catching mice. If you didn't walk by at that very moment, she'd gobble them all up, including skin and hair, after of course first having enjoyed a pleasant time playing with them. But if you put a stop to that cruel game and took the mouse from her, she grumbled with indignation. Just like a dog! The same story in the manner in which she ran into the garden, following you, to help you harvest the potatoes or pick some apples. *Ja*, in doing that she also looked like a dog, even though she already had nothing but a deep contempt for such a creature. With the tall sheepdog, which stayed with us for a couple of days, she did her best to assume the same gait and did not step out of his way. No, she would have been shamed by such cowardice. More likely she would cause her hair to stand on end and blow contempt right back in his face. That was enough for him – maybe from sheer amazement – to keep his distance, so that I could reach and grasp the dog by his collar. Really, Mieke could have completely disappeared inside that huge maw.

But I digress. We were discussing mice. I thought that was the reason Mieke looked so glum. Her nose felt dry. "Today you stay in the basket," I counselled. And in this instance that was redundant advice, as Mieke did this entirely on her own initiative. The previous day I had put her outside in the sun, but a little later she was standing on the *stoep*, protesting loudly. Her upper lip and whiskers had lifted and her lamenting "Meow" sounded so determined and reproachful that I quickly brought her inside again. Mieke was not kidding; she was not in her usual mood for gambolling and flying round corners of the house at 70 km/h, looking back to check if there was anything on her tail, quite simply for the sake of it.

Therefore, the more astounded I was when Greet, our loyal housemaid, came to us with a frightened expression while we were peacefully drinking a cup of coffee with a pastor from a neighbouring community. She informed us that Mieke had quickly had a bad turn as she was behaving very strangely – making crazy leaps around the kitchen. I went with Greet to see for myself. And see I certainly did! What incredible antics! Was the poor creature suffocating from oxygen deficiency? Was she delirious? I threw open the back door and in a flash Mieke had vanished. But where? I kept asking myself this in the midst of all my ongoing work and all the ensuing conversations. The thought of Mieke gave me no peace. According to what I have been told, when animals sense that they are going to die, they seek out a still, lonely place. Had Mieke done that? I went out into the garden to search. Was she lying somewhere under the brushwood?

"Mieke! Mieke!"

Through the clear sunlit autumn air there came no answer at all.

"Would you go and have a look as well?" I asked my husband when dusk fell. That day he had been extremely busy. But he did venture to go and look... yet without result. Then I put Mieke's haybox in the shed and went to see the girls in the *leerkamer*. It was their night for the girls group at the *pastorie*. My husband joined us for the second hour. At one point he thought he'd heard a faint little voice yammering weakly outside the door to be let in. Who knows? No-one else heard a thing.

Then at half past nine the girls left for their homes, and I went outside. It was freezing cold! "Mieke! Mieke! Puss, puss, puss, puss, puss!"

No answer.

I nudged the door of the shed open, which was already ajar.

"Mieke! Mieke!"

"Mee-ow!" A very weak, plaintive cry. My hand reached into the darkness inside the haybox. Something there... soft and cold.

"Mieke!"

"Look who I've found!" The box with Mieke and all was carried to the *leerkamer* and placed on the table. My husband, Greet and I stood around it. Mieke began to spin around. Didn't that signify something? Maybe she was deathly ill?

"Have a close look into her eyes," suggested my husband, "then you might see what's wrong."

He tried giving her a droplet of milk from his finger. Mieke did not react. Not a thing. Then she lowered her head. Couldn't she swallow anymore? No, it seemed that swallowing caused her pain. What would be most dear to her, in these last hours of her young life... so touchingly sweet? We stoked up the *leerkamer* stove fire. Mieke would stay here tonight, to give her a warm departure. We fetched flannel cloths, so that they would keep her rugged up. We laid them under her and over her little back. But she found them uncomfortable. She stood up, meowed and looked about helplessly. When we took them away she settled down again. After half an hour we noticed her languishing visibly. Occasionally she thumped her tail, which normally she only did when she was cross. Was she delirious? Can kittens live also in a world of delusion? Surely there's no way we could know. But when we scratched her head softly and called her name, then she became calmer. Her little tail that had often thumped with annoyance, lay there still again. She answered us in her weakening voice and the strange expression in her eyes dwindled away.

Finally we all went to bed. Before dawn, at half past four, Greet came again to check on her. She found Mieke by the back door. Had Mieke sensed that death was near? Had she crawled out of her basket to find a place to hide? Mieke lay there on the threshold, dying on the mat. Greet laid her back in her basket. She was limp and cold.

Before seven we came downstairs and asked after Mieke. She was holding her little white paws crossed; her head had tilted backward and her eyes were closed... just one little tooth showing from her mouth. Was this really Mieke? Or was the little rascal playing somewhere in Elysian fields, far beyond our earthly domain and was that which remained only an empty shell of the kitty she once was? I leave this question open, as I know there is no answer to it.

To be, or not to be, that is the question, said Hamlet.

Mieke was a little enchanted princess, and therefore in her case, it makes sense to ask that.

Chapter 5

Gradually the days turned colder. One evening it began to snow. A giant white blanket lay for several hours over the immense plain. The soft tweeting of a pair of songbirds in the alders, who go there to sleep, made the stillness seem even more intense. In the far distance from the east you could see lights glowing. The glow came from a German concentration camp just over the border. Seeing those lights always filled me with a feeling of tightness inside, due to all the suffering that we knew would be endured there. Suffering that no-one really knew about, but that only left you guessing. There sat a captive people, suffering hardship. Cold perhaps, and hungry. In any case they were defenceless against the injustices inflicted upon them. I stood still, out on the road in the loneliness of the wide land, to gaze at the distant lights. Were the prisoners at this moment eating their meagre rations, or had they perhaps crawled under a thin blanket? Were they mistreated? Something now rose up within me that I had felt as a child: rebellion and grief over the defenceless animal facing his executioners. A feeling of powerlessness combined with quiet desperation, in that you knew you had to do something to fight it, but could not or dared not. And then you clamped both hands over your ears and crawled deeply under the blankets so as not to hear the shriek of the pigs that were being slaughtered, and then you prayed fervently to God that this terror would stop. And then the realisation dawned within me that I, standing there alone on the road, should pray for these unknown people in that German camp.

But what I didn't know was that, on that very night, four Poles would flee that prison – probably at the very same time that I stood there on the road; the culmination of weeks of carefully planned measures to escape. For through the fields of snow, shrouded in white cloth in order not to be seen, they came across the border that night. They knew all too soon that they had arrived in Dutch territory – from the street lamps that lit up all along the main road on our side of the border. For we, in a country still outside the hostilities, did not black-out anything at all! Later they told us that they knelt down on the road to express thanks for their rescue. They could now let themselves be quietly taken to the nearest military police barracks. But soon enough it was evident that they couldn't remain there, and so they were quartered instead with our own soldiers in the local school. All too quickly they became the talk of the town. Everyone wanted to give them something. What would they like? They had only to ask. One of them, a high-ranking officer, spoke good German, his brother some French and the two others from the navy, only Polish. The officer wrote on the blackboard: *Van Houten's cocoa,* and pronounced it like this: "Van Hoeten's." Fine. They would have that most excellent iconic Dutch product, as well as tobacco, cigars, cigarettes, butter, coffee and tea. Moreover, they took their meals from the same cooking pot as the Dutch soldiers. They slept in the café, where Annemeu's room was set apart for them with four palliasses of straw on the floor. And a recreation room was readily assigned; our *leerkamer* at the *pastorie*. They proved to be fast learners of shuffleboard, and at chess and checkers they were on par with our own best players.

The girls fluttered around these interesting newcomers like bees attracted to the honey pot. I teased our own lads a little about that too. One Sunday eve I said to one of them, who was covertly observing from a corner, "As long as they're here, you don't count anymore."

"They'll be going away soon," said the boy laconically, "and then we'll be back on offer."

And between all the games there were conversations. On Sunday morning the Poles accompanied us to the church service, which was held in the *leerkamer* to save on fuel. They did not understand the sermon, but they participated in the Lord's Prayer, kneeling down on the floor, and praying in their own language. They thought we northerners were too proud in our attitude to God, in that we stood at prayer or simply sat. Was that pride? It had really never occurred to me to think so, but perhaps they were right.

That evening the sound of Polish songs floated from the *leerkamer*. It was evident that the Poles had not done this for some time; how could they sing Polish patriotic songs in a German camp? At first they sang tentatively, as if either they lacked confidence, or they were out of practice, but slowly their voices were let loose; they sang duets and trios to a strange rhythm, and with a peculiar pathos, to which the youth of Groningen listened in wonder. And what rapture was exhibited in those impassioned faces. Our boys and girls between the ages of 14 and 20 stood around them and watched the gesticulating hands and the feet stamping on the floor, but they did not laugh. "Fantastic!" they cheered, when it was over. "More! Another one!" And after each round the Poles would launch into yet another encore. And each song shot like a bolt, straight to the heart. One was about their biggest river, where heavy cargoes were carried downstream. And in its rhythm you could hear the slow measured pace of the barges in tow. It reminded me of *The Song of the Volga Boatmen*.

In response, of course, the Groningen folk had to perform **their** national songs for the Poles! They began with a folk-song from Groningen. They followed that with the Dutch anthem *Wilhelmus*. Then *O splendid colours of the Netherlands flag, O ground of our treasured place* and *Where the white capped dunes...* a long series of the most beloved songs, even those which our farm-labouring youth seldom sang in the days before the war. However, from now on these became the 'conscience' of our heritage, any objections to which seemed to be disregarded by this foreign audience. Was there a scintilla of the awareness that before long, our youth would no longer be permitted to sing these songs and that the word 'fatherland' would soon for them have a power that it had never before possessed? That evening we were late to break up, but no-one felt it was too late. They were all agreed that it had been a wonderful evening indeed.

It was a winter with deep snow, but the Poles were used to it. They laughed and joked about and kept kicking up masses of snow on the road outside the *pastorie*, by the school, and along the farm lanes. Under the care of *Vati[11]*, as the Dutch sergeant was called, and under whose authority they were placed, they were kept busy the whole day long, with a stopover for coffee and a game at the *leerkamer*. But this routine of activities was not their ultimate goal; they wished to go further, to France preferably, to where the wife of the one who spoke French had taken flight. These men were embittered and wanted to join in the fight for the freedom of their homeland in the east. This life of patient waiting did not satisfy them. And after they had freed their land, might we, Domie and I, come and stay with them? A most alluring offer, but for the time being to travel such a distance was not possible for us.

One day a car with military police drove up to the *pastorie*. They came and fetched the Poles from our *leerkamer*, and took them away to the remand centre in Groningen. My husband went to a great deal of trouble to request from the authorities in The Hague that they be released. In the intervening days we just sat there uninformed and unknowing... one week, two weeks, one month, two months... anxious under the stress that such things cause. When would the cage spring open so that our birds could fly away? The German-speaking one also asked me that question when I visited them and sought him out in that sombre establishment. The French speaker also asked it, and the two others as well, who spoke no language I could understand. But they asked with their eyes and that disturbed me even more. At least I had something to tell the two who spoke the two foreign languages that I

---

11 German for Dad or Daddy.

was familiar with, but you never felt so helpless as when you can say or do nothing at all, except to offer them a packet of cigarettes across the barrier. To the French and German speakers I said, "Don't lose courage! Domie's interceding for you and he's very persistent. Once he gets his teeth into something, he never lets go."

"*Ja*, but it's taking so long, and we're just stuck right here."

"It always takes a long time with the official authorities."

"Even here in Holland?"

"*Ja*, of course. What did you think? That such slowness only happens in Poland?"

"I suppose bureaucrats are bureaucrats – all over the world," was his philosophical reply in German.

A man behind bars in Groningen is just a number to someone sitting behind his desk in The Hague. What could we do about that? Unless there is a pesky *Dominee* from the flatlands who fills that man's head with so many arguments that you can't fit a pin between them!

You would know full well the parallel here to the unrighteous judge of Jesus' parable, who finally judged righteously just to be rid of the constant flood of complaints.

This was such a case and when their freedom was finally granted the Poles were so thankful. A card followed a little later, sent from Paris, full of expressions of gratitude. And again the invitation to visit their estate in Poland, but according to the Dutch proverb that Mother would quote, *The chance of that still sits in a wide bag.*[12]

---

12 "That's far from guaranteed," or "It's not a given outcome."

Chapter 6

The moonlight beamed softly over the young wheat in the field, upon the copper beech in the front garden, over the path going to the church with the blooming hawthorn hedges on both sides, on the lilacs and on the jasmine. I stuck my head out the bedroom window and inhaled their fragrance. A frog croaked in a canal nearby, and beyond, all was motionless; absolutely still. Everywhere was embraced by the white soft moonlight. Everywhere by this deep, abundant peace. War? Was there a war? Well, no, that must have been an oppressive dream. Our land, our fair Holland, where the dunes still lie in the moonlight and where the sea breaks on the beaches, belonged to us... and to no-one else! Or was there indeed in the still, white light, the body of a forgotten soldier half buried in the shifting dune sands?

Then suddenly a motorcycle thunders along in the night, breaking the silence with a crackling roar, discordant, noisy and disturbing. A wood pigeon flutters restlessly in the Linden trees and coos, comical, yet sad. Now the machine is rattling along our fence-line. A German soldier is sitting astride it. I can see his helmet gleaming in the moonlight. A rifle hangs on his back. Each night he takes this route to check whether our people, now brought into subjection, are behaving according to the imposed German regulations. German laws and curfews apply here, in our land! I suddenly feel the cold and shiver in my thin nightdress. I withdraw my exposed head and steal softly back to bed. My husband is sleeping peacefully. Tonight he is out like a light. I must take care that I don't wake him, as he'll then know, only too soon, the reality that we are now slaves in the hand of an oppressor. Slaves? But to whom? To this realm of lies and deceit, of might and violence, cannons and tanks? Or are we servants of Christ? I look toward my husband's face, rejuvenated by sleep, and pray that we shall remain faithful when the noose tightens. He especially, as a minister. That we will not be slaves to human thinking, but people who through Christ have been set free. *Christ overcomes,* says the text hanging in the *leerkamer*.

And I suddenly realise that it's not guns that determine the final outcome, but the Spirit. From now on we will be faithful to stand at our post. Faithful to death, if necessary. Death – then he will lie there so still, just as he is now, and this endless tenderness that I feel for him shall enfold me forever. I shall not then wish to call him back, to the ugliness of our earthly existence, nor do I wish to do that now. Then his spirit will linger elsewhere, just as he is now, in his dreams. I love him and gaze upon his finely chiselled features. I love him too much to wake him and kiss him.

Chapter 7

There is currently fighting down south along the Grebbe Line[13] and close by there lives my family. How is it going with them? Connections by post, telephone and telegraph were drastically broken and have not been immediately repaired after the five terrible days of war. My husband reads my mind. "You'd really like to go back there wouldn't you, *hè*?"

"*Ja*, gladly, but I'd prefer to cycle. With the train you can never be sure of the connections, and the railway bridge at Zwolle has most likely been destroyed."

"Cycling at this time of year sure is the most pleasant way you can do it."

So on that score we were united. And when the bicycle was prepared and ready, with my travel case up on the back, off I went one morning heading south, passing tract after tract of arable land as far as the eye could see. Wheat, barley and young sugar-beets, horse-beans and here and there a field of scented rapeseed flowers. It was not the shortest route, but certainly the prettiest. I rode on through Westerwold. Here the soil was poorer. Wheat gave way to rye. The land also undulated a little here and there, changing imperceptibly as I approached the landscape of Drenthe. And if you keep on pedalling, preferably eating your sandwiches on the bike or along the grassy banks of the roadside, then you eventually find yourself in Overijssel, where the water so clearly

---

13 Defence system using selected flooding of low-level land areas in times of invasion.

reflects the sky and the cows stand up to their bellies in lush buttercups. *Ja*, because at that time there were still a lot of cows in Holland. Just after the war began, the opportunity to make off with them back across the border into Germany had not yet presented itself, even if the general looting of resources was already well underway. It seemed to me that Holland was as a bride in the clutches of an undesirable lover, who was removing her jewellery piece by piece, all the while saying in a cajoling voice, "Keep still, girl, I've got your best interests at heart!"

Everything was in fragrant bloom – everything appeared well cared for. There were no longer cars on the roads because all available petrol had been requisitioned. I rode, a solitary figure, through the backdrop of a blooming countryside. Inasmuch, by preference, I had not taken the major roads, I saw no sign of the Germans. Only at Zwolle, my destination for this particular day, there lay parts of a dead horse scattered along the roadside; two thighs and a tail. In my mind that called up imagery of bloody conflict – stirred up by foreign intruders who were intent on crossing our mighty rivers. That's why the pretty bridge over the Ijssel had been blown up. I was taken across the river on a small ferryboat. Out of action, the destroyed bridge hung limply over the water. But it had been a useless gesture to blow the bridge. The enemy had already reached the other side, and here was I using a ferry.

In a small café along the way I ordered a glass of milk and a bread roll. The girl with her hair tightly combed back, wearing a smooth bodice and a wide, dark skirt, was a real daughter of the Veluwe. She smiled at me amiably and started chatting to me about the weather. She inquired where this *juffer*[14] came from, and she also wanted to know where I was going.

She clapped her hands together. Such a destination! And all alone on the bike... and it had only just been in the midst of war as well! And did

---

14 Regional variant of juffrouw – "young lady" or "Miss".

my mother and father think that was wise, and was I myself comfortable doing that?

"I just came here to see whether you've all already become Nazis," I said.

"If we've become what?"

"Nazis, the ones who believe in Hitler and the Holy German Empire," I replied, with some sarcasm.

"Here we have *niks* to do with Hitler and the German Empire," asserted the girl. "And we believe in something completely different, and that also the *juffer* would know quite well."

Ja, that I knew very well indeed and it comforted me when I resumed my journey to think how far these folk were from being foisted upon by theories that were completely alien to them.

I also knew that each and everything worth saving was in our own homes. I still felt a little reluctant in returning here to my familiar and trusted surroundings. It was as if, in some way or another, everything had changed after that fateful date of May the 10th, 1940, when for us the war truly began. But it was wonderful to both see and imbibe the scent of the heath and forest again after the flatlands of Groningen, to which I had admittedly pledged my heart, but where I still did not feel as quite at home as I did here in these woods. The red sun was slowly sinking below the tops of the pines. Our trusty Dutch clocks had been set forward by one hour and 40 minutes: German time. If I got a move on, I could be inside before it got dark.

Chapter 8

Under the chestnut in bloom behind the white house in which I had grown up we now sat together: my brothers and sisters, the young nieces and nephews. How did I get here so quickly? How was it up north? Had we seen much goings on of the war? They had been right in the thick of it.

The war! The war! I suddenly felt so tired. There it went all over again: the overrunning of our country, the occupation of its territory, the taking of captives. An enslaved people, who must not ever air their opinions – the papers, the radio – all under censure.

"Tell you?" I said wearily. "What is there to tell? It's the same everywhere. We've capitulated on all fronts."

"Capitulated? We've been betrayed by the NSB![15]" asserted my eldest brother, raising his voice.

"Don't shout like that. Nowadays to say such things aloud is no longer permitted."

We sat there in the midst of our family gathering. Johan spoke about the Grebbe Water Defence Line – how that was a scandal. Such an insidious bunch of traitors; how there hadn't even been a single drop of water admitted through the sluices. He gesticulated with his hands and I watched his severely emaciated face, his bright burning eyes, and listened to the passionate words.

According to the Germans we were also *Deutschen* and they

---

15 *Nationaal-Socialistische Beweging* – Dutch national socialist movement sympathetic to Nazi Germany.

thought that identification was a great honour that they had bestowed upon us. I looked at my brother and smiled. That was certainly a misconception on their part. We were surely a branch descended from different tribal stock – from the Franks probably, and therefore Johan's heart would be drawn more to whatever the French were – to France and their French heritage and culture – but definitely he was no German!

I wanted to know precisely how the current events had all evolved; how the Dutch youth had managed to persevere, sitting there and looking up at the sky, when there had been no help forthcoming from the English planes; how the Dutch army had withdrawn from conflict and how our soldiers had slumped, exhausted, sleeping upon the necks of their horses. They were so fatigued and defeated that only a miracle in the form of a heavy fog had saved our retreating forces from being bombed from the air, which would have surely decimated them. And how our Queen had just escaped to England – altogether a sad and bitter tale of the five days of war they had experienced so near at hand. And while I listened I saw Mother's hands with her wedding ring resting on the boards of the table. Fortunately my family had not been involved directly in the conflict. In Father's chair sat my youngest brother. He was avidly lending support to Johan's statements, and in-between, the voices of the women and the young ones also contributed support.

Yet they had learned nothing! In the heat of their indignation they had forgotten to talk softly and to carefully keep their opinions to themselves. But what could one do to oppose all this might? The big guns that had been paraded by us in long columns were still in active use here. If I wished, tomorrow I could go and see the villages and towns that had been shot to bits. And there was always Rotterdam... It appeared that there was no longer any righteousness or justice. And what about the treason? *Ja*, that was something that, for us as a nation, would reflect our shame down through all the coming ages. "From that perspective we as a society deserve to suffer three more years of hunger," said Johan.

A couple of hours later, when I stood before my bed in the guest room, I found I could not pray.

I had just been regaled with an array of gruesome tales. But here in the bedroom there was stillness, and from it came a voice I recognised: *Blessed are the meek, for they shall inherit the earth.*[16] That didn't sound like a mocking jest, but as a truth given to impart consolation. The Dutch poet Henrietta Roland Holst concurred when she wrote, *The forces of meekness shall overcome.*

Be of good cheer, says Christ. *I have overcome the world.*[17]

In my death on the cross I have judged them. And from my rising on the Paschal[18] *morning shall they live.*

---

16 Matthew 5:5.
17 John 16:33.
18 The third day of the Feast of Passover and the celebration of the resurrection of Christ.

Chapter 9

Silence and vastness and lark-song, and a lonely farm loft, where I may write.

"Do you want to store something up there?" asked the stable boy, when his mistress commanded him to bring a table and chair up to the loft above the granary.

No, it's not necessary that someone hides me away due to these exigent times. Not in the least, but it is a flight nevertheless. It is a desire to withdraw from everyday life – its worries and responsibilities – and immerse myself in contemplation. For the life of action falls away behind me once I tightly shut the heavy door and enter the mysterious twilight of the barn, where the bales of straw are stacked right up to the oak beams.

A wooden ladder leads to a heavy iron fire door and behind it is a veritable hermit's retreat. It's a spacious room, with yet another loft level above. If you look out from the upper windows, you see the wide land, accented here and there with flecks of red and blue. These are women working in the fields, and toward the horizon lie the cottages of the Old Dyke, and in the background the ornate tower adjacent to the village.

One level below, the loft looks through broad windows onto fields of barley and a more distant farmstead with a large barn. Harmonious are the lines of its roof, which stands rust brown against the blue sky. The wind surges through the barley stalks, inducing a silvery wave of bobbing heads.

A great and good land this is. All the vain efforts of men seen from this distance seem small and less significant, including one's own life, which you can survey from this viewpoint as if it were a dream.

I think sometimes that from eternity we shall view our earthly existence as a coloured bubble on the surface of our inner life of the soul. All passions, fears and joys will then be stilled in the clarity of our observation of reality, whereof we now only glimpse but a small illuminated part.

A large flask of milk stands next to me on the floor. One of the gifts of this land.

Do not marvel at my sudden return to material things. Next to spiritual prayer, *Thy will be done on earth, as it is in Heaven,* the Lord's Prayer sets the plea: *Give us this day, our daily bread.*

And the soil on this fragment of the world's surface does not bestow sparingly, but in overflowing measure. She is gentle in her dispensations, although sometimes she seems unfriendly due to the climate. She is like a mother, who rules her children with a strong hand and who sometimes appears sullen to those who do not know her. But insiders know that they never need come in vain to her, because she stands on her capacity to give lavishly to each one, for her heart is kind and gentle. And in all hunger and want suffered by the cities during these years of war she has never ceased to provide her gifts. But we must help her a little, for some things she cannot do unless a transformation has taken place. For example, wheat cannot simply be converted to fat. There is need of an intermediary, and for us that intermediary was... a pig!

Only to a dreamer would come the idea to build an air raid shelter and in it to house a pig. But Domie was such a fantastic realist. So he commenced digging. A large hole appeared and along with that a growing mound of earth. A small boy from the neighbourhood who resembles Peter Pan (the one playing upon his flute by the lake in

Kensington Gardens near Hyde Park) is always about and lends a hand with odd jobs. He comes up to Domie's boots. It's just like David and Goliath; the small Peter and the tall Domie. The work was progressing steadily. "That Domie can do way more than preach," ventured the workers. *Ja*, he can even excavate – something that had not occurred to them at all!

Stelmaker brought along a lot of wood. A corridor was installed in the shelter and at the end of it a chamber. No-one knew its real purpose, but everyone wanted to give advice. Our neighbour arrived with drainpipes, otherwise the shelter would be underwater for half the year, and considering the last time when there was heavy bombing at Emden, we should definitely be prepared with a dry air raid shelter. There were many objections. For instance, how would a permanent occupier there have enough light and air? The old housepainter came and built a light shaft, of glass plates and white walls, all designed by Domie.

A small chimney pipe was added for air-ducting and also two doors for soundproofing. Then later another one of straw. The wood was nicely tarred to prevent rot. Asphalt and bales of straw formed the roof, then over the top of everything a final thick layer of earth. Everyone wanted to see it and everyone also wanted to comment. Our neighbour from the big farm next door thought the long corridor so practical, but that the drainage was in any case flawed. Domie zealously defended his work. "During the actual dig I did not reach the level of the water table, but when some does accumulate, it always runs away through the pipes toward the ditch."

"*Ja, ja.* Domie can say that, but that was during the dry season of the year. But how will things turn out in the autumn and winter?"

And Stelmaker's door just would not shut. Each time he planed some timber off, it appeared to be too much, because then the door would end up with an excessive gap. And when he then glued on a strip of wood to compensate, the door again would not fit the jamb properly. He broke out in sweat, as Domie is so demandingly precise and would always want the perfect job!

The painter removed his cap, scratched himself behind the ear, lit up his pipe and said, "We'll never get anywhere with this air-raid shelter."

And finally I was able to go and take a look inside. I shared the painter's opinion, but without showing his tact. To me it was all a rather dire and risky scheme. Just imagine that it was discovered! How easily that could occur, with all the children that came and went throughout the garden. And the labourers who were already on their way to work at dawn could see clearly through the hedge – catching sight of someone walking about with a pail of feed. But Domie just had to see his plan through, although I promised him not one whit of my cooperation. The only thing that I appreciated about it was the lovely garden developments, which had come about by all that excavation of the ground. A mound of earth now adorned our garden that we could later cover with greenery. Also a sunken hollow had formed, in which my husband and Petertje had laid a stone floor, forming a lovely protected area where we could sit. Low planted embankments surrounded the feature, and there was a winding path leading to it.

"Looks just like Paradise," commented Elderling, with his heavy voice and his childlike blue eyes.

And he was right. It is really such a shame that in our earthly paradise there is always a serpent lurking.

"Domie!" called Petertje with a voice that trilled like the flute of Peter Pan. "Domie, are you down the shelter?"

No answer.

Petertje ran to the entrance and peered into the dark cavern. There, on a nail, hung Domie's jacket. Domie had to be there.

"Domie!"

"Snrrrrrrr ghrrrrff!"

Petertje stood a moment, numbed with fright. Then he turned on his heel and raced for the pantry where he bumped right into Greet.

"I got such a fright – that ol' beastie there – grunting like I don't know how!"

Greet's eyes widened with dismay. "Were you down in the bomb-shelter?"

"*Joa*[19], man!"

Well, there you have it – just as *Mevrouw* always said! Scarcely three hours with the beast in the pen (it was brought in the early hours of the morning) and the terrible secret was already out!

"Promise me that you'll tell no-one, or Domie will go in the clink," cautioned Greet.

A terrible vision loomed up in Petertje's mind – of armed Germans taking Domie away and his big pal being brought out and chained up in the prison van.

"No, not to anyone at all!" he replied, hoarsely.

"And above all, don't let *Mevrouw* see that you know about this, because she was always dead against the idea."

Petertje nodded his understanding.

"But the door must be kept shut," he said wisely.

"*Ja*, of course. Domie wants to make a secret lock for it."

"Make for what?" asked Domie, stepping into the kitchen right at that moment.

They all looked at each other cautiously.

"On the door of the bomb-shelter," said Greet. "Petertje has been inside."

"That ol' hog started to grunt," said Petertje by way of explanation.

"Petertje, can you keep a secret?"

"*Joa* – for sure, Domie!"

"Then it's all good," replied Domie in the lad's dialect. "Find me a hammer and some nails, and we'll go and make a secret lock and then not a soul will find out about it."

"Not from me," Petertje assured him solemnly.

"That I know right well," said Domie.

---

19 Groningen pronunciation of *Ja* spoken with with a more rounded sound, similar to "oar" in English.

Now Greet sets off every morning before sunrise and each evening after dark dressed in gala attire – comprising an old coat, slacks to ward off rain, and Domie's boots – down to the 'palace' as we call the bomb-shelter, in order to wait in attendance on Kaiser Nero with a pail of feed. After rain her boots get stuck in the miry clay along the winding path through the tall shrubs, which leads to the palace. At the end she climbs down the ladder, lugging the heavy pail, and stands in the pit right in front of the door. Softly, softly, Greet! So that you don't upset the hungry Kaiser who is inside, impatiently awaiting his meal. Take care that he hears as little as possible of your fumbling at the door, otherwise your fears will surface that his loud grunting might penetrate through the thick layer of earth above, and through the straw bales, three doors beyond, and your presence and that of the emperor inside could be betrayed! Greet stretches out her hand, seeking the cord that hangs concealed in a recess in the door frame. This lifts a latch on the inside of the door which when set, keeps it locked tight. Whoever attempts to push open the door from the outside will find that it does not budge. Any local trying that will say, "The door's jammed," remembering the sweating of Stelmaker, who simply could not get that "confounded door" to fit properly. However, if you pull the cord like Little Red Riding Hood did, then the door readily opens.

A shaft of light now enters the almost dark, earthy den. Immediately Nero reacts with a quick emphatic snort. A pungent odour of pig strikes Greet full on. But she's not quite there yet. She must manoeuvre her way with her pail through the narrow corridor, through the straw doors and finally through a wooden door. A pair of trotters strike against the partition wall. The Kaiser heaves himself up on his hind legs and with his head up, looks out over the pen. Greet switches on her electric torch and just for a moment she and Nero look right into each other's eyes. But Nero begins to squeal loudly then attempts to jump over the wall. Greet pushes him aside with her pail and with an adroitly aimed swing dumps his feed into the trough. The loud squealing does not abate when the pail knocks his head, but then there is the thwack of feed falling into the bin and after that silence, in which all one can hear are the satisfied and voracious sounds of a pig gorging himself. Greet is now adapted to the gloom, so much so, that even without her torch, she can see the pale of Nero's coat stand out against the surrounding darkness. Even in daytime very little illumination penetrates down inside through the light shaft.

Who would have ever got the idea that we, who knew nothing of pigs, or of animals' needs, were hiding a pig in the air-raid shelter? Not a soul! Nobody thought it were possible that we would, and even less did they think that we should be capable of such a thing. Of course that was a godsend. The more naïve we were seen to be in this province of agriculture and animal husbandry, the better it was!

"And that bomb-shelter of Domie's turned out to be quite a flop – *joa*, man, what did I tell you? Such people don't know anything. Now it's all finished they don't know how to make use of it!"

Meanwhile our pig thrived through summer and winter, by virtue of the constant temperature in his underground den.

Chapter 10

Insects buzzed under the trees, flowers bloomed in the front yard, and there was the curious zinging sound of a whetted scythe. On a deck chair, sheltered from prying eyes by a hedge of green, lay Johan. I was reading him a poem about clouds that sailed over, high up in the blue. His eyes in that haggard face gleamed and gazed far heavenwards. A silence followed in which neither of us felt the need to say anything. It was good to be together again, just as in our youth, and no words were necessary for us to understand each other.

The bees buzzed, the flowers poured forth their scent – time stood still. He was deep in thought, with those long white hands caressing the sheet. "Clouds..." he said slowly, in raptures of delight, "...are so splendid. I could look at them for hours. Even as a child I already thought them so beautiful. Shapes of animals, mountains – you can see everything in them. Sometimes they become caverns, with the light of the sun behind. Or the sky looks like a great lake, with white water lilies."

We fell once again into the companionable intimacy of silence. I let the book slide down to my lap. He wished to say more, but the words came only at intervals. Finally he said, "They didn't have to send me back, when I was so close to the edge. Right then, I felt so pure..."

He had almost died, and I understood that he was speaking of that. It really was a disappointment for him not to gain admittance to that purer sphere, the air of which he had already inhaled, and now here he was, longing to look at the scudding clouds, with the light of Heaven beyond.

"You've come here to get better," I said.

He nodded. "*Ja*, you've really done your best." He smiled. "When I really didn't need to eat so much."

"And that's just how it should be – rest and good food, the doctor said."

We both fell back into our own thoughts. The farmers had been kind and friendly. They brought cream and Westerlee cherries. We provided the best of what we had, cooked thin pancakes and put them before him with a glass of wine.

"Johan, this is a French meal – come on, have some of it."

"Wonderful!" he said, with his eyes shut, sipping at the wine. He started laboriously on the pancake, chatting all the while.

"You have to eat something too," said his wife.

Then he looked at her with a helpless, wounded expression.

"I just can't," he said, and slumped back in fatigue.

Oh, getting him to eat that food!

Sometimes we tried a softer line of attack, and sometimes we bantered. Then he just became sad. But we had to get him to eat! We had to be tough and persevere – what kind of sentimental love would calmly allow him to starve instead of pushing him as far as we could?

"Johan... Here, try some cauliflower."

"*Och*, don't nag me like that."

"You have to," I said. "You're not doing your best. You're not cooperating at all. Otherwise you'd be so much better by now."

Why do we always most vex those ones we hold dearest? Because we expect so much from them. I did want to keep him here. For me, he just had to stay as part of our lives! And so he should! Once upon a time, he also tried to hold me close, but in a different way – he was jealous in his love, but that was all long ago. Now I was the one who said, "You must" and he was the one who said, "I can't", and then with his eyes added, "Forgive me, but can't you see that you can't win this contest? I'm on a different path to the one you want me to take, and I can go no other way."

In moments like these, in the afternoon stillness under the linden tree, he was talking to me about the clouds and about that other mysterious place that he had seen from close by and to which that beckoning vision was calling him. I suspected something; of a tragedy that always seems to repeat itself.

"You're of me," we humans say to each other, "because I love you. You are bound to me with a thousand threads – from my earliest youth thenceforth."

But the Almighty smiles.

"You are of Me," He says, "from before the foundation of the world. I have given unto you this short span of time on the earth, to love people, to wonder at flowers, with music that will bring your heart delight and colours so fleeting you will wish to preserve them on canvas. But you are of Me. You shall forget perchance the short time amongst the pressures of everyday life, but in the midday stillness you shall again perceive it. Then you shall hear My voice again and just as the voice of the nightingale awakens your deepest yearnings for spring, so shall My voice awaken within you a longing for the Father's House."

The warmth became languid and sultry. Johan's eyes fell closed. I put the book down, picked up the stocking and darning ball, and I sat and darned. But the warmth drew me also under her power. I still heard the humming of insects and the regular swish of the scythe through grass, but my hands lay idle in my lap and my mind set itself free from time and place to go its own way. It returned to our parental home, where, by this much older brother, long stories were told to the little sister there in the cot, so that she no longer saw the figures of interest on the wall, but instead untamed mountain landscapes with lakes and wild animals. He guided her into a fantasy world, and at his side she roamed all through a land magnificent and mysterious, as can only exist in our imagination. Our measures of time and space do not apply there. It is populated by giants and dwarves, fairies and gnomes. The animals can speak, the flowers have faces – and everything there is vibrant and breathes in a mysterious life. The echoes in the ravines hear you, and the wind whispers through the treetops. And there, nothing is impossible.

And when she is somewhat older, he paints for her this world. Not this time with words, but with colours; she looks over his shoulder, while he mixes the paint in small, white ceramic pots and thence brushes it onto the paper. A magician is Johan! In his capable hands a world emerges that he sees in his mind, that lives in his memory. Small towns of Breton hugging a slope and in the background a sea so blue and transparent, that in it you could see reflected the sky and the sailing white clouds. And later when you're almost grown up and driven out of the mystical land of childhood, then you yourself go with him and his best friend, the wide world, to explore it all. And when you sit together to listen to a waterfall on a Welsh mountainside, that from ages past has sung its melodious song, then the child's dream returns and becomes reality, and reality becomes a dream.

"Have you two fallen asleep?" The voice of Paulien calls us back to consciousness.

"It is really so warm..." I say apologetically. "And what a lovely gown you're wearing."

Johan looks at her with the eye of an artist and smiles. "In that gown, she looks so luminous," he says, with an articulate wave of his hand. "But you must have been gone quite a while."

"Won't you sit here?" I ask and offer her my chair.

"But then you won't be able to sit."

"No... I've got to stand up. I've been sitting here dreaming way too long."

Should I not leave them alone together now? I know full well how happy Johan is when his wife is by his side.

There follow even more warm, oppressive days. Johan feels the mugginess. Outside it's too warm throughout the day, and we have no idea where to put him, as each room, even the coolest one, is for the moment warm and stuffy. The stifling heat hovers over the entire countryside. The sun rises each day to stand in the sky like a burnished copper ball and parches the earth. Whenever you step outside the front door from the comparative coolness of the hall, it's like stepping into an oven. Even the ground feels hot underfoot. No birds are singing. In this heat, scarcely anyone can be out there working the land. They thus begin very early in the cool of the morning and by midday they declare: 'oldert!'[20]

There was a man who wanted to go and fetch grass from the meadows on the floodplain. He was afraid that it would be all washed away at high tide, as it was already mown, and he needed the grass to make hay for fodder. The fellow was afflicted by sunstroke that day and then taken to hospital where he eventually died. This makes a deep impression on Johan. He has always had a deeply sensitive nature, but now he does not have much resistance left. It was only his vital spirit that yet lived on in his flagging, exhausted body.

Whatever is it that is really undermining his health? A disease of the blood, says the doctor. Everything was done that could be done for Johan – liver injections, medicines. He is under the care of one of the most skilful specialists in that field. Now there's only one thing that can help: rest and a good diet – and "from now on just let him do whatever he aspires to do."

Last winter he spoke of his will to come and stay with us. "Next Christmas I'd like to be at the *pastorie*," he said. But he was too weak to travel. At that time we didn't even know if he'd make it through to Christmas, and anyway how could you bring such an ill person here, in the freezing cold?

But the doctor had said, "Let him do whatever he aspires to."

And Johan wanted most to get well. But he could not.

---

20 "Down tools!" – announcing a pause in the work for rest and refreshment.

"Don't forget to pack my drawing kit and paints," he said to Paulien, as they were packing their cases.

He stumbled over to the work-quarters to say goodbye to the house-servants. He sat down there on a joiner's toolbox.

"I've come to say goodbye to you all, as I'm going away on a trip."

Did he have a premonition that he would not return from his journey?

Deeply sunk into the cushions of the train compartment, he looked out the window toward the beautiful fruit-bearing earth that glided by on this, his final voyage. To the sun flecked pine trunks of the Veluwe, to the green and yellow carpets of grass with masses of buttercups and the looking-glass waters of Overijssel, to the wheat fields and the heathlands of Drenthe he looked. And he knew it: this earth that you love so much, the preservation of whose beauty you have so eagerly sought, you are going to have to leave behind. Then comes the wistful bitter-sweet stillness over a man, but indeed also the tranquil awareness: I've done my duty. I now hand all this over to posterity. I shall leave, but the earth remains.

Ja, he wanted much; he wanted to draw and paint, but he could not mix the colours nor hold the brush. He wanted to read, but that fatigued him too much and he fell asleep. When he awoke, he was distressed that he could do no more. But when you talked with him, then you could easily forget how frail he was. Tolstoy and Dostoevsky, Ruskin, Vincent van Gogh and Leonardo da Vinci. All passed in review.

"Don't talk too much, old chap."

"You must not wish that on me; to just vegetate here in silence. Anyway, when's Elderling coming again?"

"This afternoon."

"Oh," he said, satisfied. He loved to receive visitors, and especially those 'with whom he could converse', as he put it.

Were we blind? Couldn't we see that he was ever slipping backwards? At least we could see that he was making no progress at all toward recovery.

If only an end to all this infernal heat would just arrive for once!

On one of these warm days a visit took place with which Johan was overjoyed.

During the mobilisation just before the war, soldiers often called to visit him and his wife at home to drink coffee. And one of these callers was a man called Akker, who was posted now to this area as a road-mender. The road running alongside our house had just been put in order, and now two road-menders, including Akker, came by to ask for a drink at the *pastorie*.

Paulien was sitting out the back with her mending.

"*Dag,*[21] *Mevrouw,*" she heard a familiar voice greeting her – and there stood Akker with his empty canteen in his hand.

"*Hé* – how did you end up here?"

"I work here on the roads. And you?"

"I'm here for the sake of the health of my husband."

"Is *Meneer*[22] sick?"

"*Ja*, he's resting inside, but I shall tell him that you are here, because he shan't want to miss this!"

Akker's comrades took tea outside on the lawn while Akker himself chatted with Johan in the study, where he was lying on his *chaise-longue*. Johan had not seen him since the war began, and Akker had to bring him up to date regarding his wartime experiences.

"Would you believe," offered Johan, "that hatred consumes my life?"

Akker looked at the shining face and nodded.

"But surely you are a Christian?" he queried.

"*Ja*, I know full well that it doesn't stand in accord, but I can't help it. When I think of the injustice and all that they have done to us, of all the lies and deceit..."

But the matter would not leave him in peace. All through the afternoon he could hear the echo of Akker's words: "But surely you are a Christian?" He had also been asked that question once by a Communist.

---

21 "Hello," "See you", or "Goodbye" – a general greeting on arrival or departure.
22 *Mijnheer* or *Meneer* means "Mr" or "Sir" – in this instance "Your husband".

A father had two sons. To the eldest he said, "Go, work today in my vineyard," and the son replied, "Yes, I'll go," but he did not. And also to the youngest son he said, "Go, work today in my vineyard," but this one said, "No, I'm not going." But then having remorse, he went after all. What do you think? Who of these two sons has done the will of their father?[23]- asked Jesus.

"Not what you say, but what you do – that's what it comes down to," thinks Johan. "That communist was closer to this truth than I ever was."

The idea is simmering away in his mind. He cannot stop thinking about it. Outside it's dead calm – not a leaf stirring. Dark clouds are gathering and in the distance sounds a dull rumble. A couple of large thick drops fall. Thank God! Man and beast together yearn for liberation from the claws of this life and energy-sapping heat monster. The thunder sounds more threatening, comes closer. A white bolt of lightning shoots through the air. Now the storm breaks forth. It is really coming on apace. The flashes and thunderclaps follow each other more swiftly. It's raining bucket-loads now, pouring out of the sky and flowing down into the glade and our shelter pit. We sit with each other in the room, kept in silence by the fury of the elements. It also causes something in us to relax. If it weren't so silly to stand there under this pelting rain, I'd really love to go outside. But it's such beastly weather!

After an hour it has relented somewhat. We can now open the windows, which must be shut tight during storms and heavy rain. A marvellous smell of the wet earth suffuses the room. The wheat that is already laden with heavy ears lies flattened in various places. A bird begins to sing. The cool air comes drifting inside and dispels the warmth. Opening the doors makes this happen even more quickly.

"Do you think the Tommies will come over again tonight?"

"It'd be ideal. The wind's already died down."

---

23   Matthew 21:28-31.

Where did all those mosquitoes suddenly come from? Were they flying in through the open windows to where the air was cooler and away from the humidity outside? No-one had a suitable answer to that question, but they were buzzing all around the study where Johan had to sleep, as he could no longer manage the steep and arduous staircase. Not much could be done about it really. To spray would cause a musty odour that Johan could not stand. So he went to bed while they were still buzzing around. In one way or another their sinister hum filled me with dread. I looked out at the night. Do we always have to have premonitions of things that are about to happen in our lives?

Toward dawn Paulien called me. Could I come? Johan had developed an unstoppable nose bleed! For hours already!

I woke Domie up.

"You've got to go and fetch the doctor. Johan has a bleeding nose."

That startled him. He shot up and scrambled into his clothes, saw the sadness on my face and said tenderly, "It won't help, lass. Don't give into grief."

Of course I must not. Giving into grief was self-centred of me, while this was always about Johan! In order to do for him what was possible, he must see nothing of the expression on my face. However, when I entered his room, I spoke to him with an unusual gentleness. "What's the matter? Have you bloodied your nose? Shall I make a cold compress for you?" I asked.

"Paulien has gone to do that," he said. "Just look at my arm – see how many times the mosquitoes have bitten me!"

I was dismayed. All over there were red spots, on both hands and arms.

But the doctor knew better when he turned up. He loosened Johan's pyjama top. Underneath on the skin there were spots everywhere.

Then the doctor buttoned up the top with a resigned gesture. Out in the hall he told me, "They're not mosquito bites."

"What are they then?" I asked anxiously.

"Burst capillaries. That's also why his nose is bleeding." And then, hesitantly, he added, "I would notify his family."

There arose a big lump in my throat and I fixed the doctor with an intense look. "Is that really necessary?"

"*Ja*, it is," he said, then turned and walked away. I let him go. There was nothing more I could ask.

My husband went with the doctor to telephone while Paulien remained with the patient. It seemed I could do little more. Because a death warrant had been signed this morning, and that warrant would be fulfilled in our home!

I walked aimlessly through the corridors, the kitchen, to the *leerkamer*. There was a pile of hay on the floor, which had yet to be hoisted up to the loft. I let myself collapse upon it. Black, everything was black as the night! A blackbird was singing. But I did not hear its song. Inside someone lay dying, and that one was our Johan. Paulien didn't yet know and neither did their children, but soon they would. For them it would also become dark, for you really wanted to hide the truth from them, but you could not do that. You had to tell them – but **how would** you tell them? Paulien would not want to accept it; they would be desperate. How did that go again – about the valley of the shadow of death?

E'en though I walk through the valley of the shadow of death, I shall fear no evil...[24]

But I was not up to that. No, I would not be ready for a long time! I definitely was afraid of the evil that was going to happen – death was already standing at the door. I had crept away and I sincerely hoped that nobody would find me. But soon the house would be filled with people; they would arrive after the phone call with downcast faces. Oh, if only they would just leave me alone in here!

---

24 Psalm 23:4.

A familiar tread sounded through the house. That was Domie, who was looking for me. He lifted the latch of the *leerkamer* door. I scrambled to my feet, feeling ashamed. He said nothing, but put his arm around me and drew me to sit with him. The clock ticked away the time in mere seconds, but which seemed like hours. Finally I broke the silence with the question: "Have you also notified his friend?"

"Who, Bertram? No, I didn't even think of it."

"He is also a part of this," I said. "He probably knows Johan better than any of us."

"I'll do that then," said Domie. "Then if you... You know, we must also think of Paulien. They must be carefully prepared for the worst."

"Does she suspect anything?"

"No, not this. She knows well enough that it's very bad though. But you'll just have to tell her."

I had to tell her just like that? That when her children came and the others, that there was no more hope? And at the thought of her suffering, my own seemed to dissolve away.

Paulien and Johan, they have always been as one!

Up the garden path they came, completely quiet: the boy of eighteen and the girl of fourteen.

"Hello, Mother – how are things with Father?"

"Go and see him," replied Paulien gently.

Timidly they went inside. The pale face of the boy became even more wan when he caught sight of his father.

The girl bent over him and kissed his hand.

"Hello, Father!"

"Is it really you?" said Johan with a happy smile. "Listen – that's wonderful!"

Did he know why they had come? Probably, for he was not surprised at all, not even when his younger brother came. Johan was the only one of us who seemed to find it all so self-evident – the only one who was not saddened and shaken.

His friend Bertram also came and that made Johan happy. I left them together in the room. When two men who have been bonded together through a life-long intimate friendship stand before the door of eternity to say goodbye then I do not belong there with them. But just as I walked out I overheard Bertram say, "We have to yield, Johan."

Later, after he had gone, Johan commented, "In the same way that Bertram came to see me just now, I once visited him when he lay sick in the Sanatorium."

Paulien clutched at this straw. Could a miracle be possible? Would she still be able to hold on to Johan after all? But when she spoke openly about it, he gripped her fast with all the strength that remained in him – and shook her passionately. No – of that hope he would no longer speak.

What was I to do at this moment? They had forgotten my presence. Sadly I left the room carrying my own burden of ongoing desolation.

That night Emden was bombed. The old *pastorie* shuddered and rattled, but inside in the sickroom a deep peace reigned. It seemed that in those recent days that life was being ever more washed and purified. It had been set free even from the hate that had previously been such a persistent element.

When we saw that calm face and all the patience with which Johan bore his suffering, then my husband and I could not help but say to each other, "How gentle he has become, and... *ja*... and become pure, almost as if he's another person who doesn't belong to this world anymore."

The locals felt empathy with us, but without daring to show it openly. On that point, Groningers are very sensitive. On days like these they are rather wary of being too much of a nuisance. Early in the morning De Lange came with fresh ice, and the neighbours offered accommodation to our family members, all the while remaining behind the front boundary hedge of the garden. Almost no-one came to the *pastorie* at that time, and for that I am still so thankful to the community – that they had actually helped in such a discreet, almost invisible and modest manner! For whosoever offers help, is sorely tempted to push themselves into the foreground. But in our case that never occurred at all.

It was as if the violence of the outside world could no longer penetrate inside this room, as if Johan already lived beyond the reach of the satanic powers which afflict this earth. Whenever a bomb fell or there were grenades exploding, then he communicated a look of mutual understanding to Domie, who kept watch, sitting next to the bed in the light of a small lamp. All that din repeatedly broke the intimacy of their conversation over eternal things, which was conducted therefore during pauses in the shelling.

Johan was now extremely frail and was often wavering on the border between waking and dreaming.

The bombardment lasted more than an hour. Domie wanted to protect Johan who was repeatedly being startled out of his slumber by the grenade blasts and the crump of heavy bombs, but he could not. Finally it became still. The pulsating roar of the machines flying overhead in huge formations dwindled into silence.

Domie read:

I know to Whom I trust my heart,
Though restless sands shift, I'm not swayed.
I know this Rock on which I build,
He fails not, who awaits Thine aid.

And at the evening of my life,
I bring, through strifes and careworn haze,
For every day Thou grant'st me here,
A purer, higher song of praise.

Johan nodded. "That is the evening song," he said.
Then he folded his hands and prayed.

It is remarkable to see such a life... how rich and full of spiritual wealth it has become, as it was with Johan. It all comes back to this single foundation. Coming out of church the previous week, I had spoken again with him about the Paschal message, but he had a better grasp of the depths of the death of Christ than I had, and our conversation had not satisfied him. "After His resurrection Jesus was like the brilliant light of the sun," he said. "He was no longer subject to the natural laws of gravity, nor of space and time. So from that point in time He only appeared to His disciples now and then."

Johan spoke no longer of the resurrection. He lived it. There remained now only the difficult crossing ahead, to be freed from the body. Later, when I brought my own child into the world, I found myself needing to think about Johan's death. What a struggle it is – to come into this life, as well as make our transition into the next. What physical duress! And how burdensome is our earthly existence, all through being bound to our earthly body! However, on the eve of the last day of Johan's life, together with his daughter, I was looking up to the vast heavens, from which the sun was setting. A sea of light shone forth to meet us, just as it must have been on Golgotha, when the sun set behind the three crosses.

And from one of them hung Jesus.

Through His resurrection He broke our earthly bonds; our sinful nature He made clean through His death. The cosmic significance of the Cross stood written in the heavens in flames of fiery red, which softly merged to gold.

The night which followed this display was quiet and undisturbed. Domie read with Johan the High Priest's Prayer – the departing words of Jesus to his disciples.

Let not your heart be troubled – ye believe in God – believe also in Me[25].

It was wonderful how such a peace and rest emanated from these words, read in the quiet of the death chamber. How pregnant with meaning each word became.

First light shimmered in through the chinks. Morning was cool and bright. We opened the shutters. It was everything Johan wished for. There should be the fullness of the light of day within the room of many books where he would die; the golden clarity of sunlight. A dove cooed in the beech tree. Slowly the blossoms opened in the light. I brought some of the white ones inside and put them by the bed. Johan nodded gratefully. There sat his youngest brother who sobbed like a child. Again the small hands folded. Was he praying for his brother? I suspect so, for on that one's shoulders now fell the responsibility for the work they used to do together.

Towards eight o'clock Johan laboured under an oppressive stuffiness. His breathing faltered every so often. Should we not help him? Should the doctor not give him an injection of morphine? Should one becloud such a clear mind toward an unconscious passing over to that other life? Would that do harm to the crossing? What would Johan himself think? We could no longer ask him. But his friend Bertram would know. Earlier, they had already spoken about all these things together. Also about dying and over the question of whether it's justifiable to lighten one's suffering.

I went out to call the doctor. He was ready and able to come over to us right away.

Then the answer to our question from Bertram resounded in the affirmative, but when we came back home it was apparently no longer

---

25 John 14:1.

necessary. About twenty minutes before, while in an unconscious state, it seemed as if Johan had already been taken from us.

"How do you know that?" I whispered to Domie. "When I left he was already just like this."

But Domie shook his head with conviction. "All of a sudden, the contact between us was broken," he replied.

Ja, that had been something beautiful, that living contact between Domie and Johan that had developed in these last days and nights, even without the exchange of words. Both these men were in strong spiritual contact; finely tuned to each other. That became for him a massive spiritual support. God used Domie's arms to help carry Johan through dark caverns and across dark abysses.

Yea, though I walk through the valley of the shadow of death, I will fear no evil...

And there was not a trace of fear in Johan. He was embraced by the strong arms of Love. Dying was arduous, yet God's way was enlarged for him, and all was well.

But then unexpectedly Johan awoke to lucid consciousness. He drove his own body for the last time to obedience, and with an extreme effort of will, he turned his head from one to another and looked at us all one by one. His gaze rested on my youngest brother, as if to say, "My close companion."

This is it – it's coming. We all knew, and were waiting in breathless suspense.

He turned his head away from my brother now, looking straight ahead toward something that we could not see. That must have been the opened gates of Heaven, as his eyes became luminous and the light of the setting sun seemed to reflect in them. Then he exhaled a massive sigh, now free to depart. Toward the light. We remained motionless for several minutes. Then grief took hold of Paulien and I led her away to another room.

"Did you see his eyes?" she asked, sobbing.

"*Ja*, we've all seen them! He has gone home, Paulien. You surely know that!"

"*Ja*, I know that," she said, sobbing upon my shoulder. "But I've been left all alone."

"Don't think of yourself, but of him."

"*Ja*, I really want to do that," she said, suddenly firm. "I'll just think of his happiness! Oh, how magnificent that must have been, what he saw!"

Loving hands dressed the world-weary, now laid-out body in linen with wide borders.

"The jacket – that he so loved to wear," said Paulien.

Now he lay completely still, in the room where the white flowers still blossomed on the table at the foot of his bed.

Nothing had changed, yet actually everything had changed. A sacred atmosphere pervaded the house, for each of us had been lifted in spirit to perceive the glory. There was no space left for sorrow. A gleaming radiance touched everything. Bertram came, after Johan's sister had left the room. We two were the first ones who stood with Johan, whom we both, in our own way, had loved very much.

There emanated a high nobility from the peaceful features, and a smile lay about the mouth.

"How nice he looks," I said to Bertram. "You're a philosopher and have meditated on both life and death. How do you see things now?"

"Man lives, insofar as he is human, in another reality than the visible," said Bertram. "When a man dies, like Johan, he arrives then at his true destination. Death is not onerous, but life."

Was Bertram right?

I thought over Johan's life, that had been a life lived large, but a difficult one, due to all the inner contradictions of his complex nature; the small, mundane daily duties that kept coming into conflict with his natural artistic talent.

"His is a 'having' spirit," said once an English friend to me, who stayed with us in our family home. "Johan is very hungry for love."

And seeing the sublime rest upon that face, there seemed now to be not a single wish nor desire for further fulfilment. Now all contradictions seemed erased, all conflicts resolved in a wonderful harmony. The hunger for music was assuaged by the harmony of the spheres that had encompassed his soul after the silver cord that bound him to his body was broken, when his wings spread out in the light, just as the butterfly drifts away towards rainbows of flowers and leaves us the dead sheath of her cocoon.

"Nothing's been lost," said Bertram. "All that he has given us remains as our spiritual heritage forever. In that sense, there is no separation."

I knew that all that he said was true, but that we could only experience this truth as long as we dwelt on the high places, to which Johan had taken us on his trip to Heaven. For in this pure and rarefied air we were lifted above our own limitations. Yet we were like the disciples, who, upon the transfiguration of Jesus on the mount asked, *Let us stay here, Master – and we shall build three tents*[26]. But He does not grant that we be taken out of the world. We must return below, to the level plain from which we came. Our work there is not yet finished. And there awaits us the familiar grief over that which we have lost; sorrow over the voice which speaks no more to us, the clothes that will no longer be worn, the books that will not be opened, the piano keys that have ceased to be stirred to life, the pencils and paintbrushes that lie there unused, because the hand that handled them lies white and still under the dark earth, but the spirit that controlled them yet lives.

Then through the long nights steals a nostalgia for memories, for a reunion. It even pounces upon us in the middle of the day, through a word which is called to mind, or a scent, a song, a picked flower that

---

26 Matthew 17:4.

once brought delight to the one we loved. Then we stand defenceless and must cede to our grief once more. One time it surprised me some weeks later, by which time the many wreaths and flowers on Johan's grave back in his place of birth lay already withered. I cycled through by-ways crossing our local *polders*[27] where the grain stood ripe in the ears, awaiting the scythe. To me this was all a vast desolation, this sea of golden yellow under a midday sun – the lonely, tilled plain, where I found myself a stranger – and always would, as it was not the ground of my own birth. For at home there were woodlands and I had wandered within them with Johan. There was the little secret grove guarded by the over-arching willows, and there I had lain in the grass with my straw hat over my eyes and there Johan had read to me from Hans Christian Andersen.

27 Reclaimed land from the sea, surrounded by protecting dykes, and mainly used for agriculture.

Chapter 11

And it came once more, when the others were all at our village church one evening and I was by myself at home with a small grey kitten that I had got from Elderling. But it was sick; this kitty was really very ill and that could very well have been my fault – that it became so sick through eating an unbalanced diet, or maybe it was too early to be taken from its mother, or it happened simply because it was born an untameable harvest cat, like the local people said. But I stoked up the fire, for it was getting chilly outside and I put the kitten in a basket right in front of the hearth. It was restless and continually showed that it wanted to go out. Then it meowed plaintively and climbed over the edge, stretched out and snuffled around my hand with her dry little nose.

"What do you want then, puss?"

But the puss did not really know what she was looking for, and I didn't know what to do either. Meanwhile one phrase from Psalm 23 kept arising within me, which Johan had quoted in the last days of his illness:

He leads me beside still waters...

Ja, he had spoken those words, and that filled me with such nostalgia. I tried to play the piano a while, but even this music brought back memories of him. I felt tears running down my cheeks, which I immediately checked. Suddenly the front door opened, and then the door of the room where I was sitting. Were they back from church already? It was Elderling.

"Domie asked if I could just go and pay a visit to the *pastorie* since things aren't too good with the kitten," he said.

There was not much light in the room, as it was already dusk, but in the glow of the fireplace he surely must have caught sight of my tears. I had to be careful to explain why. A Groninger would certainly find it childish if he thought that you were crying over a sick kitten.

"I'm not crying about the kitten," I said.

"No," he replied. "Well that will..." and then after a pause, "Why then?"

"It's because of my brother," I said.

He nodded his understanding.

"I really don't know what will help that kitten," I said. "They say that it's a field-cat and that we can't keep it."

"They say that all the time about a field-cat, but that means *niks*. It can cope well enough here."

"Maybe she was taken from her mother far too soon."

We both now glanced at the sick kitten that I had placed in its basket on the table.

"It's rather warm in this room," said Elderling.

"You've got quite a thick jacket on. But the kitten is feeling the chill. Just look at how it's shivering all over."

"Should I take it with me on the bike, and reunite it with its mother?"

"*Ja*, that seems to me to be its only chance," I replied.

So, we bundled up the kitty for warmth in the little basket – against the cold outside, and Elderling took it under his arm. He had on a thick jacket with a velvet collar. Just like the one my father used to wear. Suddenly a warm feeling of thankfulness surged inside me. He was a father also. And shouldn't you feel yourself at home in a land where the people are so good to you? I let him out and said jokingly at the door, "It is written, 'The righteous takes care of his cattle.'"

He tied the basket with the little pussy behind him on his bike and countered good-humouredly, "Domie didn't preach on that topic this evening!"

"On what then?"

"In my Father's house are many dwellings," he replied.

I didn't know if that was true, but he wanted me to remember this to comfort me in my grief over Johan.

"Thank you so much," I called, while I watched him as he rode off down the path. And I meant it from the bottom of my heart.

An elder of Groningen doesn't preach, but says a single word. And that word perfectly fits the situation.

Chapter 12

Now it is just before Christmas. The nights are long, the days short. The clothing that has been collected for the Christmas distribution by the women of both Associations has been laid out on tables in the *leerkamer*. Mostly there are jumpers, knitted in all kinds of coloured wool that we had in stock and copied from various patterns. There are some skilful knitters here in the village and in the surrounding community. One old lady actually spins the wool herself. On the dyke near the Dollart, sheep graze in the lush grass. A steam pumping station and a house stand nearby. When I arrived at that lonely place with the Christmas list, the woman let me see her thick bedspread, made of sheepskins from her own flock.

In other years members of the Church Council took me in their own cars to the farthest places afield. But now there's no more petrol, so I have to go on my bike. Therefore I got going early, back in November, because the Christmas list takes a lot of time. Visits everywhere are an integral part of it. Almost everyone gives something, but they also expect that you'll calmly sit and spend a little time with them. These are the yearly rounds we make for the community.

In the last months of the year the damp air lies low and heavy over the polders. While I'm sitting in a remote farmhouse, chatting with the farmer and his wife, a heavy hailstorm falls. It clatters against the windows, and swirls in waves over the fallow land, which stretches out, stripped bare, toward the horizon. But inside, it is friendly and warm.

The fire throws a rosy glow all over that shadowy room. On the bureau there stands a stuffed heron.

"Did you shoot it yourself?"

"No, that one turned up last year in the severe winter we had. He was half starved when I found him near a culvert. I found I could catch him easily, as he had no strength left to fly away. I brought him home, but by then he was too far gone. I couldn't keep him like that, so I then had him stuffed. Does *Mevrouw* like birds?"

In accordance with my answer in the affirmative, there followed an animated conversation about birds that breed over by the mud flats – until the storm subsided and I could get through to the next farm on my list. I sank here and there in the mud along the way, and when I returned home I was limping; the consequence of losing a heel from my shoe en-route.

That evening, Mulder came to attend the Church Council meeting.

"Look what I have here – a heel belonging to your wife," he said to Domie. "She lost it near the *stoep* of our house." He pulled my heel out of his bag and with his lower lip drawn back above his goatee, laughed a short coughing chuckle.

Toward bedtime, the wind died down. I was very tired from my long jaunt. It had been an exhausting struggle against the harsh weather. Cold winds and hail had struck me full in the face. When I closed my eyes, I saw it all again before me: the outstretched bare earth with the dark and threatening clouds above. Was it possible that here within a few months the crops would again wave in the breeze and from high in the blue sky the sun would ripen the basking grain?

And was it possible that under my own heart yet another one beat, and I felt the young life move as a light flutter now and then? Was that not a grand, incomprehensible gift? I carried it always with me, securely protected against the cold and infirmity threatening to overwhelm from outside, as a dear secret, as an inner weaving together of my life with that other, newer one. Or was this life already old, standing outside of time, deeply rooted in eternity where no more questions exist?

In the stillness I lay listening and staring at the window. Very softly, snowflakes fell outside. Minute crystals attached to each other – thousands upon thousands of them. When we got up the next morning, the earth would be white. And I would never be alone again, for something new was ever growing in an equally enigmatic way as the snow blanket – something new, that had always been there and that I had always known in the secret life of my subconsciousness; something that I had known in a dream. Or on the edge of waking and dreaming, where I was now. That is why it took such distinct forms. That is why it was so close at hand, so that I could embrace it and we could smile together as we slept.

Christmas came and the Christ Child was born anew in the barren and cold world – and there was again no place for Him other than in the wretchedness of a stable. At the back of the church, where children and the elderly sat listening by the soft, flickering light of many candles, sat a German soldier. He had crept inside since he could not bring himself to stay away, but he had the feeling that he, fully kitted out in German uniform, did not belong to Christmas. He was a native of East Frisia who knew the traditional Christmas story well. He remembered it all, evoked by the soft candlelight and our telling of children's stories. Such a bitter contrast between his current life and those remembered pictures from his youth in the *Heimat!*[28]

Had he also thrown grenades and sung, *Wir fahren gegen Engeland?*[29] He must surely have been more ashamed of it now than before, because tears flooded over his cheeks. And that meant he would become even more ashamed still, because a German soldier never cries,

---

28 Homeland.
29 Last line of the refrain of *das Engelandlied*, a patriotic German Naval song – "We're sailing against England (in battle)."

or so he was taught. That soldier was supposed to be the strong man of iron and steel, unfamiliar with real human emotions. Domie was discreetly made aware of the strange, lonely figure down there, right at the back of the church. There sat a *Duutsch soldoat*,[30] they told him. Domie walked up to him. No, they had forgotten that there sat a human being.

He became uncomfortable, like a shy bird, when Domie approached him. "Might it be alright to stay?" he asked in his East Frisian dialect. *Ja*, certainly he could stay. Christmas was for the lonely and for those who felt guilty. And did we not all stand before the Christ Child with unclean hands?

For:

...that light is come into the world, and men loved darkness rather than light, because their deeds were evil.[31]

That is the heart of the Good News recorded by John and every honest person knows that it is true.

We make compromises, and so are drawn into a net. We are not free. We are as a chrysalis, spun into a cocoon. Only when the mysterious transformation takes place inside the cocoon, only then the dying pupa becomes a butterfly, floating away on the breath of the wind. And as Christ works in us; in the secret depths of our being by the in-streaming of his light, so He makes us free. Such freedom endures our whole life long. Soaring fully in His light only takes place when the cocoon of our earthly existence is broken and we breathe in the shimmering air of eternity.

After the climax of Christmas came the jolt – back to the reality of everyday life. The local children had celebrated Christmas with us and

---

30 German soldier – in Gronings dialect.
31 John 3:19.

mainly their mothers accompanied them. Their fathers declined to be seen participating in "that do at Domie's, with cake and what not."

Incidentally, many mothers would voice the same thoughts, but it wasn't held against them quite as much by the strident working class voices, if for once at Christmas, they stuck their heads inside a church door. That would be considered more of a 'feminine weakness'.

In midwinter at 8 o'clock in the morning it was still dark. Yet on that 27th December, from our bedroom we heard someone's clogs outside on the *stoep*. "Who can that be?" we had wondered in our first winter there, but by our second winter we already knew: a package that needed to be swapped, of course. "That's for you," said Domie.

A quick dash into my dressing gown and then downstairs to answer the door. There stood a girl of thirteen with a packet under her arm. Oh, *ja*, Tetsie was returning some slippers.
"*Mevrouw*, the slippers don't fit."
"Come on in. Were they too big for you?"
"No, *Mevrouw*, too small."
"Child, how is that possible? Just go into the room and put them on."
Tetsie went in and sat on a chair, and tried to put on the slippers – size 39. They really didn't fit; I could see that for myself.
"Then what size are you?"
"Forty-one, *Mevrouw*."
"For goodness sake! You folk have such big feet, hear!"
She glanced at me mischievously, suddenly reverting to her mother dialect.
"*Joa*. But we must also work hard, and so we get such big hands and feet."
Put on the spot, I felt ashamed to look at my own hands and feet, which were not large, and which to her would surely signify laziness.
"And you thought that one size smaller wouldn't fit?"
"Wrong is what it is!"

"Well, you are right about that. But what can we do about the slippers? Can't your little sister wear them?"

"I'd rather have something for myself," said Tetsie with blunt honesty.

That was obvious. You'd rather get a present for yourself than for your little sister – especially if you were just thirteen years old and had longed for a pair of nice warm feet!

"Slippers were written on your wish-list, and you know that these days you can hardly get anything anymore. I had those ones left over from last year, and I thought that they would fit you well. Perhaps a bit too large, I thought, but that is alright for slippers."

"*Joa*, but now they're too small. Can't *Mevrouw* get them changed?"

That was a novel idea.

"Well, I bought them more than a year ago."

"They'll do that then," said Tetsie optimistically.

"Why not go yourself? Then you can have the new ones fitted right away."

"For me they'll do nothing, but *Mevrouw* has bought so many slippers there for us last year – for *Mevrouw* they'll do it, sure. And I don't need to try them; if *Mevrouw* just says forty-one, then it's right good."

Against so many valid arguments I had no answer. But I visualised before me the long open road to the neighbouring town. Nothing for it but to go by bike – one hour there, and I imagined the cold wind, which in this land you almost always seem to have against you, piercing through my clothes and chilling me right to the bone. And then at the shop this ridiculous assertion will be made: "*Ja*, look, last year before Christmas I bought a whole stack of slippers and now this is the only pair left over, but they don't seem to fit..."

And bearing a thoughtful expression, the shop assistant would reply: "*Ja*, look, but there will be no more exchanges at the moment – for slippers from last year especially – and besides we may not do anything more without a receipt."

"*Ja*, but the quality of these slippers is from before the war. And if you only had a pair two sizes larger left over... I would gladly pay extra."

"I don't know, but I'll go and check," the shop girl would respond in the most optimistic case, and then there would be a fair chance that she would go to the almost, by now, empty storeroom and then return with the announcement:

"Size 41 is sold out."

Clearly that trip was a futile idea. What about sending a courier? That didn't help either for a situation with such an uncertain outcome. No, I'd have to go there myself; there was nothing else for it. Next to me stood the sturdy country girl with the yearning childlike face. "Will *Mevrouw* do it?" she asked.

"Alright then," I said with a sigh.

But for Tetsie, there remained not a single cloud on her horizon.

"Don't count on success too soon," I said, cautiously from the *stoep*.

But Tetsie was already scooting down the garden path; she turned around and called out, "It'll be right good!"

Later that morning another mother turned up to change a jumper, of which I still had a couple in reserve – wiser now through the experiences of the previous year, and then another pair of young clients whose wishes I was also able to satisfy.

When it came to about five o'clock in the afternoon the back doorbell rang. There stood a man – tall and broad and square shouldered he was. I had never seen him before, because he was not from our village, but from one of the more remote polders. Up to now I had only made acquaintance with his wife.

He came across as an angry father, because he got straight to the point and called me to account: why had I favoured other children over his boy Eltjo? I failed to understand this accusation, understood only that the giant standing before me was furious. I had to look up if I wanted to speak with him, and by then I couldn't see much because the light was getting dim, and it was even darker outside as there was no snow lying around.

"Why don't you come in," I said. "And who did you say you were? The father of Eltjo? Of which Eltjo?"

"Benders," said the man, gruffly.

"And what is the matter with Eltjo?"

"Why weren't you fair to him? When he came home last night he made a scene and hurled his top right through the kitchen. All the other boys got nice sweaters but all he got was a spinning top."

"And then I suppose you gave him a good spanking after such a temper tantrum when he got home from the Christmas party?"

The man looked at me in surprise.

"No, because I wouldn't give that kind of present to a boy of seven."

"And you think that I gave your boy the top in order to pick on him? What pleasure would I have got from that? Apart from Eltjo, a couple of other children did not receive any clothing either, since they had no need of them, and anyway, I didn't have enough for everyone. You know very well that these are hard times. And you can't get everything that you want when you want."

"*Joa*, but why pick just on our young 'un, exactly?"

"That's what I'm telling you – because I didn't think he needed a sweater."

"Well... we're not exactly needy... but why pick on our boy right now?"

He stood there still sulking, acting just like a spoiled child himself, to whom a good spanking would do no harm.

I gazed upon his giant frame, compared with which I was almost a dwarf and thought that someone else could manage this much better than I.

"And what do you want to do now?"

"The top you can keep," said the man, and laid the thing with a scornful gesture on the mangle.

"*Weighed in the balance and found wanting*[32]," I said. But he was not exactly knowledgeable about Bible matters and so the meaning went over his head. "And so now Eltjo doesn't have a present."

That he understood clearly.

"Have you got something else?" he asked.

"I'll go and have a look. There was a sweater exchanged this afternoon, but that one was too small to be what you've come for. I would really like you, for once, to think about the fact that I had to wrap up over a hundred parcels, and what a task that was at the time."

"*Joa, joa,* that I could well believe," he said, now in a better mood. And when another sweater was actually found that should fit Eltjo well, his cloudy face brightened right up.

"I thank you," he said.

"I hope that it fits – and if not maybe your wife could alter it. I still have enough wool left over that you could come and get if you need to."

We took our leave as good friends, but whenever I saw the spurned top lying back in the cupboard, whether in summer, autumn or winter, there always came a sour taste to my mouth as I thought how far above the sullied ground of our greedy passions stands the true meaning of Christmas.

---

32 Daniel 5:27.

Chapter 13

The life of our various church associations and other pastoral work carried on comfortably in its usual and regular way. But what of results? What does one expect of such ministries? To ask that is such a habitual trait. Everyone demands results from their work – a farmer and a housewife, a doctor and a nurse. Why not then a worker in the Lord's vineyard? You just want to see fruit. However, you gradually learn that in this sort of work there is hardly anything to see, because the Word of God works in such a mysterious, hidden way.

And Jesus spoke to them in parables and said:

Behold, a sower went forth to sow, and when he sowed, some seeds fell by the wayside, and the fowls came and devoured them up. Some fell upon stony places, where they had not much earth and forthwith they sprung up, because they had no deepness of earth. And when the sun was up, they were scorched, and because they had no root, they withered away. And some fell among thorns and the thorns sprung up, and choked them. But other fell into good ground, and brought forth fruit, some an hundredfold, some sixtyfold, some thirtyfold.[33]

There are always stony places and people whom we can't reach. The unapproachable, those who have known for ages how things stand, yet don't even bother to pay any attention to the gospel. Should even one grain fall along the pathway of their lives, immediately the

---

33   Matthew 13:3-8.

birds of their intellect swoop down and snatch it away. Then there are all the thorns and lost opportunities that may tread upon the germinating seed.

Yet gradually you learn, with a certain serenity, to develop a healthy detachment from such things, because you'll be held accountable for only a small part. It's like working in the garden: I don't doubt myself if the potatoes don't turn out well or the seed doesn't germinate, since that is due to circumstances beyond my control and above my power to change, but it does no good to sit here writing if there are weeds growing up in the Master's garden, and then to start feeling sorry after the potatoes are planted late, the seed is not sown, or the young cabbages are not watered. Because those tasks are part of the ongoing job for which I am responsible.

After my exams last winter, I was officially called by the Church Council to the office of Evangelist. The congregation thought things were going just fine without the appointment, but I don't gladly do work where I have no jurisdiction, and so up to that point I had refused to teach catechism. But now things are completely different. Now, whenever there are catechism classes that must be undertaken for whatever reason, then it bothers me if I act like a farmer who has neglected to sow his crop while the weather is ideal.

Occasionally you glean from a conversation that the seed is indeed germinating in hearts and has begun to shoot forth. This is always a cause for rejoicing and a source of wonder, just as you always appreciate with joy and thankfulness a flower that grows and blossoms from that which you have yourself sown.

The plot of ground that we had been assigned to work had been neglected for years. The local adult generation was completely un-churched. Work had been done there, but among them politics often became a substitute for religion, and that authority which, for the believer, comes from God's Kingdom, was attributed to Russia by the Communists living in these parts. If he could pray, it would not be "Thy Kingdom come," but "Let Russia come here and then we'll have Utopia." Of course one could ask them a couple of practical questions, such as "There are many more farmhands than farmers, so don't you think that you would quarrel over the division of farmland, if you're already envious about a mere Christmas present?" But in the new utopia there is supposedly no place for dealing with jealousy and other base human traits which the Christian believer recognises as the old fashioned word, 'sin'. They think change must come not from inside-out, but from outside-in. Make the world right and the people will automatically show virtue. Everywhere this romantic vision wields a great attractive power over the younger people. Among our young catechists we encountered these ideas over and over again. The Bible teaches the opposite: the real revolution begins in Man himself; rebirth and conversion through the working of God's Spirit and then sanctification.

The uniqueness of the Christian Faith is nonetheless true in that it is not an abstract ideal, but recognises real historical development influenced by both environment and origins; what we have become through a long line of ancestors as well as through circumstances, even of climate and soil. But that it offers in response a whole new reality; the action of God's Spirit is like the yeast that leavens the whole lump of dough from within, or the tiny mustard seed from which a large sturdy plant grows.[34] The chain of cause and consequence that shackles us and which we drag along is broken – not by itself, but by God's power – and we are set free. A new Heaven and a new earth, with renewed, reborn people! A kingdom, that is coming, that is already established to the extent that it lives in our hearts. "The Kingdom of God is within you," said Christ.

---

34 Luke 13:18-21

As we sing:

And in each one, who belongs to Him,
The new Kingdom does begin.

But whenever folk are presented with that reality, opposition springs up. We had in the young people's group a very astute boy. One day he told us that he wasn't coming back because he did not believe, and that it was unfair to stay with the group just to have fun and socialise.

"Fine," said my husband. "If you feel that way, then it is better that you go. But listen well; God is already working on you. That's why you don't want to come any more."

The matter was now taken out of our hands and we just had to calmly hand it over to God. And there still operates today what the old folk call 'the irresistible force of God's Spirit.'

After one year he returned. Shy and reluctant, he entered the *leerkamer*. A Groninger is rather afraid of standing out, but Domie acted as if he had never been away, and accepted him back as a familiar face into the circle of fellowship. During his absence the seed had germinated and put down its roots.

Chapter 14

The night was cool and still. The motorcar made its way along the lonely, dark road. The doctor drove and Domie sat next to him. I sat by myself on the back seat.

It was the night of Saturday leading into Sunday morn. Poor Domie, I can't help it if I must rouse you from sleep on such an untimely night. But in a little while, go back home and stay calm, for I'm quite ready to play this out alone. Tomorrow morning the people are coming to church, just as usual, and you should be at your post to bring them the good news.

A grey fog hung over the land, through which the evanescent moonlight could barely penetrate. There was expectancy in the air – something of the coming spring, something familiar – in that each year it returns, yet at the same time it was strange and unknown. Indeed, my mother must have felt this when she was expecting me, as I was her youngest. But even more strange and unfamiliar must have been that awakening feeling when Johan came into the world, because he was her first-born.

Mother!

When a man is about to die, he speaks her name. Johan had called Mother's name one day before he died and he had now gone to be with her. And she who is about to face this mystery of life, of giving birth, she also calls her own mother's name, but very softly, because it is only for her, and not for the living. She must know that in this hour you are in need of her. She hears your quiet prayer; can't you now feel her constant presence? Do you not see her eyes in the twilight and hear once more her encouraging voice? *I have left this for you my child. And now it is your turn.*

Certainly, Mother, now it's my turn. But please stay with me for as long as I have need of you.

There lay the small provincial town of Winschoten,[35] sleeping in the night. Just one more bend in the road, and we pulled to a stop right in front of the hospital. A door that opened noiselessly, a night sister with a large cap, a long dimly lit corridor through which we walked, a lift that hummed as it sent us upwards. Then a room with a white bed. By the light of the shaded lamp that glowed above, I could see that Domie was pale.

"I'm going to have a good sleep now and you should too. So go home and have some rest. I'm in good hands here, aren't I Sister?"

"*Ja, Dominee.* Nothing for you to worry about. You can go back now with the doctor."

"Take good care of my husband now, won't you, Doctor?" I joked.

"*Ja*, it's all going to turn out fine," responded the doctor cheerily, while starting back up the corridor where he had been waiting for Domie.

Shortly after that Domie also disappeared around the door frame. Now stillness reigned throughout the building. I could only hear the regular steps of the Catholic sister, who kept watch and read from her Book of Hours, occasionally entering and leaving the room.

Now she stuck her head round the door.

"How are things?"

"Fine, Sister."

"Need anything?"

"No, Sister, thank you."

---

35 Winschoten is a provincial town on the railway between Groningen and Germany, about 12 km from the border.

"Press the call button by your bed if there is anything."

"*Ja*, Sister."

Again peace – a rustling profound quiet. Was I awake or still dreaming? There were Mother's eyes again, beneath that high pale forehead and there also was the familiar smile round her mouth.

"So, child... listen! You're lying here... good! A whole lot better than the woman on that makeshift camp bed, whom I once helped."

"*Ja*, I'm perfectly well, Mother. I know full well that I must be thankful for so much comfort and good care."

"Have you thought everything through?"

"All the baby clothes were brought in a suitcase by car. If you had seen them, you would have been satisfied. *Ja*, it's all been thought through properly and I've been able to get everything I need. Not in excess, but enough of everything."

"More than that you do not need."

"Of course. Less is more, wouldn't you say, *hè*?"

The smile became even broader.

"You already know it all, you hear. But how are things now at home? Have you already completed all your work or have you more or less stepped aside from it for now?"

"I had reckoned that I would be away from home before too long, so tonight I put our bank giro account in order. About 9 o'clock I finally managed to fall into an awful sleep, but I wanted to have that work all finished first. Up to then I didn't realise that I'd have to actually leave tonight, but now it's all clear to me, even the tax situation. Which is a relief. Domie hates to be bothered with such things."

Mother nodded. "It is wise of you, that you sent him off home again," she said.

"It's Saturday night, and tomorrow he must preach," I answered.

"*Ja*, in all circumstances, do your duty."

"He's coming back at midday tomorrow – he said."

"We shall hope that your baby is both for you and for him, because," – now twinkled the humour in Mother's eyes, just as of old – "men are complete heroes, but with something like this you can do better without their help."

Now we laughed together softly in the intimate familiarity of the night.

"You must get some sleep," said Mother. "You need to conserve your strength."

She – or was it the sister? – came to my bed and sat, holding my hand. I don't know any more, but it was good to lie there like that and while sleeping to watch and wait for the wonder of birth that drew nearer with every breath.

Chapter 15

Greet had gone to fetch the doctor. She heard the door shut tight and the motorcar driving away in the night. Now she is alone in the house. What should she do? Go to bed? But she is wide awake and can't drop off to sleep quickly. This is a strange night. Everything around seems to be listening. Everywhere she walks in the house her own tread sounds hollow. If only *Mevrouw* were here...

The night has been interrupted and early in the morning she must check on Nero. Should she just go now and take a look? It's really dark out there and there will be no-one about on the path.

From the bottom of the kitchen cupboard she fetches the feed-pail, into which she pours the meal from a bag. She pumps some water in and mixes it all up with a stick. She opens the kitchen side door and walks down the winding path. Arriving at the shelter she pulls the secret string. Nero is not expecting such an early visit. He has sunk in deep slumber, and only notices Greet when she is standing before his pen. Then he begins to snuffle and ponderously scrambles to his feet. He is becoming severely overweight; already carrying an ample 200 pounds. This time Greet is ahead of him. She has already tipped the feed into the trough before Nero can get up on his hind legs and start to kick against the partition wall with his front trotters. He falls greedily on his food, since a pig can always eat well, even in the middle of the night.

Now to retreat with the empty pail. Keep your mind on the job,

Greet! Don't forget to lower the bar just up there above your head, so that as soon as you are outside the shelter, the door will shut tight behind you. But the strange shapes of this night take hold of your imagination and you become a little scared of them. That's why you only do half your job and forget the bar. Greet, Greet! What are you thinking? Anyone can just go inside and discover the secret! You might as well go to bed now, but the door isn't barred. This afternoon, if you're not on guard when Domie is away at the hospital, this act of forgetfulness will catch you out!

During the day the youth at a loose end will freely wander about the grounds of the empty *pastorie* since they don't really know what to do with themselves now that the *leerkamer* is closed. So, feeling bored, they'll wander about the garden, and in particular will zero in on the bomb-shelter. Well may you go pale when you spy them going into the garden; your friend Giny is surprised by all the consternation, but the cat is already out of the bag! Fecco and Eltjo have already pushed beyond the unlocked door and they emerge aghast, yet half laughing.

And you, who have pursued them with Giny – well might you put on a wild face and yell out, "There are rats in the air raid shelter!" There is not a soul who would believe you – or did you really think that a boy of about eighteen cannot tell the difference between a rat and a pig? Poor Greet! The boys take pity when they see your startled face and begin to console you. They assure you that they are the best at keeping a secret and that "no-one suspects anything like a pig in a bomb-shelter" and "I swear ten guilders that I didn't," says Fecco.

"*Joa*, sure, man! If we'd known how upset you'd be, we'd never have gone to the bomb-shelter," says Eltjo.

Eltjo is Petertje's brother. So Petertje definitely didn't blab to him. Now both of them know, but the older brother never realised that the younger one did. So in other words, Groningers can be silent if necessary.

"And *Mevrouw* is in the hospital," says Greet. "She always thought this was so dangerous! And it's all out in the open now!"

"You're certainly in a spot of trouble with this," says Giny. "But we won't ever blab. And now you'll have to tell all of us the full story!"

Then just go and sit over there, Greet, on the steps leading down to the bomb-shelter and tell them. I don't think you can complain about an inattentive audience now. Since Giny is staying over because Domie hasn't yet returned home, tonight when you're in bed you can both talk about it all again. That will help pass the time and reduce the tension.

Finally, at two o'clock in the morning there comes the sound of a motorcar zooming along a country road. Will it stop by the fence? How often have they asked themselves that over the last few hours? With bated breath they lie there listening. *Ja*, he's stopping!

"That's Domie for sure," says Giny.

They put on their slippers and dressing gowns and go down the stairs. A key rattles in the lock. The door opens. In a rush they pounce on Domie. You can read the excitement on their faces.

"We now have a little son," says Domie.

"Oh, man! Congratulations, Domie!"

They all take each other's hands and do a little impromptu dance around in a circle.

"What's his name?"

"How much does he weigh?"

But suddenly Domie is drained and weary.

As in a daydream, he remembers the doctor's voice saying: "Give the *Dominee* a glass of water." Then there was a sister who accompanied him along the corridor in the ward, where they seated him on a bench and got him a drink. And then suddenly he was standing in the nursery room, where a sister was holding a miniature human being in a bath and that miniature was his little boy!

"Did you see him in the bath? And was he very good?" his wife had queried.

"He's a beautiful boy," he had responded to her. "And he weighs 7 pounds, 1 ½ ounces, the sister said."

Domie now wearily repeated those same words to the girls: "He's a beautiful boy, and he weighs 7 pounds, 1 ½ ounces..."

Giny and Greet went on ahead to the kitchen to cook a bowl of oatmeal for Domie. "As you haven't eaten anything the whole day," said Greet. And Giny also fried potatoes for him on the electric stove.

"And now tell us about Hansje!" they chorused. Tired or not, they would not be deterred.

What do his eyes look like? What kind of hair? What about the hands? Is *Mevrouw* bringing him home soon? And is she well? Enlivened by the girls' excitement, Domie took up the story:

"Well, when he'd been washed, the sister brought him to *Mevrouw*. She liked having him in her arms and then she said, 'Hello my dear little boy, we've known each other for a while, haven't we? I hope that we'll both have a lot of joy together.'"

At the word "joy," a shadow stole over Greet's face. Was this the moment when they would have to tell of the bomb-shelter fiasco? Now – tonight, with Domie so happy, but also so exhausted that his features looked drawn and haggard?

But it was perhaps for the best. And Giny was already launching into it.

"Today," she suddenly remarked, as she was pouring the porridge into a bowl, "some boys went inside the bomb-shelter."

Domie gulped.

"Who then?" he asked. "And how could that have happened?"

"Last night in my confusion I forgot to bar the door properly and so Fecco and Eltjo have been in there and naturally now Giny also knows."

"But we know how to keep our lips buttoned up," said Giny.

"*Ja*, Groningers certainly know how to stay silent," replied Domie. "But how could it be, just like that, that right at the eleventh hour, it was discovered?"

"*Mevrouw* wouldn't rest so easy in her bed if she knew," said Greet.

"I'd actually wanted to have him slaughtered during the time when

Mevrouw was away. Such matters are not for her. However, now it certainly needs to be seen through, right to the end. Not that I don't trust the boys to keep their mouths shut – I know them too well for that – but now the snow's gone more people are likely to be roaming about over that side of the house, so it's best that instead of being kept hidden in there, the beast should definitely be evacuated. It will be a massive relief to *Mevrouw* if she comes home and finds the bomb-shelter empty."

Greet was now looking so pleased, as if she had done them all a big favour! *Mevrouw* soon home with the baby – and Nero pickling in the brine! What would she have to say about that?

It was the midday visiting hours in the hospital. There was a tray of cups ready next to my bed. Yesterday there had been a massive crowd of nineteen here to wish me and my son well. Would we encounter the same gale force of as many visitors today?

It was already five to two when the door opened and round the corner appeared the elated face of *Vrouw*[36] Courts, and after her old Geertje, who reached only to about her waist. Just like the silent 20's slapstick duo, Watt and half-Watt.

"My word, *Mevrouw*, that you in there?" began *Vrouw* Courts. "*Och*, goodness me – how's it really going with you, and where is the young baby?"

"Down in the nursery."

"*Och*, my word – but we must have a look at him now we've come all that way from Oldiek."

"*Joa, joa*," nodded Ol Geertje, her eyes blinking. "We have to see him."

"You'll see him – at two the sister's bringing him here. But how did you get in? It's surely not yet visiting hours!"

"*Och*, I never asked them... They know ol' *Vrouw* Courts here very well. And that's right good!"

---

36 A shorter form of Mevrouw, also meaning "wife", "woman" or "Mrs". Carries more formality and respect.

"*Joa*," nodded ol' Geertje, "that's right good!"

"Did you just walk right past the sister on duty at reception?"

"There was no-one down there, hear."

The door opened and a sister carried in a little pink bundle in her arms.

"*Och,* goodness now, here comes your little treasure."

Vrouw Courts, with a competent expression on her face, took the baby from the sister without a word. And pulled back the blanket.

"*Och,* goodness, what a precious little love. Look at 'im, Geertje – what a stout lad! *Mevrouw* can be right proud of him!"

"I'll come right back," said the sister, who could do nothing more here, especially when faced with Courtsje's[37] powerful gestures and garrulous commentary.

"That's good, hear! I'll look after him well. Heavens above, I've already helped raise so many kiddies! Whole of Oldiek, roundabouts. There you'd be just a beginner, Sister!"

But Sister's white cap had already disappeared round the corner.

"What eyes, what lovely eyes. My word, he looks you right in the face! Geertje – have a look – isn't he just like Domie?"

"*Joa,* man, but he's more like *Mevrouw,*" said Geertje.

"No you old quarrelpot, how can you say that? He looks like Domie!"

The discussions over the question of whom he most resembled evidently began to bore Hansje. He began to cry. *Vrouw* Courts shushed him in her arms.

"*Lutje, potje, reert...*"[38] she soothed – and then a new diagnosis was quickly determined: "He's hungry."

"Sister has to weigh him first," I chipped in.

Courtsje looked unsatisfied. "That I'd never do," she said. "You can tell just by looking at a child, hear, if he's getting enough. He doesn't need those blessed scales for sure... just be still, little man."

---

37 "Courtsje" is the diminutive form of her surname, the -je suffix functioning the same way as -y in English names e.g. "Jonesy."

38 "Li'l bubba cries..."

"Just pass him to me," I suggested, "then he'll settle down until the sister comes."

Vrouw Courts cast an expert eye over him once more from head to toe and then reached over to pass him over.

The two old women bent over the bed with tender faces. As soon as Hansje felt my own warmth, he relaxed and lay there on my arm, gazing at the faces above him with large eyes, full of wonder. He was gazing at the rosy apple cheeks, the chin with the round dimple, the bright blue roguish eyes and the prominent forehead of *Vrouw* Courts, over which a grey coif rippled, all neatly closed by a bun, and then to the wrinkled face of ol' Geertje, with the blinking eyes.

"Let me tell you this," said *Vrouw* Courts. "You'll have to give him something more soon: a bit of *kindermeel*[39] or something."

"The doctor says..."

Vrouw Courts looked indignant. "Let the doctors prattle on all they like, hear, I'll have no truck with them! You must do what I'm telling you. Frankly, such doctors let children fade away, man! *Joa*, chilled on the outside, starved on the inside. They must have something. *Niks* better than *kindermeel*, hear! Then they grow like cabbages. That youngest one of the Joacobs family – *Mevrouw* would know them well – he was only four pounds. I dashed over there straightaway with *kindermeel*. Now he's as heavy as a millstone, hear!"

"But Hansje was already seven pounds, one and a half at birth," I said proudly.

Geertje clapped her hands together. "Hear that?" she said. "What a gift, *hè*?"

"*Joa*, he's a lusty child," said *Vrouw* Courts. "It's a right miracle, man!"

Geertje gently tapped like twinkletoes on his little cheek. His little face contorted slightly.

---

39 Literally "children's meal"; a finely milled rice grain meal for infants, similar to Farex in Britain.

"Oh look, now he's smiling at ol' Geertje. *Joa*, let's see another smile, my darling."

"You can't start doing anything useful in here," said *Vrouw* Courts. "Those sisters are giving all the orders, but once he goes home, then *Mevrouw* must do as I said before – right away a little bit of *kindermeel*. That little one of my own granddaughter – you know her well, Geertje, the one who had *terminen...*"

"*Terminen*? What's that?" I interjected. *Vrouw* Courts hadn't thought for a moment that here my knowledge of their Groningen dialect fell rather short, but chalked up my ignorance to inexperience in the field of having babies.

"Doesn't *Mevrouw* know that? *Mevrouw* hasn't raised any children yet. *Joa* – how shall I explain, Geertje? *Terminen* is... well... *terminen*. Now and then it comes on and keeps on getting worse, and then suddenly the child's gone. That little baby born to Marijke's daughter died just like that, as Geertje well knows – she went all blue."

Suddenly a light went on for me. "Oh – you mean convulsions!"

But that was a word that neither of the great-grandmothers recognised.

"No, *terminen*," said Courtsje.

The door opened and in stepped the sister from before.

"I had almost forgotten you," she said. "Oh, the little one's in Mother's arms? How spoiled you are, hear!"

And to both the old ladies, "Don't you think he's a cute boy?"

"*Joa*, it's a right wonder," said *Vrouw* Courts.

"It's a miracle," said Geertje.

The sister took Hansje from me to weigh him.

"You do that **each** time?" asked Courtsje with a suspicious glance at the scales. "That really is not worth fussing about, you know."

Her pointed remark made no impression. The sister this time round had little sense of humour, and only found the old ladies to be irritating smart-alecks.

"*Ja*," said the sister, curtly.

"At our village school, the Consultation Bureau[40] weighs the babies just once each fortnight," said Geertje.

"Because at the very least we can tell by just looking if they're putting on weight," added *Vrouw* Courts.

"We have our own methods for checking that," said sister, drily. "But now *Mevrouw* must get some rest. Soon it will be visiting hours again. So how did you actually manage to get inside the ward?"

"Through the doors," said Courtsje, waggishly. "Room 17 upstairs, Domie told us and then we were here with no-one nearby. Not that we needed help, hear. We can find the way all by ourselves. Coming, Geertje?"

"*Dag, Mevrouw* – and once you're back home," with a sideways glance at the sister, who was weighing my little one, "then do as I told you."

"Pass on my greetings to everyone at Oldiek, won't you? And thanks for the visit!"

They turned back once more at the door. "You're welcome," said Courtsje, playfully.

And Geertje added, clutching her umbrella, "We're going home to brag about your *jonkje!*[41]"

"Who were they?" Sister asked, still standing before the scales with her back to me.

"Two women from Oldiek. One of them has been a maternity assistant-nurse her whole life, and thus has had a lot of experience with small children."

"Oh, indeed?" said Sister.

"Sister – is *terminen* the same thing as convulsions?"

Sister took Hansje from the scales and turned to me with that little bundle of humanity on her arm.

"Have they scared you with tales of convulsions?" she asked sternly. "How foolish!"

---

40 Government health and welfare office which sent staff to small villages to perform health checks on children.
41 "Young 'un."

"*Och*, no. She only said that a young baby of her granddaughter had died, and it had gone blue all over."

"This afternoon you haven't had any sleep, of course. I won't allow anyone to see you before half past three."

I was thinking of the visiting two great-grandmothers, who had easily found their own way to my room. Perhaps some of the younger generation were just as smart.

"Before long you'll have another 20 grams on your baby."

"Would a little *kindermeel* be alright to give him, Sister?"

"*Kindermeel*? For a newborn infant? Where did you get that idea? Did the old nurse tell you that?"

I thought of *Vrouw* Courts and of the hundreds of children that she, following her own dictum, "had made to grow big." Even in the area of child nutrition, the professors were apparently still not in agreement.

"*Ja*, and under her care the kiddies certainly thrived."

"Some children won't die, even if you give them horse-beans to eat," said the sister, acerbically.

Chapter 16

The Churchwardens had also made plans. Before the homecoming of the young prince, they had given the carpenter the job of putting a new window frame in the small downstairs room, which would be set up as the baby's nursery. And the old painter came along with rolls of wallpaper, panes of glass and a large can of light coloured paint. Festive gatherings of women and youth groups were held, and at the pot-luck feast, as they called it, even chocolate milk and biscuits sprinkled with aniseed *muisjes*[42] had been procured, for which coupons had been put aside far in advance.

The house looked like a garden of flowers. The young citizen of the world, in whose honour all this had been prepared, allowed himself the pleasure and acted as if it were self-evident that he would be made so welcome upon his arrival. He accepted the little gifts and listened to the poems read out, all with an impassive face. He even appeared on the stage in the *leerkamer* with a long poem of his own, to make his acquaintance with all the friends present:

Hé, what has this come to, this frightful to-do,
Blest sleep which I have to forsake?
Was in my cradle at rest, wrapped up in my nest,
But now Mama has kissed me awake.

---

42 *Gestampte muisjes* – "Powdered Mice" – powdered sugar granules infused with aniseed flavouring, which is popular when sprinkled on bread or buttered toast.

She said that it's time to be put on display,
But faced with a crowd I'm quite shy.
I'm not in disguise, but am shown like a prize,
Do I have to make friends and just why?

What terrible misery one has to endure,
Your faces out there I do dread.
To smile at the thought of trying to sort
And learn each of your names in my head.

But be not dismayed when I get those all wrong,
As folk come and gawk at first meeting.
On that I'm not keen, and I might make a scene,
But that's just my manner of greeting.

When I get much bigger as many days pass,
We shall share many joys – me and you.
I know that you've come to honour my Mama
And I'm thankful your loyalty's true.

Thank you to those who brought a nice gift,
From which we derive so much pleasure.
I'm spoiled as you know, but I'm going to grow,
So I hope that those clothes fit my measure.

At two or at three, maybe things will fit me,
That Mama's carefully putting aside.
Now Oldieksters and Hörnsters, I'm back now to rest
And safely in sleep to abide.

Mama let's go off to bed and lay me down there,
These moments of joy are but fleeting.
So, on with the party and have lots of fun,
I'll see you again at next meeting.

In answer they all sang to him their version of the national song
Whoever has Dutch blood flowing in their veins:

We are so thankful and rejoice
To come united here,
To feast in honour of your child
Whose life we hold so dear.

For all of us are now a part
Of Domie's fam'ly throng,
And now we sing with fullest voice
Our celebration song.

We quietly hope your dearest son
May prosper and be free,
Perchance to follow Domie and
A theologian be.

Especially as she Him believed,
And chose her Maker's lot.
Live life together long, with joy,
Such blessings flow from God.

During the day Hansje lay outside in the sunshine and stared into the blue heavens, which seemed to reflect the colour of his eyes. He was healthy and speedily gaining weight. Only one time in his young life did we call the doctor to see him and in hindsight that turned out to be unnecessary. Sometimes he had a little pain in his belly. Barley water was then the prescription.

That Saturday evening he needed to have some of that medicine administered. Papa wished to give it to him in a little bottle, but then received immediately in return from his son a good deal of something more than barley water! Hansje seemed to show little appreciation for the gift. He constantly interrupted his drinking with howls of disapproval. "Come on, my young chappie," spoke Domie to calm him down. "It's so nice." But Hansje did not agree and kicked his legs in anger.

"Can you come take a look and check this pain he has in his tummy?" said Domie.

"Just keep on with it until it's finished – I've got to do something in the kitchen," I replied.

After a certain interval Domie came to fetch me, bearing a frightened expression. Had the fear of *terminen* seized him? We never spoke that word, but we both thought it could be. How else could we explain the unexpected sudden spasms in his tiny body as related to me by Domie?

"It is already so late," said Domie.

"*Ja*, the doctor would be in bed by now," I concurred.

"We shouldn't really..." added Domie.

"*Ja*, but for tonight... otherwise we shan't have any peace. But it is an ungodly hour to call the doctor; already past midnight!"

"I'll go," he decided, and he ran to the *leerkamer* where his bike was stored.

By the time the doctor did come, Hansje was lying peacefully in my arms.

"*Ja*, Doctor," I said apologetically, "he looks alright now, as if nothing is the matter, but Hansje was crying a lot before. And we felt a bit stressed about it."

"*Ja*, sure," said the doctor, in a good mood, "I am used to that. As the old proverb goes, *When the doctor is found, the child is sound*! But pass him over here to me and let's see what's ailing him."

Doctor got right into it; he checked Hansje over from all sides, let him bend over forwards and backwards and even turned him upside down on his head, so it seemed to me.

"Everything's completely normal," said Doctor, after his conscientious examination. "I can't find anything amiss. But what are your thoughts about it – now that all this has happened?"

"Could he have gotten too warm, Doctor?" I asked tentatively. "He looked rather pink this afternoon when he was laying in the pram. And when I put my hand under his cap, it was quite hot to the touch."

"*Ja*," said the doctor, nodding. "That is indeed possible. Today is the first really warm day we've had since winter and if you hadn't taken that into consideration when you put the pram in the sun, then it'd get stifling under that cap and so the baby would get too hot."

"So what should we do now, Doctor?"

"Nothing, just go back to bed and put the baby down to sleep. He'll really be tired from all that crying and his stomach will be unsettled from the heat."

It was clear to us that we'd called the doctor out from his bed for nothing and we were rather embarrassed about the scene we'd made. But the doctor shrugged off our excuses. "I can always count on the fact," he said, "that people, upon having their first-born, will on at least one occasion call me from my bed for no valid reason. That is one of the hazards of our profession, just as the risk of your profession is," he continued to Domie, "to be awoken out of sleep by your baby when you have to preach the next morning."

"But, have a think about this," he added at the door, "for a baby, too hot is just as bad as too cold, hear."

"*Ja*, Doctor," I replied meekly.

Then he went on his way once more, in just as happy a frame of mind as he was when he arrived on our doorstep. I marvelled at the patience with which he negotiated the 'risks' of his profession. Such a doctor always stood ready to serve anyone in need, and whatever we from our inexperience had messed up, he would have to come and put right again.

Chapter 17

The bombardment of the submarine pens at Emden became increasingly more intense. You could set the clock by it: every evening at half an hour before midnight the English fly-boys came over, and it wasn't until one-thirty or two in the morning when their droning finally ceased and the machines went on their way home. You sometimes glimpsed them flying like birds across the crescent of the moon in line-astern formation, their pulsating roar filling the air. Barrage balloons floated above Emden and everything there was blacked out, but despite that, from where we were on the other side of the Dollart, Emden was so lit up by the bombs that the English dropped, that in the light of the rosy afterglow you could almost read the newspaper. Shrapnel from the anti-aircraft fire randomly clattered onto our roof. First you could hear the whistle of falling bombs, then the loud crump as they exploded. On certain occasions aerial dogfights took place and then bombs fell all over the countryside. They even exploded behind the church – such that one night our bedroom was bathed in a brilliant white magnesium light – and they also fell on the farms. No-one felt safe anymore. The walls of the houses shook with the sound of bombs falling to the left and right around them. In such instances the cot with our sleeping baby was moved to another room, where there was less risk of flying glass shards and splinters. But would that now give Hansje sufficient protection? Could I even protect him at all from these infernal powers?

I now did for him what I'd never done for myself. I took him down into the bomb-shelter. Insofar as we are a part of nature, it is a deeply ingrained instinct to want to protect our little ones who are dependent on our watchfulness. Our reason tells us that we can never predict where and when a bomb will explode, but our faith says that not one hair of our head shall fall without the will of our Heavenly Father.

With my little boy in my arms I witnessed a terrific light show in the northern sky that would have been awe-inspiringly grand if it were not so gruesome: falling shells that painted striking luminous stripes like fireworks on the canvas of the heavens. This wasn't designed for our benefit however; it was only intended for the harbours of Emden. But how many bombs did fall over the town as well? How many mothers sat there in dark cellars, holding sleeping or screaming children in their arms? You inevitably feel a mixture of guilt, shame and disgust that we've all participated in such acts by thought, word and deed. And even if we were not in a position to act, the following day we'd still say to each other: "They've bombed Emden again," and we'd rejoice over it! However, I knew very well that we were only saying that in the hope that this would hasten the end of the war and that the victory of the Allies would once again bring security. I knew that we had endured injustice and suffering under great duress. Speaking personally, I understood the truth of the Bible text, *For they have sown the wind, and they shall reap the whirlwind*[43] – and that what we'd witnessed at Emden was therefore a just punishment for Warsaw, Belgrade, Rotterdam, London and other cities. *"Wir werden Ihre Städte ausradieren,*[44]*"* had boasted Hitler's voice over the radio. And yet, and yet...

Who among us, after twenty years, would not be ashamed of that massive slaughter of humanity that such events brought about? Wouldn't we excuse ourselves by saying, "But that act was committed by barbarians in those days. We're no longer the type of people who

---

43 Hosea 8:7.
44 "We shall annihilate your cities."

would do that kind of thing!" But all the while the germ of evil is once again being thoroughly sown in the hearts of this younger generation.

There always stands before us the Sinless One – who took upon himself our guilt and atoned for it by His death, and He did all that, when we were without strength.

Chapter 18

Those days were also marked by the forced conscription by the Germans of Dutch citizens into the *kabelwacht.*[45] Somewhere in our neighbourhood a German telephone cable laid across the countryside alongside the railway had been sabotaged – so they claimed. Therefore all our rural citizens were forced to do guard duty. One man from each family had to serve time, standing watch over the route of the cable along the railway line embankment. Excepting of course the NSB and Dutch sympathisers loyal to the *Reich*, as they would never have participated in such things as sabotage!

How long that order was to last was not explained to us. But shifts were assigned every night from ten to one and then from one to four o'clock in the morning, as the rousing song says, which was actually composed on the cable watch and goes as follows:

THE CABLEWATCH   *(to the tune of Lili Marlene)*

All citizens must stand guard,
It's really not a joke.
And it may cost your head if
Sly hands the cable broke.
Through rain and wind and biting cold,
The guard who's true to Holland's soul,
Is on the cable watch,
Is on the cable watch.

---

45 The Cable Watch.

One is wearing clogs with
A staff clasped in his hands.
One has on his farmer's cap
As at his post he stands.
And there they watch across the land,
For three hours straight their post is manned,
From ten 'til one, then 'til four,
They're on the cable watch.

You hear them rushing homewards
And slamming their doors tight.
They're shouting loud "I'm starving"
And you would know they're right.
Through rain and wind and biting cold,
The guard who's true to Holland's soul,
Is on the cable watch,
Is on the cable watch.

It really depended... whether you were assigned to be on the first or second shift. In any event, you had to stand each night for three hours along the railway line. By every telephone pole, for kilometres, there stood a man on watch. On clear evenings, when Domie had been assigned the 10 o'clock shift, our young people accompanied him to his assigned post. Domie carried a thick staff with him, and they showed a fine spirit of camaraderie when they all set off together, linked arm in arm, to escort him to his vigil.

According to the night inspection patrol you could only be let off watch duty if you belonged to the NSB, or at least if your name was drawn on the list for winter relief duty. It was all a senseless and cowardly vexing of the people, who had to work during the day then stand on watch at night. Indeed, such a vague and indiscriminate way to mete out punishment made the whole affair so exasperating. No-one knew how long this would go on. But their reprisal against the common folk reaped in us all a sense of common brotherhood. The farmers brought bales of straw on their wagons to the railway. From it they built huts as well as for the *Dominee*, the blacksmith and the school master, who couldn't do this task for themselves. All this was not permitted, of course, but the authorities turned a blind eye, and it was let through.

"Punishment?" exclaimed De Lange. "Is it a punishment – to be outside on these marvellous midsummer evenings? Isn't it wonderful now that it doesn't get dark so soon? You're sleeping through the best time of your life, man! And about four in the morning the birds are already starting their song and the blue poppies appear in the light just as the dawn mist is clearing."

With his optimistic take on life he really cheers up Elderling, stationed one pole further down the line. But altogether the dreary task lasts far too long! The rain sets in. They must wrap up so well that they parade a display of the most fantastic outfits ever seen along the road. They must pass through the slimy, muddy clay to get to their posts. Down the farm lanes it's almost impossible to cycle. The clay sticks between the tyres and the guards, so that the bike becomes clogged up and can barely roll any further. Finally they then stand by their assigned poles hour after hour in the rain; or at least that's how it would be if their comfy wigwams were not available. But fortunately they are, and from within, farmers and townsfolk alike keep watch, sometimes in twos or threes at a time. Until the inspector is seen approaching. Then they must scamper to be back at their own pole in a hurry!

A German inspector once tried to approach them unnoticed on his motorbike. He did not take the usual way, but another route instead, running through a copse of willows. That was unfamiliar terrain to him and he unexpectedly locked wheels and shot head over heels into a ditch!

But where were the sudden converts to the NSB from among these stalwart men, who could then be excused from watch duty? Whoever thinks that strategy would have worked doesn't know the East Frisians very well. Did those Prussians actually think that they could persuade these freemen of the land by force? On the contrary, it only drove them on the defensive all the sooner and got their backs up, for now it had touched them all personally! They all felt as if they had been put in the stocks! No, the Prussians had not succeeded in belittling these men – if before they had been lukewarm, they now became fiercely anti-German! It is simply a human trait, to care about matters that directly concern us.

These were certainly folk whose defiant outlook was not brought low by reprisals; even by the Germans' forced acquisition of our sizeable assets of farm horses. For a long half hour, along the road sounded the clopping of all those magnificent animals – the pride and the glory of the Groninger. And you saw very few of them return. The requisitioning of their tractors was not too critical either, thought the farmers, but when it came to bicycles, then Holland was really in dire straits. Because isn't it true that you have a bike and I do as well?

Chapter 19

One day, right in the middle of this phase of bombing and the nights devoted to the cable watch, a letter arrived. At this time, the persecution of Jews in our country was taking on ever more frightful forms. Domie and I had already considered what we could do for them. Thousands of Jews were dispossessed of their money and goods and left alone out on the dyke. How would these people then live? Then you often heard stories of Jews who were deprived, not just of their gold and goods, but also of their liberty. In Amsterdam, police vans raided the Jewish quarters and young men were dragged from their beds, or simply taken straight off the streets. Then they were sent to a camp in Poland and you never heard anything of them again – and for the most part, we'd heard it said that a large number of these young Jews had been killed.

At the editorial office in Amsterdam where I had worked, a Jewish woman photographer had regularly come in to offer photos for sale. She had sometimes shared a meal at home with us. From that original business acquaintanceship had grown a more or less casual friendship. Lily had taken our formal wedding photograph. When Hansje was born I sent her a card announcing the birth. My silent thoughts now went out to her. How would she make it through all this? Was there anything that we could do for her? If so, what? And now, all of a sudden, came the answer: "May I come and stay a little time with you? I am in great need."

I went upstairs with the letter, up to the attic room. Domie was sitting there working. He was in a pessimistic mood due to lack of sleep, thanks to long hours on the cable watch. I lay the letter down in front of him. That gesture was eloquent enough.

"Well, there you have it," said Domie, looking glum.

"What?"

"*Och*, it's all a lost cause. And all I have to look forward to is ending my life in a concentration camp."

"You don't know that."

"*Ja*, I do, and this will surely hasten it."

What now? Cancel? Don't come? It was true that a pastoral ministry at this time was no risk-free vocation. Who would dare to speak up in good conscience if the Church kept silent about the horrors happening day after day? But now this letter on top of all those concerns!

Every person by nature is inclined toward self-preservation, including a Christian. What if you had a mind to help a daughter of Abraham, when thousands of Jews were being deported? If you were discovered, wouldn't that make things altogether far worse, especially for the one you wished to help? And would you even let your husband run such a risk for a casual acquaintance when he was already wavering on account of his responsibility to the Church?

On Sunday Domie had read out a protest from the Synod[46] against the persecution of the Jews. On account of that piece and from all the other things they knew about him, our friend Bertram, who was travelling by train to Groningen, overheard a couple of NSB loyalists chatting about "...that Domie from the Hörn... such an unsuitable one for the young people. We must get rid of him."

"Go now and take this letter to Elderling," said Domie.

I complied and laid the whole matter before our Deacon.

---

46 A governing assembly of the Church, convened to rule on matters of doctrine and practice.

"Look... here she writes: *I am in great need,*" I told him, "and the whole letter shouts out a cry for help."

"Naturally there are folk for whom you would do everything you can," said Elderling, carefully. "Is that the case here?"

"Well... She is a casual acquaintance from my previous office in Amsterdam."

Through Elderling's high windows I was viewing the wide land with the ripening grain peacefully basking in the afternoon sun while in Amsterdam despair reigned. There were thousands of people who saw no hope for themselves; the most desperate had brought an end to their own lives. And one of them had asked us to rescue her. I had once rescued a young bird out of the claws of a cat. Anxiously cheeping, skittish eyes, fluttering wings – freedom! I could do it again, but now it concerned a human being. *Ja,* but when it meant not just putting my life at risk, but also risking the life of him who was my dearest beloved! And then we had to also consider another; our young beloved Hans! Elderling was very concerned for us.

When I returned home, I still didn't know the answer.

But he who seeks advice over what Christ asks of him, knows it very well.

And, behold, a certain lawyer stood up, and tempted him, saying, Master, what shall I do to inherit eternal life? He said unto him, What is written in the law? How readest thou? And he answering said, Thou shalt love the Lord thy God with all thy heart, and with all thy soul, and with all thy strength, and with all thy mind; and thy neighbour as thyself. And he said unto him, Thou hast answered right: this do, and thou shalt live.

But he, willing to justify himself, said unto Jesus, And who is my neighbour? And Jesus answering said, A certain man went down from Jerusalem to Jericho, and fell among thieves, which stripped him of his raiment, and wounded him, and departed, leaving him half dead. And by chance there came down a certain priest that way: and when he saw him, he passed by on the other side. And likewise a Levite, when he was at the place, came and looked on him, and passed by on the other side. But a certain Samaritan, as he journeyed, came where he was: and when he saw him, he had compassion on him, and went to him, and bound up his wounds, pouring in oil and wine, and set him on his own beast, and brought him to an inn, and took care of him. And on the morrow when he departed, he took out two pence, and gave them to the host, and said unto him, Take care of him; and whatsoever thou spendest more, when I come again, I will repay thee.

Which now of these three, thinkest thou, was neighbour unto him that fell among the thieves? And he said, He that showed mercy on him. Then said Jesus unto him, Go, and do thou likewise[47].

Jesus' teaching is sobering in its practicality; it cuts through all the theories about whether, in a particular case, you should do something only for your countrymen, or only for your own family. Samaritans and Jews were not kindred souls. This Samaritan ran the risk of having to pay for this act of charity with his own life, because the bandits could always catch up with him. In that mountainous region of Judea, life was never soft. It stands to reason that the priest and Levite were so keen to distance themselves from the wounded man, not because they were callous, unfeeling men, but out of raw fear for their own survival.

Our neighbour – that is not a vague ephemeral entity. It is not someone from America, or Tierra del Fuego, or the Hottentot whom you shall never meet. Such a kind of abstract perception as "you must love all people," renders the idea of love meaningless, as it's unachievable; you can only love those whom you know. But the neighbour – that is the person who crosses your path and who has need of your help. These

---

47 Luke 10:25-37.

words, which long ago were uttered by the mouth of Christ here on earth, echoed in our hearts again.

Lily could be truly thankful unto Him that in the last mail collection of the day was an express letter to Amsterdam bearing the request, "Come to us as soon as possible on the last train out."

Many know that His Spirit and His words are the source of inspiration for their deeds. Others also draw benefits from this rich well, unaware of its stream dividing and flowing throughout our entire upbringing and culture. Only when people deliberately cut themselves off from that stream of life, and put something else in its place, as happened recently in Nazi Germany, then normal moral standards are eroded and a human being lives entirely as a slave to his own nature. And that life always ends up failing to be all that it should.

The following day Domie was on the second watch, from 1am to 4am. We'd stated in our letter that Lily must catch the midday train from Amsterdam. The local station here at Nieuweschans was some distance away, and she would have a suitcase with her. He would set aside an hour to go and fetch her after dark, with a second bicycle to hand.

It was dark and it was pouring with rain. We had reckoned that she must have received our letter before midday the following day after posting – and that naturally she would have already prepared for a precipitate flight, seeing that she had pleaded with us to send an immediate reply. One hour too late could cost her her life, now that she had ignored the summons to be present at the SS round-up in the Euterpestraat – and so she would come on the last train north that afternoon, bringing all the essentials she could carry, among which was probably her precious camera.

I shall never forget the atmosphere of that particular evening. I was standing in the kitchen preparing something for Domie to take on watch, since our meal times had become irregular during all that night-watch activity. Directly after returning from the station after midnight he would grab his thermos of warm coffee and leave again for his watch out on the railway embankment.

"Take some belts with you," I suggested, "to tie the whole lot on."

"*Ja*," said Domie, "and my tent flysheet, then at least I shan't get soaking wet."

He threw it over his shoulders like a blanket, and I tied it securely round his neck with some string. Like that he would stand on watch hour after hour in the rain. It was broad enough to drape over the handlebars of the bike. So I arranged that for him after he mounted the saddle.

"Take care," say the miners when they enter the dark mineshaft. I said the same to Domie, as I wheeled over my lady's bike for our guest to use, and farewelled him and the two bikes into the darkness and rain, now on the way to fetch her from the station. "I hope you're soon back home – both of you!"

That meeting at the station was a dangerous experiment in its own right. Jews were not permitted to travel. They were not permitted even to go outside. How on earth would she manage to make the trip? Of course she would attempt it without her yellow star, and most likely be carrying a forged pass, just in case they asked for her identity card on the journey.

I went back inside the kitchen. The house around me stood there, silent and large and four-square in the night. The rain spattered against the windows, and ran in rivulets like miniature waterfalls down the panes, through the downpipes and into the water butt and cistern. Not one aircraft droned overhead; they would not come over in this weather. I thought of Domie, who was now cycling alone through the late, dark hours. Soon he would be there, standing on the un-roofed platform of the small provincial station, his eyes probing the gloom, seeking whether the train from Holland[48] was about to arrive, all smoky, wet and chuffing steam. And then a lonely petite figure would alight with one suitcase and a bag; our refugee. No-one at all must see the two of them rendezvous, her and Domie. But that event would be highly unlikely, since around midnight, no-one would be outside in this weather – and if by sheer misfortune a patrol of the military police did accost him, he could always show his official letter: that exigencies in the line of duty permitted him to be outside after curfew. Hopefully, Domie and Lily would finally arrive here like a ship sailing into safe harbour.

The alarm clock on the mantelpiece above the fireplace ticked. Greet was sleeping and little Hans dreamed away in his cot upstairs. Lateness and stillness. I stirred the porridge. That was something they would really appreciate, as soon as they came inside, all cold and wet.

Waiting, watching. Listening to the rain, to the constant gush of water into the cistern.

Finally – someone was fiddling with the *leerkamer* door latch. Were they here?

I practically flew right to the door and switched the light on.

It was Domie, but alone.

"She wasn't there," he reported sombrely.

"Oh no! Really?"

We looked at each other, devastated. Had we been too late? I imagined a dark canal in Amsterdam. Had the waters there closed over a certain frail figure?

I am in great need!

"There's nothing we can do," said Domie. The words sounded as cheerless as the dispassionate running of the rainwater into the cistern.

"You'd better be off again," I said. "Here is your thermos and your lunch box."

I pushed them into his carrier bag and saw him depart silently.

---

48 Holland refers here to the central provinces rather than the entire country.

The usual greeting, "Good night and good watch," refused to come to my lips.

Rain. That had at least one advantage. I could go to bed now. The English bombers would not be over tonight. I was sincerely averse to hauling Hansje out of his cot, to take him outside, running through the garden to the bomb-shelter under the falling shells and bomb blasts.

Nonetheless I felt compelled to fetch him from his little bed. He suddenly awoke when I switched on the light of the bedroom.

"Ssh, be still, little man."

I picked him up, contrary to orthodox recommendations, and I turned on a small bedside lamp and drew him closer to me, encircling him in my arms. This was such a sweet tryst, after the terrible imaginings of this night. I stroked his little head. He had his own little prayer: "Lord I thank thee that in your flock I am a very little lamb."

I recited it for him now.

He stopped feeding and looked up at me. Then he smiled – such a cherubic smile, that it touched me deeply.

How is it possible, I thought, that right here, right now there is such a contrast: between the devilish powers exhibited by men, who sentence each other to death so that you must flee as a hunted animal flees – and something so lovingly angelic? I imagine that Lily's mother naturally would have cuddled her own baby like this, together with her little twin sister. But then the persecutions started in Germany. The mother stayed on in Berlin, but as soon as they could stand on their own feet both her daughters had escaped to Holland. Now the spectre of those death sentences was looming here also, and the girls were without a mother who could shield them, as I do my own little child.

There remained one wish yet – one prayer: "Let her be kept from danger, help her to find the way to our home!"

All the cares for our own preservation were forgotten – lost in the tenacious disquiet over that other young life.

I confessed this to Domie the following day.

"I think about her often too," he responded.

The matter lay as a heavy burden upon us, so that we were overwhelmed by that pervasive, gnawing question. "What has happened to Lily? Is she alright? Why doesn't she come?" The answer was given a couple of days afterwards in quite an unexpected way. On a night when Domie had just departed for his assigned watch from one until four and I was lying in bed, there came a knock at the front door. I threw something on and went below, but did not yet slide aside the great iron bar that secured the door. Instead I demanded:

"Who's there?"

"Am I at the *pastorie*?"

"*Ja*, what do you want?"

"Haven't you received my letter?"

"No, I received nothing and I don't open to anyone as it's past midnight."

I had the notion that a couple of delayed travellers were standing before my door, who now were seeking somewhere to lodge. That had happened before. But I was determined not to accede to such requests. It was now dry and the middle of summer. The country lads in need of a kip could simply crawl among the sheaves that were standing all over the countryside.

A silent pause ensued, both inside and outside the front door. Later I readily understood how the traveller outside must have felt at my response. Also, now the silence spoke eloquently; I saw that I must have disappointed the young man outside on the *stoep*. Yet I could not bring myself to go back upstairs again.

"Alright then, who are you?" I asked. I would surely have known someone who had written me a letter.

"I've come from Amsterdam," came the reply.

That told me nothing. I did not recognise the voice at all.

"Just tell me your name."

A momentary hesitation. Then, so softly that I could hardly pick it up, "Salomons."

"What did you just say?"

"Salomons."

I stood there composing myself. That was Lily's surname, but in my bewilderment, because who would ever reckon on this happening, I said, "But you're definitely not Lily. You are a man."

"*Ja*, but Lily is here with me."

At those magic words all my resistance melted and I shoved back the heavy iron drawbar which bolted the front door.

A short, sharp whistle sounded once more outside and Lily, who was crouched down by the fence, stood a moment later on the *stoep*.

"Come on – quickly inside!"

I had turned out the light, so no-one could see her enter. Once the door was closed I turned it on again and barred the door behind my guests.

There they were: Lily standing like a timid bird next to a young man who carried her luggage: a rucksack and a pair of bags. Lily seemed nervous.

"It went well," said the young man. "We didn't meet anyone at the last station."

"Were you able to find the way then?"

"We were accompanied by a pair of men as far as the fork in the road. They then told us that we had to go straight ahead until we arrived opposite the church."

"A couple of times we hid ourselves in a pair of wheat-stooks," said Lily, "as we thought that a military police patrol was approaching, but it turned out to be a false alarm."

I was so grateful that she hadn't said much *en-route;* instead her friend had done all the talking. Her German accent would otherwise have surely attracted attention. It meant nothing that while on the road they had sought directions to the *pastorie*. Everyone in the neighbourhood knew that we regularly have many guests staying over.

A little warmth hung about the kitchen, emanating from the coal-burning stove. I escorted my guests there and cooked up some potatoes for them. They both relaxed a little now.

Where could I put them to sleep? Lily would go in the attic room, since she could not live openly with us, but had to go immediately into hiding. If they came looking for her, it must not be noticed that her bed had been slept in. It was a collapsible camp bed with two halves that could be folded together and stowed.

"But would they look here for me?" said Lily. "That I don't believe. If I'd murdered Seyss-Inquart,[49] then *ja*, they would put all their effort into tracking me down, but not now – I'm not important enough for them," she concluded.

Her friend would be best put in the guest room to sleep. I decided to awaken Greet and went up to her room. "We've got unexpected guests. Could you make up the bed in the guest room?" I requested.

This was all a little strange – things happening in the dead of night, but as soon as Greet saw Lily, she immediately grasped the whole situation, since Greet had lived with us in Amsterdam.

"*Juffrouw* Salomons!" she greeted.

"Do you still remember me from the Keizersgracht?[50]" asked Lily.

"*Ja*, of course! You even came once to dine with us."

While Greet made up the bed, I chatted a while with our guests. Here we were not accustomed to express deliveries by mail. For which reason, we would not have expected to receive any letter yet – announcing Lily's intended arrival. That would only come the next day, together with the rest of the ordinary post.

But why had she only just turned up? We had already been so anxious, expecting her the very next day after our letter to her.

"At first I had to take refuge somewhere else – with a sculptor I know in Haarlem," she informed us. "But that arrangement could not be for much longer. And I couldn't come earlier than today; I received your

---

49 The Nazi Chancellor of Austria who was appointed as *Reichskommissar* of the Netherlands in 1940. He intensified anti-Jewish measures and ordered brutal reprisals against the Dutch people.

50 The third canal ringing the Centrum of the City of Amsterdam.

letter only yesterday, since I was no longer at my own address. Staying on at home there was far too dangerous!"

"Alright... why don't you just retire upstairs now and have a pleasant sleep."

"*Ja*, wonderful! I haven't eaten or slept for three days and nights. It's remarkable how much you can put up with!"

Poor, victimised Lily! You will find a bed here – and rest – finally rest!

When half an hour later I ascended the loft steps to check on her, she suddenly sat up straight in bed and fixed her horrified gaze on the door.

Then she recognised me, and fell back onto the pillows with a sigh of relief. She'd already slept a while and had now been frightened awake by the sound of my tread on the wooden steps. At first she didn't realise where she was and gasped, "Oh! I thought... that it was the police."

"No, listen – it's only me. The police won't search for you here – you said so yourself, remember? But I came up to check if you needed anything."

Lily shook her dark curls. "No, I don't need anything... *Hé*, what a lovely bed," she said, drawing the blankets more snugly over her.

"Are you warm enough?"

"*Ja*, it's splendid!"

"Rest well!"

It had gotten very late – it was already about half past two.

An hour and a half to go, then Domie could again hasten homewards. I lay waiting for him, dozing a little and dreaming that the police were hot on my heels. But I couldn't figure out why. I ran through long, dark halls as I was hotly pursued by some evil power. On and off flashed a torch, which illuminated the white walls with an eerie light. I just had to go a bit further, around a corner. Now they were right behind me. A pair of long arms thrust out toward me, but there was a window. It stood open and I jumped out. I was falling, far, far below, the air whistling in my ears. With a thump I hit *terra firma* and was startled awake. I was lying there in my own bed, and the long halls of my dream became those of the *pastorie*. In the upstairs corridor the window had not been blacked out, so we could not switch on the light there. So the young man must have used his torch during the night and evidently I had dreamt about it.

Someone was walking around below. I lay there a moment, straining to listen. I heard the kitchen door-latch fall. Only then it dawned on me that it had to be Domie.

I glanced at my alarm. *Ja*, half past four; that all made perfect sense.

I went downstairs to tell him the good news.

"Lily has arrived!" I said. "She arrived tonight with an Aryan friend."

"What a blessing!" said Domie.

"*Ja*, but..." and I told him of her fearful reaction when I went up to the attic.

"Under that accursed regime they allow a person to die a thousand deaths," he replied.

Chapter 20

These days feel strange due to the pattern of broken nights. During our life involving the cable watch, war and worry, Hansje is like a sunbeam on a rainy day. Lily is crazy about him. When she catches sight of his blissful smile she forgets the terrors of the last few weeks and months and life returns once more to be wholesome and comforting. He stretches out his little arms toward her and makes little gurgling sounds with his tongue. He beats a tattoo with his little bare legs and cackles at a joke that she shares with him. He is like 'the birds of the air' of Jesus' teaching, and has not a single care – certainly not for his daily bread! But for his parents, the anxiety now begins to mount.

Lily had brought no ration coupons with her, and she could not get any more, as her registration card had been cancelled and blocked. However, we knew for sure that we would not be left in the lurch. Whoever did a good turn to the farmers received wheat and peas from 13 to 18 cents per kilogram. Not a cent of profit was made above the normal price at which they delivered their products wholesale. Nor was there a black market here, like in the previous war. Extortionate sales were never made. You either bought foodstuffs at the going price or you didn't get them at all. And when you did get them, then it was because the farmer wished to help you rather than enrich himself.

The interest which the city dweller now began to show for the agricultural countryside had a certain peculiar savour. People that could not distinguish barley from rye and hardly understood how potatoes grew, now were asking if they "could just see the farm."

"Oh, so you do have chickens? Then you'd surely have eggs as well. And butter, and cheese? Would you be able to help us with any of those things?"

City slickers seem to think that on a farm, the goose flies ready-roasted straight into your mouth. They have not the slightest concept of the amount of preparative work required.

"Do you work much in the garden?" a woman lodger from Amsterdam asked one evening when she came across me planting endives outside in the vegetable plot.

"*Ja*, why do you ask?"

"*Och*, well... I thought if I had to do that, I'd rather live way up on the third floor, as far from the garden as possible. But it is fortunate for you that you do find it so enjoyable."

"In winter I'll gladly eat these endives."

"*Ja*, me too, but not if I had to plant them myself and water them myself, then weeding, and the other things you have to do with them."

"Do you mean binding them and blanching them?"

"*Ja*, and then picking them and all the other work that comes along. No, I really hate gardening. But surely in a town even you who loves the garden would not be able to till the soil?"

"So this is not too bad, I guess. But I've also lived for six years in Amsterdam."

"That long?"

Now one of our country lads came along to ask me something. After he left she remarked, "What a fine young fellow he is. Not like your typical yokel farmer."

"You're talking just like an American, who comes to see Holland and is amazed that we don't all run around in clogs and baggy pants," I replied.

"No... but there are farmers who can barely write a decent letter."

"Then you should be seeing it this way: that they are so busy planting potatoes for you that they don't have time to indulge in such pursuits."

However, in these times a substantial number of moderately to highly intellectual types have learned for themselves how to plant and grow baby potatoes on their rented plots of land outside the cities. And that must have been quite a success from an educational perspective, because it can't be good that a human being is alienated from nature and not realise how much sweat and effort has gone into every hard won morsel that he puts into his mouth. It is so good early on a spring morning to imbibe the aroma of damp earth, to push in the spade, and hoping for future blessings, to entrust the seeds and plants to grow and bear fruit, which shall be harvested on a late summer evening or on a still autumn day. But as I already said, we were often helped with provisions of food through an individual who knew of our precarious circumstances and even by some who did not know.

Lily had now been with us for several days. Days in which she had to acclimatise and find her way along a new path of life which would endure for an undetermined time. For who would know when the war had run its course? That could be over a year away, or sooner, but most likely even longer still. We reckoned on at least a couple of years more. What would that be like for someone in hiding? Someone who could not go out into the street, and must limit contact with outsiders as much as possible? And wouldn't she feel lonely, up there by herself in the heights of the attic room? For we had a demanding life and could grant her very little companionship. And might those unfamiliar reclusive circumstances lived in for so long result in a nervous breakdown? The first week she slept a lot, in order to compensate for the deficit arising from the recent nights during her flight from danger. We brought her meals up to her. During lunchtimes she came down one floor to the guest room where it was sunny. There I sat with her for the first few days. She sat on the floor in order not to be seen through the large open window, and she mended clothing while I was stringing beans and chatting to her.

"You know, she also has a twin sister who still hasn't found safe accommodation," I said to Domie. We looked at each other and thought the same thing. Domie was the first one to voice our thoughts.

"Then she must really come here as well. Two is not as much a risk as one and then they'll also have each other for company."

"*Ja*, but again, there are also specific difficulties attached that you don't have with one. For one thing, there is the matter of accommodating them both. That little room upstairs is extremely small for two people, and also the sourcing of provisions is going to become even harder than it is already, as you have to procure even more supplies. And wouldn't two people get on each other's nerves when shut away like that day after day? We are no angels and a human is a human! And don't forget Imke! One person obviously does not chat, but two cannot resist the temptation to chat together and even if they are not inclined to do so, two people involuntarily make more noise than one."

"Then they'll just have to sleep in the mornings and stay up during a part of the night. They can apportion their days as they wish. And as far as living accommodation is concerned, they'd rather live in a hole in the ground than go on to end their days in Poland."

"But what about Imke?"

"*Ja,*" said Domie, "that's definitely a more serious problem."

Chapter 21

When Hansje made his debut into this world, we proved all too soon the truth of the Groninger's adage: *A handful of people makes a house full of work*. And to lighten the whole load, Imke came to the *pastorie* for half a day each week. She had been serving us like this for two months and that now created a dilemma, because to burden Imke in only her fifteenth year with such a big secret was not appropriate, but to dismiss her without any reason, was out of the question. Thus everything had to happen secretly around Imke. Not a pin may drop, no creaking beds, and nothing must point to the presence of people on the loft floor above.

But concerns, and these were very serious, were there to be overcome, Domie declared. He talked it over with Lily. "We shall be very quiet and in the mornings we'll whisper and sleep a lot," she affirmed. "I would find it lovely if I could have a companion here with me. But since my twin sister is just like me, you know, we always end up having arguments. However, I lived once with a friend who is in all respects completely opposite than me," said Lily in her own unique turn of phrase, "and that went really well." Lily was excited at the prospect of sharing her room, and there arose touches of blush on her otherwise pale cheeks.

Domie would now have to go to Amsterdam the following day, to first check if her sister had in the meantime found a place to stay, and if that was so, then her friend Esther could come instead, with whom living together went so well because she was not as excitable as Lily, but apparently calmness personified!

The visit to Amsterdam ended in a highly satisfying outcome. Domie brought back all kinds of things with him from Lily's house, which in her hasty departure, she had had to leave behind – and he also received there a message that a safe-house had been found for her sister. Thus the following week her friend Esther arrived on our doorstep instead and became Lily's refugee-in-arms. All tidings were happy ones. And what a treasure trove Domie had brought with him! A splendid eiderdown quilt, clothes, soap and even a pair of knick-knacks to put on the wall!

When he departed from Lily's house, her entire studio lay empty, except for a large white projecting screen that he could not carry on his back, and a pair of empty bottles. And in the middle of the floor a small yellow star lay abandoned, with the hateful word "Jew" written on it.

He had deliberately left that small lonely item behind for the German investigators, who were expected sooner or later, and would surely find it during their search throughout the empty house. But the bird had already flown!

Unlike Lily's, the arrival of Esther was hardly sensational. Naturally it occurred during the night when Domie was on cable watch, and she was again accompanied by their Aryan accomplice, who proved to be a close friend of the two girls. But this time I was prepared and hadn't gone to bed. And when I heard the bell, I knew she had arrived! I went and opened the door immediately, as we were not expecting any more surprises that night.

Lily hadn't said too much about the calm disposition of her friend. Esther and her accomplice stepped inside the hallway. She took off her coat, and in a very serene and self-controlled voice informed us that she had had a good trip. To me, the accomplice appeared much more nervous than Esther. But once we stood in the kitchen, that good old kitchen with lots of blue paint on the walls, enveloped in the warm cosiness of the coal-stove that had been lit today for the preserving and bottling of beans, he became more at ease. This was familiar territory. Again potatoes were on the menu and leftover greens from the afternoon. Cooked together in the skillet, they provided a delicious hot meal for our weary travellers.

By evening when it was dark and all shutters had been closed, Lily usually came below. But this time she had wanted to stay upstairs to welcome her friend into the attic room, which they would share together from now on. Before Esther's arrival it was all single-handedly cleaned and decorated by Lily. The desk was pushed against the wall, because in the place where it once stood, there was now a second camp bed. This one folded to make a bench seat in order to save space. On a small table stood a vase of flowers. Also, the wall decorations had undergone changes. Esther took in for herself the entire scene of that small intimate room. I don't know what her opinion of it was, but then I don't need to know. Lily was overjoyed at their reunion and all the things she had brought. With all these personal items they could really settle in and set up this nook as their real home.

Would everything work out in the long term? I asked myself, as I undressed half an hour later.

Now the risk of discovery was no longer the primary concern; instead there were all kinds of other difficulties that were attached to an endeavour like this and which arise from human nature itself.

To what extent to grant our guests freedom, how much to interfere, and how soon, if the situation lasted for weeks, months or perhaps even years. Should we rigidly dot all the i's or pour out God's lotion of gentle grace in order to avoid conflicts? Would the household be organised to give them work, and if so, what sort and how much? Were it too little, then they could suffer boredom. Were it too much, they might get the feeling of being exploited. How much of this, how little of that; in short, where were the boundaries to be placed?

When he stood responsible for the demanding task set before him the young Solomon prayed for wisdom. Why should I not likewise draw from the same unfathomable well? Why not plug my little life's lamp into the great Heavenly Power Station? Had that mighty source ever failed me or abandoned me in moments of hardship? I lay down a moment later in bed. Surely it would all go well!

In the still of the night, memories from my youth flooded back. A house full of people, especially in summer, and in amongst them Mother's face and Mother's words. How did she always manage to be so planned and well-prepared? She made her way straight through her life's days in complete integrity; said things always precisely as they were. Everyone knew what she expected of them and where the boundaries lay that she drew. You had respect for her, since her words were wise and good – and now they served as your guide for life. And one of her nuggets of wisdom was: "You must allow a person their freedom." That I would have to test during the 'captivity' of our two victims. Since I did not know where the boundaries were to be set exactly, I would have to err on the side of caution at first, by minimal involvement with my refugees, and then stepping in with more when required. Because they shouldn't have to feel my presence as an inconvenience. The loft from henceforth would be considered their domain.

Chapter 22

All good things – and happily also all bad things – come to an end. And so it was with the cable watch. Just as suddenly as it was imposed, the men were suddenly relieved of this particular burden. About half an hour in advance both farmers and townsfolk alike knew that they were now done with it; that from tonight they would no longer have to stand guard. At first that was a rare, sobering feeling. Tonight – to not stand by the cable pole, but to lie in bed. How was that possible? In the last months, days and nights all thoughts had revolved around the watch. But now, when you were no longer required to stand there, you had the strange sensation that you really would have to stand there again sooner or later. Just imagine – all those poles there, unattended, all along the railway embankment, and you sleeping in the middle of the night, actually in your own bed! That was unheard of! Everyone felt a little uncomfortable with it. The watchmen all suffered a strange sickness that you could call "cable nostalgia". However, some had already had a hunch about the way things were going. The crop was now ripe, and due to the time pressures of agriculture, you couldn't begin the harvest with a bunch of sleepy farmers, who could think of nothing else but being stationed at their posts. The harvest must be gathered in because it must be sent over the border to feed the *Reich*! The Germans saw to it that their attention was now fully focussed on the business in hand, and not on guarding the poles! When these suspicions and rumours made the rounds during the final evenings of the watch, many of the watchers smuggled things up to the railway embankment. There had to be a joint farewell celebration! Their retreat was not going to occur silently and without fanfare.

And on the final night, all along the line was heard this children's song:

A shark once held a wedding feast,
Inviting every water beast.
Fiederaldalda, fiederaldalda, fiederaldaldaldalda!

From ten poles distant, both east and west, you could hear the refrain resounding through the still night air. And Domie stood there, gazing wistfully at his slice of *Speck*[51] that had been brought to him wrapped in paper with the inscription, "For a solitary watchman on the Oranje Railway".

Those poor country folk who suffered from nostalgia for their midnight posts and who became restless at 10pm or 1am when beforehand they would be up and out of bed, but now lay tossing and thinking of their thermos and lunch box, their tarpaulins and boots that they had had to take on watch with them. And of their cosy thatched wigwam, where the rain seeped in, and of the misty dawns, which lingered for up to four hours. But one must adapt to each new situation, because the least word that you utter of such nostalgic sentiments might be sufficient to result in another snapped cable and then you'd find yourself posted once more at the foot of a pole! Your nostalgic yearnings would be granted of course, but you'd never know for how long you'll be stuck up there this time, and so your grumbling would go on. Even Domie suffered the 'pole sickness' a little, the desire to pack some sustenance for an expected night out. It was good that there were now so many other things to distract his thoughts.

With two refugees hiding in the house, security measures had to be devised. For this reason, we never spoke of the "women" guests or

---

51 Speck is a type of leg bacon, cured with salt, spices and juniper berries and then cold-smoked. Like many foodstuffs it was very hard to obtain during the war, so this slice was regarded as a real treat!

something similar, but of the "Mice in the attic". In this way we could prevent ourselves from making slips of the tongue, because having already had mice in the loft, everyone would find such a comment quite normal. Nevertheless, it would be rather odd if you said, for instance, "The Mice have been ironing this afternoon!" Upon voicing such an extraordinary declaration, when you saw the amazed face of your listener before you, you would mind never to make that mistake again! So the chances of committing that kind of slip were rendered particularly minimal.

Now it was the beginning of August, and the cable watch belonged clearly in the past. A cloud drifted over the countryside. It cast its shadow over the sea of ripe grain. In the distance rows of stooks stood ready and behind them meandered the small river on which a ship drifted, carrying a large sail. The harvest had begun. During daytime the sheaf-binder made his rounds over the field, cutting armfuls of the grain-laden stalks and tying them in sheaves, and then stooking them. From early until late, one could see them out in the weather, loading the wagons and bringing the crop into the huge barns. That was something to be envious of. Each year the land yielded its harvest; mostly a bountiful one. That process was visible and tangible and we who had been here only a few years had also worked hard, ploughed and sowed. But what had we achieved in terms of visible results? Church attendance – what about progress there? Nothing really worthy of note... as far as we could tell. Before the war folk from Oldiek would come along by bus to the Hörn and up to our church. Whereas now we had obtained the use of a schoolroom in Oldiek for the use of Church Association meetings and services. About forty people turned up there regularly on Sunday while the number of attendees in the Hörn had stayed about the same. Always looking at the numbers! But God often does things differently. He goes for the chosen few. And whoever comes to our own church does that willingly – not from tradition or social habit, as in their local situations they have had a lot to contend with which competes with church attendance. So these faithful sit in their accustomed places with open ears and listen attentively.

"Gideon," spoke God's voice, "you have too many men. Whosoever is fearful and afraid, let him return home.[52]" Then immediately three thousand men departed, those who had stood on the periphery and for whom the Holy Fire had cooled too soon.

To begin something is usually not an art form, but to bring it to completion is another thing! A suggestion to send out a calling for an assistant Minister had been made before. "It's not necessary to send out a calling," argued Domie. "We have the opportunity to go out there ourselves, committed and fully prepared, but we just don't do it."

Then he preached again in this big empty church that was built eighty years ago, as the old building had then become too small. But as the church bell tolled, now the people were embroiled in tasks at home or in their gardens, so Sunday morning offered nothing to celebrate. Nothing poetic, nothing requiring one to dress in their best and wend their way along the fertile sun-drenched lanes to church. To a place where God bends down to say to man, "Thou seekest Me – I let Myself be found through thee. I instil into thee thy dissatisfaction and thy yearning, for thou only findest the true rest, when thou findest rest in Me."

When we visited the sick, people would always argue out of their own innate religious ideas. "As long as the world is in such a sorry state, I'm not coming to church," they would say. They held our dear Lord answerable for the shards of this war, which we ourselves have created through our common guilt. Conviction of sin only comes to a man when he stands before Christ. And Him they knew not.

With the younger generation, it's best to begin at school age. Of

---

52 Judges 7:2-3.

course for them this was only tentative, factual knowledge, yet without depth, not explored nor applied in their own lives. In the questions that sometimes arose during the day, the Word of Christ was yet to materialise, in which He said, *I thank Thee, O Father, Lord of Heaven and earth, that Thou hast hid these things from the wise and prudent, and hast revealed them unto babes.*[53] There is good reason to constantly rejoice over the intuitive feeling and understanding of children.

It is a practical rule of the Church that a pastor must not go unmarried to serve in the land of Groningen. There is a witty poem in German, in which the pastor's wife is called *seine frohmütige Seelsorgerin* ("his cheerful-spirited lady pastor"). Of such a wife he has desperate need. Let him at least have someone to be a sounding board for all the shocks and disappointments. Then the next day he will be able to resume his tasks with courage and cheer; as long as she doesn't respond to everything he says with "*Ja, Ja*" and nods of the head, but also if necessary contradicts him, and always keeps the bigger picture before them, that it is never about us, but about the cause we serve.

The church tower bell of which I spoke earlier tolls no longer. Initially it hung in the tower without voice for a couple of years, because on Sunday mornings it was not permitted to be rung. But in this summer of the year 1943, it has been completely removed. The bell, which had always served to call the people to the hearing of the Good News, must now serve the foreseen shortage of metals for manufacture of German armaments, and for that purpose it was re-smelted. But if it comes to that, then it is mostly for a lost cause. Such was the case in the previous war, when the bells in Germany were also removed from their towers. After that war, the words *Die Glocken verlieren den Krieg*[54]

---

53 Matthew 11:25.
54 "The Bells lose the war" meaning that to appropriate church items used for godly purpose and use them for war will end in defeat.

were inscribed on one of the bells installed in our province. For once, two disparate things would not unite; the calling voice of God's Kingdom and the sinful purposes and violence of this world.

Meanwhile all of us had to adapt to the new circumstances as well. In just one week the size of our family at the *pastorie* almost doubled. That meant that the ordinary material things; washing the dishes, cleaning vegetables and potatoes, which were not out of range of the trifling issues that beset each household, were likewise almost doubled. But our Mice did not let themselves off lightly, and took on a great deal on their own account. In the afternoons vegetables and potatoes were brought upstairs in a set sequence. When Imke came back the next morning, they had already been done. She really must have thought that during the night the pixies had been at work. Because even the dishes that she normally washed in the evenings were stacked clean in the kitchen and the laundry that had only been hung up yesterday to dry already lay ironed and folded in the cupboard. Even the amount of mending dwindled visibly. The typist and the photographer both acquired real skills in diverse domestic affairs.

In the morning, because of Imke, it had to be very still up in the loft. The Mice used this time for reading books and to study. And in this way a fixed daily program was established – the tapestry of their lives on which they could continue their embroidery. All that remained was to discern a fine pattern therein, so that even upon this current imposed and unwanted canvas could be worked something good and beautiful.

How often do we murmur, in our freedom to choose a path, about the unwanted patterns of our lives? We say we would be able to make something out of it, if the background circumstances were suitable, if we didn't have to put up with this or that. If only our marriage were more harmonious or there were no war, or we were not bogged down with money troubles nor food rationing. But these laments don't help us at all. We have been given our only canvas to weave upon and that can't be changed for another. "Let us see what you will do with it," says our Employer. "A poor workman always blames his tools."

For security reasons we took extra precautions. The Aryan friend who had accompanied the Mice seemed highly capable with his hands. He constructed a trap door in the floor of their room which descended into a wardrobe on the floor below, and through which they could escape at any sign of danger. That wardrobe had its normal doors opening on the next floor down, but a bookcase was stood in front of them to obscure it so that no-one would get the idea to go searching inside. On top of the trapdoor itself was placed a rug nailed on for camouflage. This secret wardrobe was a good hiding place for peas and other dry foodstuffs obtained without official rationing coupons, so we stored them there. A small ladder that descended vertically from the attic room was constructed from some slats of wood. When we had need of anything, the trapdoor was opened and one of our Mice popped down to the wardrobe to retrieve it. After a couple of minutes you saw her head emerging above floor level and shortly after that a sack of wheat appeared that she had filled up below to give to one or another of the guests. Certain of the guests were initiated into our secrets about the Mice, but others not. Someone lodged with us an entire week without knowing anything. She once went unexpectedly upstairs to her room to fetch a jacket. Then she told me that she had heard something up in the loft. Did we have birds nesting under our roof? "Could be," I replied. "Everything seems to live up there. We even have Mice as well."

Our guest from the city was very scared of mice, that I knew very well; and so with one stroke I had obtained a guarantee that she would never venture up to the loft. Also, Ministers who came to fill a vacancy at a church in some neighbouring parish might lodge with us overnight. But they never knew what was happening above their heads. With such an arrangement there was always the need to compromise schedules and re-organise things, but gradually we got used to it.

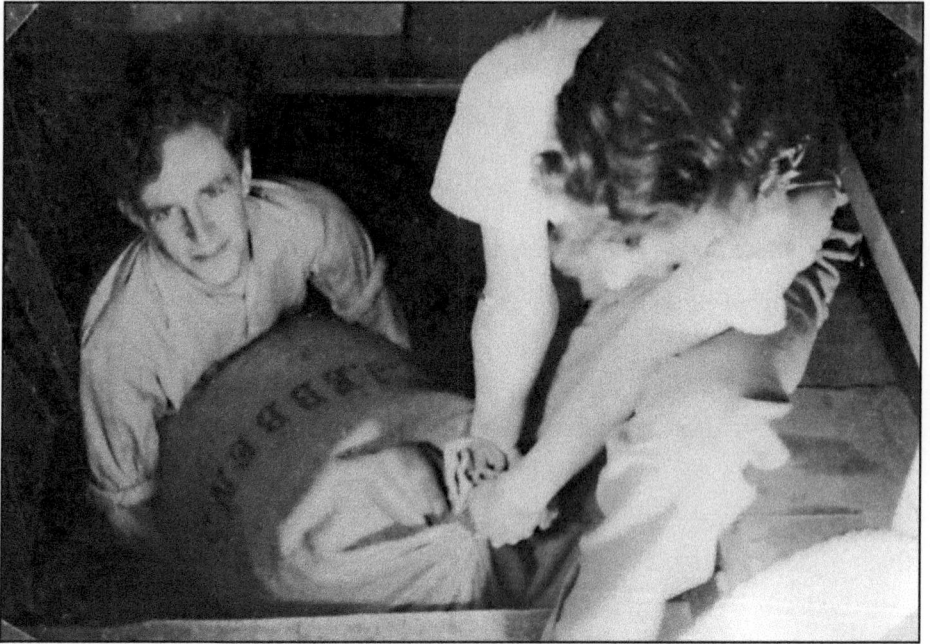

Chris and Frits retrieving a sack of wheat from the secret wardrobe, one floor below the loft.

Chapter 23

On closer examination this old *pastorie* offered even more superb hiding places than we originally thought. The *leerkamer* had a stage platform and if you could excavate a passage under the whole floor with an exit to the outside, then there would be no remaining obstacles to discourage your escape.

No sooner said than done! Our friend from Amsterdam arrived incognito with the last train, and started excavating under the *leerkamer* floor. Due to his prowess he quickly acquired the nickname *van de Mol,*[55] so that our menagerie, apart from the two invisible Mice, would now be enriched by the Mole, who would arrive through the bolt hole at any hour of the night and day. But even that was not enough. Now there were two Kaisers in the bomb-shelter, one for us, and one for de Lange, who regularly brought it feed. That happened amidst voluble protests from me. Now that we had our resident Mice, we absolutely could not risk having searches of the house. But necessity is the mother of invention, and thus one had to be daring. With so many now together in the house, you couldn't all perish together from the winter cold. Yet another pig appeared on our guest register, a legally obtained pig this time, which lived in the shed. That one had been brought with my full sympathy and cooperation. To get it I had to write letters and fill in application forms. On top of all that our goat had borne a kid and both mother and daughter also stayed overnight in the shed. Furthermore we had a large hutch hanging against the shed wall, where four young rabbits were housed.

---

55 (Of) the Mole.

One particular day a giant of a buck rabbit arrived, brought by a neighbouring boy. In good weather I dragged the rabbits outside and put them into a portable hutch made of chicken wire, which stood out on the lawn. There they had limited freedom and some food (alas also limited, so each time the hutch had to be moved over new grass that had not yet been grazed).

But the heavy buck was extremely unmanageable. It scratched me with his hind feet as I held him fast by his ears and then behaved very disagreeably toward his younger colleagues as I put him into the hutch. *Ja*, he even bit them! That was the last straw! I grabbed a basket, pushed him inside, tied it on my bike's luggage carrier and rode with him to the nearest *pastorie* where the resident *Dominee* was set up to deal with rabbits. He had collected about seventy so far!

What an achievement it was to feed all the open mouths at our place. We needed to get another goat for supplying milk. Domie meant well, but he badly misjudged the situation, since Domie, who never had had to feed animals, didn't know what gluttons they were and what an onerous task it was to sate their appetites. According to his simplistic reasoning, you bought a goat, and it gave you milk and that was it. You just put her on the grass and she ate it.

His little speech won over the Mice. They also wanted to do their bit for the food supply, and therefore they bought the goat. That evening they went down to the shed to take a look at their purchase. It was already dark, but that did not matter. A stable lantern was carried to light their way.

It was cosy and warm in the shed. The goats ate contentedly from the hayrack full of grass that they had been given for the night. The rabbits in the hutch above nibbled at a root vegetable and peeked curiously through the wire mesh. The pig knew nothing better to say than "knnnor, knnnor" and rubbed himself against the partition. And there stood the new goat; their goat, Sara, as they named her. She was white with a black stripe on her back. She had horns which she used to thrust and butt. The little kid pressed himself skittishly against the mother. Really there was too little space for so many animals here.

Ja, but Sara did give us beautiful milk. Would they like a cup of it?

A little later in the kitchen, the Mice, both equipped with highly discerning palates, tried some of Sara's milk. They squeezed their eyes shut in delight. "Delicious!" they agreed.

And meanwhile the Mole sat underground for hours and dug. He excavated a long tunnel under the foundations of the house. That digging was not the worst of it; the obstacles that he encountered along the way were not inconsiderable. In an emergency so that the people fleeing could crawl out, a heavy iron bar had to be sawn through. That was no trifle! A hacksaw borrowed from the blacksmith had to do duty for this purpose.

And so now you would hear, from under the house in the calm of the evening, the muted grating sound of steel upon iron.

I stood motionless outside, listening intently. Poor Mole, that job was no pushover!

Suddenly a realisation hit me. Had I locked the shed properly just now? I went over to take a look. No, the key was still in the lock. And how many rabbits had I previously taken inside? I counted three. *Ja,* but there were supposed to be four there! That tiresome creature! You always had trouble with him. The lantern was still standing nearby. My hand felt for the matches. They were right next to it. With the lamp alight, I ran out into the darkened garden. It looked rather like *kip-kap-kogel,*[56] when the local children on Saint Maarten's feast day go about the houses carrying Chinese lanterns or a hollowed out field-beet containing a burning candle.

If your dog went missing, then you would call him by name, and if

---

56 From the first verse of a children's song at the Feast of St Maarten, celebrated on the 11th November. There are many variants, but they all begin with the same words.

your cat was lost, you then called, "Puss, puss puss!" But for a rabbit? How would you call him? Naturally, there was nothing there now to call out to. He was already long gone. At least an hour had elapsed since I fetched his chums back inside. The best hope was to follow the example of poachers and lure the rabbit by the light – at least I could if it was still in the vicinity. I cast light around the strawberry beds. Was that a rustle over there?

"Are you looking for something?" a muffled voice said from very close by. Understandably, I was a little startled. There stood the Mole.

"One of our rabbits is on the run," I replied softly.

He was holding the hacksaw still in his hand. He used it now to probe carefully between the cabbages and then stopped. He raised a finger. "Listen!" he whispered. A soft gnawing of small teeth on a crisp cabbage leaf was clearly discernible. How fortunate we were!

Soft scuffling of feet in the direction of the gnawing sounds, then a sudden plunge among the cabbages, and the Mole had struck! He hefted the fluffy bunny aloft by its shoulders. "Terrific," I said overjoyed, as I took it from him. "Thanks so much!"

This reminded us all of the parable of the lost sheep. With a stepladder I climbed up to the hutch and reunited the young thing with his brothers and sisters. So much care, so much trouble – and for what? Surely not just so that we could eat them up come next winter? We slowly realised our contact with these animals had become personal. But the Mole had already saved the situation once again. And that was the about the best outcome for the day that we could hope for.

Chapter 24

And now I sit once more in my loft at the farm, and let all the memories flow by. After a period of dry, warm weather it is now bringing rain and squalls. Colossi of clouds hang above the broad vista of chequered fields. On one parcel of farmland, the grain is still standing but from another the wheat has already been taken in. It lies here, piled high in the barn, and the horses plough the golden stubble under, so that the fields are now becoming textured with black.

At this time the previous year the Germans were pressing onwards unopposed through North Africa, so that it appeared a certainty that they would gain command and control of the Suez Canal. Then came the hard fall. In the space of one day, Catania, a major city on the east coast of Sicily, had fallen, and so had Orel in Russia. Last year right at this time the siege of Stalingrad was fully underway. But now Mussolini has resigned and Germany has lost Italy as an ally. In recent times the turning axle has begun to stiffen and creak alarmingly, and now there is no more grease to apply: it has simply become unstable. Before November of the present year, still 1943, folk were saying, "It's all over," and even the German soldiers posted here to man the Flak searchlight, would say in their East Frisian language: "When they've bombed Berlin to smithereens, then it will all be over."

Would that really be true? So many predictions have been made already. Massive aircraft formations have flown over us on their way to Hamburg, where no stone has been left upon another. We got out of bed for the show this last week, because it was not particularly dangerous. German fighters rallied against the Allies; bombs fell and exploded; it was a terrific din, and Hansje awoke in fright and started to cry.

Here, so close to the border, accidents resulting from aerial dogfights are commonplace. Whenever a heavy American or British bomber is shot down, from our loft window we can observe airmen jumping from their doomed machines. This may happen several times during the day. Their parachutes blossom and float slowly over the countryside, carried on the wind to arrive on earth several kilometres away from their jump point. Most have come down on land, and one in the Dollart, where fishermen dragged the sodden aviator from the shallows and took him to shore. Five of these men lie buried in our churchyard; British and Americans, at whose interment only the Lord's Prayer was spoken. For that is the one prayer that is prayed by all people in all languages. *May Your Kingdom Come*... and keep holding fast... through the labour pains of these interim days of uncertainty.

Flowers bloom on their graves. They wait there for the end of the war, to then be brought over the sea to rest in the earth of their own lands. May God forgive them the guilt of their short lives and awaken them at the end of days. The wind rustles the heads of grain and forces the red Salvia on their graves to bend low, as a greeting from the living unto the dead... unto them, the many, who fought for our freedom.

A couple of centuries ago the waves flooded from the Dollart over the place where they now rest. Before that there were the massive forests, whose giants have fallen over to one side in the great flood, and whose trunks one still encounters under the ground when digging the graves. Under the layer of clay, over a meter thick, lies the moorland and forest floor, where the leaves of many eras have fallen and been pressed together into a thick, dark mass, from which we now cut our peat. Life is always changeable, and we sing but a short stanza of her eternal song. We then finally cross over to another form of being, to which our spiritual intuition witnesses, and which, from our belief in the eternity, projects back into the present.

But in the short time that is given to us here, the days can appear long and the nights without comfort, so that worries and fearful premonitions disturb our sleep. For many, this life over recent years has become a nightmare; certainly for them who were marked with a star. Back in August 1942 everyone longed for something to happen, whatever that might mean. The word "invasion" was whispered from mouth to mouth. The allies had to risk an attempt at landfall somewhere. But where? That could happen at so many places. The coastline of German occupied territory running from the south of France to the northern extremity of Norway is a very long way. And they could just as easily drop inside Frisia or Groningen and then continue their combat from here. I received a tip-off from someone who apparently knew, from "impeccable sources" that I had to make preparations to leave here with my baby. "And with my refugees as well," I added to myself. Domie was away for a week on his bike, nominally for a vacation trip, but working undercover with the Resistance. At this moment we could not manage a trip with all of us together. While travelling would he pick up the rumour of looming, threatening events? In any case we must prepare ourselves for any eventuality. So the pram was packed full, firstly with the things that Hansje would need, and secondly with the barest of essentials for ourselves. On a particularly clear night there was a heavy bombardment at Emden, from which we were expecting an invasion to follow. We sat in the hall and waited. Hansje was the only one of us who slept through it all. But apart from the bombing nothing else happened. A vague feeling of disappointment came over us. It would definitely not be easy to wander around the countryside for a few days, even if we took our goat to supply milk for the baby, as Greet had suggested.

The harvest standing in the fields would be destroyed if the onslaught began here – perhaps right by our house. But imagine the result: the

Germans would be driven from our land. We would surely be inundated with offers of provisions and chattels. We would be poor, but free again. Not to mention the glory of it all! We would again be able to raise our children without interference. I had not brought Hansje into the world to be conscripted into the Hitler Youth, to become a drilled boy-soldier for the German *Reich*. That we could even continue along this path of ambivalence, remaining under the yoke of German slavery and raising our children in a spirit that wars against our most sacred convictions, has been an odious and fearful thought for every Dutchman.

And in hours like these, in which the best could yet come to be, when even your life stood on the line, you recalled to mind the words of our Queen, that "there are things more valuable than one's own life."

A rumour always contains a grain of truth. There was an invasion, but not in the Netherlands. Only in France. Was this a test run? They wrote about it in the newspaper *De Nederlandsche*, and in the other newspapers under German control; obviously their propagandists presented it as a complete failure for the Allies. They discussed it on the radio, but I think that we will only find out about the true significance of the Dieppe raid after the war.

Chapter 25

From our perspective nothing had changed. But apparently rumours about coming events had also reached others. Such as the people wearing yellow stars, who desired liberation even more than we did, as they had not yet found havens of safety.

Now it would not be much longer, they hoped! Those who could hold on would be saved.

Among them were two Jewish men, the Cohens, friends of De Lange, who is known to you by now as the guardian of both Diocletian and Decius, the most recent residents of the bomb-shelter after the erstwhile Kaiser Nero had departed. "You need to go into hiding," said De Lange to these star-badged men. "There's nothing else for it."

Objections. Massive difficulties.

"You simply must do it," said De Lange.

"Where then? With whom?"

"I'd say with us, but they'll seek you out here for sure, since everyone knows that we're friends. But I think perhaps I know where else you can go."

De Lange is one of our Deacons. We can rejoice indeed over our Church Council members, since there are fellows here who want to do something for someone else. At the next farm beyond De Lange there live the three Wissing brothers together with their elderly mother. The oldest of the three, Hilbrand, is also a Deacon. De Lange and Wissing share many points of ongoing contact as both neighbours and office bearers of the Church Council.

De Lange laid out the matter before Wissing.

"You can't take them in, but they sure can come and stay with us," replied Wissing after due consultation with the other members of his family. The offer was made.

"Well then, if it's alright to stay with you, Wissing," said the Cohens, "though it's just for a short while... for the long term we've been given another address."

"*Ja*, sure," said Wissing. "Don't be shy, but come on over as soon as you can, hear!"

Adjoining the Wissing farm was an uninhabited farm-worker's hut. But one night it suddenly became occupied; the Cohens had taken up residence. Although this was not entirely unexpected, the timing did stir up some consternation on the farm. Ol' Moeke[57] had her hands full with caring for her eldest son, "...since he was not too well, you know," she told me later. "He had something wrong with his stomach, and then Doctor gave him something for it, but that wasn't much use, you see. *Norit* they call it – looks pretty much like the black lead from a pencil. So instead Hilbrand treated himself. He took a good nip of *jenever*[58] and grabbed five good cigars – the hard-to-get, quality ones from before the war – and with these he went to bed. And he actually got better! But then suddenly, on the very same evening, Luppo heard sounds coming from the workers' hut. He first thought it came from the byre, so he went there to investigate. But in the stall there was nothing going on, hear! Cows standing and eating clover, and the horses were in the stables. Then our Luppo walked over to the stables and stood still to listen. Blimey! *Ja*! He heard something alright – coming from the workers' hut. You must understand that was from the Jews settling in! So he went straight to our house to fetch Sybolt, and then both of 'em went over to the Cohens, to take 'em some food and things like that. But I said, 'Think about it, young'un. I don't want a lot more work from all

57 "Ol' Ma."
58 Gin made from grain, which grows abundantly in Groningen.

this, see, and our maid must not find out.' What does *Mevrouw* think then, have I done right?"

"Absolutely right! The less folk know about it the better."

"But after they had been with us a fortnight, some other folk arrived. In the middle of the night – a man and woman on a bike, with *niks* in their bag. I said to Hilbrand, 'This is all getting too much for me. Four all in there together!' And Hilbrand added, 'I know, we really should help rescue those people... but now, you see, there's a woman there as well.' And that didn't seem too good to him, since, as *Mevrouw* may well know, our boys are not too comfortable with womenfolk around. But then I said, 'A woman like her can also contribute something useful. She can teach the men how to cook meals, do the washing and such tasks, since I sure don't want any extra work from all this, hear!' And what d'you say 'bout that, *Mevrouw*?"

"No, it's better if you can do without too much of a burden at your time of life," I said. "But weren't the two original guests supposed to be only temporary?"

"*Och, Mevrouw*, you know very well how it is; those folk that promise but go back on their word when there's serious trouble, while others honour their word and so could never put these folk out on the street. As *Mevrouw* may know very well, Germans are against the Jews... they really hate them."

Ja, I also had certainly heard something like that... that Germans really hate the Jews.

"Bad people can really make a lot of trouble for you. The Germans are such filthy dogs, aren't they?"

"We've certainly already experienced a heap of misery from them," I replied with a sigh.

"But what's going to happen with those four, man? They've got *niks* on 'em."

"Maybe Domie has got an idea about that," I commented.

"Would *Mevrouw* like a cup of coffee?"

She bustled off to the stove to fetch the coffee-pot.

"No, I really must go."

I pressed her old wrinkled tiny hand. She stood next to me, and I had to look down a little to speak with her, as she was very small. She looked at me sincerely and said, "You come back again, hear... *Joa*, don't hesitate to do that."

I felt that I could gladly concur with such a friendly invitation but while cycling home I was also thinking that we now had four local refugees who were lacking the barest necessities. Once home I talked it over with Domie.

"I've already made a plan with De Lange," he said, "to get some things for them."

That seemed quite simple, don't you think? Someone in danger might have left their property unoccupied, having had to flee in exceptional times when men hunt people in the middle of the night. That really incites the normal Dutchman's sense of justice, when all that is left standing is their forsaken house, with all their property inside, ready to be looted at short notice.

"Naturally," you say.

"That doesn't even come into it," interrupts the German. "The Jews will no longer be allowed to live, thus all that they owned from now on belongs to us. That is our logic. That is German justice. It was so in the time of the Batavian tribes.[59] It was deemed to be the right of the strongest and we must return to that once more. All that came later, like the foreign influences from Christendom, undermined and weakened the heritage of the *Volk*.[60] The dumb Hollanders have learned to think incorrectly. Therefore we've come here to re-kindle the light of our culture in their darkened minds. We arrived dressed in our jackboots, which always make such a favourable impression in our own country, but the inveterate Amsterdam street urchin saw nothing impressive. He laughed and called after us, "Hey, Chief! Can you swim?" And then he mockingly whistled our battle song, *Wir fahren gegen Engeland*. Then

---

59 A Germanic tribe that occupied the Rhine delta from the 1st to the 3rd centuries, contemporaneously with the Roman Empire.
60 "People" or "Folk" – but with a sense of tribal or national identity.

whenever we honoured each other with the Hitler salute, a couple of brats would raise their arms and ape us, so that a forceful order was issued forbidding insults against the German *Wehrmacht*."

But you cannot forcefully make so many do's and don'ts in order to belittle the nation. Just as in the time of Alva,[61] the Spanish Iron Duke; when our people were like butter, which slips from between the fingers if you try to grab it and mould it. The people of the Netherlands could not defend themselves with weapons, apart from the fact that they are not permitted, because even before our time the words of Jesus to Peter held sway: *Put up again thy sword into his place: for all they that take the sword shall perish with the sword.*[62]

Our spirit cannot be overcome, but remains resilient and tough. What to do in the given circumstances? Something positive of course, the most essential action of the moment, to save the property of these people, and that as soon as possible, before it was discovered they had gone away. Because then the Germans would lay their hands on the lot as spoils of war.

---

61 The Spanish Duke Fernando Alvarez de Toledo, whose heavy handed government of the Low Countries resulted in insurgency, the Eighty Years War, and the eventual formation of the Dutch Republic.

62 Matthew 26:52.

Chapter 26

The evening was dark. Two men, Domie and De Lange, cycled along the empty road toward a certain small town in the province. In the next village, through which they had to pass, they had an appointment with the local doctor. He owned a car and had agreed to drive them on to their objective. With a car like his they really sped along. It all seemed to take but a few minutes! They had arranged to meet a trusted individual with whom they had been in contact on the cable watch – at a street corner where they agreed to rendezvous. The car stopped and they waited a little longer while they checked their surroundings.

The key slid gently into the Lips cylinder lock. With shoes removed, they sneaked upstairs, for on the ground floor lived people who must know nothing of this whole affair. A loose tread which creaked, the scuff of a chair in the room below, their hearts pounding with fear. It must be how a burglar felt; this was not the trivial everyday work of Ministers and Deacons. They also had on large gloves to avoid leaving fingerprints. Here, behind this door, De Lange had been known, as he regularly used to turn up there on a visit each week. First to the bedroom. The young woman had said that they most needed blankets and linen. It now came down to this moment: to seize the opportunity in the shortest possible time and all in complete silence.

The linen cupboard. Even an admiring glance from Domie at such exactitude and neatness! Sheets, pillowcases, hand towels in immaculate white, lay in such neatly aligned piles that you could lay a ruler alongside their edges. However, that was about to change! He reached in and started stuffing handfuls into a suitcase. Another cupboard was open. Here there were clothes, woollen underwear; suits for him, dresses for her. De Lange stood next to the dressing table. Here there were articles of toiletry – the woman had also requested some of those! A comb fell onto the floor. In the apartment directly below them, a chair could be heard shifting. Had they been heard? They waited, breathless. No, nothing! On with the job at hand. Blankets!

"In the suitcase?"

"Can't fit in any more."

"Tied up in a sheet, then?"

"Like this... add another?"

"No, that'll do. But knot it tightly."

"Now back to the suitcase... it's chock full."

"Go and sit on it, then I'll fasten it up tight with the belts."

"Could any light from here be passing under the door?" Domie queried in a whisper.

"Let's hope not... and that it's all gone well," answered De Lange.

"We've really got to get going!"

"How exactly?"

"Sliding them down the banister rail... no creaking, with blankets put underneath, and then firmly close the door behind us, but very quietly."

How they got away from there without detection, they still have no idea. They were both heavily laden and their burdens could not have been more awkward to manage while simultaneously attempting to make no sound!

Outside on the street corner stood the man on guard. He helped to carry the things over to the car. Packing it all in – this suitcase here, that one there, this bundle can go in there – now get in – step on the accelerator, change gears – off home again in the darkness of the night.

There the Mice and I apprehensively waited in the study by the stove-heater.

We had calculated it all out. So long for the bike trip, this much time for the car journey, the work inside the house should take this amount, and add on so much for the journey back again. They should already be about home!

If they had been captured, it looked bleak for all of us. A search of the house would follow. We started thinking of the secret escape route. The Mice were in danger, and it would be Poland for them if they were discovered. For Domie and De Lange, if they had been nabbed, the concentration camp awaited. How terribly long it all seemed to be taking! They should have already been home an hour ago! Wasn't this a cause for concern? I just had to keep calm on account of the Mice, who were effectively sitting on hot coals. But I just couldn't understand the delay.

"Maybe there's some other factor we haven't taken into consideration," I said. "Perhaps they've had a flat tyre or something of that sort."

Finally... finally, the sound of the doorbell, followed by the familiar knock in 4/4 time on the door.

"I'm so glad that you've come. Did it all go well?"

"Top notch! We've taken a part of the goods straightaway over to the Wissings. The rest is, for the time being, stowed safely. We couldn't take everything on the bikes."

"Oh, that's why you're so late. And what about the car?"

"We only came as far as Wierda by car; the rest of the way we cycled."

"Ah, now I understand where you've stowed the remainder."

"*Ja*, but mouths shut, remember!"

"Of course... and what do the refugees say?"

"They were absolutely overjoyed with their new acquisitions."

Domie had meanwhile taken off his coat and stepped inside.

"We're so happy that you are back," said the small Mouse. "We were all so worried."

"Whoever doesn't dare, doesn't win," replied Domie.

Should the day be more important than the night? For the lives of our souls, no. During sleep a person turns toward the inner man, and lives a rich and fantastic life. Then the boundaries of our existence fall away and all things seem possible. Sometimes those who have already long passed on come to us and we speak with them as if there were no divide. Even the boundaries of space fall away and our spirit tarries miles away from where our body lies asleep. We see colourful scenery and experience wonderful things. Often we are in a state to perceive that which in our day-consciousness is not possible. In a dream one sometimes creates poetry, the beautiful last echoes of which cannot be but poorly articulated upon wakening. One wishes to hold on to them, but they evaporate, like a thin mist before the morning sun. Things that were hitherto obscure to us become clearer in the dream... a grammatical structure, an evasive difficult word... and we awaken with that very word we sought on our lips... such as *miscellaneous*. We mumble, "*Ja*, that was the hard word that I couldn't recall." And another time, on awakening, we might say, "This earth must hold us by its gravity, otherwise we would be lost in the vast infinity of the universe."

That sentence I just quoted was the final and only one that I can still recall of a piece of prose that I once recited in a dream. For the rest... the whole is still clear during sudden flashes of perception, but if I wish it to fully materialise in the form of remembered words, then it seems intangible as filmy moonlight; in contact with daylight it evaporates.

Sometimes while dreaming we are in a condition to perceive greater things than everyday reality will allow, and our creative energy is at its most active.

Jesus knows our mysterious inner life and He knows that there is a great similarity between sleep and death. *She is not dead but is yet asleep*[63], He says of the daughter of Jairus. He went to wake her. And He has the power to do just that.

Just as we can call back someone's dreaming mind to everyday life,

---

63 Luke 8:52.

so can He recall the spirit, which had fled to far places, to return to the body, to the reality of this physical earthly existence.

The night after Domie and De Lange had been on the warpath, I had, in a dream, a showdown with a German who came to search the house.

"You're hiding Jews here," he said with a smirk as he bent down to look under the bed.

"Not so loud," I whispered, "the young boy is sleeping."

But it was already too late – from the direction of Hansje's cot came the expected short sobbing sounds that turned into a drawn out pitiful crying. He worked his way up on to his knees and sat up like that in his cot. "Shut up!" threatened the German, and he pointed his revolver at Hansje.

Then suddenly, all my fear disappeared.

I shall roar as a bear, whose young ones are taken[64] – a picture the Bible paints so powerfully and evocatively.

With one swipe I wrested the revolver from the man and threw it out the window.

"Whatever do you mean? Shooting at small children!

You don't have the right to come into my house, to come into my country. You are a foreign barbarian! Get out! Now!"

Without his firearm, the man was nothing. Did that happen because he had been taught to put all his trust in it? At my use of the word "Right" he started shrinking in size. Without it he felt powerless here – on strange, forbidden terrain.

"Excuse me," he said, while he continued to become smaller. I saw him shrink away finally to nothing, but in a dream one isn't amazed by such things.

Then I ran over to the cot, threw my arms around Hansje and said, "Just be still, my boy, he is gone." Now he had nothing more to give us trouble over.

---

64 Proverbs 17:12, Hosea 13:8.

When I later reconstructed the dream, I knew that, apart from the tension induced by the previous evening, the scene with the revolver was all thanks to the fact that I had seen a car with Germans stop in front of the café here in the village. The Germans all got out and they warily kept their rifles at the ready with the catch off. They went searching through the house because some unfortunate youth must have been concealed there. *Ja*, just keep a tight hold of that gun, I thought sarcastically. Without those things you are nothing. They are your only support and your only worth. Your profession is violence. Justice is not in your dictionary and therefore your *Reich* is rotten and shall 'disappear as the chaff'[65], as Luther would have put it.

---

65 Isaiah 17:13

Chapter 27

This morning I found my chair and table shoved aside to a corner of the farm loft, because all across the floor, spread several inches thick, lies this year's harvest of rapeseed. Instead of the huge field of yellow flowers, which I could view from my window, the loft is now full of blue-black seed from which the precious oil is pressed. "Is that used to make our margarine?" asked a traveller, who was viewing the vast rapeseed fields from the compartment window of her train. "It's such a ghastly colour!"

"But that's really a matter of opinion," as De Lange would say.

You would be familiar with the story of Gideon down in his clandestine wine-press, threshing his own grain, since he was forced to hand it over to the Midianites who came on their fast camels each year to overflow the land and raid all their crops, taking the produce away with them. The tribes of Israel had tilled their own land. Militarily they had done nothing but play at soldiers, and now were only using their weapons to gather their crops in secret. *There is nothing new under the sun*[66] says the Preacher. That story from the Bible could have been written today. For up in the stifling loft a farmer is pressing his own rapeseed oil with the aim of keeping back some of the produce for himself and his workers, who have borne the heat of the day – and for a Domie who has a lot of insight into technical matters, and who does duty as a technician for the press, working under extreme temperatures of 43 degrees.[67]

---

66 Ecclesiastes 1:9.
67 On the Celsius scale (equivalent to 110 degrees Fahrenheit).

Every evening the motor is running. Outside it cools off somewhat but in the loft, not much, since no windows can be opened, lest the sound penetrate through the quiet of evening, reaching as far as the road. *Rikketikketikketik*! These winter days supply no pork, but instead we get oil! What a bonus!

"Elderling had his workers doing seventeen litres of oil!" some people told us. But in the presence of others they held their tongues. Such reports in circulation are dangerous enough in themselves.

One of his workers has also just got hold of a piglet.

"And what do you think I 'ad to cough up for 'im?" he asked his farmer to take a guess. "''undred and forty-five guilders," he said, answering himself and then added, "*Joa*, man! My oath! But I'd rather a pig than the 'undred and forty-five, just believe you me!"

"And we're still always complaining," says Elderling.

I'm standing in their farmhouse kitchen. He tells me this while we wait for the buttermilk to separate for Hansje, as *Mevrouw* is churning it in a large preserving jar. Since she just has to go down to the cellar, her husband takes over the churning. "Alright – it's ready now," he announces when she returns. Now she pours the contents of their own improvised churn into a wooden bowl. There are huge clots of butter in it. "I always separate from the cream, and so with such a small churn you have less work than you would with milk," she says.

"How can it be that they're always complaining here?" I ask.

"Because of the climate," says Elderling, promptly. "At harvest time it's always raining, and that has a definite impact. When the harvest is due then the whole year's work is winding up. Bad weather is hard to take for the farmer and for his labourers, as this is the time when they earn the most and then they have to stop working because they get soaked."

I take a look outside. Rain and wind. The drab sheaves of grain stand wet and morose out on the land. But we just keep waiting, until they dry out a little. In this weather, you can't bring them inside.

"Provided that it gets dry before this afternoon, and if it then remains so the whole night through, then perhaps early tomorrow we can finish it," said Elderling.

While I sit here in my loft, it's pouring once more and who can say if it will stop raining by next week, or even after a fortnight? The barometer reading looks bad enough for that eventuality!

But in fact each year the harvest is always finally gathered in, thus we shall again just have to hope for the best. And there is always something left over. *One is never starved by staying right next to the larder*, says the Groninger expression.

Who would have thought that Stelmaker, who once sawed up slats for us so industriously, was actually now using electrical energy to mill grain? Because up in the farm loft sits the electrician, who has so neatly installed the contraption and who now collects the milled flour in a sack.

"Oh, is Domie down there?" he calls. "He may as well know about this."

Domie climbs the stairs up to the loft and finds there a completely installed mill.

"Look," says Monteur,[68] who always breaks into his Groningen dialect when talking to Domie and me. But his dialect is also interwoven with phrases of classic, 'respectable' Dutch, which he uses in a formal, lofty style: "We must rescue ourselves. If we comply with what they have in mind for us, we may languish in failure. What does *Dominee* say in that regard?"

Dominee finds it beautiful.

"You must also have such an installation yourself for your own loft."

"*Ja*, that may well be so, but how do I get the parts you have there?"

"That is not such a great secret. We have another mill for you. The motor you can get from Amsterdam by bartering some field crop – and then you are ready to go! I have heard reports that it's getting even

68 Literally "mechanic" – Stelmaker's nickname.

tighter for them in the city, which affects what they are willing to deal in. The rations are to be reduced yet again. The townsfolk are starving, and they even dare to come to our door seeking a gift for winter relief. The last one who came to us was an NSB woman. But my wife certainly told her the truth. "*Och*, man, did you really come with such a list? If the Germans had not come here in the first place, then we would have had enough for everyone, and then there would be no need for any of your winter-relief nonsense!"

"And what did the collector say to that?" asked Domie.

"She tossed her head back and strode away," answered Monteur. "But to return to the subject – is that mill not something you could use, *Dominee*?"

Domie is very interested and views mills and motors from all angles. The whole affair looks very promising and he has already been won over by Monteur's plan. He considers that the Mole should come over and then they can discuss together how that would all work at our own house. There is still an old bike up in our loft. Maybe they could use that to power the mill through a drive belt. The Mice no longer need to do gymnastics at the bar; instead they could ride a stationary bike. Then they could squeeze their eyes shut and imagine that they were riding down leafy green lanes, and could then report: "Today I cycled ten kilometres, and I went to such and such a place, and along that road..."

After returning home, Domie proposed that idea to the Mice. They responded with laughter and continued to embellish the imaginary picture. But all things considered, it wasn't such a fantasy; a large box of wheat was sent to Amsterdam by De Lange, and a motor arrived in return.

An old washstand, still up in the loft, was made ready as a support for the mill, with a hopper attached, made from a large sheet of cardboard. It looked rather complicated, with the motor standing underneath on the floor. But it lacked a suitable drive belt. We had quite a saga trying to obtain one in order to put the whole machine into motion, but in the end we had the contraption working beautifully.

If there were strong, cranky winds – *maal weer*[69] as the Groningen folk like to call it, then it truly was opportune, because you couldn't hear the purr of the motor above the weather. The Mice would then put on their tracksuits and don white caps to cover their hair and settle in for a long spell of milling. In the course of days like these they got thoroughly dusted with white flour, just like real millers. But whenever someone called to visit, the motor would be cut with one touch of the hand, since the switchboard with the master switch was mounted in the hall right by the front door.

Earlier Ministers' families must have grumbled over the "uncomfortable old *pastorie*", but for us it left nothing to be desired, and it seemed to have been especially built for these times. What use would be an over-planned, straight on, straight up and down house, without deep cupboards, bedsteads, and secret passages? Each nook was known and fully utilised in some spontaneous way. But an outsider would expect something else: A then B then C. Logical, routine and predictable.

---

69 Literally 'bad weather'. However the author is using the phrase in the sense of 'wild weather,' when the noise of the wind easily masked the sound of milling.

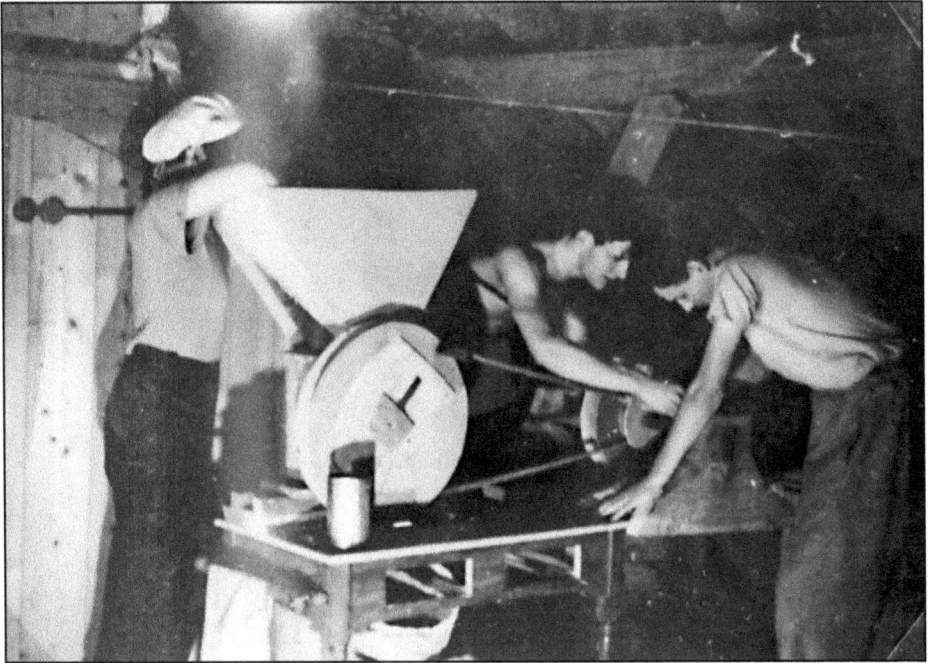

Up in the loft: Lily and the boys milling flour during wild weather.

Chapter 28

All was going well, and in early October, Miss van der Pol arrived on the scene. She was not a refugee, but an officially called assistant, assigned by the Consistory to help with outreach to the community. Oldiek was now on the up with the establishment of a local association, together with an advisory service from a vacant nearby parish. So much work, but there were still no more than seven evenings available each week! The new assistant was completely unknown to us. At an interview I requested at the College of Social Work, where I myself used to be a student, I spoke to the director about the new appointment. I asked her three questions:

First: "Is *Juffrouw* van der Pol suitable for this work?"

"*Ja, ja*, she has concluded her practicum in Bussum very competently."

Second: "Is she a good Dutch citizen?"

"*Ja*, certainly. She comes from a missionary family in Indonesia. Her parents are still out there. She is one hundred percent reliable."

Third: "Can she keep silence?"

The director looked at me in surprise and then laughed.

"I do not know," she said. "But I think so. Is that a necessary attribute for your work?"

"*Ja*, very necessary, as you well know that loose lips in these times..."

"*Ja*, of course. Well, I will not press you further on that question... But I'll tell her we are counting on her silence."

In early October I met her from the train. At the little station it was blowing fiercely. The land looked bare and bleak. I thought what a poor impression all this would surely make on someone from Indonesia and said, almost apologetically, "It's not always like this."

"No, that I could well believe," she laughed, and from that laughter radiated something of the warmth of the Indonesian sun.

"I have asked your director," I began, while we were cycling home, "whether you can keep silence about what you see and know."

"*Ja*, she told me about that. I shall at any rate attempt to do so."

"Then I'll tell you further about our secret when we get to the *pastorie*," I replied.

Domie was already standing on the *stoep* when we arrived. He came up the garden path to meet us and welcomed Polletje, as the children and we also quickly nicknamed her. And then there was Greet and little Hans, who quickly became good friends with her. He was now almost six months old. He gave her a long, serious look. She spoke to him: sweet, friendly words with a sprinkling of Sundanese among them, which sounded very melodious. He understood her completely. The sun broke forth all over his little face, and he stretched out his arms to her. She could not resist taking him up onto her lap.

"Apart from these people you've just met, the *pastorie* is also housing a couple of invisible guests," I said.

"*Ja*, that is our big secret," said Domie.

"On the way home I already dropped a hint or two about that," I continued, "and it's probably a good idea if we go upstairs right away to make their acquaintance, then everything will become immediately clear." After I'd introduced her to the tall and the small Mice in the loft, I went back downstairs to make tea. People most quickly get over their reticence with each other if you leave them alone for a while. When I returned the ice had been completely broken, and when later I stayed behind to chat with the Mice, we came to the conclusion that Polletje would be a real asset to the *pastorie*.

The first morning with us, she was to sleep in late, but used this free time to write a letter to her fiancé, to whom she wrote about the sweeping vista from her room and the sun which shone upon her bed. For her friend the sun, which had accompanied her from her earliest youth and which had made the land of her birth so warm and fruitful, had also appeared here from behind the October clouds and now beamed a moderate, glowing warmth over the wide countryside. A pair of song birds basked in its rays and twittered gently in the colour-changing foliage of the beech. The poplars were almost bare, but the beech still stood there clothed in its full glory and raised its golden crown heavenwards. A robin hopped over the garden path, and a grey cat lay stretched out in the shade of some bushes on the sunny side of the house, feeling well disposed to prey on the birds.

"I'm finding it really lovely here," Polletje commented, completely voluntarily. The late October sun must have contributed to her delight, because we noticed soon enough that Polletje was usually in her element whenever the sun was shining. But she also knew how to spread sunshine to those around her. In no time at all she had the youth on side. But how would it go among the older ones of our community?

The righteous Groninger does not like change. A provincial Hollander may adapt well to new ideas and new gadgets, but the true Groninger of the north holds only to the proven old ways. In the central provinces of Holland, whenever a *Dominee* comes as the invited preacher, the church is full, because everyone welcomes a change and wants to hear him. In contrast, the Groninger stays at home. "Our own Domie wasn't there," he says, as a convincing explanation for the fact that he himself was also absent!

"And now a new city *juvver*[70] like her..." the women from Oldiek said to each other on the evening of the meeting of their Women's

---

70 Another word equivalent to Juffrouw and Juffer. A young lady in Gronings dialect.

Association. They always arrived early, mostly a quarter of an hour ahead of time. A lot of chat always took place before I arrived. Evidently the coming of the new *juvver* was the predominant topic of the conversation on this occasion. But it later became apparent that any concerns of theirs had little foundation.

Vrouw Courts was the most senior member of the group. You have already made her acquaintance when she came to see Hansje in the hospital. She stood up to speak for them all, and wound herself up excitedly until those apple-cheeks glowed.

"Sure, we can just try it," she said, "and if it's not well pleasing, then we can all push off, hear. We shan't just go – first we'll try and if it turns out that such a one from the town is very pushy, then we'll say, 'you won't see us again, hear. We've gotten too old to let ourselves be bossed about by a young girl like you.'"

They all agreed to Courtsje's wise words, even the younger members. And they reiterated: "*Joa,* man – we've gotten too old to be bossed about by such a young girl."

It is indeed good that Domie and I, and especially Polletje, did not know how precariously poised matters were with our Women's Association at Oldiek. But we may judge the first encounter between Polletje and the women an outright success. Well might they try the wait-and-see approach. On their inscrutable faces nothing could be read, but they listened with rapt attention so you could hear a pin drop when Polletje spoke. And it looked as if, in their eyes, she had passed muster.

Here before them sat a modest young girl, that by sheer intuition knew exactly the right tone to use when preparing a speech for their suspicious ears. She said only those things that allayed their fears about what might happen.

"She says it in her *Hollands*[71] speech of course," Courtsje told me at the New Year's party I attended to share in some fellowship and

71 'Hollands' refers to the standard Dutch language.

oliebollen,[72] "but she wanted just to say, that she doesn't want to rule over us here."

"No, of course she wouldn't. Is that what you were afraid of?"

"*Joa*, man, such a foreign *juvver* – you have to think about it for yourself, hear. But I wouldn't have come again if it wasn't good, hear, and neither would the other women."

Nothing remained to argue about. I could only be happy that it had gone so well. Apparently on that first evening, when they were walking home arm in arm in a long line along the darkened roads of Oldiek, they were saying to each other that it had turned out well enough, since that *juvver* was not like the usual know-it-all from the city.

---

72 Dutch doughnut batter balls deep-fried in oil.

Chapter 29

They also had a Men's Association at Oldiek. It was, however, a smaller circle, comprising married men and committed attendees. In the middle of the season Domie picked up a skin affliction. Had it been the food? Not enough fat in the diet? The Mice got swollen ankles. Was that due to the same problem? The cured meat from Nero had been used up long ago, and we lived on what we could get with our butter ration coupons, which had been issued only for our own family and which therefore did not include the Mice in the calculations. Therefore our shared personal rations of fat were very meagre. "It's a good thing that we still have Domitian down in the bomb-shelter," said Domie.

The occupiers of the bomb-shelter carried the names of a succession of Roman Caesars who ruled in the days of the Christian persecution: Nero, Domitian, and De Lange's hog called Diocletian.

Domie's skin rash gradually healed, but an infected boil remained. It was in an awkward spot so Domie couldn't cycle, nor even sit properly. He lay with his books face down on a mattress in front of the heater and studied. The work could not be left undone: Miss van de Pol and I had to deal with a lot of pressure as a result of Domie's infirmity.

"Would you go to the Men's Association meeting at Oldiek for me as an observer?" Domie asked me.

"What do I have to do there?" I replied.

"Domie looked at me, rather perplexed at such a question. "Hold the meeting... as usual," he answered.

But I didn't find that usual at all. They would certainly get a surprise if I walked in through the door instead of Domie. I would have to take the projector with me and show a film. *Ja*, that would always grab their attention! Living in such an unsophisticated, provincial village as Oldiek, I had assumed that they would no doubt like to see something of the scenery of other countries. And when I arrived there they were sitting calmly around the stove heater, and did not show any surprise when I entered. I laid out the matter before them.

Would they like to see a short film?

"*Joa*, go ahead."

They gathered around the table. Then the lights went out and an image of the south coast of England appeared, flickering on the wall. I had been there myself, and could relate some of my experiences over there.

"Man, is that coast rocky!" they said, after the showing. "Prussia could never compare with it!"

"No, man, they'll not try climbing about over there!"

They chatted on about it and companionably smoked their pipes. At nine o'clock the oldest gave the signal to wind up proceedings. They watched with interest as I pulled the projector apart and packed it in my case. They helped me tie the case on the luggage carrier and wheeled the bike outside for me through the long darkened corridor, where they lifted it cautiously and carefully from the high *stoep* onto solid ground, on account of the breakable lamp that had been packed away.

"Thank you so very much," I said. "Good evening and take care on your way home."

"'*n Oavend!*"[73] they replied. Then their silhouettes merged with the darkness. Their footsteps sounded along the dyke path, and slowly dwindled to silence.

On the road home I asked myself – had they really enjoyed

---

73 "Good night!"

themselves tonight? There was something lacking of course: the Bible study, but that was Domie's responsibility. That boil will just have to get better, I decided... and real quick!

But the following week, there I was, venturing out alone again, with my briefcase tied on the back.

On the Monday after that, the women of Oldiek, who were seated at the tables, asked, "Is Domie not well yet?"

"No, still not better."

"That's right bad luck, man." *Vrouw* Courts, who was almost a half of a doctor herself, knew however, of a suitable remedy. "He must drink camomile tea, then it'll get better straightaway. It cleanses the blood. From tonight on *Mevrouw* must give him a porringer full... warm... before he goes to bed... What? You don't have any camomile in the house? Goodness... then I'll make it for you, hear! You must always have some in the kitchen... that's good for everything... pretty much!"

Ol' Geertje had obviously not followed the discussion about camomile tea, but had continued to weave her own thoughts into salient advice.

"Those little pictures," she said, all of a sudden. "Men see no worth in 'em."

This counsel came as a total surprise, and I must have looked a bit taken aback. Had it come to this – that I had cycled to Oldiek in the wind and rain with a heavy case on the back, only to hear now that "men see no worth in little pictures?"

But apparently they had already talked it over among themselves, for now a young wife representing the men's viewpoint suggested, "*Mevrouw* must give the Bible study talk for all of us, just as you did with the women."

Thus the matter stood as follows: the men had gone home unsatisfied despite the showing of a film depicting a far country, because that which they had expected had not been given. But the good thing was that if you had a wife, she could do the complaining for you!

"Alright... next Wednesday... Bible Study. Tell them that," I said.

Since it was a short time before Christmas, at the next meeting I decided to discuss with them the first three chapters of the prophet Daniel: the vision of King Nebuchadnezzar, who saw the gigantic image with the head of gold, the chest and arms of silver and belly and thighs of bronze, the legs of iron and the feet of iron mixed with clay. And then the stone that had been cut from the mountainside without hands, and which began to roll down until it smashed against the weak feet of the statue so that it fell to earth with an almighty crash, and the gold, silver, bronze, iron and clay fell to pieces. But the stone became a great mountain until it filled the whole earth. No doubt an ancient Middle Eastern despot would fully appreciate the successive rising and falling of world empires presented in this striking manner, Thinking about the stone that filled the whole earth... which represents the coming Kingdom of God beginning almost unnoticed with the birth of a child in the manger at Bethlehem... that was something that gave us all a good solid preparation for Christmas. We carried the blessing of that evening in our thoughts as we all set off home through the snow.

Chapter 30

For the Mice their winter season had now arrived. Their daily schedule was therefore altered. In summer and also in the beautiful Indian summer days that followed they often sat by moonlight in the glade near the shelter. If you sat there, either side of the winding path leading to its entrance, where you were shielded by the tall shrubs, no-one would ever see you. And after all, we expected no more visitors in the garden later than ten in the evening. Only De Lange would be likely to come at such a late hour, bringing some meal to feed his own Diocletian and our Domitian. He would have his heavy sack lashed on the front of his bike. From the darkness, he would softly call to the Mice, in order not to scare them, "Good evening, ladies!"

But now there was just the silence, in which they strained to listen. Had they heard something? Absolutely still, they stood by the back door. No, just the rustling of leaves, that was all. In the summer, when the nephews stayed with us, one of the boys sometimes stood on guard at the corner of the house, to watch if there was someone coming inside the fence and to allow for any unwanted visitor to be accosted. But no-one ever entered the garden, so that was a good thing. For months now the Mice had been been with us in the house without anyone seeing them. Not even Imke, who knew nothing of their existence. Or at least, so we thought! In winter Imke would arrive at eight o'clock each morning. Before that hour, much had to be accomplished; the Mice did the washing up that had accumulated from the previous evening. They also chopped kindling, brewed tea, made pancakes, had breakfast and then prepared and lit their own stove-heater. When Imke arrived, every trace of their breakfast had to be removed. Greet cleared away their plates, forks, knives and cups from the living room where we normally sat to eat, because as long as it wasn't too cold the fire burned through until morning. We put an alarm clock on the table for as long as our electric clock was broken, because it all came down to being precisely on time and ready for Imke's imminent appearance. Polletje was mostly in this early party, so the round table was customarily laid for four. In the middle of winter, only rarely did Domie and I join them for an early-bird breakfast. When there was still something to be discussed by the two of us after one of the church association meetings, we took our breakfast much later, and during the period of his skin infection when more time was required to apply the ointment, it was taken very late, more often after eleven than before.

And don't forget the Kaisers! That was always a reason for Greet to rise early. A word of praise must be said before her upcoming wedding for the diligent way she has taken care of these creatures. Because that had to be done in half or sometimes full darkness before Imke arrived, since our fourteen year old had not been initiated into our secret. Polletje was also very sporting. She volunteered to feed the Kaisers, so she pulled on the whole gala-ensemble, comprised of boots, old trousers, and Domie's old jacket, attired in which Greet always made her appearance at court. The first time she found it quite scary, to sense the great grunting heads rising up at her in the darkness of the bomb-shelter. But gradually she grew so confident with the dear creatures that she even volunteered to muck out their sty. To those readers who are missing their rasher of bacon at this time, do you ever wonder whether you would still want to eat it when you feel something for the creature that provided it? I can answer that question with a heartfelt no. Perhaps one person has need of more fat in the diet than another. When I call to mind Domie's skin infection and its probable cause, then the inner protesting voice ceases, which always arose when the names of these homely creatures were mentioned on my lips. But the danger associated with the risk of their discovery was and remains large.

Due to the extreme shortage of coal in the winter of 1941-1942, time after time schools were officially granted intervals of vacation. Schoolchildren roamed around our *pastorie* to see Imke, who had just outgrown her school years.

"I've got to pick some kale from the garden," said Imke.

"Then we'll come with you," said Ginie[74] and Binie.

If you want to go to the vegetable garden to pick kale, then you must follow the winding path that leads also to the bomb-shelter, but at the fork you have to turn left. The path was frozen over in parts, but still passable. The stems of Goldenrod and Michaelmas daisies were still standing, but were bedecked with white frost. The garden looked wintry and bare. The bunches of dark kale stood out in relief. Imke brushed the snow from their heads and snapped them off at ground level. With a basketful on her arm she turned and went back toward the house. But where had Ginie and Binie gone? In fact they had entered the sunken glade close to the entrance pit in front of the shelter.

"Come out of there," ordered Imke, "it might collapse."

Both girls happened at that moment to be sitting right above the entrance door. It was very quiet, just like in the week before Christmas. Luminous, as the folk round here would say.

All of a sudden their attention was riveted by a deep subterranean grunting sound. Had Imke heard correctly? "That's a pig!" said one of the younger girls. They listened carefully again.

"There's a pig down there in the bomb-shelter!" they exclaimed excitedly.

Imke also heard it fully now, and instantly sized up the situation.

"That's bad," she said. "It's skunks! They grunt like that too."

They scampered, all three of them, back to the house and through the back door.

---

74 Ginie is a different girl from Giny, Greet's friend mentioned earlier in the narrative.

"Greet!" they shouted, once inside the kitchen. "There are skunks in the bomb-shelter!"

Greet gave a squeal of alarm, ran to Domie in dismay, and related what had come to light.

Meantime I walked right into the uproar, having just returned from a shopping trip.

"*Mevrouw*, there are skunks in the bomb-shelter." Ginie attempted a grunting impression. "Just like a pig. I really got such a fright!"

I had heard enough! I pushed past her and dashed into the study. There they were, sitting altogether: Domie, Greet and Miss van der Pol, who already knew what was going on. Greet was on the verge of both crying and laughing. She had been Domie's ally in this whole affair. My facial features did not betray my true thoughts which were, Well there you have it. I told you so! This was surely no time for point-scoring. I simply said, "What are you going to do now?"

"Imke's already rescued the situation," said Domie, not sounding too convinced by his own words.

"Really? Do you think they'd swallow that, when Ginie gets home tonight? When she demonstrates the sound that skunks make, just like she did for me just now, then her parents will know very well that these are not skunks."

And yet in that I was mistaken. Perhaps Ginie did not do her little impression after all, because to our wonder and surprise, Ginie came back to us later carrying a huge trap – a skunk trap!

"And may Papa have the pelt?" she added. "Look – it's so beautiful when you put it on show," she explained eagerly.

If it were not for the serious consequences this turn of events could have had for us, I would have laughed out loud at such a comic farce, of which Imke and Ginie were the directors, and we the mere audience. But now, inside me, suddenly a spark of rancour surfaced. I kept my voice low as I said to Domie, "By all means do what you feel to save the situation, but I will not be part of this folly." And I strode from the room.

The whole saga fizzled out. We heard nothing more about the skunks, apart from when Ginie came occasionally to ask if we'd caught one. But the trap stood behind the chimney curtain in the kitchen, and the most we could hope for would be to catch a rat, but even that failed to eventuate. In the end Petertje, another initiated into our secret, courteously returned the empty trap to its owner.

But this 'mouse' (or might I say this un-caught rat or skunk) still had a tail!

Imke had now discovered the secret of the bomb-shelter, but in private she had also discovered even more of our secrets. But she never spoke of them. However, now, in our own interest, she began hesitantly to open up to us about them.

"That stove-pipe that runs up from the loft through the roof," she shyly mentioned to Greet one morning. "It would be right well to think about it."

"Why do you say that?"

"Marchien asks me about it every time that I come into the shop. 'What's the deal with the pipe?' she says then. And in the mornings when I come to the *pastorie* with Aaffien, she says, 'Look! Greet is burning the stove-heater up there'."

Poor Imke, you whom we unintentionally and unknowingly had exposed to such embarrassment. At such a young age you have already realised that this is a terrible time, where you, by betraying a secret, could put someone's life in danger. We had not wanted to tell you anything, since we thought it was all too heavy a burden for your young shoulders, but you could bear more than we thought. And since you are a true maid of Groningen and belong to this tightly-knit community, you have learned your art well... to be silent.

Imke suspected something – that was now clearly obvious. But what exactly did she know or suspect?

"Let it rest," I said, but Domie thought it more dangerous that she knew a half-truth than the whole. And in that regard I had to concede he was right.

He called her to him in the study.

"Imke, you mentioned the pipe and that we needed to take care, since Marchien kept asking you about it. But what exactly did you mean by that?"

Imke nervously shifted back and forth on her chair.

"Oh, Domie," she said smiling shyly, "...no, Domie..."

"Now then, just calmly say why. Just tell us what you think."

Imke blushed and then said, "Someone is up in the loft!"

The pronouncement was out... and then followed silence.

"And what did you think then... who do you think is there?"

She shrugged her shoulders.

"I... don't know.... a *Dominee* or someone."

"No, not a *Dominee*, but in fact two people... two of them up there. They had to flee for their lives. As you well know, in these times sometimes people get murdered, just like that."

She nodded quietly and suddenly looked much older than a carefree child of fourteen.

"Now when did you really first suspect something?"

"When it was my turn here in the *pastorie* during church service, when I was alone minding Hansje in the house, and then I heard footsteps on the floor upstairs... and I became so frightened, because I thought of course that they were robbers or something. I was petrified and would have run out along the garden path, but then I started thinking and then I thought: they must know all about this, as each time something was stolen it would have to be noticed that it was missing. So there must be someone they've got up in the loft. And then to be sure, I went and counted the plates and spoons and forks. There always seems to be a lot of washing up going on here, and so I thought... they have someone hiding in the loft and they don't want a word getting out about it."

"And have you ever spoken to anyone about this?"

"Not anyone at all."

"Thanks to Our Dear Lord that you have not done that."

"It would be right dangerous if I did."

"Then from now on you will of course have to keep silent, but you would appreciate well enough, that we've never told you this before, because we thought it way too big a secret for your young age. We believed that you should not be thinking about such things yet, and not have any worries about them either. Now you know everything... but to get to meet our secret guests... well you'll just have to patient... until after the war. That seems the best thing for you right now, don't you agree?"

"*Joa,* sure, I don't need to see them, Domie. It's right better that way," said Imke wisely.

Then she went back to her work again, just as usual, as if nothing had happened.

The Mice were amazed at such insight. To have known it all and yet not to have let anything out... even to let us carry the delusion that she knew nothing!

"Imke is the living proof of how well a woman can keep silent," I said.

"A fully grown woman could not have done it any better," decided the Mice.

"Would that all adult women have as much insight as Imke!" sighed Domie.

Chapter 31

Sunny days have returned but the land lies stripped of much of its verdure. It's still very early in the season for harvesting. Last year everything was still standing out in the fields during the second half of August, but now not only have all the main crops been reaped, but they are already in the barns. The barn where I've come to sit in my loft and write is packed to the rafters.

Some of the farmers are already threshing. All this activity is happening a month earlier than in other years.

In front of my window there remains only a large field of flowering clover. The beets are still growing, and the horsebeans stand in isolated clumps. The potatoes have not been cleared yet, but the major part of the work, the hectares of grain, have been harvested. That is achieved nowadays using their American machines: by reaper-binders and tractors. After a few days, the grain of this huge tract of land has been cut and the bound sheaves stooked to dry. In good weather and in hot summers they can be gathered in after a couple of days, or even by the next day, as long as there are enough hands to do the work. The barn doors stand wide open as the wagons, piled high with produce, ride inside.

Scattered here and there are several forgotten wheat spikes, a small fraction of the yield from such an enormous area of land; the gleanings which the townsfolk pick up. Most of the locals are not bothered about this practice, because otherwise the townies will get it in some other way.

Polletje is likewise making a success of gathering the gleanings. Like a petite coloured patch on Elderling's land, she bends down, just as Ruth once did on the fields of Boaz, seeking the spikes of wheat that the mowers have left behind. The sun burns hot and nowhere is there any shade, but Polletje feels the tropical heat suffuse her skin. She is almost in her element, like a fish in water.

"Warm? *Ja*, delightful!" she said, when asked about it. She came home on two occasions with a sack full of spikes of wheat, which the Mice threshed for her by rubbing the heads between their hands.

The fields of stubble are soon ploughed under; here and there are bursts of activity leading to the fresh sowing of seed: cabbage seed and winter wheat for the new crop. The land enjoys no rest, yet patiently and constantly brings forth new fruit and new crops upon which both man and beast can feed. No wonder that hymns of praise are sung about 'the good earth'. Now with the grain in the barn we can prepare ourselves for winter. Then begins our church work in the various associations and we call both young and old together.

The Mice have been with us for more than a year. We celebrated their anniversary in July. How on earth did they make it through the autumn and winter last year? By dint of hard work – much work. The tall Mouse studied a voluminous tome on historical materialism entitled: "The Low Countries Near The Sea: An Illustrated History of the Dutch People from Dunkirk to Delfzijl" by Jan Romein, in addition to which she was preserving beans, cabbage and endive, as well as painting and typing this manuscript. Sometimes the small Mouse engaged in her old profession; taking and developing photos, busying herself with flood-lamps, developing canisters and trays. She enjoys tinkering. Her hands are patiently busy for hours on end crafting puppets of a particular design that she has conceived herself: a Spanish country squire or a 19th century lady, and these materialised using coloured scraps of cloth that she found stored in a trunk. "Don't throw anything away," said my mother, "you will need it again."

"That loft..." said the Mice, "there you can find all sorts of things! Enough to provide everyone with *Sinterklaas*[75] gifts."

And they rummaged around like real mice in all the darkened corners and nooks, everywhere finding something to their liking.

The Mole came up on one of his frequent visits. No-one ever saw him come and go, because he always arrived on the last train from Amsterdam and left again a few days later in the dark hours before dawn. He brought a beautiful set of hand-crafted puppet heads, which he had carved himself... enough to stage a whole puppet show! The task of the Mice was to then clothe them using scraps from the box of bits and pieces. This collection was to make a fine contribution to the resources used by the Youth Fellowship.

And for Hans there was a knitted outfit that was intended to be a Christmas surprise for his mother, so I was not permitted to come unannounced to their attic room at all during November. And the Mole also painted the *Magere Brug*,[76] the bridge crossing the Amstel River, over which we crossed a couple of times each day when we lived in Amsterdam.

And then the day finally arrived – the Eve of *Sinterklaas:* 5th December! The Mole joined us; all the presents were opened and the poems that had been composed especially for the occasion were read out. And we were amazed that it was really possible that in such perilous times you could still enjoy celebrating such a happy feast-day.

I kept aside one of the poems. This speaks for itself, so I'll let you read it:

---

75 The Dutch tradition of Sinterklaas can be traced back to St Nicholas of the 4th Century. His habitual gift giving became the model for the traditional Christmas figures of Sinterklaas, Father Christmas and Santa Claus.
76 The picturesque 'Skinny Bridge' in Amsterdam, so named for its narrow width.

Our Dominee's house is so well-built and solid,
It's clearly not tinsel and cardboard and froth,
And early each morning from six through to seven,
Mysterious forms hover round ev'ry path.
Through kitchen and hallways full buckets are carried,
And food is got ready and kindling is chopped,
That's unexpected and seems quite suspicious,
It's not a hotel. Should such nonsense be stopped?

Hark! Up in the attic though noise is forbidden,
It's all helter skelter, mice quickly have scurried,
And they sound like the roof is being demolished,
And then there's a faint hint of a motor unhurried,
A soft raspy murmur comes on the dawn breeze,
Unwavering, gritty, like grinding somewhere,
Then Greet's classic breeding and courtesy lead her,
To lend a keen hand to all chores done up there.

And out in the garden there's something amiss,
Too much interest is shown in what should be passé.
If you so much as pause by the bomb-shelter entrance,
Then you're told off quite sternly and you're sent away.
It's odd that some people, though few I admit,
Always seem to be there like sentries on guard,
And often they wander about like they lived there,
What goes on... who knows...in that part of the yard?

I'll unfold the mystery that lies behind Domie,
He cannot be easily lured nor deceived,
He invents many ways to set up deceptions,
To avoid all surprises when threats are received.
Clear headed he acts without evil intention,
He says, "I'll not fall into traps they have set!
Should they ever get wind of the things I am doing,

I must not allow them to set up their net.
And thus to have all my pursuers waylaid,
Some more thorough measures and plans must be made."

In quiet and carefulness, so it stayed secret,
A perfect escape route was dug 'neath the floor,
From the leerkamer platform right through the foundations,
By which he could vanish and be sighted no more.
Domie was crafty... But Heaven forfend it!
So were some lads who were bored and all het up.
Thus seeking adventure and thrills to explore there,
They crawled 'neath the platform, unveiled the whole set up!

Oh, Domie, what's come is a minor disaster,
Now Eltjo and Binie and Hampie all know!
They crept through the floor-space, explored it so quickly,
Uncovered the tunnel that lay there below.
Doesn't that make you a little bit worried?
From now on exclude them from parties in there.
With this rope you can bar them, those scamps from the youth group,
Lest they have you cornered at last in your lair!

You would gather from this composition that our secret passage had finally been unveiled.

This happened on the same Saturday evening when Polletje was supervising the boys in the *leerkamer.* Domie had a duty to fulfil in a vacant parish nearby, and had already left. When I heard a surge of rowdy noise, I surmised that something must be going on. Petertje was already standing in the short passage leading to the *leerkamer*, and saying with a frightened face, "Some boys are sitting under the stage and they say there is a very deep tunnel there!" Petertje, who was already in the know regarding our bomb-shelter occupants, had an inkling that there was also danger in this discovery. And rightly so! From the expression on my face, he must have seen how shocked I was.

"Get out of there, right now!" I shouted, summoning the boys from the dusty, shadowy depths. One by one they came out of the tunnel and crept on hands and knees out from under the stage. They were four rather rough and ready lads of about sixteen or seventeen, who now stood before me, with arms drooping feebly at their sides, fully ashamed of themselves. There followed a strong rebuke and the immediate sealing off of the *leerkamer*.

After a quarter of an hour, our four gallant explorers of exciting subterranean tunnels returned. They came to ask for forgiveness. That I granted promptly. My scolding had been excessively out of proportion to their offence. Had I lost my sense of humour and my understanding for boys? They could have no idea why I had been so angry – and I could not tell them the reason. That is the tragedy of our human society; that there are so many misunderstandings. Nevertheless, they went home comforted that evening after obtaining my mercy.

Chapter 32

Everything continued as usual. At the Wissings' two refugee families were housed in their loft. In it there was also an attic room that the guests had rearranged with a minimum of furniture into pleasant residential quarters. There was a bed, a small table, and a pair of chairs. A working stove-heater was also set up. De Lange made himself very useful. He went over some nights to chat for a while with them. For those who live in seclusion, totally isolated from the outside world, they surely have need of each visit, and do value them as a welcome break in the monotony of their existence.

"I talked to the people right at the start," said Wissing. "I went to talk to them and I said: 'If this has to last a year, or longer, what do we do about it?' But that young woman must have been thinking: 'That man doesn't know any better – I believe that the invasion will come soon'."

But Wissing was on the mark in assessing their ability to adapt to circumstances; the young woman was having a really tough time of it. She always sat there shut up with three males for company, and then of course both Wissing and De Lange were also male. "Having all these men around all the time drives me crazy," she confided to me. "Couldn't Polletje and you come over sometimes for a change?"

That was easier said than done. Because the Wissing brothers guarded their house as a fortress. Grand and lonely, it stood behind its canal and high fence. The curtains, especially those that covered the hiding place upstairs, virtually sealed the place hermetically. Access to the loft where they were living was barred by a stout lock. All in all, it rather resembled the fairy tale castle of the Sleeping Beauty. Only the impenetrable hedge of thorns was missing! But our astute doctor, the same who had brought them blankets and clothes in his car, must have got involved, since the young woman had not been well for a time, and on a prescription form he wrote for her: "Visits by ladies." As a consequence, the gates of these castle-knights were opened magically to us. The draw-bars were slid aside and we gained access to the innermost sanctum of that secret dwelling, where the local society of refugees had their bolt-hole.

I brought my own medicine for the young woman: some paper and a pencil. At that time I did not yet have this special place of my own; a loft for a private space in a neighbouring farmer's barn. I would gladly have written elsewhere, but in our own fully occupied home there was not a single quiet spot where I could do that.

It was on a Sunday, at noon, when I made my first visit to the Wissing farm. First of all a down-to-earth social chat in the room of the first loft level where they lived. Then the young woman and I climbed some stairs up to the next level. There we sat together on a bale of straw. The soft rain tapped out soothing liquid rhythms against the window.

"If I had such a loft, such a beautiful farmer's loft," I said almost enviously, "then I would be sitting here the whole day writing."

That visit gave birth to the idea to put my feelers out now and to search for such a retreat as long as it took until I had found it. But the young woman was apathetic and shrugged her shoulders. "What would I write?" she asked.

"About your lives here... that is interesting enough in itself... thoughts about your feelings and sentiments, your companions and your guardians... or rather guardian angels, the Wissings, all of which, line by line, are worth the effort you put in. If you just did it just as a kind of emptying yourself... as you poured out your heart on the page you would see how you were going in keeping your spirits up. That would at least be as much help to you as I found it was to me, and the advantage is that you always will have paper and pencil at hand to journal, unlike myself."

"I'll try it," she replied. But I never heard anything more about it from her, so I fear that particular diary will never come to fruition.

It was always fun when De Lange paid a social call to the *pastorie,* because he could so wonderfully relate, or rather act out, a domestic situation, as he got inside the character of whoever he was portraying and imitated their voice and manners precisely, so that it wasn't any longer De Lange sitting there, but one or another of the village types that he was imitating. He even did a fine impression of the Wissings, as follows:[77]

"We've already requested a bucket a few days ago," said the refugee guests, "because we just wanted to mop our floor, but we haven't been given one yet."

Now De Lange melodramatically puts his forefinger up to his lips, looks nervously around and whispers forcefully in a conspiratorial tone, *"Pssst! Prisoners of war! The maid can't know anything of this!"*

"But the maid knew the first day though, that we were here," counters Inge (the name of the young woman with the blonde, completely un-Jewish features). *"She saw us down there on the work floor, but she didn't really want to see us, as she quickly turned her head away. She holds her tongue well, so he need not fear."*

De Lange remains completely in character. He once more becomes the Wissing brother:

"May as well talk to the maid about it, and tell her, 'things won't get the worse for you, my girl, if you don't blab about it,'" says Wissing.

"Alright, then you can take the bucket upstairs," I say.

---

77 This performance of De Lange's is a comic pastiche of snippets of upstairs and downstairs conversations to entertain and illustrate the personalties involved, and may not be entirely factual. The matter of the bucket may be euphemistic: alluding to the indelicate subject of personal ablutions.

"No, no," says Wissing. *"The maid mustn't know that there are prisoners of war up there."*

"Och, man, do you really think that the maid is trying to find something out?" I say.

Wissing says, "Don't you think so?"

Then, up in the loft, Inge asks Moeke, "Where do you say the bucket should go?" and of course Moeke just has to reply, "Upstairs!"

"Ja, it can just as easily be kept anywhere – like upstairs," I say. "At my place, there are buckets on the work-floor, behind the house and who knows where else."

But Wissing simply retorts, "Prisoners of war... concentration camp! They had nothing on 'em to begin with, hear! And that cabbage that I left near the bridge the day before yesterday, hidden in the nettles – have they got that yet?"

Inge's answer comes back, "Cabbage? We haven't seen any cabbage."

Wissing exclaims, "Darn! Then it must still be there."

A little later, someone comes up the stairway to the loft. It's the oldest Wissing brother.

"Wissing," I say, "that cabbage... you know the one I mean... that we were just talking about before?"

Wissing takes his cap off and slowly and thoughtfully scratches his head.

"Joawel,[78]" he says. "That's still there right enough, among the stinging nettles. Joawel, it's still there next to the bridge."

"It was supposed to be their supply of food for today," I say.

"Joa... well today they had buttermilk porridge. Not too nutritious, I must say. But anyway, we've got good preserved cabbage as well. After all, they are prisoners of war. Don't you agree?"

"Ja, sure, man, you must not become reckless, but you can also exaggerate the risks."

"No, no," Wissing replies, slowly, emphasising each word. "You can never be too careful."

---

78 "Yeah, sure."

And that was it. De Lange indeed has the gift of the gab. And Wissing listens respectfully but is stubbornly planning to just keep doing what he is already. "Safety is the best policy."

Both De Lange and Wissing were present at the following meeting of the Church Council. One Deacon comes all the way from the Dollart by bicycle, because he lives on the very edge of our parish boundary. He's always the first to arrive, along with Mulder from Oldiek. Then after them, Elderling arrives with another church elder. The six of them sit in the study. Domie makes up seven, the sacred number.

I usually wait ready with the tea service until De Lange, who acts as secretary, has read out his neatly written report. This concerns the upcoming Christmas celebrations and therewith the many practical matters to discuss and sort out. Who in Oldiek should be provided with a Christmas gift? How much money has *Mevrouw* already raised from the Christmas list, or is she not yet done with it? Will they be generous with money, does she think? And how many Christmas trees should we provide?

That's a responsibility always given to Wissing. He sets off into town each year to search out supplies of trees, since no-one quite has his talent for all the requirements of the task. And decorations – does *Mevrouw* still need to buy more? Because last year – "as you well know – our Christmas tree fell over and damaged so many of the ornaments." At the meeting standard Dutch is spoken, but the remarks and comments offered liberally throughout are in the local *Gronings* dialect.

And now Domie has one more request. He has received a letter from a church in Amsterdam, which has asked that if we have here any spare ration coupons, could we pass these on to their folk for buying vegetable pulses for the annual Christmas children's party in Amsterdam?

"That ration coupon nonsense is a waste of time," opines Wissing.

"We can do better by sending them some actual beans ourselves," agrees De Lange.

Now they discuss it with each other. The conversation is totally in Gronings dialect from this point on. Once they reach an agreement, Elderling officially takes charge of the matter. Domie is to write a letter to the *Dominee* in Amsterdam and explain that they are going to post a carton of peas as a Christmas gift for the children. In that way they will receive more peas than the quantity for which spare coupons could be exchanged in the city. Domie is in his element. Wonderful – he will do that. But how many Christmas trees are we now expecting? Two or three? I see seven pairs of eyes focussed on me. The *lutje Domie*[79] must surely have an idea. Three, I reply; one here in the church, another in the *leerkamer*, and also one at Oldiek. We also did it like that last year. De Lange notes that down... three... and then the conversation continues, the deep, steady cadence of male voices dissolves into the background. But I no longer am listening. Something else has captured my attention... a memory of our Christmas party last year with the women, where the tables were covered with white decorative runners, on which the home-made cakes were set among sprigs of evergreens and glowing candles, and in a corner, the softly luminous Christmas tree, then the Christmas story so dear to my heart being read aloud, because no-one can ever enter the Kingdom of God more easily and safely than through the stable at Bethlehem. To us, the incomprehensible comes close through that Child. It becomes visible and tangible to our gentle hands. The Word became Flesh. The great secret of God, Who reveals Himself in human form, that we might learn to understand Him and love Him; that is a wonder which our eyes perceive in reverence, as did the eyes of the medieval painters in their frescos of the Madonna and Child.

How did that old song go again, that the Youth Group sang last year in their performance Cantata?

---

79 Literally "Little Domie" or "Assistant Minister", here used colloquially to refer to the author, as wife of the Dominee.

Thou strengthen'st me with tender hands,
And fill'st me with Thy mighty breath,
To free me from oppressive bands,
I fully live now through Thy death.

I had reached the selfsame point in my thoughts at which the men's discussion had arrived, because De Lange then asked, "This year – are we going to have a Cantata again?"

"It will have to be the same one," said Domie. "I can't develop a new one each year, because there is a lot of work involved."

Ja, they also understood that very well. We would then need to draw up a program for our Christmas pageant as it seemed best to us. Were there now any more points on the agenda? *Ja*, but nothing more that related to Christmas. There were other activities that awaited my attention so I left the study. I only came back to see them once more that day, to return the empty bottle for the milk and to especially wish a safe trip home to the men who lived so far away that they would not arrive home until after dark.

Chapter 33

A few days after this meeting a terrific storm suddenly broke loose. Unexpectedly it howled across the fields in its unabated fury to swoop upon our roof. One of the chimneys must have been its prized target: its entire four-cornered cap was wrenched off and struck the skylight window of the Mice's attic so that the fastener broke and the window snapped open on its hinges. Then the cap continued relentlessly on its downward trajectory, driving straight for the kitchen below, but fortunately not striking any of the ground floor windows. The Mice were stunned with shock. They yelled to us downstairs. In a moment we dashed up to join them.

"What's happening up there?" we called as we ran.

Domie was already standing on the table in the attic. Stretching his arm through the gap in the skylight, he managed to seize the frame and hold it firmly. The wind howled through the skylight into the room, and snowflakes whirled around his head. He looked like a sailor aloft in the rigging of a ship at sea in stormy weather. Above the hurricane his voice called for a rope and a sack of flour. When these items were rushed up to him, he tied the skylight frame to the weighted sack. Now the skylight could not fly open, otherwise the wind would have to lift the sack as well.

For the time being there had been a temporary fix, but the smithy and the joiner would need to pay a visit, not to mention the Deacons. So then... where would we put our Mice for the duration of the repair? Ah! In the secret wardrobe! We would also have to make use of it for this specific purpose on other occasions – for example when the chimney-sweeps came, or the gutters were being cleaned out up on the roof. And we even used this strategy once previously, when Imke brought hot coffee up to Domie, who was working in the loft. And that was before we knew that she knew! She told us later that she was looking curiously about, to see where the mysterious occupant of the loft might be, but she never caught sight of him. She thought he must be hiding from her in the closed attic room, since you could quickly run over and disappear inside.

In an unanticipated moment one day, the smithy arrived and set up his ladder against the house. The Mice were just warned in time and were evacuated down into the wardrobe in a few split seconds. So the smithy and his apprentice were now looking down on an empty attic, just like *Sinterklaas* and Black Pete of Christmas tradition who had also recently glanced through the skylight window.[80] When they had detached the last torn shreds of zinc plated metal from the top of the chimney, and the two of them had climbed back down, they loaded the heavy chimney cap onto a wheelbarrow and set off back home. Now it was the joiner's turn. He had to enter the house to work on the skylight, and therefore could not suddenly surprise us as the smithy had. I kept him engaged in polite chit-chat while Polletje hurried upstairs to warn the Mice. *Roetsch, roetsch, roetsch...* they crawled down the ladder for the second time. With the trapdoor above their heads shut tight, the attic was empty once more. I went up with the joiner and he inspected the skylight.

"That's got right twisted off – and quite a few tiles have also been blown off the roof, haven't they? *Och,* man, that was really some storm!"

Suddenly he put a question that really shook me.

"Was that put there just to protect a secret?" he asked.

---

80 In the Dutch Christmas tradition, Sint and his helper arrive at each house and look down inside to check on each child's behaviour to ascertain whether they are worthy to receive gifts.

I was far too embarrassed to show fright, but I was genuinely scared that the Mice would hear him and become apprehensive.

"What do you mean?" I countered, interested nevertheless.

"Here," he pointed with his hand.

"Hé, I've never seen that before. Must be something our predecessors did."

How was it possible that the fellow saw it? I would never have noticed were I the stranger. He somehow put two and two together and deduced a connection between the bell wiring circuit and the portable mill, which he saw still standing in the loft. I let him keep guessing.

Indeed, it **was** for warning the Mice! Everyone had already been playing with it; it was an old circuit that had already been installed in the house many years before we arrived – in order to call some past maidservant to duty. But now we had rigged it with a buzzer attached to the hidden wardrobe that could also be heard above in the loft as a warning to the Mice. At least if it were functional. But a fault must have since developed somewhere in the wires, because we could no longer get the thing to work. Domie and the Mole and Polletje's fiancé all tinkered with it, one after another, but no-one could locate the precise spot of the open circuit.

One time, in all innocence, Imke gave Domie a terrible fright by pressing the button for the distress signal, all without her ever knowing or suspecting a thing. The Mice scampered in panic down to their secret wardrobe and Domie legged it downstairs, white as a sheet, and all for nothing. All for a curious young girl who wanted to try switching on a lamp in Greet's room, but then accidentally pressed the alarm button instead. But *ja*, that's just the way things turn out sometimes, says the Groninger.

I told the joiner nothing more; especially of those images this black-sheathed electric wire evoked in me, but went below with him while he told me what materials he needed in order to repair the damage.

"When will you be back?"

"Tomorrow morning, I think."

"*Ja*, but when exactly? Early or late morning?"

He looked at me rather non-plussed. I'd never put him under this much pressure before. Well now, you always return whenever things best fit in, *nietwaar?*[81]

"Why does *Mevrouw* ask?" he enquired.

"So we can sort things out with the Mice," I had almost blurted out. But instead I said, "Because I'd dearly love to have it fixed again as soon as possible. If we don't agree on a time, then the morning may just roll on by and then we'll be putting off the job until the next day."

"No, early morn, 'bout eight o'clock – *Mevrouw* can count on me being here then."

"That's fine," I said, and then I thought to myself – tomorrow will have to be a very-early-to-rise morning. Now that the question of timing was settled, we could have the Mice moved to the guest room before he arrived.

The only one here in the house who was immune to these DPD's was Hansje. (We called these small or large fright-inducing incidents DPD's – an abbreviation of the Dutch *dagelijkse paniek dienst* which means 'daily panic service'). By mid-January Hansje had turned nine months. He messed around in his box, crawling here and there on all fours, sometimes rising to his feet. He had first stood upright and come forward on tentative steps precisely on the day he turned seven months. He also really enjoyed a game that you played with his little hands: *Tower, tower cask of powder*, from the lines of a children's song which you sang to him. He also loved the noise he made on the piano when the keyboard cover was opened and he could reach the keys. How interesting and beautiful life must be, each day fresh and new again for that little man. His bathtub was made ready each morning, and set down nice and warm on the floor, and he would gladly get in,

---

81 Translated "Isn't that so?" or more loosely, "Don't you think?'

clothes and all! When he finally sat there, he would vigorously splash with his hands while looking triumphantly around. Was this really all so new for me? In a certain sense, *ja*, inasmuch as everything that is really beautiful is new, but on the other hand, it had by now become over-familiar.

When I was a young teenager I also bathed a young baby boy every day, the child of my older sister, who had sadly died after his birth. In the holidays my growing young nephew came to stay with his grandparents. I then largely took care of him. I found that baby as sweet as I now find my own. I had bathed that child and put him to bed and considered him to be a small miracle. Later more small children were born. They seemed to always approach life with laughter emanating from their blue eyes, as if nothing but good was expected of it. And all too soon that feeling came to me that what was so confident and trusting about life must count on our protection; and we had to keep away from their childlike eyes all that is base, filthy and mean. And now that they had reached about twenty years of age and were in the prime of their years, Hitler had committed to attack and undermine our youth. "All manly young chaps sign up for the Waffen S.S! There is still a place open for you," calls the fowler, seducing them with his sweet piping. But only a few foolishly allowed themselves to be enticed and to volunteer for the Eastern Front. They still could even now be voluntarily sticking their heads in the noose. Later, might they be forced to?

"But then I'd keep them in hiding," said my brother. *Ja*, by every means necessary we must find a way to escape, so that this Moloch[82] never gets a chance to take our boys. Never!

The tragedy of Napoleon at the Battle of Beresina[83] would not be repeated! They would not be aimlessly and callously slaughtered on the Eastern Front. Had their mothers brought them into the world and

---

82 A pagan, Canaanite god associated with the repugnant act of child sacrifice, which practice was fully condemned by God in Leviticus 18:21 and 20:2.
83 The 1812 battle of Napoleon's troops against the Russian army.

nurtured them with tenderest care for such a purpose? And had I put my little nephew to bed with a lullaby and a story toward that end?

I suddenly realised that it did not make much difference if it were your own child or another's. Our youth was truly exposed to this danger, and therefore an obligation fell upon those of us of the previous generation. For how could they begin to resist if we did not help them, and what gave us the right to say, "Don't go!" if we afforded them no shelter nor stood as surety for them? The Russians only have to fight more fiercely, and the English and the Americans should accept the hazards and fly lower, face danger head on and risk being shot down, thereby losing their lives, but we don't have to do anything, right? If only we could just sit here with our cup of ersatz coffee and listen to the radio news of how others are fixing up the world for us.

We also must do what our hands find to do. We must commit to passive resistance. That was our duty. That was also our way of warfare; the only possible response, and furthermore the only one permissible. Not "taking up the sword" but a stiff passive resistance in a spirit of tough invincibility, a refusal to bow before the usurper who is violating our rights and our law.

"I believe in the power of Good," a young farmer said to me one day. That all sounds very nice and understandable in less tumultuous times, wherein life is as a tranquil lake with a mere ripple on its surface. Then we can prudently speak of "God, virtue and eternity," the familiar trio, and say that we believe. But then the folk of the Middle Ages sounded the depths and the dark abysses of life far more comprehensively than we have. They truly experienced the demonic powers that rule over mankind, the eternal battle between good and evil, and being translated from the kingdom of darkness through Christ, who conquered both death and hell.

A young Minister was introduced to his new church community at a service where he preached a civilised and thoughtful sermon. Sitting and listening from the pew was an old professor, who afterwards said to him, "You believe in God. Now you still have to learn to believe in the devil." For us that is not so difficult. We see his might everywhere, grasping for and affecting everything around us. In recent times we really have got to know and believe in the incarnation of evil. Before that we were not so accustomed to it. Paradoxically, in the beginning there were some incidents of active opposition to the Germans. When the Jews by the thousands were robbed and led away in the most disgraceful and inhumane manner, a massive strike broke out spontaneously in Amsterdam. But little by little we got used to the oppression and started to weaken; we lay down and withdrew. But that means now evil has acquired even more power over us as a nation.

Because: *Offences will come*, said Christ, *but woe unto him, through whom they come!*[84]

The German people are busy heaping up great guilt upon themselves. Whosoever placidly and impassively quotes the first part of this prophecy in regard to the Jewish people and their exceptional history must seriously keep in mind the second part, and know that he, as a Christian, is accountable for the fate of his fellow men. Should everyone do his duty then nothing can harm us or our young men. As a nation we stand for each other; in unbroken fellowship we are made strong against the attacks of the aggressor. However, every step we go back means a step forward for the enemy. Always he is attempting to see how far he can go. He doesn't make his attacks suddenly and openly, but cunningly, little by little, so that most people do not even know that he is busy stretching his net.

At first there was just a very innocent looking piece of paper. You had to respond to one question asking if you had any Jewish ancestors. Most readily filled it in without thinking. After all, hadn't they done that

---

84 Luke 17:1.

sort of thing in the past? What devious use was surely made of that information! Thus followed the immediate dismissal of all civil servants who had Jewish forebears. A new provision followed: one was no longer allowed to employ Jewish personnel in service; Jewish businesses were 'expropriated' or should I say 'confiscated,' sounding all very civilised, and an administrator was appointed for this purpose. The rightful owners, dispossessed of their property, were unceremoniously put out on the dyke.

Shortly after that followed more rules: Jews could no longer travel, they could not own a radio, telephone nor bicycle, they could not make use of nor linger around trams, parks, hotels, cafés and other public places, and finally, they were not permitted to enter the homes of Aryans. So that they would be recognised everywhere, where they could be robbed and raids held against them with impunity, they were branded with a star. Ultimately they were outlawed altogether and handed over to the wicked lusts of their evil tormentors. Since Christians, especially the churches, are *the salt of the earth*, and the *light of the lampstand*[85], they must protest against this maltreatment of humanity. And they have done so. The attitude of the Church is unquestionably praiseworthy at this time. Now the wheat is separating from the chaff in almost apocalyptic terms.

But he that is a hireling, and not the shepherd, whose own the sheep are not, seeth the wolf coming, and leaveth the sheep, and fleeth[86], says Jesus.

Some of the most faithful servants of Jesus Christ, even among our friends, have sealed their testimony with their lives, while many other Ministers are still languishing in concentration camps.

Submerged beneath all the superficial spume and spindrift of life that

---

85 Matthew 5:13-14.
86 John 10:12.

manifests in times of relative peace and prosperity lie eternal truths hidden deep within the heart of the Church; truths that point beyond our temporal state and with which we are to be clothed throughout the ages to come.

That the power of evil is depicted as a serpent is extremely apt. Smooth and slippery are the stratagems that are employed by the enemy at this time. False and venomous are his slogans, with which men are brought into a stupor so they do not see the peril facing them and fly as easy prey into the open maw. Had we not yet learned enough from the methods they practised on the Jews? Must we learn the lesson all over again from scratch when it concerns our boys? The Church had protested against the forced deportation of labourers to Germany.

"Just wait," said the German authorities. "Now we shall take the sons of your bourgeoisie as well, who study here at the universities. Such a life of study is just a waste of time. Our own boys don't do such meaningless things. They do useful work – they soldier for the *Reich*!" (*Ja,* really? Any genuine productive activity on their part is completely inconceivable!) "Aha... simple! Those little Dutch lords behind the front can at least be employed manufacturing our ammunition for us."

"What?" respond the young Dutch capitalists. "That would be treasonous action directed against our own country!"

"Alright! Shut their mouths by closing the universities, which are all hotbeds of resistance anyway. Bury those old fossils of their professors in a camp and have students sign a paper stating that they are all in accord with what we wish. When we've collected all the papers, then we'll see. If they all sign, then it means that they are under obligation to be deported at any time and that we therefore have a free hand with them. We can thus take them without a fight. But if only a small number sign the paper, what can we then expect from this stubborn people? Make those ones' reward to stay back home and the rest will have to be taken away. Among the few compliant ones we see no problems here however, because they most likely will be already members of the NSB."

Then the unexpected happened. The card system with all the names of the students registered at the university at Utrecht was destroyed in a fire. That was a drawback for the Germans but they would take their captives nevertheless, by the old tried and tested way they had utilised to catch so many Jews. They held raids in a street where many students lived. They came with police vans and hauled them from their beds during the night. Or they sealed off the university campus with its laboratories and instigated a manhunt within the cordon. Some students fled right up as far as the collar beams under the attic roofs, but in the minds of these minions of the devil resided no hint of shame over such a godforsaken practice. They took along their powerful torches, especially manufactured for a manhunt, and shone them into the darkest corners.

"Hey! Is that someone huddling up there on the beam? Come down! Immediately!"

A moment of nervous silence; the boy is not stirring. Then a revolver is drawn. "Get down! Or I'll shoot!"

A trembling boy lets himself down. Nicely done though! Beautiful! Brave heroes of the Third *Reich*!

But the boy apprehended could have been our nephew Chris, because small children quickly grow up and become tall. The baby I had taken care of when I was a young girl was already a head taller than me and a student there in Utrecht. That, for us, was very disquieting.

Chapter 34

I had already written Chris a warning letter couched in covert phrases but never received a reply. It certainly was not written with enough clarity to mean anything to people who did not understand the coded terms of our "hidden language". But were I to write explicitly, that would be dangerous. The Mole provided us with a solution to our problem. He had just been with us for a few days and was about to travel back to Amsterdam. He volunteered to go to see Chris and his father and to pass on our offer that Chris could take shelter with us.

"Hiding out?" responded his father. "No need for that! You shouldn't be so afraid."

Evidently he had learned very little about the methods of the Third *Reich*. Courage does not underestimate an opponent, but it acknowledges the enemy's power and astutely sees through all his intentions. Prepared thereby, courage effectively counters all his shrewdness, toughness and endurance in a resolute passive resistance, by which all his attacks are thwarted. But just try convincing anyone whose opinion differs and they think that you have too little faith in God. A little while later when we were down there together on a visit, we had a conversation about this matter and I justified to his father the taking of special measures to protect Chris.

"Trust in God alone is no insurance against the dangers of life," I said. "But it is the belief that God will help you as you do your duty. Which in this case must be to ignore a call to go to work against your fatherland – for a regime that is of the devil."

"So far it hasn't happened," said my brother-in-law.

"But eventually, it will," I replied.

About a week later the station in Utrecht was cordoned off at nine-thirty that morning and everyone's identity card was checked. If the word 'student' appeared then you were packed into a car and later swiftly transported to Germany. Chris was already aboard his departing train with only three minutes to go before the nine-thirty round-up! Indeed the time had now come, agreed my brother-in-law. And one early morning, completely unexpectedly, there came a knock on our kitchen window, where the tall Mouse was alone out the back, busy with her morning activities. She scooted up the stairs and yelled, thumping on our bedroom door, "Domie, there is someone by the back door!"

"It must be De Lange, surely," we reassured her. But this was someone completely different: it was Chris, who had finally come to take cover under our roof.

Happily he was safe! Overcome with thankfulness, I could just hug him, and that I did! He had stayed overnight in the waiting room of the station and had set off here by foot in the early dawn. It was still dark and no-one had noticed his presence. The usual recipe: a plate of porridge and after all the emotional stress, a good bed. He would be allocated the guest room. He was still busy telling us the story of the Gestapo raids and his flight from danger when Imke turned up.

"Imke, we have another lodger staying with us that you must not say anything about!"

Imke shook her young head and laughed. "Oh my... well I guess that's just the way things go," she replied. We had no better philosophy to offer than that.

Chris was thrown in right at the deep end, because Domitian's life needed to be brought to an end and Chris, in training as a veterinarian, had been taught some anatomy by an expert butcher. It doesn't appeal to me to dwell on such matters. I must confess that I have kept myself aloof from this business, since I feel an aversion to every aspect of it. I know that they use a vast array of equipment and that soaking and scrubbing goes on late into the night. But we also needed to be up next morning for the usual daily tasks, and to care for Hansje, and that was my role. Next on the supply list came De Lange's Diocletian... and then finally the shelter lay empty. Within a fortnight it no longer had an occupant. What a relief! But Diocletian no longer wanted to eat when Domitian was taken away. And they say that pigs have no feelings!

Chapter 35

Early February came and it blessed us with a foretaste of the coming spring. The snow upon our shelter melted away and hazardous gaping holes appeared in the roof of straw bales, which were slowly rotting beneath the layer of earth. It might be better now to allow it to collapse gracefully, once the precious wood down there had been salvaged! It would have to be dug out, and that could be nicely done by the Mice and Chris during the evenings, when spring came a little closer and it became milder. Chris had planted crocuses in the autumn grass, all while wearing a pair of large boots. They proved quite 'handy,' Elderling said, at which we all laughed and then added that in this case 'leggy' would be a more apt word than 'handy!'

When Chris first planted the bulbs, he had just become a free man. Now he was looking at their first budding flowers through a crack in the blinds. But he welcomed the approaching spring, as we all did. He adjusted himself remarkably well to his new life. For the Mice who had already been resident here much longer than he and who had a more difficult time of it, this colleague of theirs was a great asset, a sentiment that we discerned in a poem Lily wrote in honour of his birthday, given together with a doll that her patient fingers had wrought in the intended likeness of his girlfriend:

Dear colleague sharing our stronghold,
Blond man of peace, so calm and bold,
Not ever seeing how you cope
With ease, and face each day with hope.

But we old friends, we trusty two
Who love you dearly, clearly do,
Although we're often sharp and sour,
Which, ja, gets tedious by the hour.
Yet times are bad and so constrained,
And sad moods to these times are chained,
But if we raise an awful din,
Your calm prevails. Your joy within
Does keep you even tempered, true;
We sure appreciate knowing you.
To show our gratitude we provide
This youthful beauty for your side,
Who gave you comfort in dark days.
So when you cannot stand our face,
Then look upon her lovely smile
And you'll feel better by a mile!

Ours was a nice little community that brought out the best in each other.

Chris had discovered that they could also profit from the sun whenever the large hallway window upstairs was opened. Whenever you lay down directly under it, the sun shone directly on your skin. From now on the sun was greeted with jubilation. The refugees pampered themselves as agreeably as the birds which already were carefully slipping through the opening. In the beech perched a blackbird. Each evening he sang his best melodies as the red sun slipped down behind the finely laced network of the budding treetops.

Our thoughts turned to the garden. On account of the dangers posed by the unstable bomb-shelter, it still hadn't been dug out last autumn, thus it had to be done now. After all, the shelter was empty and so it didn't matter if someone came to work in the garden. *Ja*, but who could do that job? I did all the light work myself, because there was then no worker available for hire. In recent years there has always been a great shortage of manpower since many able-bodied men had been conscripted to work in Germany. Domie could have done it, as he had now fully recovered, but was far too busy with other things. Elderling helped us out of the dilemma. Visualising a fruitful season ahead, he sent three of his own farm-labourers to take the manure pile mucked out by Polletje from the Kaisers' habitation and use it to fertilise the soil. The men brought their own spades and knew how to use them. They spread the manure over the garden and continued to dig it in.

"The rubbish pit also needs emptying," they said to each other. "We can do that nicely into the bomb-shelter." They slapped themselves with their arms to keep warm, since they had removed their jackets in order to move more freely. They spit on their palms and grabbed their spades again.

By ten o'clock I called them inside for a cup of coffee. They traipsed into the kitchen and sat on the chairs that Polletje had already arranged for them round the stove.

"Last cow's late, shut the gate!" said a short fellow with beaming eyes to another lanky bespectacled chap who had been last to come in and had left the door open. The third was of average height, but of stocky build.

"We thought," said Berends, the short chap, "to empty the rubbish pit into the bomb-shelter, then that'll be all cleared away for you."

"Don't you think that's a good idea?" asked the fatter one, who was studying my face.

"Right now it's not the best idea," I said, "since there is a lot of wood down in the shelter that needs to be lifted out first."

To them that was a point of view they'd not considered. Yet Berends already had his eye on one of the heavy beams for his own pig-pen.

"Oh, does Domie want to take them out?" he asked.

"*Ja*, of course, wood is now very expensive."

"You can say that again," said the stocky one, "I'll tell you!"

"It's right dear and scarce," added the oldest of the three, with a lugubrious, commiserating expression on his face, while he gazed down through his glasses at his cup of coffee which Polletje had passed to him.

"*Joa*, man – dear and scarce and *niks* more to get hold of, hear, *niks* more! It's already all gone!"

But Berends was not going to change the subject so quickly. He sat there, musing over the rubbish pit.

"Farmer must know..." he said. "We'll ask Farmer where we should throw out the stuff from the rubbish pit, since it can't go inside the bomb-shelter passage."

Suddenly he had a bright idea! "Down the gully!"

"Down which gully?"

"Next to the bomb-shelter!"

"But that's become our special garden glade now!" I replied, startled. "In summer we sit there and Hansje has his box there. You mustn't fill that up!"

Now they laughed. "Sure... but we could make the slope a bit more even," said Berends. "Not so mountains-and-valleys, but more gradual."

"*Ja*, but I like to represent myself in the garden, seeing the hills and slopes of my place of birth. For me it all doesn't need to be so even and level."

"Have you ever been to Frisia?[87]" now asked the stout one.

"*Ja*, indeed... a few times."

"There it's also flat everywhere, just like here," said the tall one. "We go there every year for the hay-making."

"And we take our horses," said the stout one. "It was sowing season here then, but over there it was green land everywhere, you know, and so we went there for the hay."

Polletje gave me a look which meant, "What is he saying?"

She frequently had trouble still understanding the locals and so I

---

87 The north-western coastal zone of the Netherlands west of Groningen, including the inhabited off-shore chain of islands from Vlieland to Schiermonnikoog.

translated: "Tjammes says that they often went to Frisia with the horses, since the sowing had finished here, while there they were short of hands."

"Oh, *ja ja*, sure," said Polletje, "I understand."

"Then it's alright then," says Berends, roguishly. "We just speak peasant language here, does the *juvver* think?"

"*Och*, no," replied Polletje, "I find it very distinctive, very unique!"

I wasn't sure if they followed her, and so explained, "*Juffrouw* finds it very nice."

They laughed together, a little unbelieving.

"Now, y'must not talk twaddle," reprimanded Berends.

"No, honestly, I mean it!" Polletje assured him.

"But the Frisian language, that's something," said Tjammes, changing tack. "I can't understand a thing, man! They can really take you for a ride there."

"They are completely different folk than here," said the stout one. "And food is also very different, hear. Not much good – and there's not a lot of it," he added with some disapproval. "Morn' at six, we only got two slices of bread – same again at eight. 'I can't work on that, hear,' I told the woman. 'Then what do you get at home?' she says. 'Pancakes,' I say, 'a couple of thick ones with white bread... a whole lunch box full, and then at midday beans and bacon.'"

"I now see why you're looking so well," I commented, but he didn't respond to my banter, for he was firmly away on his hobby horse and would not be deterred.

"And at midday there was a bowl of rhubarb on the table and they all dug in, man! 'Twas a miracle. But not for me, hear! I say, 'Keep that for y'rself, and give me just beans and bacon!' On that y' can't work, man, on that y' can't work," he repeated once more, emphatically.

"Otherwise they're the best people," says Tjammes, who also had something to say on the same subject.

"*Joa*, but each finds it best in his own place," opined Berends, and with a gesture which signified 'I summed that up rather nicely, I think,' he placed his mug upside down on the tray, the sign that he did not want any more coffee.

The stout one – Klaassens was his name – chewed phlegmatically on his bun. "That I could well believe," he said. "In that man and beast are the same. You remember, Tjammes, that old horse that Farmer has, the black one who was right homesick? He would not eat, or drink, *niks* more! And then he had to be sent back from Frisia, and when he was home at the farm, he was alright again. How is 't possible, hè? What an animal!"

"They are more headstrong and clever than a human," said Berends and at this remark, he glanced at Polletje's face, as if seeking her approval. But she looked at me helplessly: the meaning of the phrase had completely escaped her.

"Berends says that animals are very smart," I said.

"Absolutely!" she concurred enthusiastically. "Do you have such a clever horse?"

"No... Farmer's horse! What would I do with a horse? I'd rather a pig!"

Now all three of them broke into laughter. They stood up and Klaassens added as they left, "When Farmer comes, then we'll ask him about the rubbish pit."

"You do that by all means."

"*Mevrouw* can already speak a bit of *Grunnegs*[88]" said Tjammes.

"*Joa*, but not so well as Domie. That's more natural for a younger man, isn't that so?"

"*Joa*, that could well be so."

"There is Farmer now," said Berends. He caught sight of the dogs running along in front of the hedge and into the garden. Now Elderling himself also appeared around the corner of the house.

"Elderling, what should we do with the rubbish pit? We want to shove the waste in the bomb-shelter, then we're rid of it, but *Mevrouw* says the wood must be taken out first."

---

88 The Groningen dialect – as pronounced by a local.

"Well, what's wrong with that?" asked Elderling calmly.

"*Joa*, may well be so," said the energetic Berends, "but we thought we'd be done with it then, y' see."

"Domie has gone to Groningen," I explained, "and now they want to tip the rubbish into his cherished entrance pit. So I need to stand up for him a little."

"Naturally," acknowledged Elderling. Without paying too much attention, we'd been strolling along past the bomb-shelter. The men dropped down, pushed the door open and went inside.

"It stinks in here!" proclaimed Berends. The others also sniffed the stagnant, fetid air.

"*Joa*, goodness, man, it reeks to high Heaven in here," they reported.

"That's the result of that rotting straw," Elderling said to me.

"Among other things," I replied, and both of us cast our minds back to those "other things", since Elderling was also in the know about all that!

There was now a great hole in the bomb-shelter, through which the daylight penetrated. The men looked curiously around. And that they could do freely. All trace of our late Kaisers had vanished apart from the lingering odour that betrayed their former presence. Their pen had been demolished and the feeding trough had been removed. A little later we stood outside in the sunshine again, which was already pleasantly warming our backs.

The trio found no support from Elderling to level our sunken glade in the garden, which is part of our earthly paradise, as he once called it.

"Then dig another hole and throw in the whole kaboodle," was the general conclusion.

"We must get back to sowing at the farm," said Elderling, "but you mustn't wear yourself out with all this. This must all be cleared properly. The raspberry canes need to be tied up and Domie also has a bit to get on with – that would be a nice little job for Domie."

All three men nodded. Then Elderling turned toward me. "Was there still anything to discuss?" he asked.

"No, I don't believe so. Not today anyway."

"Then I'll be back again tomorrow."

Then he mounted his bike and rode away. The dogs ran after him, barking.

Chapter 36

The balmy days returned and with them the mild nights. The garden lay dug and prepared, the potatoes were planted, the beans sown. For the most part, farm crops such as spinach, summer wheat, barley and rye were sown using the mechanical seeder. Cabbages had been sown earlier in autumn, and now the young plants graced the fields, as did the winter wheat. The horses pulled the machine that scattered the fertile seeds along the ploughed furrows.

This is the time when in man is birthed a strange call to action. It is hard to remain inside the house. A bird and his song allure us over the course of the day so that at night the silence becomes almost audible. On such mysterious moonlit nights Chris and the Mice worked together down in the shelter. Domie had torn off the fragile roof by daylight, so it appeared as a deep trench surrounded by high walls. Screened by these walls they could work in safety. It was a massive job: the Mice shovelled away the earth to form a substantial mound over a row of raspberry canes. This year we would not be eating many raspberries. It was so still out in the night air, you could hear your own breathing and the dull sound of falling clods of earth. The soft enchanting glow from the moon shone into the open pit and upon the three who worked silently, or at most whispered a few words now and then. They listened intently to the sounds they made themselves, and paused when they thought they heard something out of the ordinary: voices out on the road, the rustle of twigs in the shrubbery that surrounded the garden and behind which they worked. Many nights were needed to get the entire job done. On certain evenings formations of aircraft came over and were shot at by flak guns; on others our workers had to take cover behind their earthen wall and watch the bright flashes of light as the port of Emden was bombed. Afterwards the silence fell again and the unperturbed moonlight once more flowed gently over the countryside. Nature pays no attention to the strident, jarring noise of humans and simply resumes her duties immediately when the opportunity presents. The bombardment, which had broken the peace, had been just like a stone that is thrown into a deep pond. Just a splash... then the water closes over again and the surface remains inviolate. Water lilies float on the smooth, softly undulating liquid mirror that betrays nothing of the secrets of the deep.

Sometimes, when, from some way off, I observed our house standing there quietly and innocently, I recalled this image of the pond, because no one could guess what was happening behind those white, closed curtains on the upper storey. Our *pastorie* was just like a true native of Groningen, whose taciturn face does not betray the matters that engage his heart. Life is often much like a book, wherein are words that we cannot spell. Nature is mysterious and enigmatic and we never tire of her wonders.

One evening I came into the shed to take care of the animals before going to bed. I suddenly became aware of soft squeaking in the dark, a helpless sound made by small living things. It was a familiar sound from my childhood. This squeaking belonged to a downy litter of young, hairless-chested creatures with small tails and tickling paws. Each had a tall, square head with wide mouth, snub nose, blind eyes and long, silky ears. They were young rabbits!

With the same sense of excitement I had as a child at such a discovery, I went inside to fetch the lantern. In a corner of the crowded shed I could see the nest. When she sought out this place the mother had not taken into account the door that was always being opened and closed. It narrowly slid across the cradle of down, which she had plucked from her bare chest. A newborn bunny was on the cold flagstones beyond the periphery of the nest and was crying piteously. Groping with its blind snout, it pushed forward, seeking his siblings, his mother and warmth. He might fall into the kitchen drain! I carefully lifted him with my warm hand and at this nurturing gesture, he suddenly fell silent. He lay on his back in the sucking position and scratched around with his paws flailing aimlessly upwards. The mother looked at me suspiciously. "*Ja*, he is yours, you know," I reassured her. "I wish only a moment to put him with your other children." I pushed him gently down to one side in the nest, which had seemed almost lifeless up until that moment, but with my contact there was an immediate swelling, squeaking sound of many living creatures. How many would there be? I could not count them easily; they squirmed around and over each other so much, but according to my lowest estimate there were at least twelve. They seemed to be hungry and therefore were in a frenzy, for the touch of my hand had awoken a longing for their mother's nourishment.

If I left now, she might fulfil that responsibility so I went away with my lantern. The shed with the many animals, the young mother and the babies, lay again in darkness. But I was still uneasy about this. The lives of all the very young ones were under threat from their worst enemies, the rats. With her brood right beside the door and that drain hole – a cover must be put over it, a plank or something similar. I couldn't do much about that, because the mother would probably become unsettled. There was a risk admittedly that she might leave her little lad in the lurch too, but from the outside I could seal up all the gaps around the door.

Having come into the house I announced, "We have a nest of young bunnies!" They all had to go and have a look. "But not for too long, and not too often! They won't handle that amount of attention, because they've only just been born and are still lying outside the nest," I added.

Their gazes softened as they saw the downy nest and the small Mouse exclaimed that the bunnies were so cute. The short visit over, they then left.

"I'd really like you to help me," I said to Domie. "We must make sure that all the other rabbits that roam around freely are back in their hutch and that gap in the wire mesh through which they can get out is blocked. The old one should have a little bowl of milk and some oats, and we need to seal off the gaps and cracks around the door."

Domie sighed. "Always on a Saturday night," he complained. He was most likely thinking of Hansje, who had tired him out upon his entry into the world.

"*Ja*, that's unfortunate," I replied, "but there's nothing we can do about it. You were so crazy about the time with Hansje, so just think of this as getting more of the same for free!"

"Alright, but what are we going to do with all these rabbits?" he asked, now all practical and down to business.

"Sell the three biggest ones and keep this one for Hansje. Once they're big enough we can transfer them to a proper rabbit cage in the garden."

"*Ja*, Hans would really like that," said Domie.

He started on repairing the wire mesh while I transferred the other rabbits to the hutch, covered the drain and fetched some oats and milk. Domie then patched up the cracks around the outside of the door. In this way we had done our best to care for the babies' welfare during the night.

Chapter 37

"Truth is stranger than fiction," as the English expression says. I can't help that certain situations may seem to you improbable, or if you think they are just written for a book and that such coincidences of circumstance appear to be contrived. I assure you that I sit here in my loft without any need to invent complications and plot-lines. This book is being written entirely from real life.

Greet wanted to train as a nurse. She had to be approved officially by the provincial *Groningse Diakonessenhuis.*[89] But during her interview and medical examination it came to light that she had a mild infection of scarlet fever and she was therefore refused enrolment at that time. For the same reason, neither was there a place for her in the dormitory block. Indeed they even brought her home in an ambulance. That gave rise to some concern. Hansje could go to the Elderlings, but the Mice would certainly be very susceptible because of their peculiar reclusive life and if they both got scarlet fever what consequences would that bring upon us?

However, Greet's disease in itself bore no cause for alarm. Her bed stood before the window and she gazed out at the workers sowing the wheat. She also received many visitors. The Mice would climb down into the hidden wardrobe, which was in Greet's room, so they could freely chat with her from behind the thin partition. Naturally they did not come into any physical contact with her. Neither did the friends who waved to her from the road below. There was a big apron standing by. I

---

89 Groninger Deaconess House, a Protestant hospital founded in 1887.

put it on whenever I had to be with Greet and there was also a bowl with diluted Lysol. I washed my hands with this whenever I was about to leave the room again. We hoped that these simple precautions would prove sufficient to prevent any further infection.

One midday the sun shone through splendidly inside, and to enable us to fully enjoy it, we had a shared tea party up in Polletje's room. In the midst of our chatting the doorbell rang, and I had to go below to open to the doctor's wife, who had come with a warning. The Germans were apparently undertaking a search of De Lange's house and might arrive here at our home any time soon, looking for stores of wheat or barley or some such. The whole village had got things from De Lange, and certainly we had as well. And this warning proved spot on. In fact a motorcycle with a side-car had pulled up at the De Langes' and four men got out. I thanked her for the message and dashed quickly upstairs, where I had to disturb the peaceful idyll of our tea party.

The kitchen cupboard had to be cleared of stores and whatever foodstuffs were up in the loft must be hidden in the wardrobe below. How quick and resourceful we can be at such times! Imke, who was with us for several whole days during Greet's illness, exchanged a bucket of pig feed, which was set and ready for the evening, for the toilet waste bucket and placed it up on the W.C. No sleuth in his right mind would lift its cover seeking contraband provisions! The loft floor was swept with sacking and the small Mouse found a bowl of oats that Chris had used to feed a sick rabbit and which had inexplicably ended up in the small bathroom.

We were all busy, when suddenly the doorbell rang again, loudly and emphatically. We stood frozen to the spot. Were they here already? If so, they were very unwelcome. We were not at all prepared to receive them. Polletje looked at me, and I looked at Polletje – it could be someone else though. So I stepped with some fear and trembling toward the door, and pulled it open.

There stood *Mevrouw* De Lange, who pushed her way agitatedly inside. I felt very uneasy. Her impromptu visit must of course be related to the search.

"We are already working as fast as possible to clean up any evidence," I explained. "We were already warned by the doctor's wife."

"Really? What did she say?" demanded a tense *Mevrouw* De Lange.

"She said there was a house search going on at your place, because there was a motorcycle with a side-car standing outside in front of the house."

"So, what else did she say to you?"

"That because of this, I had to hide all our wheat and so forth."

"It's not about wheat," said *Mevrouw* De Lange. She hesitated, as if in two minds and then continued. "*Ja...* well of course I know things which it is better not to know."

"Then it's about the Jews," I concluded, and Polletje, who was standing in the hallway behind us, said later that my face had turned as white as a sheet. At any rate, Polletje had heard enough. She raced to the loft, snatched the bowl of oats from the small Mouse's hands and insisted: "Down in the passage, quick! There's a search on for Jews!"

In a moment all traces of our residents were removed from the loft. Everyone had been trained for this moment. Even to crawling quickly through the tunnel while escaping.

Chris did not say a word, but grabbed all his stuff together, as well as the coat belonging to our small Mouse, who was all very nervous, and in a few paces was down the hatchway. Also the tall Mouse knew what had to be done, and in this crisis she did so in quick, efficient and controlled movements. Once down the shaft they crawled under the stage in the *leerkamer*, one after another, over to the tunnel, then disappeared inside, closed the door and slotted the latches in place.

Meantime I had started up the stairs with *Mevrouw* De Lange to the loft. I had asked Polletje to sprint ahead upstairs again to check the attic; everything was in order; they had been properly warned up there.

"And do you think we shall also get a house search here?"

"I don't know that. Of course I have no idea if they are following a lead, or whether it's just a suspicion since they must know that we have been friends with a Jewish family."

"Have the Wissings next door to you been warned also?"

"*Ja*. After they had searched our house, I told them, 'The local *Veldwachter*[90] is well known here around the farm stables and barns, so he will continue to direct you', and then I left them to it while they were busy finishing off, and I rode like the wind on my bike over to the Wissings'! In itself that was dangerous enough, but I had no other choice."

"Has anyone seen you coming here? That would awaken their suspicions that something was to be found here and so you came to warn us ahead of their arrival."

"No, I don't think so – but I doubt that would arouse suspicion. Everyone would understand that I'd get a shock from something like this and naturally would find relief by pouring out my heart to my friends. Anyway, they practically accused us right on the doorstep: 'We were told you have Jews in the house.' But then I immediately replied: 'Well then I don't mind your searching my whole house, but don't omit anything.' I believe that my immediate reaction made a decisive impression and that they thought right away, 'We must be mistaken.' But I am so glad my husband is not at home... that at least he was not in jeopardy."

"Domie is also not at home right now."

"They had a good look down in the coal cellar with their big torches, but in the conservatory where anyone could have been sitting under the table they hardly even looked. They checked in all the cupboards and discovered all the instruments stored from your music ministry that we had hidden there before the requisitioning of copper – about seven of them. And then they said with a sneer, 'Your husband must be a musical prodigy!' But there was nothing they could do about it as their raid concerned the discovery of people in hiding!"

"What a blessing that no refugees were found in your house, but had

---

90 Literally "field-warden", a rural position of the police constabulary.

been moved to the Wissings' instead! I dread to think what could have happened had they not gone there!"

Suddenly we observed a motorcycle with side-car and police escort coming along the road.

"There they go," said Mrs. De Lange. "Could you let the Wissings know that the Germans have gone? It'd be a bit silly if I turned up there again. I'd prefer to return home as soon as possible."

Suiting action to the word, she stood up.

"Very many thanks for what you have done," I said, but she desired no expressions of gratitude. She mounted her bike and rode away. Now the first thing was to find our refugees and reassure them.

"The motorcycle just passed by and has gone away again!" I called out, bending down under the stage in the *leerkamer.*

First there was no answer. Then a muffled voice. "We'll just wait a while longer before we come out."

"*Ja*, it could be a trick, but don't be alarmed; I really think the danger has passed. I have to go over to the Wissings' as soon as I can to tell them they needn't stay stewing in such miserable tension. Will you shut the door behind me, Polletje?"

When I set off on my bike, out in the crisp afternoon air, a wave of relief surged through me.

How like spring the breeze felt, and how wonderful was the freshness of its scent! How was it possible that men on a day like today could occupy themselves with such infamous work and go on a man hunt? At the gate of the Wissings' I looked around me. No one to see. Then I rode into their yard. At the back door stood Ol' Moeke. I sincerely hoped that she knew nothing of all this. Why worry her?

"Is your son at home?"

"Do you mean Hilbrand?"

"*Ja*, your eldest."

"He's on the barn floor. Come along this way, *Mevrouw!*" She opened a door for me; the entrance led there.

Inside all was still. I heard only the milk rhythmically gushing into the pail from the cow that Ayol was milking. Wissing was standing in the middle of the floor when he saw me. His dark silhouette was etched against the light from the open barn door behind him. His tall herdsman was standing next to him and a calf opened his gaping mouth and foolishly bit upon Herta's ear. But the dog took little notice, moved his ears a little, evidently thinking, "That calf is getting no wiser!"

This whole little performance was something so peaceful and so contrary to the nervous tension that I had just lived through, that I wondered if they had really been sitting here trembling in panic.

"They've gone now," I softly said to the elder Wissing.

"Oh, gone forth, are they?" he softly asked in turn. "That's right better. What I will say is... *Mevrouw* just must not talk about it, because it's like... dry straw... and flame... I'd be saying." Then a highly meaningful glance of his eyes. "*Mevrouw* would understand me right well."

At that moment I finally discerned, in the surrounding quietness, the latent tension that quivered through his few baulking words.

"No, of course I'm not going to say a thing! One word too many can be life-threatening for both of us. We're in the same boat."

Wissing seemed reassured. The spurting of milk into the pail was once again the only sound that one could hear across the vast work floor.

Through the open barn door radiated the sweet clarity of spring. Framed by the dark interior I saw the bright green wheat and the golden rapeseed fields stretched out under the blue sky. Once more we had been rescued from grave danger and in that beautiful silence we were so thankful, the Deacon and I.

Chapter 38

One by one our own animals were sent away: first Sara who had not given birth to a kid by spring: then the little kid that one of Elderling's workers had got for services rendered in cleaning out the barn lofts, and finally the old goat, who went back to his former boss. But we benefited from a few lambs in exchange, which I had always longed to have, because a sheep gives milk, wool and even meat if the worst came to the worst, and they were low in maintenance costs and time.

Hansje came back home as soon as Greet had recovered. He found the new woolly playmates such wonderful company, as if he were like a twin and couldn't part from them. His first tottering steps across the grass were to them. They were in the apple orchard behind the house, where the trees were all blooming. Hansje reached out and grabbed them by the head. When they bleated, he started imitating their sound so well that for our Mice sitting under their open skylight, it was difficult to discern whether Hans was responsible or the lambs!

In this period our new girl Froukje came to serve in Greet's position. Greet departed for the hospital to start her training after a farewell party in the *leerkamer* was given in her honour by the Youth Fellowship. The bomb-shelter trench was filled in by a couple of lads from there and flowers were planted on top. There were no more underground adventures to be had!

It was so wonderful to enjoy the spring, the sun, the birds and the flowers, which knew nothing of war and were just as exuberant as each new spring arrived. And it was wonderful to stand in the garden among the red poppies and gaze deeply into their dark mysterious hearts. One member of their family, the European blue poppy, also flourishes here in the big fields. The pale lilac flowers with purple spots on their slender stems gently rock in the slightest breeze. And in moonlight a large patch of flowering blue poppies is transformed by moonlight into an enchanting thing of beauty. One must take the time to enjoy such loveliness, even amidst a busy life... *ja*, especially then, otherwise there is the risk of our feeling jaded and dull. And those who receive nothing from such gifts will soon have nothing more to give.

On one of those moonlit nights I heard a terrible squeaking coming from inside the food cupboard. I thought it must have been rats fighting, which still live below the floor, and that they must have gnawed through the bottom shelf to get to the barley. But when I opened the door I saw that they were not fighting; there was just one rat with his paw stuck in the trap that Chris had placed there.

To suffer the sound of an animal in pain is a miserable experience, even if he is one thousand-fold your enemy. I ran upstairs and reported, "There's a rat with his paw caught in the trap."

"Excellent news," said Chris, "at least now we've got him."

"*Ja*, but it would be best if you could get him out as quickly as you can. For the rat it can't be a very pleasant situation."

"No, but what would you like me to do? To drown it?"

"Might as well, even though I don't find the thought attractive."

"But remember, he eradicated an entire nest of rabbits."

"*Ja*, when I think of the baby rabbits, he more than deserves it."

"Alright – then keep thinking of it that way," advised Chris.

We both went below. Chris could not expose himself to view; it was still too light outside.

I pumped a bucket full of water and he took hold of the long chain attached to the trap jaws and lowered the trap and rat into the bucket.

The rat swam back toward and dangled momentarily on the chain then climbed up the trap to reach the air. We tried again, and then once more with the same result. We both started feeling miserable and rather nervous.

"This isn't going to work," he said. "He keeps getting back up to the surface. The water's not deep enough." And then he added hesitantly, "In the water butt outside, that would be better."

"Then I'll have to do it."

"*Ja*," he concurred. "It's still too light outside and the moon is rising."

"It's all the same whether you or I finish off this hellish job; it's got be done," I concluded sadly.

He accompanied me to the *leerkamer* door. Then I took the chain and trap with the floundering rat from him and firmly attached a second much longer chain to it and let the whole contraption sink below the water in the water butt. I recall how the silvery moon at dusk shone through the young leaves, which cast little patches of shadow on the ground; the enchanting lustre of this sultry, peaceful night was in poignant contrast to my murderous assignment.

Below the animal was jerking and pulling at the chain while fighting for his life. I did not dare take a look too soon. When I did so, I noticed that the rat had climbed up the chain and was above water. I had to let the chain sink deeper. But after a moment the result was the same. Deeper still the chain must go! Surely I must realise what I was doing! Water had also once covered my head, and that was frightening. I had been deprived of air and I could only just push my hand up above the surface. That was my only means of calling for help; I could not scream, as I was standing on the bottom with my mouth full of water. Then a familiar voice called, "Come here," and someone reached down and grasped me from above.

The beast was now undergoing the same deadly panic. But there was no one who came to his aid. On the contrary, if he managed to come up struggling for air, I pushed him back under the water, the horrifying, terrifying water. He did not give up. It seemed to take forever, but the end had to come soon. He could not last; he was getting too exhausted, and the battle for his life would end in capitulation. That moment finally came. The jerk of the chain ceased.

Would he be dead? Or unconscious? He surely could not recover, because then the torture would have to begin again. I stood quietly at the water butt and waited, with the rat still underwater. A quarter of an hour? Twenty minutes? I do not know, but the moonlight filtered through the young green leaves and an owl flew soundlessly over my head. You could hear the silence! I finally dared to draw up the chain. At its end hung the rat, my enemy, to whom I had sworn revenge. The front legs were kept bent, the left hind leg was pierced by the trap jaws, a sharp white tooth protruding from the muzzle, eyes big and staring, wide open and scared. Had they bulged from distress, or had I just imagined that? I had defeated him, but I felt neither triumph nor gratification. On the contrary, rarely have I felt so ashamed than at that moment. There still remained one duty; I laid the dead rat by the back door. Chris could bury him after eleven, when there were no more people out on the road.

Chapter 39

Our various Church Association groups wound up rather late in the year, due to Pentecost falling so late and because the end of the ecclesiastical calendar usually coincided with the end of our busy season. Polletje was now completely involved in the youth ministry. She successfully led the games and activities part of the Boys' Fellowship, played handball with them on the playground and even came home blushing like a peony after one evening out at Oldiek. On that last night of the boys' meetings at Oldiek, they seemed to be in a solemn mood. After the games she called them inside. For once they were as meek as lambs. They did directly what they were told, calmly walking through the school hallway and sitting down calmly at the tables. She was generally accustomed to something entirely different, so such compliant behaviour was pleasing. Domie had taken the Bible talk earlier during the first session of the evening, to which the boys had listened quietly and reverently. In that time an item must have been secreted somewhere close at hand in the classroom.

For, now at the end of the meeting, one of them stood up and produced a package, evidently in the shape of a book. It was so quiet you could hear a pin drop. All eyes, including Polletje's, were on the boy who was elected to hand over the book and along with it give a speech, just as they had agreed amongst themselves. Now he must surely start, thought the boys, but their spokesman, who was always known as such a windbag, found the accompanying silence and attention extremely nerve-wracking and just stood there with an open mouth, showing all his teeth. He gulped... and then gulped once again.

"Go on, boy!" whispered his neighbour, forcefully giving him a kick under the table. The shock suddenly loosened the speaker's tongue.

"*Juffrouw* van der Pol," he said solemnly. "On behalf of all our members..." He swallowed and there followed a painful silence. Polletje glanced at her nails.

"Come on!" the prompt again coming from the lad next to the speaker: "We present..."

"We present to you this gift, because you have always been..." He desperately sought for words then suddenly followed their urging with "...so nice in playing with us." Then he handed over the package to Polletje. She was a bit embarrassed by all this and very surprised, and she let it show. The parcel was unwrapped and the book appeared. "The Life of Jesus," was the title, and it was by a French author. "This book must have been obtained with great care by some of you," she said, as she held it up so they could all see it.

"There's also something written in the front," said the former spokesman.

Polletje opened it to the title page and saw a letter enclosed there.

"Read it out!" yelled all the boys.

Then once more there was silence and Polletje read aloud:

Dear mejuffvrouw,

We found it good to give you this gift because you have always been in our fellowship.

We hope that you will enjoy the book and not say the book is nothing much. We really need you on these evenings but we haven't always acted as you thought good.

We want to ask for your forgiveness.

Your willing servant,
JAN HARMS

"I find that an especially lovely letter, one I shall really treasure, hear!" she said.

"We should all sign it," called out a pair of boys enthusiastically.

The boys all crowded around, heads bent over the book. There was a difference of opinion about who would sign first, and about how you had to sign: only your first name? Or including your last name, or even adding your address as well? All important questions on which, initially, they heartily disagreed.

But finally a satisfactory solution was arrived at by all and the book was passed along the row. Each in his turn was allowed to sign. Their names had to look good in there. They really did their absolute best. Some signed with their tongue poked into their right cheek. When that was done, Polletje took the floor for a final word. She said that she was very touched by this demonstration of affection and appreciation. They had now come to a period of rest, but in the autumn they would indeed start up again with new vigour! Finally they sang the Evening Hymn, their young, powerful voices supported by the organ, and all departed for home.

Chapter 40

The night is cool and clear. Thousands of stars have been lit; the Milky Way runs as a delicate sparkling white ribbon above my head. I have a plot of ground which I had to have cleared of plants, because the lads are now digging for buried copper; things are moving swiftly toward an end to the war. The Russian front is collapsing, the Allies are advancing in Italy almost unopposed and the English fleet lies off England's south coast, preparing to cross the Channel toward the continent. Any day now an invasion can be expected.

It is the beginning of September. The migration of the birds has commenced. I hear them in the air overhead. Their raucous cries rend the silence. I have nothing more to do tonight. I sit on the edge of the cold frame. A line from a psalm comes to my mind: *The night shineth as the day.*[91]

The poetic beauty of the Word of God!... Isaiah, Job, the Song of Songs...

"Our people only know really grand, deep poetry from the Bible," wrote De Eeden.

"As we grow older, we become more discriminating. I do not read much anymore, only the Bible, or Shakespeare. My collection now comprises merely the very greatest," said a woman painter to me one summer.

And I hear again the insistent voice of Catharina van Rennes, when we sang "The Creation" in the Utrecht choir, which I joined as a young girl. "Too dull and flat!" she said to us. "You do not believe in what

91 Psalm 139:12.

you're singing. Have you never read something beautiful? Have you never once read from the Bible?"

For the Minister who was visiting with us today and who has spent six months in a concentration camp, that book was the only one that he had carried with him. But it could have been forcefully taken from him right at the camp entrance, together with his fountain pen, his wallet and his wedding ring, if one of his fellow prisoners had not smuggled the book in between some blankets. Having a Bible was a punishable offence, and occasionally the rooms were checked for the presence of this dangerous book. Yet in secret they formed circles around the Minister to share in Bible readings. One of them who had been sentenced to death was baptised there in the concentration camp. Unconquerable is the living Word!

Psalm 139 states:
If I make my bed in hell, behold, thou art there...
Even there shall thy hand lead me, and thy right hand shall hold me. [92]

Even in the hell of the concentration camp, God's Spirit can break through. I felt I had to meditate on all these things while I sat on the cold frame under the stars. The heavens which are stretched out above my head like a sheer curtain were as one of God's poems. You could read that in two ways: you could just notice the letters, without sense or cohesion. Seeing it like that, you might say that this just came to be that way, all by itself. Or you could hear God's poetry resounding in the song of the stars, just as Isaiah's soul caught these cadences and interpreted them for us.

He that planted the ear, shall he not hear? He that formed the eye, shall he not see? [93] says the Psalmist.

---

92 Psalm 139:8-10.
93 Psalm 94:9.

Behind our finite intelligence stands the inexpressible: *He that conceived the worlds and they were.*[94]

Naturally then, the worship flows, resulting in the feeling of being cleansed from all smallness and one's own inventions, one's own concerns and desires. Then the human life becomes large and spacious and peaceful, because one knows that God's Spirit will permeate all things, including one's own heart – if that opens up before Him like a flower to the sun. Then, all unhealthy ties and all other fears fall away. However, there is one more thing: surrender, obedience to our call, the divine compelling in us to work deeds yet unknown, just as for the young birds that were born here this year; they cannot but obey the mysterious call to fly south over my head, bound on a voyage to distant, unknown lands.

---

94 Psalm 136 from the Dutch Psalter.

Chapter 41

We had three refugees at the beginning of the summer, but now we have six. That is, three more were added to our number: one in early August – Frits, the son of my deceased brother Johan, Miriam, the sister of one of the guests hiding at the Wissings' farm, and Naomi, like Miriam, a young nurse from the Jewish Hospital in Amsterdam. Each of them had his or her own history and their own methods whereby they had arrived at our *pastorie*. We had not sought them out, for when a difficult period extends into a long time, then a kind of malaise sets in.

Initially Frits just wanted to register with the Labour Department. "We'll keep a spot open for you," was all we said. "You can go in Chris' room." But he told us that he had decided to return home and then go straight to the work camp, and this short visit in June was to say farewell. We did not expend any more effort to dissuade him, only hoping that the war would be over before they could transfer the boys to Germany, because they who were taken there in the short term still ended up on the Russian front in the much longer term – we were convinced of that! But when push came to shove, he ended up staying here after all. The thought of his father stopped him. The Churches kept warning earnestly against the ill-fated influences of going along that route, especially warning against the seductive propaganda which was rife in the work camps. When he had finally made up his mind not to go, he took his bike and left on a road trip, keeping continually on the move and one step ahead of his pursuers. Of course, a vigorous house search followed. In the middle of the night they raided the address where Frits had been staying in order to visit the M.T.S.,[95] the historic technical school in Groningen. The master and mistress of the house, a.k.a. my sister and brother-in-law, were not at home at the time, only the household's hired help. She had to suffer on her own the threatening bright torches, which were aimed all round the home and which had got her out of bed. But the search did not faze her. She claimed quietly that they would not find the boy, because he had gone to the labour camp in Mook. So they had to leave empty-handed, but with the promise that they would return another time. The bird had truly flown, but his days were numbered as he was soon spotted everywhere by vigilant eyes. So the time had come for him to say goodbye to his days of wandering freedom.

God's guardian angels all look different. In Frits' case it was in the person of the servant-girl who had endured the Germans' house search for him. She was sent to meet him and then brought him safely through the dark hours over to our *pastorie* with a couple of heavy suitcases carried between them. He was the last refugee we took; on that score we all agreed that our home was now full. All the beds were slept in and if there were to be still more, the safety of all of us would be severely compromised.

Fortunately Frits didn't encounter them, but when he arrived on our doorstep, the 'Greens' were fairly close at hand. Those men of the *Ordnungspolizei*[96] conducted house searches in various districts of our province and occasionally here and there they found something or other that was worth their effort. On several farms already several people in hiding had been picked up by the Greens. We had to be on the alert; they must not catch us sleeping. So we set up a night-watch roster in teams of two. One sat in the study at night reading by the light of a small lamp; the other slept on the couch and was awoken after three

---

95 *Middelbare Technische School* – an intermediate technical college.
96 ORPO – the Nazi police force, or *Grüne Polizei* (Green Police), whose green
    uniforms also incorporated green on cap, shoulder and collar insignia.

hours. The watch lasted from midnight to three and then from three to six. During the day we kept all doors locked.

Every evening we conducted a practice session: to crawl the entire route from the loft to the hidden tunnel as quietly as possible in the shortest possible time. Domie and Polletje listened from the *leerkamer* door for any give-away thumping sounds. I stood with a watch in hand, counting the seconds off.

Three minutes... too long... far too long! Over again! Two minutes, twenty seconds – that was better! A few times more. And so on – every evening we practised to perfect the evacuation upon which so much depended.

On one of the nights during that time of excitement and tension the mayor dropped by on a late visit. He knew of our situation and so I thought that perhaps he had come to warn us. But he had no alarming report about the activities of the Greens; he had only one request for Domie: to bury an American pilot who had been shot down. Domie was not home, so a Minister colleague from a neighbouring village was approached to perform this duty. In these recent days Domie was often away travelling through the country on secret business which did not involve any self-interest at all.

"Were you standing on watch?" asked the mayor. "You opened the door before I even rang the bell."

"I saw you coming along the garden path, and in the evening after ten we are always on guard," I said, "because our guests are downstairs at that time."

"What a stressful daily life you live!"

"It's par for the course if you have to hide people in the house, but you get used to it in time."

Chris, Lily, Frits and Esther. The small Mouse and the tall Mouse together with the boys became the first members of the Aders' refugee family to call the pastorie 'home.'

Miriam and Naomi, two Jewish nurses from Amsterdam, whom Domie rescued and brought to the pastorie to join the growing refugee family in hiding.

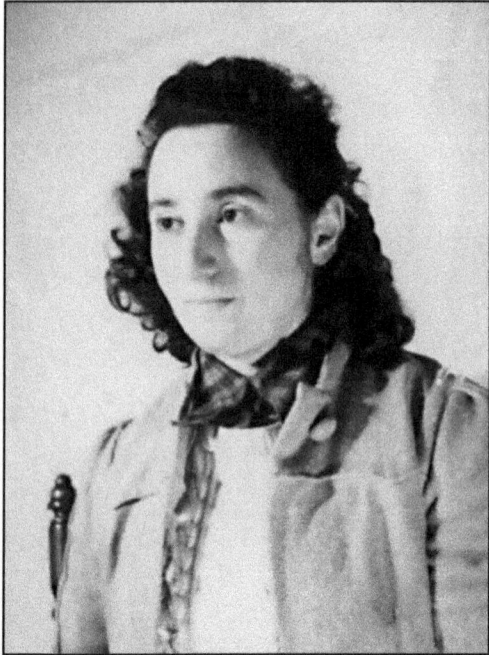

Chapter 42

And so life just goes about its business. There are the daily repetitive chores, there are the people from the village who must not notice anything unusual happening with us, there is the delightful warming sun, which rises on both the good and the evil of this world, and which in this autumn shines again every day. "Farmers know just what they want from the year," said old Oentje, who was raking up the leaves in the garden. "Not in forty year 'ave we 'ad such an autumn." And Elderling agreed. Such absolutely beautiful September and October months in which you could get everything properly dry in the house; from potatoes to sugar beets – these were indeed very rare times.

Elderling and I paused by the Michaelmas Daisies and the Goldenrod along the path that led to our earthly paradise. Down in our sunken garden awaited a pair of wicker chairs. In one of them last April the Mole had been sitting and drawing; it was a bright morning on which he had arrived early from the station. He had passed the night in the station's waiting room, since between the hours of 11 and 4am a curfew was imposed. When he arrived at the *pastorie* at five o'clock, all our residents were still in deep sleep, and the Mole went over to one of the same wicker chairs, in which Elderling and I now sat, and he drew the then still young shrubs against the sloping bank of the glade, which now with their golden and purple crowns stood in splendid array in the glow of the autumn sun. He also drew the capricious and unshapely apple tree, the back of the *pastorie*, the half-open skylight under which the Mice were asleep, and the church.

Elderling sat quietly enjoying the golden clarity of the light and colours of the flowers. We engaged in a theological conversation, which I had quite often with Elderling. He spoke slowly and clearly. There are all kinds of people, but there are few who in accepting the gifts of God are as grateful as he is. In his room hangs a text burnt into a plaque of wood:

Stand still, and see the salvation of the LORD[97]

This could be his life's motto. For him, the regular changing of the seasons, sowing and reaping, had never become humdrum, but creation has remained a constant source of wonder. Jesus said that we can only receive the Kingdom of God as a child. Later, when we perhaps shall have no longer lived here in our village for a long time, I shall still recall to mind this elder of Groningen, and think of this: that he never had to pretend anything, not even to God, but was always thankful for the light and for the flowers and the endless horizons of his country, and for the fact that he was alive to see it all.

He was also always interested in everything we needed in the house to provide shelter. And each increase in our "family Schuilenga"[98] by which name the *pastorie's* residents could well be known, was taken to heart. Certainly young Miriam, the Jewish bride that we had taken in agrees, because she is still today a good friend of both Elderling and De Lange. Miriam knew all the local farmers, because before her training as a nurse she had accompanied her father to buy grain in this district where they went from farm to farm in their little car. Then De Lange had asked Domie to go to Amsterdam, to the hospital where Miriam worked because he had received a note that she was in distress and was

---

97 Exodus 14:13.
98 Taeke Schuilenga, a businessman of Surhuisterveen, was an influential Dutch anti-Nazi who was shot in reprisal during 1943 for the killing of an NSB man by the Resistance.

about to be deported. De Lange himself was incapacitated by an injured leg, but could Domie go instead? Well, Domie did as requested and made an effort to save her from the clutches of the Greens. I told Domie, "She can stay here temporarily, but then you'll have to look for someplace else for her. You know yourself that we are full. All our beds are in use and I think four people here are sufficient, as do our own refugees, who have enough concerns and troubles of their own to end up being 'stuffed in', as Lily says, simply due to the notion that we have room for a fifth person. And I can understand her feelings. If we feel pent up, we can let off steam in various ways, but they always just have to sit and look at each other and they can't ever go outside."

"*Ja, ja*," said Domie. "First let's see if I can manage to get her out, then we'll take it from there."

One dark evening he arrived back home on his bike from the station with Miriam riding pillion. She had been collected and protected by our sympathetic 'Chief': an *Opperwachtmeester*[99] of the Royal Dutch Military Police, who thought it his duty to know better than the imposed laws of the occupying power, because if he did what they wanted from him, he would have had to betray Miriam as well as Domie, instead of taking them under his care.

I was writing in the study when she arrived. Miriam was introduced to me then and there. In the ensuing conversation Domie spoke as if it was altogether a done deal that Miriam would be staying with us. But I was afraid that would not impress our family very much.

"We had agreed that it would be temporary," I said.

"You should not have said that," Domie confronted me when we were alone.

"Then why bring me into such a difficult predicament? You virtually forced me to make a remark, even though of course I myself did not altogether find it a pleasant one for someone who feels herself under a

---

99 An NCO of second highest rank in the *Koninklijke Marechaussee (KMar)* – the Dutch Military Police.

safe roof again after a long time on the run. But when all is said and done, she has not become attached to us yet and she will not mind going to another equally good address, if they are immediately informed and know of her whereabouts."

Domie then began to tell me about Amsterdam and what he had seen and experienced there. About the Jewish homes, from which people were removed by force and the furniture looted or destroyed; over the anguish and despair of hundreds, nay, thousands, and how good things were for us in comparison, and could we not arrange things to make do?

"I know for a fact that if you had also seen what I saw, that you would have responded exactly in the same way, because we may well have to take in a sixth one, should the need arise," he concluded.

"But you're seeing things as a man and arguing from a male point of view," I countered. "That's why you do not understand that you fail to take into account all kinds of practical household concerns. What exorbitant demands six people will place on my linen cupboard alone... in a time when you can't purchase extra, and then the washing. How do you get that done and dried during winter with such a large household... and where do you want the people to sleep at night? With five here we are already short of sets of sheets and blankets. And you want to take a sixth in!"

Yet the thought of a sixth arrival would not leave me, and I slept badly that night. We could perhaps muddle through and do our best to be resourceful and accommodating – if we made our utmost effort to overcome all the obstacles we faced.

"If there is still someone to come, bring them along then," I said the following day to Domie.

Now he looked shocked. I was sending the ball back into his court.

"Be very sure of what you say," he said. "Of course there is someone... there are dozens in fact... and I will first look elsewhere for places for them. At my parents they could perhaps take in a few, and with this one and with that one..." He continued to suggest families and we discussed the various possibilities.

But the plan for the sixth arrival did not go down well with our undercover family. When I took Hansje to bed, I heard Lily whispering agitatedly to Chris at the door to the loft, and mentioning my name more than once. "What is it?" I called quietly, not to wake Hans.

"There's going to be a sixth person here," Lily said, with large dark eyes.

Chris stood like a statue of stone, his arm holding the water jug which he had just filled.

"*Ja*, I know it's difficult," I replied softly, "but extraordinary times call for extraordinary demands from us. But look, come downstairs now, both of you, since the tall Mouse is sick, and you can make your concerns known."

The 'clandestine' doctor from another village, who had helped De Lange and Domie transport the household effects from the Cohens' home to the Wissings', had visited the tall Mouse and diagnosed angina. Upon seeing Frits, who that evening was busy filling all the water jugs, he, rather amused, asked if we had gained another son, because he had not ever seen this boy before.

If you came here anywhere around ten o'clock at night, you'd run across any of our refugees on the stairs, in hallways, bedrooms, kitchen and cellar, because everywhere in the house they had some task to perform. But after the work was done, on this Saturday night we gathered in the study. The small Mouse shared her worries and the boys raised their concerns about our overall safety, which little by little was being eroded. But that would now have to be the last. We would see some more adjusting and squeezing, for the sake of the sixth who was yet to be rescued, but with that number we would have reached our absolute limit, if not exceeded it.

The very next week Domie set off for Amsterdam on his mission. He did return with our new housemate, but now for a change, the Chief had her on the back of his bike instead of on Domie's. When she arrived, she had a lot to tell and was very talkative for the first little while. She had only just turned eighteen, but had experienced more in her short life than many of eighty; parents deported to Poland along with two brothers. Miriam's mother had also been deported, but her two brothers and sister-in-law were safe at the Wissings'.

In this conglomeration of people, each one had their own concerns, their own sorrows and hopes, their own wishes and longings. Including Imke, there were now eight women in the house, of whom four were Jewish. Eight women, who all had their own understanding of how a household should run, and then there were four men as well, including Hansje, who also put in his pennyworth.

When all goes smoothly, then Paul's words of exhortation above the door testify: *Forbearing one another in love.*[100]

And may there be fervent prayer ascending, requesting some of Job's patience and Solomon's wisdom, along with a healthy sense of humour, which serves to help us navigate the stumbling blocks of ordinary life. For he who always sees the humorous side, things naturally always seem to go well.

For reasons of security we had not told Frits' mother that he was lodging with us; likewise with Chris' father. Since the Greens interrogate the next of kin under duress, it is indeed easier for them not to know where their children are hiding. Now there had been a minor issue regarding the rising time of our folk. In their own best interests I preferred it to be scheduled regularly and promptly at a certain hour each morning. Our Mole, with whom I discussed this, agreed with me completely. We all need some stimulation, he said, otherwise you'd notice very soon how slack we'd become.

---

100 Ephesians 4:2.

There was nothing I feared in our particular situation as much as a kind of apathy; people kept undercover in the same place for long periods sometimes tend to become caught up in a cloying, monotonous life. Vibrant living under all circumstances always makes sense. And it had never been so that a person could think to themselves: Why do I need to get up? Because life always involves service to either a small or larger community. Or, as the tall Mouse wrote to a friend, "my time in hiding has been a positive experience."

So the not very pleasant task awaited me of having to play bogeyman and wake up everyone early at the same time each morning. When visiting Frits' mother, she told me things gleaned from his own letters to her. She told me that he had been in hiding with another boy. In the evenings they were tasked with peeling potatoes and doing odd jobs and then afterwards they went outside, often at a very late hour. On a few mornings after these late nights they hadn't got up until ten. His landlord had said something about that, but Frits had said nothing back. In that he was right, I thought to myself. King Solomon, in his wisdom, said *"He that ruleth his spirit is better than he that taketh a city."*[101]

I lay next to her in the other of the twin beds while she related to me this account of Frits' demanding landlord. It was fortunately quite dark in the bedroom, so I did not need to control the expression on my face. But after the war, Paulien will certainly be astonished to discover who that ogre of a landlord was!

---

101 Proverbs 16:32.

Chapter 43

In the *leerkamer* now hang several nice drawings in the form of a newspaper style montage on the wall, which is changed every month. Members of our Youth Group think Polletje is so proficient with pencils and paintbrushes, but whoever makes it upstairs as far as the boys' room will notice Johan's drawing box and his paint pots, even that little white one with the chip which got knocked when I, as a child, looked over Johan's shoulder at what he was painting. Now it is used here by Frits.

Do not be sad, Paulien! With God's help, we will keep your lad safe for you until after the war, and then he will again fill the vacant seat at the drawing board belonging to your husband.

Domie is often away nowadays. Once you start to help people who are in need, you always find that even more work comes your way. I am like a sailor's wife, spending whole weeks alone, because only at the end of the week does Domie return home. There is only one difference: a sailor's wife is not usually left with the responsibility for a house full of refugees as well as a congregation to care for. For the latter, I was vigorously supported by our assistant Minister, and at home there was loyal and dedicated assistance from Froukje and Imke. These girls knew the ropes absolutely and completely, so much so that I could leave them to it, and until mid-September, I could afford the luxury each morning to go to my farm loft to write for a couple of hours for this book. Until then Polletje filled my place in the kitchen. Then the winter ministry started up and she was released from all morning kitchen duties. There were potatoes to be dug and apples to be picked. I kept going every morning to the farm loft for a couple of weeks in September to write, when most of the local women had already begun harvesting. When they saw me riding along on my bike as they knelt at their work in the fields, they probably were thinking, "There's *Mevrouw* Domie. She can right afford the time. Not us, we have to dig potatoes."

But by afternoon it had become my turn, as we also grew potatoes in a big patch behind the house, and they must be dug out. Help? From whom could I request that? Polletje faithfully helped me on a few afternoons, Froukje also a few times, but otherwise I had to do it myself. Ten *mud*,[102] twelve *mud*, fourteen *mud*, there were always more. "We had a good yield of potatoes this year," said the locals. All the farms were short-handed and the workers spent every free hour to bring in their own potato crop. It was like a competition to see who could finish first. They were nervous and irritable folk, and seemed to live only for one purpose: "The potatoes must be dug out!" Potatoes and beans. Who indeed would deny their valuable nutritional status? If you sit in the train these days, all you hear about is the current food supply. Especially if you're travelling with gentlemen. From Zwolle to Groningen I sat with four gentlemen in a compartment, and they talked about nothing but food. Material things seem to take a very large place in our existence. In times of plenty we may not realise that – but in times of want it becomes obvious. Matter and energy. A potato is a potato; clay is just clay. Is there then no place for awe and wonder? For most of us it is as if Einstein never lived; he speaks to us about matter, which apparently is not dust, but ions and electrons, like solar systems in miniature, but we just smile, unbelieving. For the most part we sit here still caught up in a materialistic worldview that has become ingrained in us over the previous centuries.

Now the potatoes are in the cellar, the apples in the loft, the beans in

---

102 A *mud* was an archaic measure of capacity in the Low Countries and varied according to the location and period of history. One Groningen *mud* is roughly 2.5 English bushels, or about 88 litres.

the barrel and the winter work of catechism classes and the various fellowships is also in full swing. The pen has remained resting there for some time; to me it does not appear necessary to hurry this book to completion, because the war now, by mid-November, is still not yet over. The fall of Italy presaged that the end was in sight, yet scarcely any notable military events happen anymore; steady progress forward is only occurring in Russia. 'Patience, courage, and faith' is again the watchword.

Now it is the beginning of February. It's been a mild winter with many thunderstorms, and in the last days of January we already had one day which was reminiscent of the end of winter. But now a change of season is gradually being heralded. The sun shines into the rooms and the snowdrops are already nodding in the grass. The hazel blossoms and the dogwood and chestnut buds are swelling. Indeed the promise of an early spring beckons.

Chapter 44

In the upstairs guest bedroom blooms a single hyacinth on a bedside table. Adorned by the fragrant pink flower, the solitary Jewish bride lies dreaming in her salmon-coloured kimono, her naturally dark curls framing her face in even darker contrast. For Miriam remains alone; now she is separated from her companions and the house is silent and empty. No longer "a hive of industry from loft to cellar," as Monteur once described it. Now one no longer encounters people everywhere in rooms and along hallways. These evenings I lie in bed and hear no creaking of the loft stairs above, nor stealthy feet and soft voices admonishing: "Shhh! Tante[103] Jo is sleeping!"

A great responsibility has fallen on my shoulders, along with the daily tension that everyone can identify with, which is to shelter those on the run; I feel responsible for their well-being and above all for their safety. The bed next to me has remained unslept in for lengthy intervals; more often empty than occupied, and therefore there is no shared responsibility between myself and Domie, but the full responsibility rests on me alone. Six adults under my care is a lot. Six people, all of whom face danger if their presence were discovered at the *pastorie*. That leaves me almost no personal freedom. The awareness of a very real and looming threat permeates my subconscious, calling into being constant vigilance and unbroken tension. I listen and awaken upon the slightest sound, like a hare sleeping lightly, because danger lurks on all sides. That apprehensive

---

103 "Auntie."

response becomes second nature, just like that which hunted animals have always possessed.

We people of the twentieth century have once again to deal with persecution. We hide either ourselves or others away to escape the punishing grip of the German juggernaut. We live in an insane world in which the power of the Antichrist is revealed and we brace ourselves to neutralise it. And this keeps the bed empty; Domie is again on the warpath and I lie here and wonder where he is... what he is doing. Should he come home on Thursday night, he'll once again have much to tell. But the work he is doing is dangerous – extremely dangerous. It means nothing more or less than saving people from the clutches of an all-devouring monster. He is a modern Saint George, but he can't employ physical strength to defeat the dragon, but needs all his ingenuity and wit to fight against it.

What about divine protection? That is certainly a truth, otherwise all would have gone badly long ago. But faith is never without challenge. It is never our role to just passively sit down in our life's little boat while the storm rages at sea and then say: "Now God will keep me from harm." We must still reef the sails against the tug of the lashing wind and weather the storm. Always there remains some action of which we must partake. That is our human responsibility.

And there is always our house full of people who were put at risk by Domie's exploits.

"Should you do such and such?" I would feel compelled to ask. "Think about the people living in this house."

"Should I **not** do it?" he would respond. "Think of the people who cling to me in hope; those whom you would allow to have all their hopes dashed."

By that answer I was silenced, and I lay again alone at night, listening to the storm and to footsteps; up the stairs, down the stairs. Pails were emptied, water jugs filled, peat stacked and tallied, firewood split into kindling, the baskets of peat taken upstairs. In the kitchen dishes had been washed, breakfast set out, vegetables and potatoes cleaned for the next day. Sometimes the oil had been pressed from rapeseed, using the mangle for several days and nights in a row.

As a rule these household chores were commenced at half past nine, directly after the various fellowship meetings concluded, and we were all finished by eleven. Only then did a more convivial atmosphere get going up in the cosy attic room. Sandwiches were removed from the lunch boxes and devoured with gusto; sometimes with an apple, and accompanied by plenty of hot coffee which stood bubbling on the stove heater. Then later, much later, I could hear careful footsteps sneaking down the stairs. That was the boys, who were going to bed. And then the house fell into its own rest. Just as soon as I knew everyone was in bed, my eyelids dropped and closed.

Sharing fellowship and a simple evening meal around the kitchen table.

Lily and Chris chopping wood for the stoves.

The boys printing parish newsletters on the Cyclostyle duplicator. This machine was also utilised for printing of clandestine news to be distributed via the local Resistance network in Groningen.

Chapter 45

But now the thing that we most feared has happened! What we had foreseen, the refugees as well as I; somewhere a safety fuse has blown. Someone with whom Domie had a trusted relationship has been arrested. What did they find in his pockets? What will he say? Will the danger reach as far as our secluded *pastorie* and will a police van stop in front of our house during the night to take Domie away? Then what if they find even more here? Evacuate! That word sent shock waves through us like wildfire. The *pastorie* empty? Danger? Protests from left and right. You see... you see! I told you! That's done it now! Hansje also talks like this. If he performs risky stunts on top of a chair, then Froukje warns him, but he still continues and tumbles off, then he reacts: "You see!" And we have nothing more to say to that.

"Nothing has happened yet, but our plan is in order to prevent further troubles," says Domie. "All these warm slept-in beds, when they come at night – well, that can never be allowed. But if you've already got out of here, then I can easily make it on my own, to creep under the ground, under the *leerkamer*, and then there won't be a trace that indicates my presence. No warm bed either, since I share one with Tante Jo, so they won't catch me."

Have you ever poked a stick into an anthill? The disturbance in our house now resembles one. The fixed paths of the industrious insects within the nest have been abandoned. They run around each other, leaving their abode, carrying not eggs, but luggage. This had to go, and that had to be taken, off to their new addresses, which Domie had sought out for them, one pair at a time. The Mice would leave together and so would the boys. He called them out two by two, so they wouldn't know each other's destinations. The Mice were to be sent to a large farm in the neighbourhood, the boys to the doctor's house, Naomi to a neighbouring village and Miriam to her brother, who was hiding with his wife at the Wissings'. The latter arrangement was therefore based on a real family connection. Wissing came to me in the evening with his concerns about it. But I knew how much Miriam would love to see her brother again, and thus I thought I'd managed to win him over.

"No more beds you say? You can surely take this woollen sleeping bag and a pair of blankets. Look, I'll roll them up together and put a string around them, then it'll go on the bike with you."

The elder Wissing glanced at the large woollen bundle with a suspicious expression, and seemed to hesitate. Then I called Miriam. Her appearance would surely inspire trust. *Ja*, she affirmed – she would gladly do all that he asked.

"At our place it's not so... you'd be in a loft by yourself..."

Ja, she said, she would gratefully take anything they could offer; she had been camping on occasions and was used to roughing it.

Her reassuring demeanour had the desired effect. Wissing lifted up the roll of bedding and took it outside. At the door he made his last wish known that Miriam should leave here unaccompanied at exactly a quarter to ten. We could certainly manage that as we have exact time by the radio. He would then wait for her by the dam on his farm.

Everything seemed so cut and dried, but unfortunately looks can be deceiving. At half past nine that big, brown roll of bedding – the sleeping bag with blankets, was back in the hallway.

"My brother won't have it," was Wissing's comment. Then the door was shut again and a bitterly disappointed Miriam remained on her own, standing behind me. All the others had now departed.

Last night I had prepared something to sweeten the bitter goodbyes;

fried pancakes with eggs and sliced apple, but however fond they normally were of these, the pancakes remained cold and untouched on the table in the loft, and the small Mouse sat on a chest with an arm around me and looked at me with her dark imploring eyes. "Oh, Tante Jo, I don't want to leave," she said sadly. "We were so at home here!"

"You'll come back," I consoled. "It's just for a few days."

"*Ja*, but when we come back, it will be dangerous all over again. Oh, that crazy organisation! When we do get back, the eight of us must go and sit on Domie to make him get out of it!"

Suddenly there arose a peal of Homeric laughter from the attic room. Her words had penetrated through the thin door, and they had all heard her from inside. Lily was unmoved; she was too sad to laugh along with them. She was still seeking comfort and protection from me, but I also knew there was nothing else that could be done. If real danger threatened, then it was much better that she left here for a few days. I tried to explain that to her. Maybe nothing would happen, but just in case...

Then I caught the words: "...so sorry for Tante Jo!"

"Why are you sorry for Tante Jo?" I asked Chris, who was just emerging from the attic room.

"Since we haven't eaten the pancakes yet, we'll share one now among the six of us," he promised.

That was a testament to how low the emotional barometer had fallen. Share one pancake among the six? Usually one person would eat six of them!

"Come on down to the study," I said, while I was finishing off my share of pancake. And do get yourselves ready. The Mice are being collected at a quarter to nine."

Domie and Polletje had "service" that night in the *leerkamer*, so they could not attend our little farewell in the loft. But later at dinner, with a very pale face and a gloomy voice, Chris announced to Polletje, "One more hour, Polletje."

I do not know what the pretty Groningen girl who came for the Mice would have thought of us Hollanders, but our parting was so heartrending and they embraced so fervently, as if it was for life, and as though one was going to Poland, and the other straight to the Eastern Front. Whenever I think about everything again, sitting here behind my bureau, I smile. What close ties were woven among the members of our little undercover community and with us!

Freedom! Freedom was the maxim, but what friendship and love had grown during this time of imprisonment! That cluttered loft... "We are so *ingehuisd!*[104]" the little Mouse had complained and thereby she had created a word that did not exist before.

Then finally they were... oh, great adventure... walking down the front path of our house, after eighteen months, into the wide, dangerous world again. But it did not look at all dangerous outside. Silence and starlight.

"What a fairy tale!" whispered the tall Mouse. On that short walk all her fear of capture was lost in the enjoyment of the moment, but the small Mouse did not enjoy it. She began crying softly and had the distinct feeling that she was going the wrong way and simply must turn for home; nevertheless, they kept walking further and further away from us. She didn't have all her things with her and that made her feel unsafe. I decided that I would take her backpack to her later. That would give her much necessary comfort in her new surroundings, without which things could look rather grim.

When I later took Lily's backpack outside I saw the doctor's car approaching from the next village to pick up our two boys. The doctor tooted a couple of times – the agreed signal – and then drove on. He intended to stop at a house down the road where a newborn baby was expected any day now. Such a halt would not arouse suspicion. The boys and I followed the car on foot. We could see the red tail-light in the distance. The house that the doctor had entered stood a long way back from the road. We made it up to the car and opened the door for the

---

104 Literally "en-housed". This word was not used in Dutch during the war, but is now used to mean the process between commissioning of a building and when the occupiers, residents or tenants move in. To Lily it meant feeling fully at home.

boys to get in. There was not a soul in sight – fortunately for us! But there among the shadows inside the doctor's car were hiding another two people! He had better not be caught harbouring them.

"I'm just going to drop a backpack off," I told them, awkwardly. "Maybe you'll still be here when I return."

But when I did turn up again the men were no longer there. The doctor had meanwhile come back from his visit. The conversation inside the house must have been rather short.

"Two men?" he asked as he stepped on the accelerator. The little car was on its way.

Back home I found a very disappointed Miriam – due to a planned celebratory sleepover which was cancelled at the last minute – and a returned sleeping bag lying disconsolately in the hallway near the front door. I also returned to a very overweight Naomi sitting inside her bedroom. That corpulence found its cause in the fact that Naomi was wearing all the clothes she owned; six shirts, five bloomers, petticoats, pyjamas, dresses, pullovers and finally over all that a pair of track suit pants and a jacket! No wonder she could hardly stand up from her chair, but an even greater miracle was that the bike on which she rode with Domie to the neighbouring village did not collapse under her weight!

And so only Miriam stayed behind with us. She kept her feelings subdued by doing the dishes, so off she went to wash up in the kitchen. I helped her. We had the strange sensation that we, including Hansje, who was asleep upstairs, were the only living creatures in the house, apart, of course, from a countless number of real mice that are always invisible but sometimes audible.

But Froukje, who had the Wednesday afternoon off and knew nothing of the whole emergency, had to hear the whole story from scratch when she got home.

"I wish that they could come back here again by tomorrow," she sighed at the end of the story. And Miriam and I agreed wholeheartedly.

Chapter 47

After much struggle, the flu has finally beaten me down and I am lying in bed. A setback just like many we face in life. And yet when one finally yields and rests, things do go a little easier. Much easier than when one is like a mere shadow, coughing and spluttering while roaming through house and garden. A gardener is needed to come and spruce up the front yard, with drastic changes to be made on all sides of the house. Can one then lie uselessly in bed? Domie has already spent some time lying there; also a victim of the flu. Now this morning he is up and I'm lying back down. It's windy and raining. The showers confer one advantage, as the cistern had recently become empty again. An enormous wash happens each week; so you may become rightly concerned when I tell you that our secret community has now been extended by two. The danger to our home has faded away; both Mice and boys are now happily back with us. But a couple of older people whom Domie had placed with the clandestine doctor suddenly had to vanish as there was good reason to expect a house search there. The good doctor had indirectly received a tip from an NSB member who was apparently well disposed to him. Meanwhile our own doctor was entertaining some invisible house guests and was also privy to our own secrets.

Our 'orphanage' now has a resident father and mother. The gentleman had been a cook and confectioner in the Jewish League, a 'doctor of gilded[105] letters', as he wittily calls it. He made biscuits with

---

105 A play on words: the Dutch word for 'gilded' also figuratively means 'sweetened'.

cranberry juice on the stove-top for one of our birthdays. "If I do well, may I stay?" he asked.

He was someone who once owned a flourishing business in Deventer. But what is left to you when you are deprived of everything, other than to humbly ask a favour? For I felt his superficial banter covered something deeper that was being communicated in earnest. In such a helpless position people of noble stature again become as children that require protection. Especially if they are not altogether physically healthy and are still suffering the after-effects of surgery. The impossible then becomes again possible: we also took them into our midst.

Another storm! I now have the time to listen to and watch the still bare branches whipping back and forth. A storm broke on our wedding day too. There was a large room above the canals of Amsterdam: our simple home – eleven metres long and six metres wide. On the floor, boards were laid where the groom had built our furniture. Furthermore there were flowers on the piano and table and a couple of dear friends had come to help me to prepare everything, because I did not want to seek any further favours from my employer at the editorial office. Nothing more than I was entitled to, and there had to be some time and money held in reserve for our honeymoon trip. My friends were struggling with getting my hair right under the veil. "Leave that thing down," said the bridegroom when he returned from a tour of the city. "Otherwise it'll blow right into the canal."

I felt a little offended by the absence of poetry in his comment. "That thing," he had said and he meant my veil, to which the girls were busy pinning flowers. But they continued their task unflustered. I would still have my veil and two bridesmaids gently carrying it in support, one at each side of the steps at the entrance to the Church of William the Silent, on the facade of which the bust of the Father of our Nation is displayed. And when we entered through the vestibule into the church, the organ started playing the Wedding March and the light streamed through the high windows, because the sun had broken through right at that moment. Never have I felt so happy as I was then!

I lay in my bed and looked out at the clouds being mercilessly driven across the landscape.

Was it symbolic – that wedding in the storm, that shining light in the church, the bust of William the Silent above the entrance – his motto engraved on our rings? S.T.I.U. *Saevis tranquillus in Undis – Calm amidst the raging waves.* A seagull, floating quietly amidst the spume on the mountainous white-caps! What did we know then of what would come to our land and people? Why did we choose this motto, and was it coincidence or destiny that we ended up in this particular church, when we had really preferred to be married in the *Nieuwe Kerk?*[106]

However, we have occasionally had a premonition that our lives would not be easy.

Domie, who at that time was not yet a Minister but a student, wrote me a long poem about Baucis and Philemon[107] whose final wish sought from the gods was for them to die together. One evening, when he came to me with a great bunch of marsh marigolds in his hand and we went out to greet the setting sun, my betrothed said, "I think that what awaits us is an eventful life."

Guided by these feelings, we chose our wedding motto. While we are amidst the raging waves, may that rest always be granted to carry us through, and among all setbacks and insufficiencies may we be enabled to remain faithful, that the light may break through with an overwhelming might, as it did on our tempestuous wedding day!

---

106 A grand church on the Dam, next to the Royal Palace.
107 Characters in a moral fable by Ovid.

Chapter 48

Whatever is wrong with me? A languid fatigue suffuses all my members. I need to work in the garden, but can hardly muster enough strength. I haven't been motivated to do anything and have not achieved anything anywhere. First Domie went down with the flu, then I had a couple of days of it. Two days in bed, then Hans caught it. He had been to a birthday party and started crying uncontrollably when he came home. "Mama! Mama!" A restless sleep ensued, interrupted by crying again. At seven o'clock the next morning he was sitting in the study on my lap and clinging to me. He was really sick. The doctor arrived and diagnosed influenza. Hansje's cot was moved to the study. I tried to sleep the night through right next to him on a makeshift bed. But sleep was elusive. He called out for me frequently. He suffered feverish bouts of dreaming, and only felt safe when he felt my arms around him.

The fever lasted two whole days and nights, but then it ceased very suddenly. Early in the morning Hans sat up in his bed and began in his childlike prattle to tell me a story about his dog. Then I gave him a little water to drink, put it down, covered him up again and said that he now had to go to sleep a while. Then we sang his little song together, but by the time we reached the very last line he was no longer singing; he was already asleep.

I sat on the edge of his bed and looked at him. One hand lay on the coverlet, the other fist he held to his mouth, which was now breathing quietly. The blond hair on his head was mussed up and his eyelids with the long lashes were closed. A wondrous being, so beautiful and tender was my child! A wave of grateful emotion hit me. He had been ill, but he had now recovered. He was sleeping at last. The small body had healed and I had nothing more to do here except to calmly go and get some sleep myself. Above my head I could hear thumping sounds; Polletje and Froukje getting out of bed. *Ja*, it was half past six. Fragments of last night's conversations re-surfaced in my mind, which I had put on the back-burner yesterday at eight, because I was just so preoccupied with Hans. But I recalled it was something about Miriam. Apparently there was a place in Limburg found for her and now she would be able to go there. What was the sense in only Miriam going away if the seven others remained behind? The word 'evacuate' hung in the air once again, but if this was really necessary for safety reasons, why now Miriam before the rest of them?

How she actually felt about this herself, I had no idea. I had hardly seen her at all yesterday to talk to, but now I really wanted to see her. I walked softly up the stairs, so as not to wake those still asleep, and stuck my head round the bedroom door.

"Miriam, are you awake?"

"*Ja*, Tante Jo!"

I crawled into Polletje's empty bed right next to hers and then a hand thrust out to me in the dark, reaching over to touch my face.

I clasped that hand.

"Miriam, what is it?"

"Oh, Tante Jo, I find it so awful to have to go away!"

I thought of Hansje whom I had just lulled to sleep. Are we not all children, if it comes to that, who want to feel safe arms around us in a grim and barren world? I stroked the black curls and comforted her as I would a child. No, she did not have to leave; I would look for another solution and propose it to Domie. The sobs subsided and I told her of Hansje, and the sudden retreat of his fever. Could we both get some sleep? Surely she would not have had much sleep last night?

"No not at all."

"Then shall we just try to get some right now?"

Through the cracks between the shutters penetrated the early morning light, accompanied by voices of farm-hands on their way to work, then the rattling sound of a car's motor out on the road.

But the room was quiet. I lay listening, until Miriam's regular breathing showed me that she was asleep. Then I also drifted off.

Had I not been given sufficient time and space to be off sick? How was it that I had so little resistance this time round and the feeling of hardly being able to involve myself in the worries of my house guests? Or was this a premonition of an impending catastrophe? My inner reserves were now exhausted. I had no new initiatives or plans. Did they all labour under such a depression as I was feeling now? To my surprise I noticed time and again that they still tackled things, had plans to alter blouses, to produce stencil work, to busy themselves with photographic processes. Wherever did they get their motivation and energy? I was a real pessimist; every time I listened to the radio I longed for the liberation to break forth and thus end the war. Then we could at last be free from that oppressive threat that hung over our house. But I was lacking in both faith and courage, and I felt so guilty about that.

The author with her firstborn son, Hansje.

Chapter 49

Then one morning a couple of German officers came by on their bikes and entered the gate; one in blue and his companion in a green uniform. I caught sight of them from an upstairs window, and a sudden arrow of panic penetrated straight to my heart. What on earth were they doing here? Were they from the dreaded Greens? If so we were lost! Half of our refugees were still asleep, the other half dressed. How did you get eight people within a fraction of a second from their beds then down under the ground in broad daylight? Impossible!

I decided to do nothing at all. I stood paralysed with fear at the top of the stairs. Then there beside me stood Naomi. She had certainly seen them too. She continued quickly down the stairs and upon her own initiative, she entered the *leerkamer* and crawled into the tunnel under the stage. "Inside is best" she must have been thinking. I still stood listening intently, heard them rattling the door-knocker, but the door was locked. Then a loud call. Polletje opened to them, and in her most pleasant voice received the gentlemen. Meanwhile, a third turned up, a newly arrived young *Dominee* from a neighbouring village, but in this illustrious company Polletje assumed he must have been an NSB man. She wanted to leave them in the study, but the pastor said, "I do not belong with those men, you'd better allow me to wait in a separate room."

"Oh," said Polletje, because suddenly the light dawned in her head.

Polletje always says that you can catch more flies with syrup than with vinegar and so she continued to play out that role. She escorted the

Germans cautiously into the study and the young pastor into the living room. He looked shocked, as though he'd received a sudden blow to his head. Glancing at the closed study door he whispered, "They are not to be trusted!" But Polletje let nothing show of her inner turmoil. She returned to the Germans in the study and asked with an amiable expression how she could be of service to the gentlemen. They requested from *Herr Pastor* a copy of a baptismal certificate of someone who had lived a hundred years ago and was registered in our church records.

"*Herr Pastor* is not at home," said Polletje, sounding all helpful and willing to assist them in such an innocent matter of duty, "but I will ask *Frau Pastor*."

She came up the stairs to my room. "What do these people want?" I asked.

"A baptismal certificate," said Polletje, "from a hundred years ago."

"Let them go and walk to the moon!"

"If you don't give them any trouble, they'll go away again," insisted Polletje. But as willing as she was, I was just as reluctant. Must our baptismal church records be misused in this way, so that Nazi Germany could now confirm that this young man who was to be married was of the Aryan race? And if not, he would not be granted a marriage license. Not to mention the Church giving out baptismal evidence, the Church which has always stood above differences in nationality and race. "In Christ there is neither Jew nor Greek, free nor bondman.[108]" Polletje's eyes kept looking at me expectantly.

"Tell them that I'll search here in the archive chest, but there is very little chance that I'll find it," I said. Notwithstanding, a little later I came downstairs carrying an old baptismal register under my arm.

"*Was wollen Sie?*[109]" I asked at the study door, and Polletje later said that my voice at that moment had sounded as harsh as that of a sergeant-major.

---

108 Galatians 3:27-28.
109 "What do you want?"

Oh dear! What fine uniforms, yet what clumsy chaps! Were they really something to be afraid of? These men appeared to be enlisted in the Navy and were stationed in Delfzijl, so they told us, but if they had been wearing a similar kind of uniform, but with a different insignia, then they could very well be from the Greens and would have the authority to drag us out of our house and put us in a camp or even shoot us if it were deemed preferable. But should we be afraid of such people? That was beneath the dignity of a Christian!

Their ancestors came from East Frisia, they told me. Hence a certain Peter Zweig had been baptised here in our church. They talked to each other in the East Frisian dialect, which is also customarily spoken around these parts, but their speech was also punctuated with a lot of German words. Would I be able to find Peter Zweig's entry for them? I sought out the desired year: 1844, and passed over the register to them. On these pages they would just have to search for themselves.

It was not that simple; the ink had faded and the entries were written closely together. Good! If they didn't find it, then it was for the best – then they could blame no-one if they had no baptismal certificate to take home. A rough finger slid down the list of names.

"Ah, that's it! That's Peter Zweig!"

Now I retrieved an official blank certificate and sat behind the desk to write while they dictated the names. The German made one mistake in his spelling. Was the whole precious piece now ruined?

Well no, for such contingencies we do have an eraser.

"Shouldn't a line be ruled through that? And do you also have in Holland similar papers for those who are getting married?"

"No, with us it's all done without needing so many documents!"

They were only partly attracted to that idea. To them life seemed important only if it were necessary to have a whole heap of official documents at hand.

There! After much effort the names were copied, black on white. I opened the stamp pad.

"What are you doing now?"

"I'm putting the ecclesiastical stamp of the church underneath." They looked quite delighted at that. As if it couldn't be any more genuine – with such a beautiful official stamp at the bottom! And looking just like the register of baptisms. "A wonderful book!"

Ja, you could find everything there, even names from more than a century ago!

These gentlemen apparently did not have much understanding of the Church, but they still had respect for the official administrative aspects of its function. Moments later they set off satisfied, with evidence in the pocket that the descendant of Peter Zweig came from Aryan parents. If only they had realised that they had just been in a house rife with Semitic influences! But I trust that none of them will ever happen to find out.

When they had gone, now it was the pastor's turn. One can be so wrong in making assumptions! And so it proved once again. The Germans, who looked so threatening to us, had come up with a very innocent request, but the pastor, of whom we were not expecting anything negative, now brought us an alarming report.

Chapter 50

The Germans had broken open a hub of the Resistance in Groningen, with which Domie had been in direct contact. After the pastor left, the message was relayed up through to our folk in the loft and during their meal they were intensely occupied in discussing the ramifications. I could not join them, because I had to take a catechism class at one. But during it I was interrupted by a knock on the door and there stood Polletje. I briefly popped into the hallway as she had something to ask me. The refugees were anxious and had asked her to look for other safe places for them to go. Should she go ahead with that? *Ja*, that would have to be done, however miserable a job it was. Eight people so very dear to us! And to have to ask others if they could manage to provide shelter for them! But the risk that came along with that! You'd much rather be responsible yourself than let others take charge. But Polletje used her tact and powers of persuasion, and by that afternoon she had obtained guaranteed places for six. The doctor from the neighbouring village was also trying to place the two older ones who had originally been staying in his house.

Again the same preparations for departure as before, but this time because they felt the actual need for such measures themselves. Once again farewells in the study and a passionately crying Naomi. New shelter-parents arrived and left, shielded by the darkness, to fetch our foster children, mostly in twos. Monteur also took our radio cabinet away, from which the voice of the world would henceforth be silent. That afternoon Elderling had already crammed his bicycle panniers full of forged papers for our refugees to take with them.

There remained just two more who had not been yet been collected – the older couple. Doctor could not find any place for them to go. In the home of our own doctor this problem was discussed at length. He already had three people staying there: two of his own refugees and our Miriam. He could take no more! We had already become reconciled to the idea that they would need to continue to stay with us. That was a very unsafe option for them, but in regard to my own safety it would make no difference if I were caught with either two or eight people hiding here. Our escape passages were no use in their situation, because at their advanced age they were not agile enough to navigate the demanding route quickly and in silence. I looked at the anxious faces of my guests. They were very nervous. It was up to me to stay calm and reassuring. They needed to get some sleep now anyway, so whatever came to pass, I decided that they were my aunt and uncle who were spending a few days here with me. After all, it was worth a try! But fortunately at last a message arrived from the doctor's house saying they could go there.

When I escorted them hastily out into the darkness of the night, they frantically grabbed at my arms, and were panting to keep up. Oh my! What if they were ever caught?

Wandering, wandering from one place to another with nowhere safe!

When they were safely deposited at the doctor's, I came home to my now empty, silent house, alone with Polletje and the sleeping Hans. At eleven Froukje also came home. With a tight feeling in my chest brought on by the uncertain fate of all these people, I bolted the door.

From a distance I feel I must now take a good look back on that time and reflect on how everything really was going and what really was happening. In the glow of this placid spring evening on the first of May, with the bright and early sunlight gracing the green of the plants on the banks which Domie landscaped in our garden, and the verdant fields beyond interspersed with patches of rapeflower already awash in a yellow haze – all those events together look rather like an improbable nightmare. A nightmare from which someone wakes up the next morning, rubs the sleep from his eyes and goes to the window to allow the cool morning air and the goodness of the sun to convince him that his dark dreams have been like sinister bats in his imagination, fleeing the daylight.

But all the goodness of the earth, the warmth of the sun and fragrance of the blossoms cannot gainsay the fact that there are dark powers that menace our lives.

It all began that fateful afternoon with a telephone conversation between Domie's Resistance network and the doctor's house: *Tante Jo must now once again see to her own health and take the evacuated children on to other addresses. Moreover, Wil and three others are seriously ill and they feared complications.*

My first thought was: Had Domie also received that message of alarm about the Groningen network? Those 'evacuated children' were already out the door; they departed last night, but what does the serious illness of Wil and three others signify? Were they arrested? But that would be terrible! Wil and her forged ration coupons – that was punishable by death!

Polletje set off south to Amsterdam to intercept Domie en-route and to tell him that he should not bring any new fugitives to us. All addresses in the village that were suitable were already engaged in sheltering our folk.

They would only be home after midnight and I had again asked the Chief to collect them.

I was waiting in the study. How slowly the time dragged! After all, at a quarter past midnight, they should have been here, and now it was about half past twelve. Could something have happened along the way? I could do absolutely nothing about that. I was not even permitted out after eleven. Neither were they actually, but Domie had a special note: *Wegen Ausübung des Berufes!*[110]

What miserable tension we lived under constantly in those latter days! First there was this calamity, then that, and what would happen next? Again that wretched, crippling fatigue and pain in my back! However, I would wait, even if it took all night. Who goes to bed in such circumstances? I turned the big ceiling light off and switched a small lamp on instead, then lay down on the couch with a coat over me. In any case, it was better that way. Rest... would I ever get any? Or a completely normal life? But these times were not normal. A reprimanding voice said within me, "How could you ever lead a normal life and distance yourself from the whole mess and not attract blows?" Praying for the protection of those who were dear to me, I fell into a light sleep.

A gentle tapping against the window – the famous signal, four times quickly in succession. Thank God, they were here! I looked at my watch: it was half past one. Surely something unusual must have delayed them? I opened the door. On the path I saw a gleaming row of shiny buttons, white braid and a tall peaked cap. Before me stood the Chief.

"Where are Domie and Polletje?" I asked as I let him in.

"Gone round the back with the bikes."

In the bright study I looked at his pleasant, open face. "Is there anything particularly wrong?"

"No, *Mevrouw*," reassured that familiar tenor voice of even metallic timbre. "We had to find accommodation for a lodger who originally was coming to stay at the *pastorie* last Easter."

Lisette, surely, I thought as I stepped backwards... a Jewish girl who looked Aryan and was now under a new name and with new papers provided by Domie's colleagues in the Resistance. I slid the bolts on the

---

110 Authorised pass for carrying out the professional duties of a Minister.

back door. Domie and Polletje stood there with their bikes in the dark of the night. "So... you're really here at last," I said without enthusiasm. "How late it's become!"

I helped them with the bikes and the luggage. Even Polletje had lost something of her usual cheerfulness. Exhausted, she leaned against the wall in the hallway. Domie looked ashen from lack of sleep and food. These days he was looking like this more often and it provoked in me a slight feeling of annoyance. I could not make up for the vital forces he had lost in a week with just porridge and eggs.

I poured coffee. "What about something to eat? Sandwiches? Porridge?"

"No, nothing."

"A piece of cake, then?"

He ate it mechanically, sitting bodily here in the room, but his mind was entirely elsewhere.

"What has actually happened?" I asked.

Then the flood of words began. Wil... also a colleague of Domie, had been apprehended together with everything she had with her, from ration coupons to forged identity cards. This was achieved by treachery, which arose simply due to the fact that she was Jewish yet could move around freely. She had been staying at the house where her parents were hiding. They had taken her with her bag to the headquarters of the Greens in the Euterpestraat in Amsterdam, while her parents and brother were deported to Westerbork[111] Transit Camp. We would certainly never see her alive again. She had stored some poison in her bag, so she would not betray others in the Resistance before they shot her. She'd always had a plan to make an early end to her life if she was arrested. But they had removed the satchel from her. Now she was begging for poison and had written a note to Margo to ask for it.

---

111 Located on the desolate moorland of Drenthe, Westerbork was a deportation camp for Jews and Gypsies on their way to the Nazi death camps in the east. It was an uncomfortable place invaded by hosts of flies in summer. Anne Frank also passed through Westerbork, leaving for Auschwitz on 3rd September, 1944.

I said nothing. Terror had seized me. The consequences of this disaster were incalculable! If Wil unleashed a word under torture, there would be the bullet for Domie and raids to search for him. They would not find him here, although they would eventually track down our refugees who were placed everywhere all over the countryside. They could also arrest me to interrogate me about Domie. And what about Hansje? Poor, poor Wil... begging for poison! She was familiar with the mysterious actions of various substances. She was, after all, trained in analytical chemistry. "Give me salicylic..." something... a name that has escaped me. And that note she wrote in her desperation to Margo, my own niece, whom Domie had also helped. If that ever fell into the wrong hands! Margo was nineteen, so she was a minor. They would then grab my brother in order to get to his daughter.

"And what are you thinking about doing now?" Domie interrupted my thoughts.

"I am staying right at home. If they come for me, they'll let me go again after a certain period has elapsed."

The Chief nodded. "*Ja*, three months' detainment is the present period for that. As long as you don't say anything you'll be set free again."

"If I go into hiding, the danger becomes acute, because then everyone will be asking: 'What's happening at the *pastorie*?' Whereas if I stay home and everything goes on as normal, it can only be seen as due to my being sick. That way I can still look after the interests of our refugees and Hans need not leave."

"But I would recommend that you remove all things of value from the house," said the Chief. "You can count on getting a gang of thieves here soon enough. The methods of the S. S. at such an interrogation are inhuman. This one looks like a girl with a very strong will, but already so many have succumbed to their treatment, so don't be too quick to assume that she doesn't tell them anything."

Then the Chief stood up to leave. *Ja*, we mustn't fritter away all our time here. There were a hundred things to be done. We had to wake up the neighbours. They would hasten to our aid and store a few items for us. I went upstairs to get a couple of things together. Domie followed me. Now for the first time we were alone. I was suddenly filled with a burning reproach.

"Now it's finally happened! You have put us into deep misery! Everything, everything for others! Nothing for ourselves."

On the dressing table was the portrait that Johan had painted. A couple coming out of the church of William the Silent, followed by two girls in white, carrying the long veil. One of those girls was Margo, then quite a little thing. We were that couple, and above on the facade was the bust of William of Orange who had spoken that motto, the initials of which are engraved on our wedding rings: S.T.I.U.

But I was not ready to be like that: *Calm amid the raging waves.* Not at this time! A great bitterness throbbed in my heart, because I saw nothing but darkest night ahead of me.

"I could do none else," was Domie's simple answer. "It's always the same ones who are asked to take on burdens and pull through." His reply softened me. And in reality I knew what he meant. Needs, emergencies on all sides, the demands which came upon you. Should not your life be given to others as a Christian, and to your fellow countrymen as a Dutchman? What would Prince William have done differently? But there was really no more time for philosophising. We had to act! Domie woke the neighbours up and I searched to get our stuff together. In the dead of night, our neighbour appeared... a little untidy, with unkempt hair, but determined to help, and do what he could.

Here's the typewriter, that camera, the projector lantern, the Cyclostyle duplicator... such things that we tend to become attached to.

Also the silverware and some blankets and linens. The Weck[112]

---

112 A home preserving system, developed by the J. Weck company in 1900. It uses glass jars with a rubber ring, in which the produce was boiled and steamed using a water bath on the stove-top before sealing.

preserving jars as well... with potted meat from the small freshly slaughtered pig? No let it go, you can't transfer all of that! Froukje had also woken up to all the trudging up and trotting down the stairs. She sat shivering by the study stove while Polletje informed her about the sudden, painful developments. "That's dreadful... really dreadful!" is the only thing that she could say.

At last we were alone again, my husband and I. The icy aloofness had melted into sadness. Would we ever see each other again, and if so when? He had to hurry. It was already five; soon we would be overtaken by the dawn light and then he would not be able to get safely away. Our farewell was really memorable. But we could not pray together at that moment. That would only come later, much later.

Chapter 51

Now the days all seem to run into each other. There are the regular visits to our family of friends hiding in various homes, which I continue so as to not let them down! "*Ja*, but you have got to be careful," they whispered after one or two weeks... apparently I was being shadowed. Domie had meanwhile vanished without trace, having become sick on his journey. Nowadays so many people are disappearing from the scene. "Something's definitely going on there in the *pastorie,*" was the thought that gradually dawned on the locals.

When Domie left, it was the morning of 6th April 1944: Good Friday. That evening at 7pm we held Holy Communion in the church. Obviously Domie could not take his place to officiate. An elderly pastor came from a neighbouring parish to stand in for him. I made preparations for the simple platter of bread and covered the table, where I had set the beautiful old silver chalice. Meanwhile the sun was shining in through the tall windows and it was so lovely in the empty church where I was so busy, yet alone. The silent clarity of God's presence enveloped me and I heard the words of Christ there in the silence, where from the cross He spoke to me, "I did this for you; what will you do for me?"

Then all my heart's defiance about the threat to our own existence broke, and gave way to a profound peace.

Good Friday was followed by a restful Easter, accompanied by beautiful bright spring weather. Polletje was out and Froukje had taken

Hans home with her for a day and a night, so I was all alone in the house. I now had time to think about everything, including the imminent visit of the Mole, who was coming to pick up the Mice and accompany them on their journey south. Reflecting on these matters in the study, which was suffused that evening by unveiled moonlight, I considered him the best option for their safe departure. At the present they were placed on the same farm where they had stayed last time, but that address was only temporary. Now the Mole would come to fetch them for a return to Amsterdam. The same evening I went to tell them the terrible news. Their house-mother was all compassion. "*Och, och, ja,* how dreadful! And they're sitting there so carefree in the little room like sparrows on the sand." Sadly I was there to put a cruel end to those carefree days. But after the shocking tidings there remained at least one positive: our trusty Mole was coming to pick them up.

And so they left very early the following morning, sneaking cautiously along behind the large barns, heading for the station before dawn so as not to be seen by the early-birds among the workers. Polletje went charging ahead on the bike, but the Mice had to walk for three quarters of an hour. They eventually wrote a letter from Amsterdam that I'll share with you here, because their trip and Esther's first impressions on seeing her home town again are much better described than I, who did not go with them, could relate:

Dear Polletje,

I imagine you sitting there waiting for the report of our successful journey and arrival here. You already know how we got to Groningen. I must have put on a silly face when the train pulled away with Lily on board and we were left behind on the platform! I really felt rather miserable at that moment; yet I did not dare to jump on board with three packages in one hand, and being so short-sighted without my glasses. But I was glad when we were reunited again on the station at Amersfoort.

It was chock-full on our train, but there was a polite gentleman who stood and gallantly offered me his seat, for which I was so grateful, because my legs were almost collapsing from fatigue after the strenuous days which had preceded this one. That was also one of the reasons why we decided at Amersfoort to immediately push on to A'dam.[113] It would normally have been very tempting to profit from the beautiful weather and spend an hour out on the Heath. But we were too tired, so on we went to A'dam. We had a compartment to ourselves, just the three of us – explain that, hè, at this time – and took advantage of this favourable opportunity to remove our muddy gumboots because several co-travellers had already looked at us in astonishment. We spruced ourselves up a bit, because we found over and over again that we looked too wild and unkempt like that to go into town and therefore made an effort to present ourselves as ladies – only with moderate success though.

To disguise the Mole as a man was obviously an impossible task, not to mention that you would not find it necessary. He would not enjoy the experience and so we did not even try. The trip went incredibly smoothly – no delays, no checking of papers (I would have really liked to have seen the ticket controllers at work on such a full train – we were packed in like sardines), and so right on time we steamed into Central Station.

Amsterdam welcomed us with an air raid siren; it started up when we were waiting for the tram. With that familiar slowness and reluctance the travellers retraced their steps back under the station roof, where we amused ourselves for three quarters of an hour watching audacious people, who despite the warning, calmly continued on their way. When the 'all clear' was sounded, there were so many people milling about at the tram stop that we decided to leave our bags in the left-luggage depot and proceed on foot to Lily's girlfriend's, where we would spend the

---

113 Amsterdam.

afternoon. We were almost there when this time, without any air raid alarm, a terrifying shooting party started up right above our heads with heavy machine guns: an aerial dogfight. I was really feeling so uneasy, but we had only a hundred meters or so to go and just walked on.

We were received with great courtesy into a cosy, sunny and artistically appointed home. I also knew our hostess from old times, and so we felt immediately at ease, talking nineteen to the dozen, eating all together around the table etc.

As you know we were supposed to catch a later train, and thus we didn't want to head over to the Mole's straightaway, so as to not to arrive there in the midst of their cleaning and preparing the guest room. So we stayed on until the appointed hour and then the Mole came by to collect us after he had also retrieved our luggage.

At the Mole's we received a really nice welcome – there was a lovely Limburg vlaai[114] to celebrate our arrival and there were flowers arranged everywhere. A lot has changed in their house since our last visit. In honour of the guests, extra cleaning and tidying had been done – at any rate that immediately brought to my mind Domie's saying, that "on the table a place must be laid for an unexpected guest." Of course we still have a long time ahead to chat with everyone about anything and everything. It was getting on for one o'clock when we finally were in bed. I was able to stretch myself right out in that gloriously spacious bed. Actually it had been made up for both Lily and me together! But Lily gave up her spot for my sake and instead crept onto a divan.

Well now, I finally want to inquire – how are you going? It is not due to a lack of interest that I only do so now – but the whole travel story does fit well together and that is why I didn't interrupt it. Would you believe Polletje, that I no longer feel at ease here? That it's all so

---

114 A fruit filled flan from the southern province of Limburg.

foreign to me – with so many people all living in tall, narrow houses along the canals, the noise and the crowds and the Amsterdam accent? For as long as you have worked in the north, you become more accustomed and attached to the people there than you yourself realise – which you will also notice if you take sufficient time off back in Bussum.[115] Actually, it's all been rather disappointing; I'd imagined great emotions being stirred within at seeing my beloved hometown, but I found it such a dirty, noisy heap of bricks and mortar. For that reason I'm having bouts of true homesickness for our fresh, wide open spaces of the north, for the simple unpretentious people of the land and their cosy patterns of speech. I can hardly keep myself from sprinkling my sentences with plenty of Gronings (so as not to forget it).

And thus they had arrived safely, without train checks of their identity cards etc. It was worthy of heartfelt thanksgiving! May it indeed continue to go well with them! When you have given shelter for so long to those staying under your roof, then your thoughts keep going out to them always.

For love is a beautiful thing; with it you can reach out and cover a multitude of people, both near and far.

And over this beautiful Easter season, when Christ's resurrection and victory over the dark powers of sin and death seem almost tangible through the triumphant life and goodness of nature around us that serves as an emblem of this hidden reality, I have rediscovered a happiness that lies deeper than the ever-changing circumstances of daily life.

---

115 Bussum – Polletje's hometown in the province of North Holland.

Chapter 52

Occasionally Domie came home on stealthy visits during the night. Just a brief hour sometimes, and then away again on his 'vacation'. One time he came into our bedroom at three o'clock in the morning. I put on a coat and went below with him to fry eggs and boil some milk. He appeared emaciated. We sat by the stove fire that was still glowing and forgot about the time. We were greeted by the first light of dawn. Thus Domie could not leave; there were already too many people out on the road. Without speaking I pointed out to him the blooming daffodils, hyacinths and tulips in our front garden. "Beautiful!" he said softly.

He had just enough time to make it over to the neighbours, who received him warmly and made a bed available where he could sleep. Domie had become a poor vagabond, driven out of house and home, hunted from one place to the next, and whom we could only see at ungodly hours of the night. He was one of the many people who were sharing such experiences during these dismal days, but before he went to sleep in the strange bed he recalled yet again, as a sweet consolation, the sleepy voice of little Hans, who, upon being asked his question: "What are you and Daddy to each other?" promptly replied: "Close chums."

On that day there was a pre-marriage confirmation ceremony in our church, which I led at the request of the young couple. Domie, from his vantage point nearby, saw people arriving and entering, but had to ask the neighbours what was happening, as if he were completely excommunicated from the life of our church.

The rounds of ministry amounted to preaching engagements on Sunday; all other work went on normally at its usual pace. Polletje took the youth, I the catechism classes. That in itself was not news; we were already used to sharing the duties together during the last time when Domie was away. A couple of farm-hands helped me out with the garden. I planted the potatoes with the assistance of Greet, who travelled over to the *pastorie* for her few days off from the hospital.

But in the midst of such peaceful pursuits a terrible message arrived: the Mole had been caught together with the tall Mouse who was staying with him, and two others as well! They were all taken to Westerbork Transit Camp, even the Mole, who is not Jewish.

Had we sheltered her for almost two years in our home, only for her to finally end up at the Westerbork camp? There was still one hope for her: that the invasion was coming any day now, before she could be taken to Poland! However, she had been given the designation "S" for *Strafwürdige Jude,*[116] because she had been in hiding to evade capture. Such people were always deported first.

We started working from all angles to plan to rid her of that letter "S" and to free Wil also, who was being immensely brave. Every evening under interrogation the damning pieces of evidence were placed on the table in front of her and she heard the same question: "How did you get these? From whom did you get the ration coupons and identity cards?" And always the same answer was given: "You can threaten me and execute me, but from my lips you will be none the wiser." Now it is nearly four weeks after her arrest. Wil is bruised and bloodied, and after

116 A Jew regarded by the Nazis as deserving of severe punishment.

each interrogation she is once more kicked back into the cell. But she is not cowed and says nothing. *"Verdammte Jude!*[117]*"*

Our prayers ascend like a wall around her. We strive for her in the heavenly places, that she will at last be acquitted of all those pieces on the table! But even then she will still be sent to Poland. And only God knows what will happen to her there.

---

117 "Damn Jew!"

Chapter 53

A dark, rainy night in May. There must have been a storm somewhere, since the weather of the last few days has suddenly changed and become so bleak! But maybe that's a good omen for our present mission. Not the lanes of muddy clay; I'm referring to the darkness and the uninviting weather. No personnel of the *Landwacht*[118] will be on the prowl for their own pleasure tonight.

Three Jews from our house must connect with the train: Naomi and two men to whom I have granted shelter for the past week, because they couldn't go anywhere else and I didn't have anyone I could ask. If there were attendant risks I would have to bear them myself; it already was a major risk for me with my Domie presently undercover and with the consequent suspicion that hovered over our house more than any other in the neighbourhood.

The danger of a search here was not far from becoming a reality and they were already doing me the honour of keeping me under surveillance, or so I was told. Therefore it was imperative that I no longer enter any house where fugitives were hiding. The Wissings', the doctor's house, the farm where the Mice and a lot more besides had been hidden; places where they had already gone hunting with their house searches. They were all off limits to me.

---

118 "Land watch" – A Dutch paramilitary organisation inaugurated by Germany in 1943 which functioned similarly to the British Home Guard in providing surveillance, particularly after curfew.

And now my guests would be leaving on this stormy, windy night which was shaking the delicate blossoms from the trees. Domie would be waiting for them at the station. One night he had arrived back home. Upon knocking softly four times in a row, he had heard both the men who had been sharing the night watch in turns scrambling away down our secret passage. So he had decided to come and collect them as soon as possible. But in the evening after the eight o'clock curfew it was out of the question for them to go via the main road and paths. Thus at half past eleven their shoes were exchanged for boots. Their luggage had already been taken away the previous day, so that the only remaining items were a satchel with shoes and a thick staff with a white rag tied around the top like a pennant. This would be placed as a marker right by the railway embankment so that, during her return journey along the same route, Polletje would know which side path she had to turn down in order to come out directly opposite the *pastorie*.

Why did I think it was right that Polletje took on that dangerous job? And why did I not do it? I asked myself, after I had closed the door in the darkness behind the departing foursome. On the pillow of my bed I found a little verse written to music, and created by Naomi. *Until we meet again! Here or at the River of God!* it began. Naomi took things quite dramatically, and yet...

I listened to the strong wind gusting. Most of the tree blossoms would have been blown away by now, but that no longer mattered since many had already set their fruit. I got dressed softly by the light of a small lamp in order not to wake Hans. To blossom is to bear fruit. Life perseveres, despite the storms. It had wrought its work in me and I had not even known it. I had accepted its terms reluctantly. Had not that delicate life within me suffered from the many shocks and emotions over the last few months? Would it remain as a nervous child? But I was not really nervous and my joy was destined to break through as witness to a miracle!

But I was more sensitive than usual. Earlier this evening there was a bird trapped in the hall, with a white belly and grey plumage elsewhere. Chris' father, who was staying here last week, had observed him outside in the garden, and said that it was an unfamiliar songbird, a migratory species. Yet now he was sitting with us in the hallway and I tried to help him a little to get back outside. The hallway doors were opened wide, but each time he flew against the fanlight above the door. Then I took a mop and coaxed him down. Tired and anxious, he lay sprawled on the floor, and I did not begrudge him that rest. Then he launched himself up and away, out through the door, then flew low over the ground. Now things would happen! He was swooping low over the path when suddenly a black monster jumped up and grabbed him. A cat! Who would have thought? The bird chirped heartbreakingly and I ran chasing after the cat, but it dashed quickly under the hedge with the bird still in its mouth. Nothing more I could do to rescue it now. Defeated, I collapsed upon a garden chair down in our sunken glade. The flowers were blooming and the wood pigeons cooed in their nests in the trees, but behind the hedge a cat was busy tearing apart the small bird with the anxious eyes. Was I to blame? But how could I know that the cat was at that moment crouching right by the *stoep*?

And now I had let Naomi leave home. After all, wasn't it safe enough for me to go with them? Down the wet clay paths they were walking in the pitch black! Their boots would be sucked repeatedly into the squelching mud. An hour that journey took... and then the return trip back home again! I would be dead by now or have become at least dead-tired, so I was grateful to Polletje that she had volunteered. Not on account of the danger, which was all the same either way. If they were discovered tonight, the Germans would be here soon enough to take me away to Vught,[119] since I had provided shelter to people who were on their wanted list. And that was a crime! I had let our people become as

---

119 Camp Vught was set up during 1942 in North Brabant. Under direct SS control, it was a place where captives suffered cruel treatment and absolutely deplorable conditions. Those imprisoned were Jews, Gypsies, political prisoners, Resistance workers, and other 'undesirables.'

unprotected prey for the prowling black monsters that might jump on them and destroy them, just as the cat did to the unfortunate bird.

So... they had apparently already seized Esther. And Wil? Could I surmise from the letter which I received from my family, that both Esther and Wil were now incarcerated at Westerbork? How else could they "have kept so close to each other," as my sister had written? So the Germans must have given up on their torrid inquisition. The interrogations and the torment therewith had ended. Wait until Polletje gets back. She would know more as Domie would speak to her at the station. They would have to hurry. Domie was leaving with a transport of six fugitives (including two Jewish girls who had been staying with my parents-in-law) and Lisette, his assistant, also Jewish, with their departure scheduled for a quarter past one. Places for them had been found far down south in Limburg.

I must have slept. When I woke up at the sound of a door opening, there was a light on in Polletje's room. I saw it shining under her door and so I went in to see her. It was half past three by my watch. A hot water bottle lay enticingly in her bed. "Just crawl under the blankets," said Polletje who saw me shivering. She still had her coat on as she sat down on the edge of the bed and gave me her report. Indeed Wil was with Esther in Westerbork. Esther was suffering severe homesickness, but now they were able to comfort each other, and see each other every day. Domie might even have parcels sent to them. That was at least something; so they wouldn't need to suffer hunger. Polletje wrote a letter to the boys about her experiences of the night just past:

The grand tour is now behind us, but before it has faded from my memory I'm sending you a report of how it all went and the outcome. The journey on foot, bound for N.S.,[120] fortunately ended well. At about 11:45 we left the house and I took the door key along. With our four, like

---

120 Nieuweschans, the terminus of the northern railway line, just inside the Dutch
border with Germany.

dogs unaccustomed to the track, we set off down the path to the lane opposite, for which route we had taken a white cloth on a stick to mark my journey back. On the way there it also served as a walking stick to keep us on our feet. It was pitch black. The eldest one walked arm in arm with me up front, and the youngest with Naomi close behind. When we sighted various lights in the distance we stood still, trying to discern whether they were stationary or moving. Mostly they were moving. The oldest kept halting our progress by stopping and standing still, but I had him firmly grasped by the arm and forced him to walk on. Finally, we arrived at the railway embankment. I pushed my stick into the ground close to a telephone pole and we crossed over the track there on account of a light that was coming our way. As it passed us we were lying flat on our stomachs in a neat row, and we watched till the light dwindled in the distance. With the clear realisation we could then take the path to the right of the rails all the way to the station, we set off once more. It was a long way, but we arrived at the railway yard and saw, what seemed to me at least, a familiar light coming toward us.

Two men passed some way ahead of us without saying anything, but I kept my thoughts to myself. I stepped forward from our party to go after the men so that a meeting could take place. They turned out to be Domie and the Chief. The very last section was very exposed and windy and we were not allowed to make any light. It was all very well organised, thanks to the best Chief there is, who has won my heart through his cooperation and support.

No more beds! Polletje in her sleeping bag catches up on some much needed rest.

Chapter 54

I wanted to leave this chapter out of my book and out of my life altogether, but a history does not always have a happy ending, and certainly not a true history. I had heard nothing from the small Mouse in a long time. I had criss-crossed Amsterdam one afternoon to find her, but without success. I was told that the people at the house where she was staying were very careful. I thought it a pity that all my efforts had been in vain, but then again it was a calmly reassuring idea that she was so safe living with extremely cautious people. From what I understood she had ended up in rather luxurious surroundings. Esther had also written something about that when she was staying with the Mole and had jokingly said that the small Mouse, who had a mania for cleanliness, could now splash around to her heart's content in hot and cold running water. And that experience must have been reminiscent of her own home environment before the war. I was so glad that she was in her element, until another letter arrived from Westerbork and the letter was written by Lily. Hesitantly Polletje brought up the matter with me. She had long known about this, but Domie had thought it better that I did not know, because I would take it so badly. That's why they kept it from me, but now Lily had asked in her letter for blankets and warm things that still remained behind of her things here, because in that camp it was so very cold. So now I had to be informed. But Lily? Lily as well? And she was so safe! How on earth did she end up in that camp? I thought of the little bird that I had coaxed out of our home, and which had been seized on the path by a cat. I left the room. I didn't wish to know anything more today. But the next night, a Saturday, Polletje told me the whole story. Lily had been staying with a lady who had a son. The son was a childhood friend of Lily and he now had an Aryan girlfriend. It seemed that this Aryan girl must have become jealous of Lily and so she turned her in. Later however, this rumour was proven false. Someone else who fraternised with NSB-ers had betrayed her, a girl whom the Mole knew and who would therefore have betrayed both him and the tall Mouse. What could it all mean? That these two had been caught was certain. Domie had entered their house just after the Greens had raided the place. From the great mess of garments and other things lying scattered all over the floor he ascertained that they had either fled in haste or had been arrested. The evidence before him showed that the latter was the painful truth. It was all just so grievously sad!

The Mole had a body and constitution as strong as iron. I also rated Esther a chance of pulling through, but Lily was such a delicate bloom that I felt especially concerned for her. No warm clothes at all... she had nothing with her. She had been attacked in the house and rushed as she was straight to the prison on the Weteringschans in Amsterdam. Then to the camp in Westerbork. All their warm clothes were still here, up in the loft. If only there was a way for us to send those and some blankets as well! Via a circuitous route we also received a letter from Esther. Esther was serving food in the camp kitchen, just as they had done here for our clandestine community, when wonder of wonders, she and Wil met up there. Wil had also been sent to Westerbork after they could not pry anything more out of her. If only they could stay together! It was already bare and bleak on those flat heathlands of Drenthe during this cold spring, and the bitter wind blew around their ears (for that reason Lily had requested a headscarf). But they were at least still in the Netherlands and we had not lost all contact with them. Perhaps even now we could do something for them.

They had asked for Bibles and Domie had spent Ascension Day writing long letters to them. We wondered if they'd ever received them.

I do not know, but the subsequent Monday we received a letter from a Captain K., the erstwhile protector of the Polish refugees who had escaped at the beginning of the war from the German camp near Emden and had crossed the border near here. He had been billeted at our neighbours' house in those days, but the Mice had never met him.

That letter reads as follows:

Friday afternoon while I stood on the station platform at Winschoten, a long train full of Jews was passing through from Westerbork. From one of the cattle cars with barbed wire strung along the sides, and standing behind an open hatch, three women called something out to me. I could not get too close, because the whole platform was cordoned off by Grüne Polizei who constantly kept the people at a distance from the train. But I still succeeded to get close enough, and then these poor unfortunates asked me if I would convey their greetings to you, which requested duty I gladly now discharge.

Yours sincerely,

Captain K.

Without saying a word I brought the letter into the kitchen, where Polletje and Froukje were busy washing the breakfast dishes, then fled to the solitude of the study where I surrendered to my grief. I could visualise the cattle truck with the open hatch over which barbed wire was stretched, and behind it three pale, hungry faces. They sent **us** a greeting? The last one ever? So they were not embittered. But I felt intense remorse. The Mice had been caught because they had had to leave the safety of our home. What could I care if at this moment dozens of other unknown people were saved? I had no connection with them, nor any direct responsibility for them, not like I felt toward our three! Poor, poor Mice who had sheltered under our roof for almost two years! We had taken care of and watched over them incessantly, and now... all within sight of port... they had been shipwrecked on the bar... And Wil, for all her heroic suffering, had deserved something far better than transport to Poland in a cattle truck! Would the small Mouse ever survive the trip? How long would it take? Probably days, because such a train was usually kept waiting at sidings en-route. No food, no drink, no ventilation, but many... far too many... people jammed in together in those squalid, stifling cattle-trucks.

Was that the end? When the train began to pull away after that brief chance rendezvous with Captain K., they would be just leaving Winschoten and seeing the colourful fields of rapeseed pass by, whose sunny beauty they so often had looked upon from their skylight last year. They would very soon view the farms of our village and then the tower of the church rising above the trees and realise: If we could only jump off the train here and turn down that muddy lane running two kilometres through the farmland, then we will be home! But there was no one to protect them, even I myself, who knew that they were travelling on possibly their last trip to an unknown future beyond whose walls no messages ever penetrated to inform the civilised world. All contact was now forever broken. Poland! The place of horror. How many have not waited in fear and tension as a death sentence was announced; their names read out for transport, once again departing from Westerbork?

One youth wrote a letter to his girlfriend. I have that letter in my possession and here provide an extract:

Westerbork 6 July 1943

It's now four o'clock and the names of the next batch of deportees have just been called out. It is now my turn. But what can I do about it? Darling girl, you know how I feel. I find it terrible that I have to leave here, because I am already far away whenever I receive your letters and packages. Your last just came into my possession, and it gave me a joy which is indescribable. There was so much love pouring out from you, it was as if you are always with me. Dearest Elly, though I'm writing with tears in my eyes, and that happens quite often, you are always with me.

Darling, I hope that you will never have to follow me here, so please always take care that your papers for Palestine or Hachera are carried with you, because there you will have a future. Make for yourself the best possible life while you are at the NIZ[121] and do not grieve for me, because that is not my will. I must, I will see you again, come what may!

The letter is written in a highly emotional style. For those who work in close contact with all this suffering, it is very hard to bear. All those people, so torn apart and clinging to Domie. Should I not be like him? The girl to whom this letter was written was also rescued from the NIZ by Domie.

But what of the Mice then? They had become victims while in the care of the underground work done beyond our own control and away from our home. They always warned us and said, "Beware, or we'll still end up in Poland." And now they were on their way there! If we never see the Mice and Wil again, then the end of the war will bring little for us to celebrate. Rather, it will cast a very long shadow over the reunion they would be missing, even if just one of these three were missing. Domie had wanted to get them to Limburg. If only he had managed to do that!

At such moments of despair, the world is black and it seems no ray of light will ever be able to penetrate the gloom. Then a man struggles with his faith... until finally trust again overcomes and all his rebellious whys are transformed into a prayer for those who are seemingly forgotten and left to fall prey to evil, just as the bird was to the cat.

---

121 *Nederlands Israëlitisch Ziekenhuis* – the Dutch Jewish Hospital on the Keizersgracht in Amsterdam, from which the Greens deported half the staff and half the patients in one day during May 1943.

Esther had written to the boys:

Wednesday, 17 May 1944

The time has come when we are going to leave our dear land and the even dearer people in it. And with that we are understandably getting rather worn out with anxiety. But I will not leave here without once more sending the two of you a special greeting, for together we have had such a wonderful time, even though it was not always so easy. Thus far everything has turned out better than expected and hopefully it will continue like this later on; as long as you face it squarely, it seems that when it's time to go, once that happens, then you can skip through it all without trauma. Lily is a bit more under my care now. I have many acquaintances and friends here and am actually quite settled in during the two weeks head start I had on her. But she is doing well, you know – and is miles stronger than I thought. I was terribly shocked when she suddenly came and was standing there before me – I least of all expected that! And Willy is terrifically sweet company for me also. She also sends you her heartfelt greetings. I think of you so often – you won't ever forget us will you? Of course we do live in hope to see you all once again. But first there will still be a bitter time ahead. I fervently hope that you get through all this in one piece. In all our shared misery it's a consolation for me to know that you're safe. Have you received our previous letters? I trust that you are keeping well – like we are. We must all go through this difficult time together. Fortunately, yesterday I received a letter from Greet, Nel and Bep. I can take it along with me. And also – I still have your photos here.

Then Lily wrote:

I long for you with such homesickness and for everything associated with you. I wish everything was just a dream. But we must go through this, because it can't be otherwise. If we are destined to make it through, then it will happen, and if it not, there is nothing to be done about it. But we haven't given up our hope of course. And I hope at least that things work out well for you. I have a little picture of you both. Unfortunately I can't get hold of my own photos now. I don't really know what I should write at all. I keep thinking of our little attic room. I'm glad to have Esther and Willy with me. Another piece of the past that is worth so much to me. Boys, do not forget me, I hope so badly to see you again soon and to preferably lie somewhere outside in the sun together where we can finally rest. Well, I have to go now, the adventure is about to begin; that's how you have to see it.

Chrisje,[122] I wish you well and meanwhile may you have a happy 26th of May.

Rest... so longed for by the small Mouse. A desire you'd willingly grant. Because she was dragged from one place to another. To the prison on the Weteringschans, to Westerbork, and now finally to Poland!

From Wil there was also a note addressed to Domie, in which she said goodbye to him because she saw an unbearable future ahead from which she had no hope of ever returning. She was very sad. "I can fight," she wrote, "but not so... not in this way." She said farewell to Domie, also to the boys and to us, her country and indeed to life. Such a courageous, militant Wil, who braved all the beatings and insults of the Greens when interrogated; yet she is just a sad young woman with an overwhelming need to be loved and understood.

---

122 The – je suffix confers a diminutive status on the noun or name. It is used as a
   term of endearment for children and among close friends. Similar to "Chrissie" in
   English.

Chapter 55

In that disastrous year of 1944 one catastrophe followed hard on the heels of another. The capture of the Mice had hit me severely. It rendered me immune to other things, immune to my own peril. Why should I still lie in a nice warm bed every night with woollen blankets and equipped with a reading lamp while many others, including my own ex-housemates, were cold and destitute! They were constantly on my mind. One night I dreamed that all three of them were standing outside the back door. I let them in at once. They had jumped from the train and so had fled captivity! My joy knew no bounds. Unfortunately though, it was only a dream – projecting my innermost yearnings onto the screen of all my hopes.

The reality was very different. The Chief had overheard a conversation between a notorious NSB colleague and another NSB-er, a former member of our Youth Association, who now emerged on the scene as a Judas. His advice was that they needed to carry out a house search at Domie's because Jews were in hiding there. He was not sure how many, but it was worth the effort, since there was a price on each head and the doctor was in it up to his neck as well, so there could be even more Jews around. All the work of that damned Domie!

The Chief made sure that the whole village was given the alarm, as far afield as where the refugees were billeted, and Domie himself appeared in a yellow electrician's overalls on the second day of Pentecost to lead them away to safety. Of course he was spotted however. Some older teenage boys had seen him coming over the fields and had spread the news that an English pilot had been shot down.

These messages were not reassuring. In order to avoid suspicion Domie could no longer come home and I did not go to meet him anywhere. However, they held conferences on a large scale in the home of some newly-wed friends who were hiding another Jewish couple. De Lange and Wissing also did their part for the benefit of their people who also had to move on. Arrangements were speedily made. Domie and Polletje went along with them and the owner of a garage also pledged his cooperation by taking them very early the next morning to another station further west down the line. The village was now virtually empty of our secret guests and likewise our home, to which Naomi had only recently returned in distress. Only the boys were kept provisionally at their address and I stayed at ours by myself, awaiting the coming developments. I found that I did not need to wait very long, because in the evening of that same day they all arrived in force!

I was now burdened by a major disadvantage; I was expecting my second child. Women are so vulnerable! Not in a self-centred way, but due to the life that we are destined to bear! For we have in the first place a sense of duty arising from an innate urge to protect our own child at all costs, whether born or yet unborn. And it is therefore one of the great temptations in a woman's life to allow herself to become restricted through caring. This was also apparent in my relationship with the Mice. They were living under our roof, and I therefore became very personal and familiar with each of them. Like the nesting hen, which shelters the chicks under her wings, I had become emotionally invested in these fugitives. But now I had to give them up for the sake of others, for strangers, with whose needs Domie was acutely familiar. But would I find myself able, if necessary, to now weigh the welfare of my child in the balance and so boldly live on God's risks that I would not capitulate, but would stare Vught and other horrors courageously in the face? For such a thing one can only pray, because it is after all entirely of grace if one receives it. And that I did now fervently.

How small a mere human is in the great struggle of life and how much he finds himself always standing in the conflict between good and evil, between the impulses of the heart and the deliberations of the intellect. And how would a man know the way amidst all these contradictions, if the promise of Pentecost were not true in his life; that the Spirit leads us into all truth? And such finally became my experience on this mundane, lonely Pentecost of 1944.

Chapter 56

Great events cast shadows ahead of them. That is indeed a good thing, for then a man or woman can be spiritually prepared and ready for when the blow falls. And yet I was terrifyingly shocked when the police van stopped outside our home after curfew on that quiet evening, the Tuesday after Pentecost. A whole gang from the *Landwacht*, known generally by the collective name of *Jan Hagel*,[123] abandoned their bikes along the roadside and climbed over the garden gate that I had deliberately kept closed to the gentlemen whom we knew would come. They ran across the grass to all sides of the house to take up positions there, so no one could get in or out. One even dropped flat onto his stomach on the bleach-field.[124] A second showed great interest in a gap in the hedge, where one night only last week a Jewish boy, who had sheltered for a few days in our house, had been able to escape. A third crept down into the glade, and all of them had their rifles at the ready. Pure Wild West theatrics!

That morning I had got up very early and was now intending to go to bed early. I had just helped Hansje, who sleeps in the room with me, and had him well covered up, and had just got into bed when the van stopped right by the *pastorie* fence. With a shock I flew to the window through which I spied the approaching gang. The tower clock struck ten. Then the doorbell rang. "Shall I open it, *Mevrouw*?" asked Froukje, who was still in day clothes.

---

123 Literal translation "John Hail". Members were equipped with shotguns, and were
    mostly sympathetic to the NSB.

124 Open plot of ground for bleaching fabrics or drying laundry in the sun, either laid
    out on the long grass or hung from timber A-frames.

"*Ja*, but right away, mind!" I shouted back. "I'm getting dressed first." I dashed into the most essential things; a pair of red strap shoes that were there by my bed, a flowered dress that hung over a chair. Then to do my hair. To my annoyance my hands were shaking. I was expecting this... but was still very much in shock; I had no time to recover, but had to go down now, because they were already busy.

In the kitchen they were rifling through all the cupboards.
"Who gave you the order to do this?" I asked.
"Our chief."
"And who is that?"
"The Inspector of Police."
Meanwhile their 'chief' came over and stood before me.
"Are you *Mevrouw* so and so?"
"*Ja*, I am."
He looked at me intently and asked, "Do you have any strangers in the house?"
"No, none." Thank God, it was true. Had there been any, I didn't know if they would have had enough time to reach the hidden passage with that swarm of locusts who had so suddenly and thoroughly besieged the house inside and out!
"You don't have Jews in the house?"
Again the piercing look, which apparently came from a manual of the techniques of his craft as an interrogator.
"No."
"You've had none?"
"I'm telling you that at this moment no-one is here except members of the family. Froukje, the girl that opened the door to you, and little Hans."

The inspector and the *Landwacht* captain now entered a small room from the hall. I remained standing in the hallway by the garden table and heard them say to each other:
"She was really nervous! She knows a lot more than she lets on!"

"*Ja*, she can probably tell us a great deal!"

At that remark my self-control returned. Close by the front door stood Froukje, guarded by some valiantly heroic *landwachtman*, naturally with his gun poised for action!

"Must you just stand there, Froukje? Or is it possible that you might accompany me into the study?"

My voice was again very ordinary, with a tinge of mockery even, at this whole ridiculous charade.

"I would suggest likewise," said the brigand chief, friendlier than one would expect, to judge by his warlike stance.

I went into the empty study and prayed. I then felt a perfect calm and quiet descend upon us. Above my head I heard the tread of heavy boots. Now they were in our bedroom. Would Hansje start to cry? But no, apparently the little toddler of two years of age was in his bed, watching with great interest how the black uniformed men moved the twin beds[125] apart and looked inside the cupboards behind.

I poked my head round the hallway door. The inspector was there.

"Should I go with them?"

"You may," he replied, "but it's not necessary."

"Then I'd rather stay here. I have no interest in it."

But Froukje just had to tag along. Down in the cellar she regaled them with comments about the Weck preserves, and Froukje explained that we had just had the meat butchered this spring. They did not notice the churn of oil standing there, or at least they didn't look inside. And up in the loft they said nothing about the sack of wheat and the dismantled mill standing forlorn, nor about the hoard of large copper pipe we had not officially submitted to the authorities. If the *Landwacht* wished to establish a musical society, here they would already have the makings of a beautiful instrument. With imperious expressions on their faces they tapped along the wall of the attic room

---

125 *Lits-jumeaux* – two single beds that appear as a standard double when adjoined. Used often in European houses for mobility and space saving.

and noted that there had to be further space behind it. Then they shone their bright torches into that dark interior, but they did not discover the hidden shaft beneath the desk. There could well have been someone concealed inside.

The *leerkamer* also attracted their attention. They shone their torches underneath the stage, but didn't creep under it, because they would have had to do that with their stomachs flat on the floor, crawling along beneath the low beams and then their pretty outfits would get dirty! The hatch entrance to the tunnel was nailed up. Froukje and Petertje had done this job. Froukje had sealed all the gaps with handfuls of dust such that the hatch was not easy to spot, especially if you had not crawled under the stage. But that was a good thing, because in the hidden passage was a spare radio set of Domie's and a piggy bank with copper coins belonging to Hansje.

Although it was covered in sand, if they discovered the passage they could dig it up! But they contented themselves only with the remark that there was no one under there and then looked behind the stage curtains with the same negative result. Meanwhile, the inspector accompanied Froukje on a tour of the house. From her he thought he could learn something. She also learned something in return. What would she care about hiding strangers here? Why should she have to go to prison for the sake of others? If she reported what had happened in this house and where those people were now hiding, she would not be included in the count of those arrested.

Go ahead, Froukje, calmly betray your mistress and a whole bunch of others! What difference do strangers make to you if you can keep yourself out of trouble? That's National Socialism! Socialism assumes some form of community, but let me give you a piece of 'popular' educational lore which addresses the baser human instincts: the desire for self-preservation under the motto *Am I my brother's keeper?*

"What have you got to do with these strange people anyway? Come

~ 314 ~

on, Froukje – your mistress is not here, so you don't have a single obstacle to putting yourself out of harm's way, so come on; just talk!"

But Froukje knew better. She had not been steeped in the doctrines of National Socialism, but in the pure teachings of Christ. And so Froukje did not commit treason to save her own skin, but remained silent.

When that blackmail did not work, the inspector approached me in the study.

"I know that you have had Jews here in the house," was his opening gambit.

"If you are that sure, I need say no more."

My composure caused him to abruptly run out of steam. He said angrily, "And you will inform me of everything and tell me where they have gone, otherwise I'll arrest you and a long agony of confinement will await you, either in prison or in a camp."

"For me that would not be so bad but I'm expecting a baby; doesn't that make a difference?" I asked.

"Even if you were expecting three babies," he said, "that would not make a single difference."

In retrospect, I was sorry to have mentioned this, because now he had forged from that information a new weapon for combat: my love for my own child. With this weapon he was attempting to reduce me to a lesser being, forcing me steadily toward betrayal.

"You can save yourself a lot of misery in these circumstances by telling us everything."

Again the same seductive motive as used against Froukje, though he delivered it to me not so thickly laid on: just the simple threat of terror, which I could escape by condemning others as the price for my own safety.

"You're doing everything possible to put your family in jeopardy for Jews! Because you have had eight or ten Jews in the house!"

"Why do you not say twenty?"

At that he became furious. Irony and humour are never appreciated by Germans and their sympathisers. It was as if I had committed *lèse-majesté.*[126]

"You're under arrest," he said. "I am the Inspector of Police and you retort with such an answer? You will now tell me where they have gone, otherwise you will bleed for it. And I'm arresting your servant-girl; all for the sake of others, of Jews, who will all be caught regardless!"

"Today we all suffer for the sake of others," I said, thinking of Wil, who had endured the most terrible things for our sakes, including lashes with a so-called 'blackjack'.

"*Ja*, we certainly do." He sailed off into a long, furious tirade against the English, who had ruined everything for them. And how it was such a scandal that there are Christian people siding with them!

It was useless to contradict him and say that it was not British and Americans who were the problem but our own countrymen. He was furious and therefore not open to rational argument. It seemed best to me to just say nothing more and to go along with him. He snapped at me that I had to immediately go outside to the car. In the hallway, he swept by and I instinctively turned my head away toward the hall-stand where my coat was hanging. I really thought that he wanted to give me a slap in the face.

"Out! To the car," he shouted. "I have tried to treat you like a lady, but you are a..." There followed an expletive that I will not repeat here.

"Thank you," I said at the compliment. His impotent rage did nothing to perturb me and he noticed it.

"I haven't loosened your tongue yet, but so far I have only been doing you a favour! But I can act very differently from being polite!"

"I noticed," I almost said, but swallowed the words on the tip of my tongue. What profit was there in provoking the man? He was so pitiful in his angst, his fear of Englishmen and other phantoms, most probably most of all by his evil conscience. I found him anxious and insecure and therefore so out of control. I had the strong impression that he had completely lost his nerve.

---

126 Treason against a ruling monarch.

By now I had retrieved and donned my coat. The *landwachtman* standing by the door with his gun now repeated like a parrot the words of his captain in atrocious Dutch: "*Veuroet, noa d'auto![127]*" and he indicated the door with the barrel. Then I remembered something. If Froukje also had to come with us, who would care for Hans? He couldn't stay by himself in the house overnight!

I turned back into the hallway, the menacing barrel notwithstanding. The inspector was already halfway up the stairs. "What will happen tonight with my little boy?" I asked.

"I shall no longer exchange a single word with you," he replied, and turned away from me.

But Froukje had heard him. With her he would perhaps like to exchange a word or two about the fate of a child of two years!

Then out I went to the car. A *landwachtman* with a loaded gun followed me up the garden path. Without such weapons in their possession they were nothing but a bunch of cowardly, uneducated louts. My respect for the institution of the *Landwacht* after this first experience of them at close quarters was not greatly enhanced! Once the car door clicked shut behind me the chauffeur who had driven the gentlemen here hastened to assure me that he was not a party to this arrest. The good man was evidently afraid that I would think that and therefore he was feeling severely ill at ease.

The other 'comrades' who were so very brave in the backyard, stationed in the bushes and lying flat on the grass in the apple orchard, ready to fire at the first stowaway who fled the house, now stood down and relaxed, according to the neighbours who viewed the entire drama through their telescope.

After half to three quarters of an hour, the initial tension had

127 "Out to the car!"

dissipated and it now seemed their chances had passed of a big game shooting party in the wilds, targeting fleeing people. What a pity about those promised bonuses! They were now at ease; they stood around in desultory groups and lit cigarettes. The points of reddish-orange light gleamed through the branches of our late flowering apple trees. It was on that day, the 30th of May in the memorable year 1944...

I was still waiting in the car. The gentlemen now had the house fully illuminated. Evidently they were not required to follow the blackout regulations. All the lights in all the rooms were burning simultaneously, shining out through all the windows. I watched them from the car; they were nosing around the desk in the study and standing there reading our correspondence. Then the front door opened and there on the path appeared Froukje, carrying a large pink bundle: Hansje wrapped up in a blanket. Of course she was closely followed by a *landwachtman* who held a gun trained on her. Ooh, she might even make an attempt to escape with a heavy boy weighing thirty pounds in her arms! If that happened they would shoot her down at once. But Froukje was taking Hans to a family close by in the neighbourhood, where he sometimes played with a couple of older boys.

They had been given strict orders from the inspector that *Mevrouw* was not permitted to even see him. However, I did not know that and so I edged closer to the window. How long before I could see him? The blanket had fallen open in front of his face, and there I observed his tiny nose. A small finger was pointing and then a little toddler's voice said, "Car – doctor's car." Had he seen me sitting here and should I call Froukje to give him a kiss? Better not. He would then say *"Mama sootje*[128]*"* and start to cry when he was taken again from my lap. So I simply looked at him with eager, yearning eyes. The emotions of the driver surfaced visibly. He swallowed a lump in his throat and then said

___

128 "Darling Mama."

with a choking voice, "Damn!" That is the only time that I have ever appreciated a swearword.

In the six or seven weeks since Domie's departure we really had time enough to dispose of each piece of paper that could incriminate us. When the gentlemen were finally through with the house search and nothing had been found, the church was next on their list. It was now after eleven. They had to get the key from the sexton, who of course was already in bed. He ran agitatedly about the house in his long underwear, since his radio had been hidden in the church tower. Here everything was ransacked, but once again nothing was found. They even scoured the tombstones in the churchyard, shining their powerful torches under the overhanging coping and then taking a sharp look over the entire ground. Nor was our shed forgotten, where the newly shorn sheep with his yellow-green eyes astonished the visitors and looked back at them, blinking against the bright light. Finally, the investigation was considered over, but to my surprise, the car moved off in the wrong direction. It appeared that the NSB mayor of the neighbouring town had been drinking with our "peasant leader" during the search, and that we now had to go and get him.

When His Honour got in, he was accompanied by a strong smell of alcohol. I scarcely recognised him at first, he had become so fat. One fellow from the rear seat had to move to the front to accommodate him. So there were now three of us in front, but we just managed to fit. Then the car turned and drove back past the now abandoned *pastorie*, standing silently in the darkness of that May night. Our driver had another stop to make, at the farm where the Mice had been hiding for a few days. This too must have been discovered by betrayal, along with the fact that they had been harbouring students, because every time it came back to this common point – betrayal! Once more the mistress, daughter and son of the household would be startled by a house search. That was a miserable experience, but I found peace in the knowledge that the farm was now empty of 'illegals'.

That search was also unsuccessful. Froukje had to go along with us now on her bike, accompanied by an escort of the *Landwacht*. In the car, the conversation was about aircraft machine guns. What else would they talk about? They suddenly seemed so very human. Even that frightful inspector turned into an ordinary man for whom tobacco constituted a very important part of his life.

Chapter 57

At the police station, the inspector once again brought up his accusation of the day. The restated theme was that I had been transferring Jews into hiding with other people.

"Out of the question."

"Stop telling lies, woman!"

It seemed better not to continue any conversation on those terms. A young policeman with black curly hair was instructed to take me to my cell. He escorted me upstairs and right into the cell itself. Then I suddenly felt a hand grabbing my shoulder. I turned to look full into that open, honest face. He put a finger to his lips. I understood him immediately – it meant "SILENCE!"

"*Ja*, fine," I responded. Then he closed the door behind me.

But in the middle of the night, he switched on the light in my cell. The young agent stood once more next to my bunk where I had been sleeping fully dressed under my coat. There were no blankets, nor a pillow, only a hard straw mattress.

"Did they find out anything?" he whispered. He had witnessed the brief interrogation in the office because he was there at the time to register the names of all arriving prisoners, and did so with mine, also writing down the charge against me.

"Nothing concrete – they suspect something's been going on, but can't put their finger on exactly what."

"Then under all circumstances you must keep silent," he replied.

"*Ja*."

"Does your housemaid also know about all this? Shall I go and see her as well?"

"*Ja*, please – and tell her that if they say to her that *Mevrouw* has already confessed – so tell us everything – she must pay them no heed, and also tell her that she is not alone, and that God is with her and that she is fighting for a good cause."

He nodded, switched off the light and softly closed the cell door behind him.

I did not fall sleep again. There was too much noise for that. A few men with rough, bearded faces had already witnessed my arrival from behind their viewing hatch.

"Hé, *Juffie*,[129] what are you in for?" they had called in a rather collegial tone. Their speech carried the unmistakable cadence of the Amsterdam accent.

"That can't possibly interest you," I parried.

Now I heard these 'neighbours' snoring loudly. In other cells men chatted and swore – the sound of footsteps up and down the corridor. A drunken man was brought in, full of bluster and shouting loudly.

After long intervals a clock chimed somewhere in this big building: three o'clock... and after seeming endlessness... four o'clock.

Then suddenly a blackbird burst into song. His melody was so comforting that I fell asleep with the lines of Werumeus Buning's poem, *The Blackbird* coursing through my fast dissolving consciousness:

My God, who filleth all the world with flowers
And sun and light and joyous hearts hath made,
And me, to witness all thy wondrous powers
To taste thy waters hath my thirst assuaged.
For those in cells imprisoned call a prayer
Like swallows longing for their home and nest.

---

129 "Missy" – yet another colloquial form of "Juffrouw".

And only those who have thy bread to share,
will in their grief find comfort, peace and rest.
Just as the ploughman rips the fields asunder,
You plough my soul that further sleep is stayed,
Yet send me at each dawning this true wonder;
The blackbird's song that all my fears allayed.

At half past five I awoke. I looked around for the facecloth, soap, towel and pocket comb, which Froukje had packed together for me, and called out for permission to go downstairs. When no-one came to let me out of my cell I insistently called out again and again.

"What's all the hurry here?" asked a semi-gruff voice. It was the young agent from last night.

"I would like to have a wash down in the bathroom," I said, "because there are no facilities to do that in the cell."

Once gain the key grated as it turned in the lock. He let me out. Downstairs I saw Froukje walking along the corridor ahead of me. I thought she looked pale and upset and I felt sorry for her.

"Froukje, how are you? Did not you sleep?"

"No, not at all – I feel so badly homesick. But that nice officer gave me two peppermints. Would you like one?"

"Come on, Froukje, would you like to have a wash? Here's a towel and some soap. And did the agent pass my message onto you last night?"

"*Ja...* No, I won't say anything."

"Good girl, Froukje. You've thought it all through then?"

"*Ja*, but he knows a lot."

"He's only guessing... he knows nothing for certain."

"Don't tell them that you have had this contact with each other, because the rule says no contacts and no visits allowed!" said the young officer, a little concerned.

"Of course, I won't make any trouble for you."

Then it was back up the stairs – into the cell – and close the door.

"Could you put the light out, then I might sleep a little longer?"

I spread my towel out at the head of my straw mattress (I might pick up a few little pests here) and put the toiletries in the large satchel that the Mice had made for Polletje and which Froukje had handed to me through the car door window right at the last moment before we drove off.

At least I had just had a refreshing wash and combed my hair and was feeling human again after the nausea which I suffer from every morning to varying degrees, and particularly now in this dank place. When the light was out, it was pitch dark in the cell, because there was no window.

At eight o'clock I would hopefully get my breakfast. At seven o'clock I now definitely decided to get up and asked if I could read something. They gave me a book: a ten-penny rag of twelve murder mysteries, quite in keeping with the Wild West performance of the previous evening, which was still so fresh in my memory. They returned at eight with three thick slices of bread and jam. Almost straightaway I devoured one of them. Instead of tea I asked for water, which they thought was stupid, but I was happy with the choice.

Visiting hour was at eleven. But not for me; for my neighbours. The cells were overcrowded. A mother and daughter came to visit their son and brother "who had not wanted to go to Germany". Now they'd really got him, and he would be sent off to Borkum. They also peeked in through my hatch to where I was sitting to catch the slightest breezes of fresh air which wafted in from outside. On that warm morning I felt as if I was suffocating in the cloying atmosphere of the cell. They asked me compassionately why I was in jail, and out of sympathy gave me a boiled egg. I ate it up immediately and, like a little child, also ate the bacon sandwich that they passed me through the peephole hatch. They promised to go on my behalf to see Bertram, the headmaster of the Grammar School here in town. Bertram would do anything to help me find better reading material than I could ever get here.

When the attendant returned, he asked if I wanted some stew consisting of potatoes and sliced beans.

"Of course, I still have to eat!"

So now to wait for the food. I'd just as soon lie down on my bunk, because I was feeling a little dizzy. How long would all this take? And what would I say eventually when they called me again for an interrogation – would I have to stay here indefinitely after all? Under no circumstances could I admit to dealing with fugitives who were still in hiding. That would mean betraying them together with those who were protecting them. All those ones had to be exempt from any mention on my part, and that I could do, by appearing to give a full cooperative explanation yet revealing nothing. He definitely knew something; we had been betrayed, that was absolutely certain. The Chief had indeed come to warn us of the danger. Now it came down to this; to limit the fallout from the disaster to the smallest possible proportions and to say only those things that hurt no-one apart from myself. If I told them about the Mice, he would not be able to catch them. After all, they had already left for Poland. The six or eight others I was charged with sheltering could be attributed to 'popular' exaggeration. For me, however, the sentence remained the same, no matter whether I had harboured two or ten. They could send me to the camp at Vught, ransack our house and property, or do both if they so choose, but it would now be up to me at the coming interrogation to grit my teeth and only mention things that would not harm, because in such circumstances I carried the fate of many people in my hands. I stood surety for them... my life for theirs. That was an appalling responsibility to carry, almost too heavy for one to bear.

And ye shall be brought before governors and kings for my sake, for a testimony against them and the Gentiles. But when they deliver you up, take no thought how or what ye shall speak: for it shall be given you in that same hour what ye shall speak.[130]

---

130 Matthew 10:18-19.

That was true, too. Jesus had said it. The Apostles were often brought before the heathen authorities to be held accountable in regard to one thing or another, and God had enabled them to turn this into an occasion for Christian witness.

That for which I was on trial was a matter of conscience.

A cowardly attitude was not appropriate. I would have to defend my belief fully and squarely over against his. After all, when it came down to it, it was better to save a life by showing Christ's love than to destroy it out of hatred and racial delusions. Surely this truth must be so patently evident to everyone that it seems foolish to devote many words to it. Had the world then become such a vast madhouse that you had to try to prove the obvious; that white is white, and black is black?

Our Lord had but to give me the words to speak "in that very same hour" as He had promised He would.

Believe in God, that is: Trust in His Word, I read one time on the wall plaque of a pastor's house in a neighbouring community. I would dare to take my stance from that text.

A deep plate, piled with sliced beans was pushed through the hatch window.

I had just taken it inside when a message came that I was wanted by the inspector. The time had come! The iron cell door swung open and a moment or so later I was standing in a large room which looked out on a square, where the red hawthorn was in flower.

It did me good to see the trees in the sunlight again while I was waiting. While the inspector was dealing with one of his subordinates, I was permitted to sit at his desk, directly opposite him. Meanwhile a song came to mind; one of the hymns that we often sang at our church fellowships with Domie:

If God, my God but for me is
Though foes are sorely pressing,
Through stresses, sadness, work withal,
He brings my soul a blessing.
Compassed round by angels bright,
I see their stars shine out at night
And flowers gird my pathway.

Whate'er the threats that rage around,
My Saviour still doth lead me.
In darkened vales I fear no ill,
His rod and staff do guide me.
He leads me onwards to the goal,
His waters flow to heal my soul,
In meadows green he hides me.

It became apparent that Froukje had been interviewed just before my hearing. She was completely outside of this whole affair, the inspector again assured her, and therefore no punishment awaited her if she told him who had been in our house. She had simply been arrested according to routine procedure, but in order, by threats and bribes, to induce her to commit treachery! "Furthermore," the inspector continued, "no one will ever be aware that you have said anything. Your name will not even be mentioned at all!" With me the case was a little different. The previous night I had pointed out that a married woman under Dutch law[131] was considered voiceless and unable to testify, so they were legally on the wrong footing with me. But the inspector assured me that I would nevertheless be held responsible.

"Domie they won't catch – he is too slippery," chuckled our neighbours opposite the *pastorie* who had watched the whole raid from

---

131 The position of the woman was defined legally as a *femme covert*.

behind their windows. These gentlemen of the police apparently thought likewise. And so they came to get me. First to see what I would reveal under duress about Jews and their hideouts, and if I proved to be easy prey, they could start anew on fresh leads to track down my husband. Not all at once, but step by step they'd draw nearer to their goal. But although I had not yet been questioned about my husband and the inspector had even deliberately sidestepped that subject, Froukje has been questioned extensively about him. How long has Domie been gone? Did he ever give lessons to Communists?

"Lessons to Communists?" said Froukje, highly surprised.

"*Ja*, he has been charged with giving English lessons to Communists, for later on; so that when the English attempt to invade here they can serve as guides."

"But Domie never gives any lessons," Froukje said. Her astonishment was so real, that the inspector was clearly disarmed from continuing that line of questioning.

"*Mevrouw* teaches English, because she has studied it. She teaches it to me too, because I work under the G.O.[132] and for that you need some knowledge of one of the foreign languages. And she teaches many others – also a few farm workers, but not English... later maybe, but first Dutch because you have to first know that well," said Froukje by way of explanation.

"Oh, so the pastor did not give lessons?"

"No not a single one," Froukje replied.

Who were his friends then? Whom did he often visit? Who brought the groceries round?

She had to divulge everything that she knew, because when she was later transported to Groningen, they would make her feel their iron fist! Here she was still treated humanely, but there were German methods of interrogation such that the biggest brutes usually succumbed within

---

132 *Georganiseerd Overleg* – literally 'Organised Consultation' – A human resources network that handled placements, work conditions and the like for member employees.

three days and confessed all. However, would she, as a young girl, be able to endure that?

Again such foolish confusion! As if their savagery had anything to do with moral courage and inner strength!

Froukje thought of Wil and said bravely, "Sir, I would hate to be sent to Groningen, but if that is your duty, you must do that."

So, nothing to go on here. He was on the back foot now and forced to compromise so as not to lose face.

"If you tell me now where the *Dominee* often went visiting, I'll let you go."

Froukje heaved a sigh of relief. At least this was a perfectly innocent question.

"To visit the members of his Church Council," she said. But wouldn't it be odd if a Minister was not doing that? That would be a sign that something was really amiss.

"Who are they?"

She named various members of the Council.

"Does Captain K. sometimes come to the *pastorie*?"

This was the name of the captain who brought us the greetings of our Mice and Wil from the cattle truck passing through Winschoten station on its way to Poland. Who had betrayed him?

"No, in the year since I've been here, the captain has not been in our house once. Maybe sometimes in church."

"Has the pastor sometimes visited your neighbours?"

"*Ja*, sure, but only because they were neighbours and not because it had anything to do with hiding people, I reckon."

"If you had made that statement last night, about whom he had been going to visit, I would not have needed to arrest you," said the inspector.

"*Ja*, but you didn't ask me that last night," Froukje said. "You asked me a lot of other things instead!"

He did not take the matter any further, only saying that he was pleased to be able to grant her freedom.

Bah, what a job! To be a police inspector in these times, and an NSB inspector at that! It seems to me that you could only succeed if you have boundless ambition and hope to get ahead via your connections with the NSB. To me his naked ambition seemed completely out of all proportion. This due to the fact that his toes had been mightily stomped on when I stood up to him, that imperious inspector whose power over me I had been obliged to feel, when he arrived to net his eight or ten villainous Jews.

When I came in, he opened the interview with the words:

"I was able to grant your maid her freedom to return home, and would like to do the same with you."

Freedom! An enticing perspective for someone who has spent one night and a morning in a damp, dark, locked cell. But beware! What viper lurks here in the grass? If I had to obtain my freedom at the expense of the liberty of others, I did not desire it.

"I know certain things affirmatively," he continued, "and it's up to you to confess them and not to be rude and defiant like you were yesterday. I would prefer that we talk together as human beings."

He did indeed put on a manly tone and I decided now that I would say to him that which I could not say last night, because he had pompously asserted himself then as 'the inspector' who was on the hunt with his foxhounds.

Touched with the delightfulness of this sunny morning and the calm atmosphere of the spacious, well-furnished room, all threats and fears lost their monstrous proportions and dwindled away back to normal.

"What you said about eight or ten Jews was just a shot in the dark," I said. "That's why I facetiously replied with 'Twenty'. But we're here now in private, and so I want to tell you something, not in your role as a police inspector, but to you as a man!"

He nodded.

"You spoke yesterday about Christianity. This means that according to our faith, we should be prepared to help anyone who is in need, whatever that entails. Therefore if somebody came to us who was persecuted and their life was in danger, and asked us for protection, we would willingly offer that to him or her at the expense of our own security.

He nodded again.

"And so... and you may assuredly regard this as an official statement... a Jewish photographer, who, when I was working at my editorial office in Amsterdam, had offered me press photos for the magazine I was working on, then wrote a letter at the beginning of the Jewish persecutions in which she asked for shelter under our roof. According to those same convictions we could not nor wished to refuse her. We took her in with another friend, who was a typist. They were with us for a year and a half after which they returned to Amsterdam. Later, I got a letter from them saying that they were being held at Westerbork and from there they were taken to Poland."

Silence fell. Last night he had said angrily to me that I didn't have to sacrifice myself for Jews who "would all be caught anyway" but now my revelation seemed to grant him no further satisfaction; that these juicy targets had both been captured and their eventual tragic fate in Poland had not been forestalled.

"But your husband has cared for as many as eight or ten," he remarked, surrendering his ground. "I'm sure of it."

You really have no idea that there are actually about two hundred, I thought, but said nothing.

"And where did these young Jewish women arrive from, when they came to you?" he asked.

"They were picked up from the station," I said.

"By a Jew?"

"No, by an Aryan, a friend of one of them, who is now himself sitting in a camp, probably at Amersfoort, for helping the Jews."

"And how did they make their journey? By car?"

"No, just on the train."

His curiosity seemed satisfied.

"Would you submit what you just said as a formal statement?" he asked, reaching for a notepad.

"*Ja*, certainly."

He took notes. "These will go to the German authorities," he concluded. "You are now free to go, on the condition that you promise me that you will remain at your home address."

"*Ja*, that is my firm intention anyway, otherwise I could have easily departed much earlier together with my husband, and would not have waited for the arrival of the *Landwacht* whose eventual coming was completely foreseeable."

I had promised him to stay at home and realised exactly what purpose that served. The Germans could come and get me at any time – for whatever reason – particularly to be used as bait, with which they hoped to catch my husband. Hopefully he wouldn't be so careless as to make a flying visit, but instead stayed far away!

The inspector was sufficiently thoughtful to call for a taxi for me, but a further half hour passed before it arrived. So meanwhile I dashed over to Bertram's house. When he saw me, he looked like Rhoda must have looked when she saw Peter standing before her on the threshold in the night, after the angel released him from prison. Similarly, he seemed to see me as an apparition, because he knew from a student in our village what had happened to us. He uttered an astonished exclamation:

"How did you get here?"

"I've come straight from prison," I said, and had to tell him the whole saga. There was food on the table and I was able to get to work on that while awaiting the taxi's arrival. I took it gratefully, because my appetite had not suffered at all during my ordeal.

The special taxi now picked me up at Bertram's. In retrospect it was indeed an honour to be picked up by the police, although the chauffeur re-educated me on that point, because he turned quietly confidential and spoke of his own experiences in joining the 'good cause' for which he now worked. But how soothing it was to see the flowers again, and to feel the sun on my back and how lovely it was to come home!

Froukje was feeling a certain heaviness in her spirit, since she had told the police that Domie came home to visit the Church Council and all its members. She set off by bike along the road to tell them that we were now free and to confess what she had said to assist the process. At that moment De Lange was with Elderling to consult about what they could do as a Church Council to have us released again. "We can't do without her here," said De Lange, "and we must bring those people to understand that."

They were still busy deliberating when they saw Froukje cycling along the path.

"Well I'll be...! There's Froukje!" Both of them raced for the door.

"Come right inside, my girl!"

"Both of us have been freed!" said Froukje. "But I gave them your names and also said that Domie often came back to visit his Church Council."

"And what is that to us?"

"You could right well get a house search from them soon."

"Let them come, you hear! With pleasure," said De Lange. "We're happy to deal with them. Did you say anything else?"

"No, I said *niks* after that."

"Well how about that! Look at you! You did right bravely well, lass. Where's *Mevrouw*?"

"Went home by taxi, but I wanted to bike back, since I brought it with me."

"You're quite right, lass!"

Froukje now had only one remaining wish, and that was to come home as soon as possible, so they let her depart.

Chapter 58

I hardly knew my luck when I was back home. Increasingly people came to congratulate us on the outcome. An old working woman shook her head when I met her on the road and said,

"Beasts, that's what they are. Man, oh man, they are beasts!"

Even Petertje ran around to the *pastorie* to see us. He had not wanted to go to school that morning as he had to look after our sheep! But Moeke had sent him off anyway with the admonishment, "The sheep can look after itself right well!"

"But I just won't learn anything!" complained Petertje.

"You'll get going anyway!"

And so Petertje went to school, but that much was learned that day I very much doubt.

Afterwards I was assured that was the case – on that morning there were others as well who couldn't keep their minds on the work they were supposed to be doing.

All this activity showed that the village sympathised greatly with my plight and that I need not feel lonely here for long, even with Domie away. And I could bring Hans back home as soon as he'd had his afternoon nap!

However, there was a sting in the tail.

A few days after our release, the *Landwacht* showed that they had indeed taken note of our current food stocks, because one morning three men in black uniforms again appeared on the *stoep*. Their leader did the talking and told us they had come to relieve us of six *mud* of wheat.[133]

"We don't have that much, but by all means go up to the loft and see for yourselves what's there."

A quick tally showed that there were only four sacks of wheat plus a bag where the boys had discarded the bran from the last milling. However, I did not find it necessary to point out that fact since they had neglected to check inside. They had been sent by their captain to requisition six *mud*, but the most that they could return to base with was five sacks.

"That bag has been attacked by mice," said the leader, pointing at the bag of bran. "We must have another sack, because there is a big hole in that one. Where did you get these from?"

On the bags were stencilled several names: De Lange, Elderling and certain others.

"From various farmers round about," I said.

"Which farmer who provided some wheat lives the closest to you?"

"De Lange."

"Well then, that little peasant must come back here to carry the sacks down from the loft for us," decreed the leader pompously. I thought immediately of the great size of the 'peasant' De Lange, with his long strong legs and arms, and who was about the size of two leaders! Well, he would see for himself shortly, because he set off forthwith to visit the De Lange farm. And in all other respects as well, our own 'peasant' stood head and shoulders above this leader of the raiding party. Would the fellow himself actually notice? It seems that our noble *Landwacht* is not generally endowed with much sense of proportion.

After their leader departed, I stayed with the other two 'gentlemen' in the loft and thought how sad it was that my plan to give the farmers their wheat back, or to get it all out of the house by some other means, would not be fulfilled. Recently there had been something different

---

133 About 400 kg.

happening each day, beginning from the date that the *pastorie* was evacuated. Last week had been the celebration of Whitsunday. Obviously Monday was out as far as moving things; Tuesday we were taken away ourselves, so these large accumulated stocks, which had been calculated to feed eight guests for a time, had been left in place. Well, nothing could be done about it now.

The leader had been away for some time and both black-clothed assistants had stationed themselves in the attic room. They sat there by the desk, totally at ease, as if they were quite at home. And in the Mice's room, if you please! Then the insolent voice of the boldest of them rang out through the loft, "*Mevrouw*! Come here!"

I walked into the room and asked from the doorway,

"What can I do for you?"

"What is this room?" he inquired sternly.

"An attic. My husband used it to develop photos."

"*Ja*, but these photos, they're Jewish!"

"Oh really?"

He sat with his legs crossed on a chair, and against the light he was holding a small negative taken from an opened box. His colleague sat on another chair, over which Lily's travel rug was still folded.

"*Ja*, see! It looks like a Jewish gathering."

"That may well be, but they could also be Turks or Arabs. They are in any case Orientals, as you see by their clothing."

"How did you come by them?" He continued to play the role of his inspector.

"My husband once made a long journey, all the way to Palestine."

"Why? Intentionally to help the Jews?"

"No, at that time they were not considered so important. It was before the war. But surely you have heard that a Minister is supposed to know something about the Holy Land?"

"A beautiful country, Palestine," commented one *landwachtman* to another. He obviously had some geographical knowledge about such matters. "Why ever did the Jews come here?... one may well ask."

"It's been a very good while since they came here," I rashly remarked. Now the gentlemen felt themselves on very thin ice. History proved not to be their strong suit. The previous speaker changed tack.

"Why don't they go back there?"

"The Arabs do not want them," the other replied.

Among these silly ramblings the brusque one suddenly returned to his line of questioning. "This is no room for a pastor! There is way too... too much..."

"Not nearly enough refinement, do you mean? *Ja*, but we regard warmth and comfort far more important than elegance. When I sat for an exam, I was working up here too. It saved fuel."

There sounded the boots of the leader again on the attic stairs, followed by Klema, a farm labourer of De Lange's, who was carrying a large, empty sack.

"Right! You need to carry these other sacks back down," he commanded Klema. "You originally brought them up here."

"Not me, hear!"

"*Ja*, indeed you did. You're a farmer."

That blunt assertion of the townsman betrayed all his contempt for the common man of the land, whom they always collectively called farmers.

"Me? Not me, hear!" said Klema once again.

"Here... load up and get moving!"

Klema did so, then swung the first full sack nimbly over his shoulder and descended the stairs. I went in to bat for them. "Our farmers have always been very keen to get their empty bags back."

"Not going to happen," said the leader. "These were seized and so they will be marked as such. Do you have any labels we can use?"

"No."

"Then we'll make them ourselves."

They now dusted their pants down, brushing it from their knees, after having dragged all the full sacks out from behind the cupboard.

While Klema carried the sacks one by one downstairs, it was the leader's opportunity to resume his questioning. He picked up the negatives and examined them.

"So, Pastor has travelled that far – all the way to Palestine?"

"*Ja*, and all the way by bike, too!"

I assumed with good reason that such a worthy sporting performance probably would make more of an impression than Domie's studiousness, and I was not mistaken.

"Well then!" he said, clearly impressed. "How long was he away?"

"Six months."

"And all the way on the bike? No travelling by boat or train or something?"

"Bike as far as Egypt, *Ja*... except of course the Bosporus crossing. He couldn't get over the water there with just a bike. But on the return trip, via the Mediterranean, he caught a boat to Italy and then travelled on the train back to Amsterdam, where we were living at the time."

"And he is now in hiding?"

"Ja."

"Why?"

"He will have his reasons."

"Where is he right now?"

"Fortunately for me, I don't know."

"I don't get it."

"Well no, but disappearing has become commonplace, especially among pastors."

"If you have a clean slate, then you don't need to go into hiding."

"*Ja*, I'd say that's true."

Now Klema was all done and we were able to go back downstairs.

My people are destroyed for lack of knowledge[134] says one of the prophets of the Old Testament.

---

134 Hosea 4:6.

I find myself musing on this truth. This young man was not evil, but through the total absence of basic wholesome life experiences, was inclined toward grabbing everything he could for himself.

People with his kind of ignorance tended to believe anything, and so they also became victims of a bad kind of populist faction. If they had known something of the 'Old Book' they would have had at least a more substantial historical and geographical knowledge, and more understanding of people in general as well as of the Jews in particular, and furthermore a sound knowledge of good and evil. In all these respects, they are presently blank sheets of paper, awaiting the Divine Scribe.

The leader asked for a clothes brush for him and his men. They were handed one. They gave themselves a final brush down out on the back steps, then they moved off round to the front of the house. They produced more labels for the bags which were then placed on a cart. "Seized by the *Landwacht*", the labels read. Klema had been ordered to take them outside to the leader. Our fence-line was packed with children watching the proceedings.

One of the *Landwacht* had absent-mindedly left his gun in the pantry. I took it out to him on the garden path.

"That's not a toy," I said, handing it over. He gave me a suspicious glance.

"Our little boy might want to try to cock it, so it is better that you take it with you."

Then Klema set off down the garden path pushing his rattling farm cart loaded with sacks.

"What a pity!" observed the schoolchildren. "Now we'll have to bring some bags over tonight.[135]" And the leader of the raiders also said

---

135 The local farmers kept secret stocks in reserve, out of which they helped their community. The children are intending to return later with fresh supplies of grain for the *pastorie*.

something in the same vein: "We can certainly take all this away," he said, "but tonight they'll have it back again. And to Klema he made the point that, "You can easily tell from all this wheat that they had people hiding in the house." His conclusion was not so lacking in insight, after all.

Chapter 59

It is a mild summer's evening at the beginning of August. The rowans are already adorned with orange-red berries and the roses are in full bloom in our garden. Sunlight sparkles on the tops of the pine trees under which I had walked with Hans not long before. The sky is a delicate blue. The peaceful silence is reminiscent of anything but war. Only when a noisy plane flies low over the rooftops and Hans is startled awake and starts to cry in his cot does this reality become almost palpable along with the memory of a recently suffered, vivid nightmare. Because I'm far from home, away from the land that will be bathing in this evening light; away from the precious Groningen *pastorie*, whose image is almost continually before my eyes.

I've not written in a long time, because the flow of my life has wended its way through fairly quiet country lanes: community work, catechism classes, house visits and visiting the sick, garden and housework, the constant care and education of Hans, the expected growth of our new baby. All together enough to make a life rich and full, and to instil a profound peace, which gracefully heals both mind and body, after all the emotions of the previous months. But a week ago, Polletje, who was working elsewhere during the summer months, cycled up our garden path to where I was minding Hans and a little girl playmate by the front door. Hans was so glad to see Polletje; he walked over to her and gave her a kiss. But Polletje did not seem her old happy self, so the surprised joyous greeting died on my lips. Why was she here? Was she bringing us the tidings of Job? She propped her bike against the wall of the house, stepped into the hall and began sobbing desolately with her arm around me.

"What is it?"

Then the realisation dawned that Domie had missed a meeting yesterday with De Lange, and I recalled how worried that had made me. Surely Domie would not forget an appointment like that?

So then, he had not been able to come to the appointed place for one reason or another. There was always something bad behind it. The old fear from last night surfaced again.

"Has Domie been arrested?" I asked flatly.

Polletje nodded. We went to the study where the sunlight streamed in through the tall windows, but we sat there, dejected and defeated. Polletje finally began to talk, by fits and starts, but it seemed as if the words came from very far away and I could not grasp the full import of their ominous message.

A policeman, Klaas Rodermond, who worked secretly for the NSB, had managed to win Domie's confidence, and when after a few weeks Domie had told him everything, the man betrayed him by handing him over to the *Sicherheitsdienst*[136] for a handful of tobacco and the promise of promotion. But when the *Sicherheitsdienst* came to arrest Domie, Rodermond played his role of trusty confidante so well that he almost got arrested himself. So Domie still does not know precisely how this happened and whom he has to thank for it.

Polletje had brought an anonymous letter with her from Haarlem. "You probably have heard," stated the letter, "that your husband has been arrested here in Haarlem. He is now in the local prison and is facing all his circumstances very bravely, because he knows how to draw strength from his faith. He wants you to know that he loves you dearly and you must also be brave. Soon something will happen. Take courage!"

---

136 The SD – the Nazi Security Intelligence Service of the SS.

It was not possible to calculate which consequences now could ensue for both him there and for me here. A painful insecurity... the feeling that you can't even analyse your dilemma step by step... was frightening. What was I to do in the circumstances? Would they now come to haul me off for interrogation? How much did they know? Was Domie caught using his own name? Must I flee? Had they ransacked the house where he was?

"You must also be brave..."

I swallowed the lump in my throat. Janny was busy making preserves of beans in the kitchen. She had replaced Froukje who was on vacation. I would go and just ask her to continue with that task until I returned, because I urgently had to go and see Elderling. Nothing of this should be talked about, but the Church Council had to be informed. I told Janny that I had to leave for a pressing matter.

"Not to do with Domie?"

My face was clear to read, that it was indeed something that concerned Domie.

"*Juffrouw* Polletje is here. Go to her and... " But Polletje had just entered the kitchen.

"Just tell her, would you?" I said. "But she must not speak of it to anyone, as that makes it more dangerous for Domie."

Then I collected my bike and rode away.

It was at the time of the pea harvest. *Mevrouw* Elderling told me I would have to go out into the fields and there I would find her husband. The field boundary lane was of hard, compacted clay; I could cycle along there. Right up to the very end, where the embankment rose to the railway line, the land was entirely planted with peas. When he caught sight of me, Elderling came over.

"Domie's been caught!" I said promptly and without preamble. He looked intently at me for a moment. We walked together further down the lane and I told him what I knew.

"What we have feared for so long has finally happened," remarked Elderling.

In the far distance, from the other end of the lane, someone was cycling toward us. "Is that De Lange?" I asked. It turned out to be the case, but when I could at last make out his carefree, smiling face, I added, "He doesn't even suspect a thing."

And so it proved.

"*Mevrouw* told me I would find you working out in the pea fields," remarked De Lange. "Is there something the matter?"

Then sounded the same dull refrain that also clanged constantly inside my head as if it could find no exit: "Domie's been caught."

The face before me tightened and the arm that fumbled with a hand in his pocket remained stiff and bent. His whole figure seemed suddenly older and careworn. He first said nothing. What could he say? Another ship that had run aground within sight of port?

Finally he managed to utter, "...That's why Domie was not at the meeting yesterday."

"*Ja*, my anxiety was justified."

"I never would have imagined! Man, man, I never would have imagined!" lamented De Lange.

The two men were so overcome with emotion. Now the three of us walked back down the lane, but we said nothing. Each of us was filled with our own oppressive thoughts. The sun was shining and the land was green. A pair of pigeons flapped high above us. Poor Domie; he could not do likewise. The free bird had been caught and locked up in the dark. He had also been physically abused, but at the time I did not know that.

"Maybe Vught... or worse," Elderling said at last. I knew only too well what he meant. Domie had worked on such a large stage. He knew that he was putting his life at risk. Many soldiers on the various fronts died every day; every second in a great battle there fell dozens, hundreds, maybe thousands. But had he sat safely at home, waiting for others to stand in the gap? No, he had also fully committed himself to the ongoing fight. Domie left me a poem written by one of his comrades who had been shot. That poem was completed by Jan Campert in his cell only one hour before his death:

The Eighteen Dead

A cell is but two meters long
And scarce two meters wide.
Yet smaller is the piece of land
Where I shall yet abide.
Where nameless I shall find my rest
Beside my comrades all,
And we who number eighteen men
Shan't see the evening fall.

O sweetness fair of air and lands
From Holland's free foreshore.
But once our foes o'erran these strands
No rest would reassure.
What can a man, sincere and true
Yet do on such a day?
But kiss his child, and kiss his wife
And join the futile fray.

I knew the job I had begun,
A task of troubles dire.
The heart that could not fair resist
Makes naught of threat nor fire.
It knows how once this country fought
For Freedom's honoured prize,
Before a cursed violent hand
Had willed it otherwise.

Before our oath could raise the fight
The relentless foe, unbound,

Broke Holland's strength, and trod her neck;
Their fire destroyed our ground.
Before appeals to rights were made
For justice and relief,
Our land was made their place for spoil
And plundered by a thief.

The dark Pied Piper of Berlin
Pipes now his melody.
As surely as I'll be dead soon,
My dearest I'll not see.
No more to break our family bread,
Nor sleep with her in rest.
Beware of all their snares and plans
That put you to the test!

Remember, you who read these words,
My comrades in distress,
And stand by them through thick and thin,
In all their troubles, bless!
For we did also think of you,
Our land and people proud,
For every night there dawns a day
Whence fadeth every cloud.

I see the early morning sky
Reach through the window high.
My God, make me Thy dying light,
And hear my anxious cry!
Just as each of us can fail,
Forgive me all my sins.
Now make me face death like a man
Just as the race begins.

That afternoon I had an interview with Elderling at his home together with the Chief, who no longer dared to come to the *pastorie*. I told him what had happened as objectively as possible, then added my own analysis. There were two possibilities, it seemed to me. During the raids which the *Landwacht* had conducted a week ago on several farms, including over at Elderling's, they openly admitted that they had come looking for Domie. But now that he was in their clutches maybe they would leave me alone. The other more likely possibility, however, was that they would now also arrest me for interrogation, in order to play the two of us off against each other. The Chief nodded. "There's only one way for you," he said. "You should leave here and not fall prey to those diabolical methods of the Germans. Because of the satanic nature of their system, you don't want to be exposed to any interrogation of that sort. You must never make any personal acquaintance with their sadism."

"But how can that work if I leave everything behind; the church, the lads in hospital who were wounded by the shelling of their train, etc.?"

"What about arranging for an assistant Minister," was the reply.

"And our home? Won't they take everything away when I'm gone?"

"*Mevrouw*, if we come out of this war, and we still have a shirt on, then we should be happy. I did not hear one Jew still grieving over the loss of his furniture, as if they were an issue of life or death. Those material things do come back to us in time."

"It is easy to reason that way when you're not facing the possibility of loss yourself. I could just as easily say to someone, 'Go on! Leave the whole lot behind', but there is also such a thing as a nostalgic attachment to the books we've collected, or to the furnishings that my husband built or those that we bought together."

He laughed an unconcerned laugh.

"That's always the way with women: attached to their stuff."

"It's probably one of our weaknesses, *ja*, but all the same I hate to leave it all. Even so I shall listen to sound reason and follow your urgent advice... for the sake of my husband and our good cause."

Chapter 60

There was not much time to lose. If we were to act, we had to be quick. It was already late in the afternoon. I decided to go that very same evening, taking Hans with me and the most essential clothing for both of us. The sandwich which Janny had prepared for me I only ate under sufferance. I did not have much of an appetite. My mind was full of last minute arrangements: money, ration coupons, insurance stamps, this and that... all these I relayed to Janny, and asked her to make up a list, which was an even better idea.

Hans toddled around us, not having to go to bed. He could not fail to notice that something unusual was afoot, and readily discerned from the tone of our voices that it was nothing to be happy about. Finally the suitcase was perched up on the back of my bike and Hans was seated snugly in the basket on the handlebar. It was getting on for nine. Without a puncture we could still reach our destination by 10pm, when curfew fell. We would seek shelter at Bertram's for the night. My life would now resemble those of the many fugitives on the run during the current reign of terror.

"Bye, Janny, take good care of everything. I do hope to come back here again."

"Bye, *Mevrouw*, I'm going to fetch Froukje tonight, then we'll be here together. And tomorrow I'll bring another suitcase to the station for you."

"But Froukje is on vacation."

"*Ja*, but she said I had to warn her as soon as you left, or if you were arrested."

Touched by such loyalty and devotion, I rode down the garden path and cast a last look back at the good old house. Janny closed the gate behind me. Passing by familiar farms, here and there along the road we came across groups of children. "Hello Hans!... Hi Hans!" they shouted. "Where are you going?" Hans asked me that as well, when we failed to enter a single gate, but kept cycling on and on, as far as Hans had ever been, and as late as it had ever been on a bike trip. "Where are we going, Mama?"

"We're going out tonight to stay somewhere, and now you have to be very sweet with all the aunts and uncles where we're staying."

Och, he really did his very best, no doubt about it, but by the time he had slept in four different beds over two days (including for his afternoon naps) the latent reaction finally burst forth after all that travelling and trekking. When I came upstairs one evening, he was crying dejectedly. I took him beside me in my own bed.

"Mus' go home, Mama, mus' go home," he sobbed.

He began coughing, then vomiting, over myself, his own clothes and the bed. I got up and bumped into a chair in the darkened room. In a strange house you can't find your way around so easily. He vomited once again. Where was something I could use to catch it all in? But it was too late; the whole stream had already spattered over the bed. Alarmed by this he cried again and I felt such deep compassion for the small upright waxen figure that sat so unhappily in his cot and longed for home. I forgot there and then my own distress and concerns about Domie, about whose fate I had no other certain knowledge than that he was in prison. My thoughts had continually been turning to him in his cell, and I prayed almost constantly for him. I was almost certain that he did that for me too, and that in the solitude of the night, our prayers and thoughts reached out to each other and joined hands. But now the care of our child had become my acute concern. How Papa would have softened for him, when he saw him sitting there with his pale little face and the dirty lines around his mouth! When I was sure that there was no more to come, I washed him clean, dressed him in fresh clothes and then gave myself and the bed a clean-up. Hansje stood chattering away in his cot.

"In Mama's bed," he pleaded. "I'm Mama's li'l pet."

So I laid him down in my own bed, switched off the light, got in and held him very close to me to warm him. I spoke to him gently about the farm where we fetched our milk every day and about all the animals there that he knew. He relaxed, the tension draining away, and fell happily asleep. In his imagination he was back home, back once again in our own familiar surroundings.

But that night I decided to seek out a fixed address where we could stay for a longer while – for Hans' sake at least. The wandering life was not suitable for such a little chap. I couldn't turn to my own family for help, because the enemy would soon be looking for me there, but I still maintained one strong friendship that dated right back to my childhood. I would go to this friend and I would certainly be received there with open arms.

I had a lot of difficulty finding a curate for our local ministry. I had initially consulted with Elderling, but to no avail. The professor from Utrecht to whom I turned informed me that there were no churchmen available at this time. My parents-in-law had already set out for the *pastorie*, where they would care for it in the interim. It only remained for me to glean any information regarding my husband as soon as possible. Therefore I paid a visit to my brother, whose 19-year-old daughter belonged to Domie's team of Resistance co-workers.

What my brother told me of the situation was very alarming. Domie had been seized in the company of two deserting German officers and an undercover Jew. At the 'hearing' they had pressed him to name names. To this end, they had mistreated him. His legs, nose and ears were all beaten with a truncheon. The Resistance was steadfastly working behind the scenes on Domie's behalf, but for the present we stood before a solid wall that barred our passing. They had originally wanted to liberate him from the prison in Haarlem on the coming Saturday. All previous plans to this end had been very thoroughly prepared, but on the Friday he had suddenly been transferred to Amsterdam. They could not effect an escape from that infamous Gestapo prison on the Weteringschans. *Ja...* escape! Surely that had been their original plan. In the anonymous letter, they had communicated that something was about to happen, and as a consequence I had to change my address quickly. And now, to our dismay, they did not dare risk an attempt because he had been transferred to the formidable Weteringschans. Their surprise assault which one week ago would have succeeded, had failed to materialise. And now Domie was in the clutches of the enemy with no chance of rescue. I had no more words to express my distress, but fled to the loft of our family home where my brother now lived. In my childhood days I had always headed up there for shelter when I felt sad. But what was that in comparison with the dark hours that I was now going through? Pitch-black night seemed all around me, without resolution, without hope. All the hours we had lived through together were now being vibrantly relived in my mind. Would I never see Domie again? Not one single message to him could get through. Would I hear no more of him, never know how he felt, or thought, or prayed?

I had last seen him at Bertram's home, when I had received word that he was there and that I could go to meet him. He had turned up in town to attend a large church meeting.

"But if you feel that's too risky, I will not go," he had offered. He had been so soft toned, almost meek. He was enjoying the room where we were sitting together to eat. "It's as if we have gone out to dine together," he observed with a smile.

"I can't stay too long though," I replied. "This afternoon at one I have a catechism class at the Hörn."

"Please... phone them to call it off."

"*Ja*, but that's not really the right thing to do."

"For just this once. We see each other so little."

I had complied, of course. I did as requested even though it was with a heavy heart. But now that Domie was no longer free, I had to be doubly faithful.

On that blessed afternoon together we would not be separated from one another. We had realised that each time we met could be the last. However, Bertram's room needed to be used for another purpose; there was someone coming to visit that afternoon. A few times we received a gentle hint to that effect. I would have preferred to accompany Domie to his local church appointment but could not countenance that. Domie was incognito, wearing electrician's overalls while outside in the street. In the vestry of the church he would take them off again. But if I walked alongside him, he would attract attention as we were both known here in this town. However, once I had left Bertram's place I simply could not resist the temptation to follow him via another route to the church. Maybe I could still watch him from a distance, or hear his voice, because he would be speaking there that same afternoon. At least I would be in his presence, though I would be a long way toward the back of the church. Hesitantly I opened the church door. A hum of voices, no organ music. On my toes, I stepped through the vestibule. Then I pushed open a second door. Just inside was a man who manifested such a look of surprise, right from his head to his toes. A woman, for goodness sake! What next? And above the inner door to this meeting was a sign which said in no uncertain terms: "Entry of women forbidden."

In that one moment of dismay, 'Cerberus'[137] and I looked at each other. 'Cerberus' made me clearly feel that I had no business to be in attendance. My unique presence as a sole woman here in this illustrious company of men was a supreme embarrassment. I threw one longing glance inside, to see if I could spy those familiar blond, wavy locks among all those present. In vain! I dared not stay longer under the fixed stares of 'Cerberus', but turned on my heel and walked out with a big

---

137 In Greek mythology, Cerberus was the gatekeeper to the underworld.

lump in my throat. That marked the end of my physical encounters with Domie here on earth.

The gates of Heaven will probably be less exclusive than the door of this church – I hope.

But thank God it was not the end of our spiritual contact! Because I know, thanks to his letters from prison, what he has felt in his captivity, what he has thought and prayed. I do not know whom I should thank for accomplishing the dangerous mission of smuggling out these clandestine letters and poems. Perhaps it's someone who may read this book, a jailer or a fellow prisoner who was later released. In any case I am very much indebted to them, because these scraps of paper, written with a pencil stub that would vanish away into the lining of Domie's vest, represent an inestimable value which cannot be compared with gold.

For the following lines Domie composed a simple melody which Bertram later harmonised for me.

Sunday in Cell A 1/19

I know Thou ever seekest the pure of heart, the meek,
He who waiteth for Thee, having this bless'd surety;
That Thou wouldst not leave me empty in my need,
But wouldst fill my contrite heart with peace in Thine own time.

But this I did not know: that Thou Thyself wouldst appear
And e'en so bend to enter by the low-set door,
Commanding golden light to stream in through the window,
To flood my wretchedness with heav'nly sound and bright colour.

And in high reverence these bare walls would rise
And speak thus: Thrice holy is Thy Majesty!
The naked vault with folded hands would praise Thee
As of old and now, that all Thy ways are mercy.

And I? With bread and water I stammer my petitions,
Feasting at Thy table with all Thy Church worldwide.
Here is Thy great Name by angels and by me confessed,
And all earth and Heaven doth bless Thy unsurpassed works!

How is it, O Lord, I crumble swiftly in my weakness,
Yet this vile being may find an entrance to Thy throne?
Such poor speech I offer Thee, Who shall soon receive me,
United with Thy will, redeemed at the appointed hour.

When I my folded hands do place in Thine,
My heart is moved by Thine almighty power.
My eyes uncloaked see nothing but Thy greatness,
And in my weakness, all sufficient is Thy grace.

Although the dread knock troubleth me with fears,
That knock that calls me to my final walk,
Thou me with Thee hast already reconciled,
And deep inside my hymn sings proudly of The Christ.

Pass on in peace! Who goeth by Thy Word,
Blessed parting! Lifting high the trusting hand,
For him who is of Thee, and Thine entirely,
Naught is destroyed for truly Death is Life!

I will share more about his time in captivity from the following, his very first letter smuggled out from prison, which was written over many days and so reflects the changing circumstances:

The thought that there might be an opportunity to write to you secretly, and to be connected with you and share things with you for the first time since my arrest, evokes a feeling of happiness in me that I simply can't express in words. I don't know when I shall have a chance to write again, because it's a miracle if we even succeed to communicate – and others are running great risks to get this out. But that's why I'm so grateful for this time and want to profit as much as possible from it. What will interest you the most – I'm doing fine and the chance of a death sentence has dwindled. There seems to be no longer any risk. I'm currently in Haarlem, arrested on suspicion of terrorism and it seemed at that time to be a completely hopeless case for me. That was on Saturday, and on the same day I was rather ill-treated by the Dutch who arrested me. In Haarlem this battering and bruising caused quite a stir with the result that the matter needed to be referred to a higher authority, and therefore I still am being detained as a witness about that mistreatment.

One adverse effect on me: an injury to the left ear which has still not completely healed. But the rest of the Haarlem police staff's kindness to me has been touching, and there are those few who have literally risked everything to save my life. I am indebted to them that such a recovery has been possible after the way I was abused. Fine fellows and a lady too! Methinks that you've already received a message from them, sent from Haarlem. Such a lot has been going on behind the scenes to gain my freedom. But before the time arrived to be liberated (Friday afternoon was the plan) I was suddenly transferred to the Sicherheitsdienst HQ in Amsterdam. It became clearly apparent that unless Germany collapses within a couple of weeks, it was again looking hopeless for me, and for three others who were arrested with me. Still others (some deserting German officers in hiding) will be executed very soon, unless I can succeed to turn the whole affair and stretch it out by naming names of refugees, who are no longer at their previous addresses. That has partly worked: one of the three got away, but two others I've lost and are almost certainly no longer alive!

The preliminary interrogations here were far from favourable. I've kept myself very tough, but so much incriminating material has come to light, and it would be almost impossible to maintain a resolute facade in response. But behind the scenes, a better solution was being worked for me – and the evidential material has never appeared on the table. So I am detained here now, not for terrorism (requiring the death sentence), but for 'illegal work': Jews, forged ration coupons etc. I only had to admit to a very minor proportion of my activities. The rest amounted to "Keine Ahnung.[138]" A final hearing was carried out six days ago on Thursday, but it was all so very much more innocent than the first time.

I then had to sign a statement concerning the ration coupons and regarding a few Jews... I had virtually nothing else to admit. If they realised at that time what they had almost uncovered! I also mentioned a few names, but only of those who were already in Poland or had been moved to another location. So fortunately I haven't made anyone into a sacrificial victim. Here in Amsterdam I'm never abused at all. I was once at the SD in the Euterpestraat. They asked me if I, as a pastor "glaube daß der Herrgott mit meinem Tätigkeiten einverstanden sei.[139]" That I answered with a wholehearted "Ja!" I've now been in Amsterdam for 12 days already, in the detention centre on the Weteringschans next to the Leidseplein, Deutsche Abteiling, cell AI-19.

As I already said, I'm very well. But all this time I've been very greatly concerned about how it has been going with you and with the baby that you're carrying. I know that there may be a chance that you can write back to me. If so, put all your thoughts down honestly, would you? As I do as well. I have had such tremendous concern for you. Because I know how emotionally sensitive you are, especially in such circumstances as these. And let me also know how our kiddie is managing, as he won't be informed about his Papa from now on. And also something about the church. But I won't ask again. You'll know best what to write. Don't keep anything back... and use very small writing on little pieces of paper, otherwise it's so hard to carry it by

---

138 "No idea" – that is, the Germans never knew about most of what Domie was doing.
139 "That the Lord God is in agreement with your activities."

hand inside prison... and so risky. Right now I have certain relevant instructions as well, which I gladly anticipate that you'll carry out to the letter on behalf of both my and others' interests. You are a good listener.

But first something about my inner life. It's obviously a hard thing when you know that your life has probably come to its conclusion. So the same goes for me, your lover of freedom and adventure. There is no immediate danger, but certainly a risk of death remains ahead. It may now seem that's not the case, due to recent improvements in my treatment and through factors over which I could not speculate. Over whatever troubling blows I was dealt in those first days, a few fragments of verse that I append here will perhaps speak far better than many rambling words. I have found peace for myself, but alongside that I have felt so terrible for you, because I was afraid that by losing me you would simply break down, and I would not be proud to be accountable for such a thing. While within myself I have felt as a king, coolly surveying the whole situation regarding you and the little lad, my companions in the struggle and my hatred for that whole accursed system, I was planning to sell my life as dearly as possible, but not to the extent of saving my own skin. In Haarlem I sat chained in my cell, but here no – which is something new. Nevertheless, I was proud to have suffered like that, and still am.

Well then, our children are most likely not going to have a father. What you can bear yourself, only you know, but one can only poorly judge another's capacity for pain. But, apart from the fact that you never know how it is right at the final moment when captives face death (methinks that for me it won't be so pleasant) my angst over the danger of a death sentence has completely gone. What I now have to bear are just everyday things that don't weigh too heavily on me. To me, all the worry has already occurred during the earlier interrogation. At the last one, the charge was only put down in writing; but that also will count heavily against me. But to avoid at all costs having that dreadful word recorded against me would be extremely burdensome. I still at least can save an accomplice, though I'm immensely sorry for the other two we lost. 'Terrorism' was the first indictment they made, and they had only had to hear the slightest sound of their alarm bell ringing to act on it. Indeed just the bell clapper would be enough to set things rolling. Moreover, it was almost unavoidable that they would finally get on the track of my plan to crack Westerbork wide open. Nevertheless, that's something that I can morally justify and it all slotted together very nicely (using a team of 200 men) but in their eyes such an operation certainly falls within the scope of "terrorism". And the captain certainly will not pardon that. Yet it has all worked out well; that there are no new victims. But two German soldiers by their desertion and supplying uniforms etc. can't be saved, to my regret. (Those were the two which I referred to at the beginning).

Ja, well – and how do I feel here in my cell? Sometimes almost happy – and that coming from a world traveller. (My own travels suitably impressed all the gentlemen here, by the way). Now you may know for sure no matter how or when I die, I will never be alone. I have always had God with me and when I prayed to him to ask that my burden may not become too great to bear, He has always answered me. Because much worse than the certainty of death has been the ongoing task to console and encourage three others to make the best of their circumstances that can be achieved. But at last the tension has now flown away.

Another thing: I hope that telepathy really exists and that you and your young baby are receptive to it. May you often feel the tender sentiments that I am filled with for you. I want to caress both you and Hansje on the head and say I love you so very much. I often imagine you in these beautiful days out in the garden. The beans will already be fairly plump. What fine luxury those will offer on the dinner table! It's the last few hours of the day before it gets dark in the cell and I have to go to sleep soon. I usually lie here thinking of you. Fortunately I have a cell all to myself. Also reading matter plus a Bible. Read just once through the verses of Psalm 27 (our wedding psalm, remember?) But just once. I have truly experienced them!

And now I sincerely wish that after the war the world could return to what it was, that we can just live there in peace without having to go and help so many others. I would love to make you and the children so happy. Be aware that I do not yet know when I'll be able to come home. But we should love and celebrate each other. Because we have nothing better than one another. That's the thing that I really can't forget. But I have to deal with the years that God has allocated to us. I already knew ahead of time what would be required of us if we were to remain in this land during the war. For me it's been the only possible way of life under these circumstances and so I would never want to take a step back and do it all differently.

I have been able to hold to my course for a very long time indeed, and know the satisfaction of having been able to save many lives. I have been consistent in the view that under this regime of marauding and pillaging the only legal way of living is illegal. That I'm a pacifist at the bottom of my heart does not mean that I am a coward. I've been a good fighter on the domestic front. And I hope that our children will later know that and learn to appreciate their father.

Now down to business. If I seem to ramble, you'll have to sort through it all yourself.
These next instructions are concerning what to do with all sorts of people and things. I am just putting them down as they occur to me. So, I guess I'm not the business type after all.

Of course, pass on my greetings to Elderling, De Lange, Froukje, our neighbours at the pastorie and others. The gentlemen here know nothing of all our relief efforts in Groningen. So no danger looms for your little corner of the country. Speak further about some things by all means, but *avoid talking about my letter in the village. That could lead to difficulties or surveillance. And don't wait too long for any reply from me, because I have no idea how long I'll be staying here. It may still be a while yet (not impossible). Or I may be transferred to a camp very soon. But actually, that hardly interests me at all. My time here is very short. You must tell me something of the world news outside, but I do believe that I am already being kept well up to date.*

I never get bored here. I have too much to think about. These few poems are about rain falling. Darling, take them for what they are. I myself attach no more value to them than they already have and maybe it's also the only time in my life that God will strike sparks of that kind from my soul. I present them to you, as the very best that I can give at this moment, together with a few melodies that have been flowing within me. A little sun streams into the cell every day. I can see the sky, and every day I am in direct sunlight for fifteen minutes, which time I spend with God, with you and the children. I think quite often of our unborn little one and of my many good friends. All of this bounty is in the spirit. But it makes you so rich. I hope you feel as happy at the moment as I am.

My hair has still not been given a crew cut. They don't do them here. Only when you arrive at a camp. So I have a luxurious thatch now, as the mirror clearly shows.
I do worry about my parents. If you wish, let them know immediately that I'm doing fine. I hope that they don't take it too badly.

And that's all I have to report. Later, you'll hear more details. And now I'd really love to caress you and take your hand and tell you that you're such a sweet, brave girl. I'm proud of you. I know that many congregations will sympathise with you. And maybe a little with me also. In any case I am very grateful to them for all the good that they offer to my own sweetheart who one day, with her sun hat in hand, came running to me in the Wilhelmina Park. This sweet memory is still with me, but alongside that, in this still miserable world, there is always so much yet to do. But when I'm home, I would like to make you happy. In any case, that will surely come to pass when our baby arrives. Even sooner. If that whole event passes and I'm still not at home, do not get immediately alarmed. I'll be back as soon as I possibly can. And just as I am right now, I'll climb right back in the pulpit on the very next Sunday.

So much for Domie's letter. I was staying in Amsterdam and on the Sunday morning after receiving it I was up until five o'clock in the morning to answer him. Thank God that by the very next day my reply was in his hands. At nine o'clock on Monday morning I had to visit a lawyer who wanted to make up a biography of Domie using all the facts in my possession.

As a child he moved house. After primary school he attended, from Ede, the secondary school in Wageningen. At that time he desired to be a railway engineer, and had acquired an immense technical knowledge of the railways. But during this same period of *Sturm und Drang*[140] he became aware of His call to the ministry. Then he transferred to the Deventer Gymnasium,[141] where he showed great interest in the workings of church pipe organs. Simultaneously with his final exams, he competed for the position of resident organist at Lochem. A year later this instrument was entirely restored under his supervision. Then finally, war work.

While providing these facts in such a cursory, businesslike manner, it struck me again how multi-faceted his life was. "I will never be able to accomplish all that I must do," he sometimes uneasily said to me. "This life is so short! I should have six lives!" *Ja*, it had to be difficult to be so

---

140 A stressful time of often stormy expression of emotions and individuality against social rationalism.
141 A senior Grammar School providing programs which lead to University admittance.

contradictory and diversely gifted. A highly developed sense of technique was coupled with a mystical artfulness. And then there was his music, his doctoral studies, his community church ministry work, his company of innumerable refugees in hiding.

And now he just sat there idly in the prison cell on the Weteringschans, and here I was sitting very close by to him. The street where the lawyer's office was situated led out onto the Leidseplein where the prison was.

Chapter 61

When I exited onto the street, I felt strongly compelled to walk along past the prison, first approaching from the rear. He had written that he could only see a small piece of sky. I spied some small windows with bars. Behind which window would he be sitting? I observed them from over the water by the *Nassaukade*. If I could just get a little closer, just go over to the main entrance, then enter through it and perhaps pretend I had come to collect his washing, for it was Friday today. I could easily try it. Underneath the gate... past some amiable Dutch guards... and into a courtyard. Germans!

"Wer hat das Schein, bekommt die Wäsche[142]*"* they snarled. I had no '*Schein*'. To be so close to him and not even... but it was impossible!

Last night I didn't get too much sleep. Whenever I dreamed I was restless. They were conducting another house search at our place and the mayor was there too. Did that imagery come from the terrible news that I had only just heard, about Hungarian children? Of children aged two to eight years, of the same age range as Hansje and his five-year old friend. What is a child of two years like? Just like Hansje. He plays in the garden and during his game he comes up to Mama, clambers up onto her lap with a flower that he has just picked for her, gives her a cuddle and a kiss on her face and says, "Darling treasure." Or he looks in awe at a tiny bug in the sand. He fills a bucket full of it and turns it out again. He crawls at night into Mama's arms to shelter from a low-flying plane that seems to want to come at us right through the window. He

---

142 "Only those with authorisation can collect the washing."

stands in amazement, one finger in his mouth and the other hand behind his back, listening to a singing violin. At the sound of this music, accompanied by the piano, his memory awakens to recall someone who also always makes music, and he suddenly breaks out exclaiming: "Papa! Papa!" He has a toy phone made of tin and calls: "Hello, are you dere?" And he sings "*Klokje klinkt, Vogel zingt[143]*" with a high voice. He lets his bear eat pebbles and encourages a plastic duck to swim in a bowl of water.

I once knew a little girl, also of that age, with black curly hair and dark eyes instead of the blond hair and the blue eyes of my little boy. But that was, I thought, because the father was Hungarian. He came one day into the editorial office in Amsterdam and offered us some photos of his country. Beautiful pictures... Most of them were backlit shots of his people wearing colourful surcoats; a herdsman leading his cows in the evening light to drink at a well. They had long curly horns. In our kitchen in Amsterdam this Hungarian once prepared for us a dish of goulash. But I heard from my former director that when the Germans came, he suddenly disappeared. And actually, we once received a letter from him in Hungary, before the country was at war. Von Vajda had returned to his father's estate. There was a snapshot enclosed of Anneke, his daughter. It appeared from this letter that he was a Jew, which I had never known, and that he truly loved his daughter, which I had always known.

Now the recent news reported that six wagons crammed with Hungarian children aged between two and eight had been taken away and transported to the gas chambers of Kraków.

Could anyone who came to hear of such a thing not be stunned to silence by that horror, and not try to make the flow of such dreadfully graphic images cease? Trying not to hear the sighing of the parents nor to see their silent grief, nor to discern the cattle cars where children are

---

143 "Bells ring, birdies sing" – the leading line from a short children's folksong.

packed in on top of each other, nor to hear their cries as they call "Mama" while the train pulls away? But there is no one to protect them and when they finally, after much crying, collapse from fatigue, there is no place to lie down, and the little ones are trampled by the bigger children, for the older siblings of up to eight make no effort to protect the little ones. But it's all to no avail, they are heading for a common gruesome fate. The gas chambers of Kraków.

Was Anneke von Vajda also among them and did her dark eyes bulge with fear and dismay as the gas penetrated her lungs? As it diffused like an insidious poison from there, through her blood, finally numbing the victim?

And what of Esther, along with Wil and Lily? Her last letters to the boys only reached us just last week. They were written in Westerbork just before their departure. Fourteen days ago I heard a report about 9000 Jews who were gassed in Poland. Were they also in that group? My thoughts are often with them; I dream of them and pray for them, that they, through the Bibles which they took with them, have learned to find the Way, and that the memory of our last shared Christmas spoke to them from a different world; a world other than this gruesome one, which for them offers no place. And all for helping these children and adults, my husband has been trapped as a felon, cut off from the sun, the flowers, his friends, his church, his little boy and me, in complete solitude. "I have participated in the sufferings of the doomed..." But then he told me that even were he to be caught and put to death, I must know that he would never take a backward step, because he could never have done anything else. His love for his own little boy enlarged his heart with enough room for others. And this love drove him to perform great deeds.

How much longer will this fight continue we ask ourselves every day? Today is August 6, 1944. The Allied armies have this very day overrun Brest, St. Nazaire and Le Mans and are on their way to Paris. Turkey has broken diplomatic and economic relations with Germany;

the Soviet armies have emerged from their land of vast rolling steppes and are knocking on the door of East Prussia, Hungary, Romania and the Baltic States; American divisions have already passed through Avranches and are also storming the German positions at Florence. There is a well-founded hope that the end is near. And in that hope, we live.

The risk of interrogation for me was now over, so I could return home. A friend, who worked for the ministry of food supply and was therefore permitted to drive, brought Hans and me home in his car. At Rolde we stopped to pluck some stems of blooming heather. And it was not long before the Groningen landscape came into view. There had been much labour expended over the three weeks we were absent. When I left, the grain was still on the stalk, but now everything was already stored securely in the barns. We came home and Hansje jumped and danced down the hallway. He has a true heart and judging from his joy, seemed to be intimately attached to his surroundings. My parents-in-law and aunt were still there, looking after the house in my absence. Janny was also there and of course Froukje. They had taken good care of both house and yard; they had worked in the garden and preserved all its bountiful produce. Should a person not be happy about all these things and so express their joy to the full? It all looked so neat wherever I glanced; everything was familiar and trusted, even our going to church on Sunday morning, where the acting Minister spoke from the oft quoted text: *Ye of little faith, why did ye doubt?* During the three weeks of tension that lay behind me I also had shown a faith that faltered. I had doubted, although there were times of quiet surrender to both life and death. But one dwells on the heights only through practice... season after season. At times, we must repeatedly grapple to avoid sinking in the mire of despond.[144]

---

144 Alluding to the fictional bog in John Bunyan's *The Pilgrim's Progress*, where Christian sinks due to his burden of unbelief and perceived guilt over his own unworthy spiritual state.

I sat there in quiet contemplation while the light streamed inside through the tall church windows. After the service I was greeted by the Church Council members and Deacons. They did not say much, but looked pleased because my homecoming was proof to them that the coast for Domie was now clear. I asked the Deacons to accompany me home to the *pastorie*, where we were able to piece together a draft of a biographical testimony. This would be forwarded on through the lawyer that I had taken in tow, all to the benefit of Domie. It was good to be together in the study, where flowers stood over the fireplace, on the spinet and the table, and the aroma of coffee gave us a fragrant welcome upon our arrival. What seemingly insignificant trifles we sometimes can later recall! I remember how I luxuriated in the soft restfulness of that aged room with its many books, and how good it was to listen to one or other of the Church Council members who had responded to the request with his own draft, and have it read to you.

It was hot outside, insects buzzing, but inside it was cool. There sounded the heavy bass voice of Elderling, who was reading his piece. A murmur of approval. So it was good. Not a single word needed to be added or subtracted. A few plans for the new season were discussed while drinking a cup of coffee, and the smoking of a pipe, all so peaceful and warm-hearted, without the slightest suspicion that within 48 hours this same room would become the target of a gang of pirates. But before that time came, I received first thing on Monday morning another secret letter from my husband:

It's Friday evening now, about half past seven. Everything is quiet here... a perceptible tranquillity. Very different from the agonising screams the moody and brutal guards seem to enjoy here every morning. A little evening sun almost confers an atmosphere of consecration. And now I once again take up a piece of toilet paper and my pencil to write to you. For whom should I be besotted with more than you, even though you are a couple of hundred kilometres distant from me? By the way, that's nothing more than how it was when you lived here in the City. You could not talk to me then either. It is a miracle that these epistles are even getting to you. There is a good chance that my first letter is already in your hands by now. Thursday has well and truly gone. If you haven't got it yet, I think you surely will tomorrow. I do hope so much that you are well, and our second little one also. That to me is still a major concern. And despite that concern and uncertainty, perhaps I will still need to stay away a while longer, because the chances are very high that one of these days I'll be taken off to a camp. I'd say Vught. Incidentally that makes little difference to me anyway. It can't go on for very much longer. I believe that the Allies are busy getting ready to make one last great push. Paris will fall, and perhaps they will also make a new landing somewhere? And the Russians will race through Danzig and penetrate deep into the heart of Germany. If not in August, then the end might come in September. This year, 1944, is just like 1918.

And what I do want to say to you is this: if I leave here soon, to my very, very great regret I shall no longer be receiving your letters. And at this moment that can make so much more difference to me than anything else. If you have my last letter already, you'll realise that I'm making the best of things. You know that I always was determined to be adaptable. So let that be your consolation. This afternoon I have written down on these sheets of paper a kind of little sermon with prayers and songs for the three inmates who were assigned the task of bringing us food every day. This is for them, for next Sunday, because there is never a Church gathering here. But I have noticed that they strongly desire something spiritual. One of them is a believing Catholic. Thus one must learn to exploit the opportunities that come your way. At least there are questions asked about spiritual things and a real openness. The absolute lack of that in our own church has always made me feel so very sad and powerless. And I'm afraid that in these four years the situation has changed very little.

Oh well, I am not here to moan and groan, but I do have the firm intention to do my very best to be with you together again soon. At least there needs to come a time of security, order and tranquillity. I hope that our lives then will no longer require so full an interval spent addressing the needs of others. I would give anything to know whether you have my letter already and what you were feeling while reading it. And if it's still going well with you and the children. It is the most important question that I need a quick answer to, because any day now I could be put on a transport out of here.

By the time of my arrival back home my hair will be shorn and I'll resemble a plucked chicken! In our little Groningen village I'm sure they will find it very funny. Well, they'll just have to get used to it. Seriously, will they still remember their Domie? I do not believe that they were all that well disposed to following me through all the changes we've endured. So it's good then that you've been that vital link connecting me with them. They really must have thought hard when they heard that I had been taken into custody. Well, there you have it. The exact circumstances under which I was arrested (three drawn revolvers and voices yelling "hands up!"), and how that came about you'll hear about soon enough. It turned out, in retrospect, that they actually thought they'd seized someone completely different. But I could no longer avoid being identified, and had to immediately give my real name, because the man with whom I was closely working only knew me as a Minister of the church, and not that I had been secretly transformed into an Agricultural Inspector by all the ruses of deception. Therefore my beautiful forged papers were of no help at all, and from then on everything immediately unravelled. Please inform the S. and also Driebergen about that.

And then there followed 14 days I'll never forget. But that's all over now. And it was perhaps the most blessed time of my life. I've never been so close to God as I was then. I just found it very difficult to intercede for you and the children in regard to your future life; to bring it all before Him and leave it in His safe hands. But for myself, I was ready for whatever should come. I hope that my life will long remain as it once was. But it's so easy to be distracted by attachments of all kinds. Even now I find it so. But that's just how it has to be for now, I think. That willingness to let go... God will give me that in His own time.

While I was in Haarlem, I was in the hands of a bunch of 'New-Order-Dutchmen,' who were exceptionally and peculiarly mindless scum of the worst kind. But here I was treated very moderately by the gentry of the German Sicherheitsdienst. Their underlings, who serve as guards are nothing special. Most of them are 'Schnauzen.'[145] But at least they keep their hands to themselves. The Hauptsturmführer[146] that conducted my interrogation virtually presented himself as a friend. The real work would be done behind the scenes, of course. But it is a fact that he systematically avoided the most objectionable practices; instead he offered me lemonade and shook my hand. I felt sure if I had not been undercover and he need not have done something for the honour of the Haarlem gentlemen, he would have let me walk out free. (That sentence doesn't flow well – excuse me). Now he's putting me in a camp as soon as possible. He is a tricky one, in that he reduces things to the smallest proportions, preferably wanting to know as little as possible, showing such decency for both my benefit and for the other ones we lost. He had no idea about what was really going on with our plans, thanks be to God indeed! Otherwise he might have had to strike back hard after all. But I do not think I'll ever have that experience. In Haarlem I was able to give a nice debut display that demonstrated fortitude. Afterward I noticed that a puddle of sweat had formed on the floor that had dripped from my forehead throughout the interrogation.

With just one word I could have brought the whole charade crashing down. But that would have made things much more difficult and I would have betrayed others. I will always be proud that they got nothing from me, despite their resorting to so much violence. They were such senseless brutes! Anyway, that's all over and done with, and I don't wish

---

145 Underlings who just bark orders; copying the stereotype of authoritarian Nazis.
146 Paramilitary rank equivalent to a captain.

to indulge in any post-mortems. I have long since forgiven the wretches and I'm not about to bear a grudge. I wish I could lend my voice for their pardon. But I'm sure that as soon as the day arrives when things are on the other foot, that they will be shot down without hesitation. The fury that most of the good police staff feels toward such low-life runs so deep. These good men were the ones who despite the pressure they faced, refused to lay a hand on their prisoners.

But how I must bore you, relating all those past events on such a beautiful evening as this. You're not yet by my side. But when we are together as a couple, I shall tell you everything.

Now it's beginning to slowly darken inside my single bed-sitter, and I have to start thinking about retiring. I know the One who watches over us all. I hope that you have my letter. It will give you more peace. Time has flown so quickly. I can't imagine that by tomorrow I will already have been a prisoner for three weeks, not only of men but also of God; and that thought has been so healing. That same benefit I would wish for all men. And if the rest of my time passes as speedily, then I'll soon be home again.

Home! Men do pledge such wondrous vows! At times, when I found it hardest to leave you in God's hands, I have made such childish bargaining promises to God that I would always dutifully brush my teeth and fold my pants along the creases if he allowed me to come back to you again. These are such trifles, but I so much want to see you happy. And such love is often found hidden in a whole pile of trifles.

And Mondays we'll hold sacred for our family. Some evenings that might not be possible, so then we'll take another evening for ourselves instead, say Thursday. And you will have time to care for yourself and make some special requests of your own to benefit you! I desire this so badly because you are so precious to me!

Now it's getting dark. My neighbour has just knocked on the thick wall between our cells and called out, "Rest well!" Will you give Hansje a goodnight kiss from me? I imagine what a chatterbox he is now. Sweet dreams!

Saturday night

I do not know how much of an opportunity I will get to write this evening, because being careful about clandestine letters is paramount. And may yet still be, as I understand that I have a few days more here, although this is by no means certain. It gives me a reason to care about something: I'm connecting with you, from heart to heart, but in the camp there will be far more censorship. At any rate I have a better chance of receiving your letter if I stay here a little longer. When I do finally leave you'll be informed of the fact after a couple of days.

Two things of importance were encountered today:
I've received a bag containing my washing. And inside was also my pocket Bible. Behind all this I noticed the little things that Lisette had taken such faithful care over... or was it Margo? At any rate, if you are so minded, please pass on my heartfelt thanks to them for the attention and care they have demonstrated to me. That does me an immeasurable good, to know that I am not forgotten. Let Lisette know that she should not take any risks. Now we're so close to liberation, she mustn't end up at Westerbork. Don't let her go by the B road. Much too dangerous for her! However, next time they can (that is, if I'm still here) hide a note – or several – in my clean laundry. But they must do it properly. For example, sewn up inside the hem and such places – it can't harm me being secreted there. Only they should not be putting in dangerous things. You never know what may happen. But I don't think anything will, because I trust their good, safe hands. Also let Lisette know that, for the moment, that there are still 1,500 guilders stashed away at the house of S.'s brother. She doesn't know that but she will have need of money very soon to cover various expenses.

The second event of importance today: I was called in for an interrogation by two 'Dutch' detectives. I thought I was rid of all that carping, and held the advantage, should their little game begin all over again. I do not really understand why that even had to happen. And lo, behold, suddenly they produced a rabbit out of their hat! The gentlemen had come to ask if the pastor couldn't just possibly mention some addresses of Jews still in hiding, then they could possibly do something for the pastor. All as sweet as honey.

They'll never use violence on me. After Haarlem, they know that it would be ineffectual. But the two gentlemen had set up a rather stupid attempt to blackmail me. They said there had been Jews arrested who had named me. And even if I did not feel disappointed by that, I hardly needed to be loyal to such folk. Indeed it can make a lot of difference when you are sent to Vught, whether you are there for six months or for a whole year, or even for the duration of the war. You could see from their faces that they were lying. I gazed at them both for a very long time in silence and then I turned all affable and smiled. While they waited for my answer they started on a pseudo-scientific theory about the inferiority of the Jewish race. When they had exhausted that theme, I sat down in an armchair and lit up a cigarette, and then another and another, all the while not betraying a single thought. This served as a reply that they will long remember. Very good; they wanted to talk over the big picture – social policies etc. Let them! I then told them that I would give them the benefit of the doubt, because they really knew no better due to a lack of both knowledge and the wider experiences of travel. And that I had a right to an independent opinion about such issues but apparently they did not. And that much was clear from the way they parroted the biased contents of several newspapers. Of course they could not seriously expect that I would inform against men whom I'd once wholeheartedly supported. So they no longer pushed that particular line. And then I gave them a further lecture for another hour. Not one riposte formed in their throats! Nevertheless, at the end they just had to come up with this lame statement: "The pastor can safely name the Jews, because all of them have been arrested anyway".

My answer: "Then why did you need to even come to ask me who and where they were?"

And this one: "The pastor perhaps fears that the Jews would be hurt?"

My answer: "I am hardly afraid of that, especially if they are to be interrogated in Haarlem at the Nassauplein." I would be the last to blame arrested Jews for naming my name under the severe duress and physical abuse meted out there.

Another attempt: The two of them claimed to have been raised at their mothers' knees as fine upstanding Dutch Protestant Christians.

"Which makes your failing so much the worse. It is high time that you again read over the parable of the Good Samaritan, and what Paul writes about these things: In Christ there is neither Jew nor Greek, etc."

All that remained for those sad-sacks was to admit defeat, return to their boss and say, "We were not able to get anything out of him."

So their final effort: "Should the pastor refuse to name even one Jew, that's bad! Otherwise we'd have let the Aryans in his cell block go free."

"I'm sorry that I can't do that," I responded, "even for the sake of those gentlemen. They know and understand my position."

And then the conversation was over. Mr. Van Zaanen[147] has many flaws. But he is not a traitor. And these losers appeared to know nothing of me. It was for them simply another session of probing for information. What a stroke of luck that they still promote such types to this kind of detective work. Oh, ja – in another context, I could have told them that I hoped that when the whole case was out in the open (of which possibility they seemed very apprehensive), then sure... the NSB-ers might uncover the address of an active safe-house, but more from

---

147 Domie's pseudonym while working for the Dutch Resistance.

accidental blundering about rather than through incisive, intelligent reasoning.

I could say all this so calmly, because I am still standing firm and I'm still detained here under German authority. What these two little fellows find out, with or without my help, the Hauptsturmführer does not care a whit!

"Yet there is a new world coming," they decreed.

"If you wish to establish that by cajoling pastors to betray men, then I do not see much order in your Order. I would rather turn the matter around: what must you think of me as a pastor, if I thought even for a moment to go along with your proposal?"

To cut a long story short, those two were certainly no match for me. Brains – nil. But I was still happy to act out that little charade. What a couple of rogues! That will be the last occasion that they dare challenge me.

A few days ago, I had to be on my guard. All my belongings, wallet, purse etc. were brought over from the Euterpestraat. (and that's a sign that the investigation is now officially closed). My forged identity card was still with my Ausweis[148] which described me as an agricultural expert. The guards wanted to know how I came by that identity card. But you can play them off so nicely against each other: "Ach was. Das hat sich ja alles schon bei der Vernehmung herausgestellt.[149]" I did of course have to pay a lot to obtain the documents, or so they thought. They really have no idea about our way of thinking. They simply can't imagine that we would engage in such risky activities purely on principle, rather than for profit.

It's a wonderful affirmation, when you can sense that your ethics and intellect are several notches above the average, and then know that the same applies to the majority of those in this category, not necessarily to

---

148 Papers providing credentials to permit free passage through a checkpoint.
149 "Ah, well! All that has already been explained at the interrogation."

the ordinary refugee in hiding, but to the Nazi's so-called 'terrorists' and (less seriously) illegal workers.[150] So, now you're back on top of the pack.

And the bell in the great hallway has just chimed eight-thirty. Which means: who wishes to go to bed, may. From that bell through to nightfall is always the quietest, most beautiful time of the day. You will definitely no longer be disturbed. But it's getting darker even earlier these days. You can already sense the days becoming shorter. Have you been able to sit outside in the evenings this summer, or has it been too cold there?

Up to now I've managed to organise myself really well during my time in detention. I indulge in various activities. I have definitely been able to hold on, just like a submarine having to submerge for a while under the sea. That's if you manage your time properly. I have been learning a little Arabic from a book by Karl May. And I've also been exercising. I am really happy with my pocket Bible. My mind is now drawn back to thinking about sermons, even though that first time back in the pulpit will feel a bit strange. It will also be very difficult to share what I have so very deeply felt, and impart that to others: "Though I pass through the valley of the shadow of death, I will fear no evil."

I was convinced that sooner or later, but probably within a few days, I would be standing in a field early in the morning before a firing squad. And I'd be strong. I would have the strength to console the others with me, and at the last, give my priestly blessing, "May the Lord protect you, and make His Light to shine upon you, and give you peace."

As for me, even as the damp mists swirl around us in the cold, pale dawn, in endless compassion, Thou wilt hide me forever in Thine everlasting arms.

---

150 Such as those who take great risks, being active in resistance, in forging papers, ID's and ration coupons.

If you have felt like this, you will have such compassion for the two poor wretches that persisted in quizzing me this morning, and who in earnest will bring about the arrest of real men and women, and destroy their time on earth with such pathetic fervour.

And now all will have already become silent in our own village. I do not know who is preaching there tomorrow. But I keep Sunday here in my own way. Together with a few other chaps, brave fellows who have to serve us daily. Fellow prisoners. One thanked me today for the beautiful prayers. A really good man; a devoted Catholic. Another put a very pious letter in my hand which he had received from his father.

So I already have a congregation here, although it's a small one. May God now watch over both my congregation in Groningen and my congregation behind bars. And God forbid that any of these should end up in Westerbork. What a pity that the plan to break Westerbork open can no longer be implemented. It was such a beautiful plan, and there was a very large company involved. I had an over-sufficiency of personnel to draw from. And they all made a splendid team. For military expertise we even had a Lieutenant-colonel. Moreover, all contingencies had been allowed for and 200 men were available. But that planned action is apparently not to be. All that remains is to play out the cards that I have been dealt.

I figured that when I'm back home, I'd really like to learn something from you; you must teach me some English poetry. It will be nice to spend time doing that together. I want to fathom more of its quiet nobility, which I suspect runs in deep currents throughout such verse.

And now it's getting really dark here. In a short while I won't be able to see. Hansje will have long gone to sleep. He now knows nothing further about his "Pappalap[151]" – he has now forgotten that. But nevertheless I will be happy to live my life for both of you. God has led me along these rocky roads and I feel like a free man. I'm even thankful I got to experience it. I now have a much better understanding of the Apostle Paul. But enough of the theology!

Sunday noon

A welcome opportunity presented itself for this note to be sent to you sooner than expected, which I duly snapped up. I hope you will get it first thing tomorrow. And that a reply from you will soon be in my possession. As you see, I am still here in Amsterdam. When the clean batch of washing is prepared to be sent here it should not have too many letters tucked away inside. It seems it's not so safe yet.

I do not know how long it will take before you hear from me; there is no reason for concern if it takes a while – please remember that.

With me nothing much else is happening, other than their deliberations over whether to let me sit here for a while or send me to a camp. September or October is still the end, I believe. My darling girl – I hope that you are staying close to me in spirit. Let's think a lot about each other and pray for each other. Greetings once again to all my familiar friends. But let there be no leakage of information about our secret exchange of letters. Tell Lisette, as far as possible, to avoid the Blasiusstraat. I still don't trust them. The Haarlem gents hinted to me that they always return after a few weeks (3,4,5 or 6).

I once again bid you farewell. Once this evil empire is gone, I hope to soon be with you again, my faithful companion in life. How will I ever be able to say how glad I am to have you? With a heart full of love I'll soon be with you again and I wish you all the best now. May God also

---

151 A child's intimate family term of endearment meaning roughly "Papa dear."

be there when the liberation begins. Here, with our small squad of guards, it will be fine. Give my kisses to the children. I hope that they are both doing well.

Chapter 62

I had sat down to answer his letter the following morning after receiving it: Tuesday 22nd August. I had by then also become reacquainted with the benefits of being back in my own home after returning from my wanderings, and for which I was truly thankful. So I went off to fetch the milk with Hansje from Elderling's farm. But I had only just arrived there when Froukje approached, pedalling briskly along on her bike. What was this all about? In her eyes I read fear and in her voice I sensed anxiety. "*Mevrouw*, there are two Germans for you." Germans? That did not bode well. What did they want with me? She did not know. It could be, I thought, that they have come to arrest me, or it could also be that it was related to Domie in some way. I had been to see my Amsterdam lawyer of course, and this could have something to do with that collaboration. Froukje had been given the message that they had very little time to waste. So I decided immediately to turn around and go along with her. While I cycled all the way back, I came up to a group of schoolchildren. "*Mevrouw*, there are Germans at the *pastorie*," they warned. Was I running, with eyes wide open, fair into their opened jaws, I asked myself – and should I keep away from there? But I thought of Domie and kept going.

The Germans were standing by the fence, waiting for me. They were two Greens. And there were also some Dutch labourers standing next to a large van, who appeared to belong to the scene about to be played out. However sinister it altogether looked, I had not the faintest idea what it was they had come for.

"Are you the pastor's wife?" they opened the conversation.

"*Ja*, do come inside won't you?"

My parents-in-law and aunt waited in tense silence in the drawing room. They had seen the Germans peeking through the windows of the study, and had heard them remark: "A lot of books!" Now they asked themselves in disquiet why the short fat *Oberleutnant*[152] and his much taller and slimmer underling wished to speak with me. These gentlemen had come in a little yellow car, but the big van accompanied by four removalist fellows rightly aroused their suspicions.

"Your husband has already been away from home for five months?" Oh, so this was about Domie.

"That's so."

The short fat one produced his orders for the day.

"We have an order to pass on to you, that you must leave this house as quickly as possible."

It was a struggle to overcome my giddiness. I felt no pain, only a kind of stupor, and so responded in a flat voice, as if an entirely unexpected but not unpleasant announcement had been given which I took simply as information.

"Oh."

By that response, it occurred to the gentlemen that I did not appreciate the full ramifications of their announcement.

"What is all this about, then?" I queried.

"You and your husband have had Jews in the house. But you must hurry. You only have half an hour in which to gather the most essential clothes and family things to take with you."

Again the stupor descended.

"When?"

"Right now, immediately... so hurry up!"

Only now did the full truth penetrate my consciousness: I was about

---

152 Rank in the German military equivalent to a First Lieutenant in the Allied Forces.

to be put out of my house by the Germans, because it had provided shelter to the persecuted who, with just a bundle of clothes as their only earthly possessions, were likewise thrust out of their homes by the Greens. In Amsterdam I had seen the dreary rows of houses where the wallpaper hung half torn off the walls, and here and there were scattered about the floor a few items of wrecked furniture. Our house would become like one of those and I myself would become as destitute as the people who had been our duty to help. The Greens had clearly desired this encounter as an opportunity to strike back, but they would never humiliate me. Not like this.

I went into the other room; the gentlemen followed me down the hallway.

"We have to leave the house within half an hour, and may only take the most necessary items with us," I said to my lodgers in a matter-of-fact voice. But it distressed me that they had to go through this, because it would cause them a lot of grief.

Mama tried to appeal to the common sense of the Greens, and Papa suggested in the middle of her speech that essentially the war had been over for 14 days already.[153] What purpose did it thus serve to leave the house empty? But neither of them could prevail. One can never argue with armed robbers. There was no time to lose. In the kitchen, the girls were busy with preserving beans. I told them how things stood.

Then they immediately got to work at lightning speed. Everything for the meal was cooking on the electric stove. "Turn it off; we won't be having hot food today." Now I really had to get my brain functioning, because time was short. Clothing, he had said... and things that I was attached to: family heirlooms, for example.

Quite recently I had been given a plaque of Aunt Marie with the text

---

153 The south had already been liberated in late 1944, the north followed later, then the west finally at the general surrender May 1945.

burned into the wood: *This I know, that God is with me.* I grabbed that from the wall first. The Green who kept following me around on foot glanced at it and laughed scornfully. Those dumb Hollanders! Wasn't there anything better to grab, something more valuable than that wooden thing? And even if you translated it what could you do with it? And when they came to clean out your house, you'd throw it out onto the cobblestones! You would then darn well find out how much God was with you!

Above hung the head of Christ, by Toorop, which also went along, and a few framed drawings by Johan. Then books from the study. I also came across a few borrowed items.

"These are not ours."

He nodded, I could take them out. He reminded me once more to hurry. What was I doing running around in the study? I had to make sure that I got some clothes... a modest array, and money, I thought... and rescue some valuables from a box. Then I rushed upstairs to fetch Hans' clothes... and mine. The girls were bringing their own stuff down. Everything got jumbled and mixed together; each one of us grabbed whatever we could and threw it out the window, since there was no time to pack.

"*Mevrouw*, what do you want now?"

"Coats and dresses. Grab my suitcase but empty it first. Domie's too, as long as it's still there."

I walked into the bedroom. There stood the old dressing table from home, with all our letters in a drawer. Those had to be taken. Then over to the linen closet. Froukje grabbed my clothes. My wedding dress also hung there... and at the very bottom of the closet lay the *Sinterklaas* costume, and the *Black Piet*[154] suit that we had used for years at home, and which, now restored, again did fine service at our various church fellowship Christmas celebrations. I bent down to take

---

154 *Zwarte Piet* – Black Pete – is Sinterklaas' helper.

it, but *Herr Oberleutnant* was afraid I would take the bed linen and therefore said,

"You may not take that with you."

"I realise that... I just wanted to take the fancy dress costume."

That concession was graciously allowed me, because our roles were now reversed; I was not the boss now, but the Greens. Things were no longer mine, but had fallen into the hands of a band of "generous robbers", who permitted you to take some of their captured spoils.

But his generosity and patience only extended so far. "That's enough," he said, when twenty minutes of the promised half hour were up. "Time's up."

We had no choice but to leave all else behind and make our way out of the house.

"There is still a suitcase with clothes owned by our assistant pastor in this room. He must have them back."

"*Ja, ja...* that's in order."

On the rear lawn Hansje was playing peacefully with a puppet made by the little Mouse amidst all the clutter we had thrown down there.

"A few toys for the child?" suggested the tall Green. So I threw outside a wooden tram that Domie had once played with, and a few cars.

"That's enough," the German said again. Then, before we knew it, we were also standing on the lawn behind the house. There was an empty box there, which I offered to my parents-in-law to use as a seat. We, the younger ones, sat down on the grass and thought about all the things we still needed to take.

Only then did it occur to me that I had no undergarments. Only Froukje could request the big favour; to be allowed to still get some further items, because she was, like Hans, regarded as 'innocent' in their eyes.

The window of the baby room was open and the tall slim one was busy inside.

"*Mevrouw* still hasn't any underclothes," Froukje called to him. "May I go and fetch some?"

That made him angry.

"You kept on speaking of books! Books!" he said. "But you should have first thought about your clothes."

Then he slammed the window shut with a thud. But Froukje persisted and finally she was rewarded by an armful of underwear which they threw out by the same window. I stood underneath to catch everything while peering inside the windows like a beggar. There, on a chair, was draped my summer jacket. I had completely overlooked it. Would I still be able to get it back? I did not dare to ask; the measure of received grace was already full. But Janny spiritedly climbed up and over the sill and retrieved it.

Also on the table by the window was a grey tablecloth woven from Norwegian wool. It was there for the taking, but I could not bring myself to reach over to grasp it. It was as if I was stealing. Roles can be reversed just like that within an hour and the world turned upside down. Our eastern neighbours had brought us 'a Newer Order', in which all values of Christian compassion and the knowledge of 'mine and thine' were replaced with a new kind of 'salvation', which from start to finish remained unacceptable to the Dutch people. And what about the influence of the Bible? Undoubtedly, it was still present. Even where this Book is not read and known, its influence is still working through our civilisation, our laws and our whole society. And it is not surprising that one must seek the NSB-ers for the most part within the ring of the completely disenfranchised, who deliberately turn away from the Gospel.

The light in the cellar flicked on. Now they were definitely going to start on the Weck preserves. Eighty bottles plus all the work that was related to garden and kitchen. But it flicked off again almost immediately. Then I understood. They were actually searching for alcoholic beverages down there and had almost certainly taken away the communion wine. Thank God the precious silver vessels were no longer in the house: the old silver pitchers and chalices of the church, dating back to 1700, which would otherwise have certainly been removed. Those they would have kept for their Bacchanalian revelry, as did the late King Belshazzar at his pagan Babylonian feast.

I walked slowly around the house. Evidence of demolition was already accruing in the hallway. I gazed inside through the side window of the living room. It was still intact, but by the dresser the tall Green was squatting and eating the cookie jar empty. I nodded once in a friendly fashion to indicate that I'd seen him. If he still felt any shame and whether this would even show, I did not know, but it did look as if he was rather embarrassed. However, this may have been my imagination, because moments later he shouted at us through the window – that we must now go away and leave the garden. At five o'clock I may return, I was told, but only I... alone... so I would finally understand why... They were apparently in no need of snoopers or bystanders.

Elderling had meanwhile turned up on behalf of the Church, and had declared that everything in the *leerkamer* belonged to our pastorate. *Herr Oberleutnant* was sitting at ease behind the desk in the study and kept himself occupied reading through our correspondence. Aha, sir! You were not stationed in Holland for this long in vain; you obviously already understood the written text, especially if you spoke East Frisian yourself! That he spoke it was Elderling's discovery. Postcards from our trips, especially those sent from England, now captured his utmost attention. English maps from long before the war might even contain secret codes! If he had given up hope by now that the beautiful war song *Wir fahren gegen England* would ever be fulfilled, and that promised land might now only be seen on postcards, in reality that signified that he would never make it over the North Sea.

After we were chased away from the *pastorie* grounds and the neighbours gave each of us a sandwich in place of our forfeited meal, Elderling went back again to tell the Germans that the bookcase covering an entire wall belonged to the *pastorie*.

It had been agreed by all that I should not return there at 5pm all by myself. The consensus opinion was that it was perfectly natural for me to have such a desire, but then the Germans might take me away in their car. *Ja, ja...* just come back! And then... have me arrested... sure!

Even so, I was not going to run away from all this! Buurman[155] protested vehemently. He would go in my place, accompanied by Elderling, and the girls must see what they could do as well.

The Greens had not finished their job to clear out the house by midday, so all our books remained there. They were partly packed in crates. Our neighbour grabbed an armful and carried them away. The whole village was watching. All of a sudden the school children became emboldened; they jumped over the fence and brazenly dragged several crates of books away. That went on several times, each one dragging off some of our possessions into the bushes. De Lange also came over as soon as he heard what was going on; he came straight from the fields in his work clothes, covered with dust and sweat, as these were hot August days.

Herr Oberleutnant was becoming impatient. For him there were far too many people around. He had just had a conversation with Buurman, which had terminated unsatisfactorily. He had also been squatting on the dresser, not on the side where the cookie jar stood, like his colleague, but on the other side where the silverware was kept! Now all that remained in sight was one lonely cake fork. "Is this silver?" he asked Buurman, and without waiting for a reply, dropped it into his sack. Had Hans' silver serviette ring also disappeared into the bag, the one he had received at his birth from the women of Oldiek, and upon which they had had his name engraved? I really don't know. There is still a very small chance that on the night of terror when Domie came home with all these terrible messages, I may have packed all the most valuable items

---

155 *Buurman* means neighbour. The author uses this as a nickname to refer to their actual neighbour next door to the pastorie.

of silverware and passed them on to Buurman for safekeeping. But I have the dreadful feeling that in the confusion and hurry I may have forgotten. And so it's probably missing. So Hans will never be able to say "Some old ladies had this specially made for me," as one of the women predicted that he would do once he came to appreciate its value and significance. The christening garb that the women from the Hörn had presented to him had also gone.

All in all the yield of silver ingots was disappointing, and *Herr Oberleutnant* could not conceal his disappointment.

"Such people must have more silver than this," he insisted.

"Oh no," said Buurman,"not at all, since they are not attracted to wealth; they don't care for such things. They have put every spare penny they had into their books."

"We've got no gold or silverware in the van," the removalists assured me outside. "They take all the valuable stuff in their own private vehicle." There was still a small gold medallion locket from Father, with a tuft of Grandmother's hair inside, which he always wore on his watch chain. Later I found the box in which it had been kept somewhere on the floor. It was empty, as was the case which used to hold mother's crystal *eau-de-cologne* bottle with the gold cap.

Any money which they found also went along in the private car. We had put aside some cash for the baby set in a drawer of the dressing table. I never saw it again.

Several boxes with savings from our Youth Association were in the cupboard. There had originally been notes stuck on the boxes, which I discovered later:

34.65 guilders Children's Club – Polletje had placed that one.

25.15 guilders, Kindergarten.

12.95 guilders, Women's Association,

and so forth...

Altogether I estimated there were about 150 guilders there.

Janny saw that they were busy wrapping all those boxes in a napkin. Then in her indignation she forgot caution. "That's the money from the children," she suddenly blurted out. "You are thieves!"

At her feisty reaction, they laughed. "Lass, don't be so cranky," they said. "We surely couldn't have known that!" Well, they would certainly take it all away now and check out the contents later. They tied the napkin up tightly and deposited it for safety's sake somewhere inside their private car. Nothing was going to happen to the young people's money under their extra special care!

They did not return the next day, but the day after that a few other representatives of the Greens appeared at the *pastorie*. On behalf of their colleagues they handed over a small tin, which contained perhaps a generous sixty cents! Their Green brethren had also relayed a message that they were returning the money given by the Church Associations. What honest fellows they were after all! So touching! They were returning all the savings collected for the youth ministry! Amongst all their misdeeds, the Nazi regime nevertheless always tries to maintain the facade of justice and 'fair play'. This was a small example of that!

But the overall value of the spoils of silver objects had been disappointing to them and that had caused the emotional temperature of *Herr Oberleutnant* to decline. When De Lange came in, it had already reached to below zero.

"What are you still doing here?" snapped the Green.

"I've come to save what there is to save," replied De Lange laconically.

That answer did not please the German.

"We don't have time for this," he insisted.

"Time enough," replied De Lange, calmly.

Then the German completely lost control. He began to scream and rant that he could subject the four neighbouring farms to less than pleasant interrogations.

"Listen to that!" said Petertje, who was outside on the road, and who had helped carry out our books.

Herr Oberleutnant chased everyone out of the house, except for Janny, who had hidden herself away somewhere when the storm broke. When the blast finally subsided, she emerged into the daylight once more.

Buurman waited for his chance and went in through the back door after the man's anger had been vented.

The Greens had now discovered that the sofa in the study could open to reveal a storage space underneath. Curious, they looked inside. There were clarinets and an oboe stored there.

"Those are from the Church Musical Society," said Buurman.

"We also have an orchestra," said *Herr Oberleutnant*, and stuffed them in his sack. Those would certainly now be travelling via the 'private car' route. Here and there were toys scattered around the house, a little pony, a wooden car, a little pig. They generously offered Janny the opportunity to take them all away, because, "The child has no guilt, and is not responsible... but the parents are a different matter!"

"Then he should be allowed to keep that beautiful little cabinet," pleaded Janny, "because that is also his. That's where his clothes are kept, and later *Mevrouw* will need it again, because look, the top is used as a dressing table for the baby."

But they would hear no more of it. No, no, there was to be no question of that ever happening. That cabinet (given by Paulien in thankfulness for when we nursed her husband Johan) was destined instead for a Children's Home.

The gentlemen were running late. They were supposed to be away by five o'clock, but it was already six and they still had not finished. The moving van was packed and the house was now left an absolute ruin. Fragments of blue china bread and butter plates were scattered over the floor, plus a cracked commemorative tile of Queen Emma. And what would still get broken during further transport of the boxes? China cups of Delft blue, from my mother, were already in the van, but their saucers I found afterwards; wrapped in newspaper and stashed in a corner. They had apparently been forgotten. The men finally went away, but they were intending to return the next morning to pick up the rest of the inventory. Above the hallway the large window was open. *Ja*, but that did not matter to them. If there was a break-in tonight, *Mevrouw* would be arrested for the crime!

Then they finally departed, the small Chevrolet in the lead, and following on behind, the large moving van with all our furniture, which represented a lot of personal history from our own lives. We had collected those things with much love and joyful expectation; most purchased piece by piece before we got married. Over time our furniture ensemble had expanded. We started off like students in digs, with the most necessary items first: a divan bed, a personally designed and "made by Domie" wardrobe, a table, a bookcase. Beautiful? Oh no, there are much nicer pieces of furniture in the world, but ours were treasured by us through the special memories that were attached to each of them. For wouldn't a man prefer to sit in a serviceable chair made by himself than on a comfy armchair that he had borrowed from someone else?

Various friendly folk offered to let me borrow items for our now empty house, but I could not bring myself to take them up on their offers. I had personally witnessed our possessions being taken away. From the neighbour's house I had seen the removal van set off down the road. There was one consolation: it went in the direction of Groningen, not over the border to the east. Perhaps when the war soon came to an end... but that was far too good to be true. That I might ever be able to reclaim it, or at least a part of it, I almost did not dare to imagine.

Chapter 63

I slept that night at the neighbours, but we all slept very badly due to the heat and our acutely pent-up emotions. Hansje was upset again and began a bout of vomiting. At half past six I got up. The weather promised to bring a very hot day. At seven o'clock I called my brother and told him what was going on: that they had been busy pillaging and emptying the *pastorie*. Could he go to the notary to obtain a copy of our marriage contract and as soon as possible bring that up here? *Ja*, of course; he would come today and stop by the lawyer to learn whether there was still any Dutch law that could thwart the Germans' actions. The Greens had told me that I could register a complaint at the Scholtenhuis[156] in Groningen. But would it help at all? At any rate, it was wonderful to have that family contact and to be reassured that someone would attempt to support me. To go on my own to the Scholtenhuis would mean my venturing into the lion's den, and most likely they would not let me leave there after all that had happened.

We waited all day in vain for the removal van and the small military car. Had the protest call of the lawyer had an effect? But the next day, the van drove by again, not preceded by a yellow car this time, but instead by another vehicle with two Germans riding in it. I saw it pass by from a window of 'the Lord's' house. This old Churchwarden had immediately shown his support by sending his maidservant over to offer

---

156 A very large old former home of the Scholten family, requisitioned by the SD for
   the interrogation and torture of prisoners. It was known by locals as the
   'antechamber of Hell.'

us shelter. *Always desire to show hospitality.*[157] Domie had preached on this biblical text two years ago. 'The Lord' at that time had hosted one of our refugees in his house, therefore he understood the Scripture well. And Domie had later made use of that sermon again. On the second occasion, however, he had certainly not thought that it would be necessary for his parents, his wife and his little boy to be sheltered elsewhere. And 'the Lord', who had served faithfully as a Deacon for years and had maintained the church affairs during the long times the *pastorie* had stood vacant, told his maid when he sent her to fetch us, "This will be my very last involvement with the *pastorie*."

We had always helped others; it was now their turn to help us. Homeless and without any earthly goods. What a strange feeling! I was dependent on others and had to ask for everything. I did not even have a single piece of thread to darn a stocking. If we were wholeheartedly received in such circumstances, with understanding and accepting love by people who did not make us feel that we were a burden, then that was something to be really grateful for.

"*Mevrouw* will want to leave here," said 'the Lord' after my parents-in-law had gone home. This made me feel awkward and I really felt that I did want to pitch my tents elsewhere.

"She is with you and she can stay with you," said the son, tersely and succinctly. And yet Hansje felt right at home there, feeding the chickens with *Opa,*[158] as he called 'the Lord', taking turns to blow on a white flute carved from a sheep's bone, and walking hand in hand to the farm next door to fetch a bucket of duckweed from the ditch. There was *Opa* in his frock coat and with his white beard, and blond tufted Hansje running bare-legged in his shorts. When they set off together like that, silhouetted against the setting sun, they looked like Tom Thumb and the Giant.

---

157 Hebrews 13:2.
158 "Grandpa."

I'm so sorry that my parents-in-law and aunt were thrown out from the *pastorie* in such a cavalier, insensitive manner. When one is younger, one tolerates these things better than when stamina declines and one's health becomes more fragile. But they were in fair fettle when the removal van came back to get the rest of the contents. Those who had been sent this time were lower in rank than the high and mighty lords of two days ago. They were also far more reasonable. They didn't send me rudely away. Neither did they dismiss Elderling, who had just arrived at the same time, nor Janny who came back when she learned that the gentlemen had turned up again.

They told us they had been instructed to disassemble the bookcase and take the treadle sewing machine. Elderling then explained with insistence that the bookcase belonged to the *pastorie* and I also asked if they did not have enough sewing machines collected already? They had already taken mine away, also a Singer model. But this one was owned by Greet, our previous domestic help. Finally, they believed me: it was so obviously true that one did not normally need two machines in one household.

Also they wanted the spare reams of Cyclostyle duplicator paper in the attic. "That's been confiscated," they said. "But it's the church's," said Elderling. Then I had an idea. I asked him if he would be willing to trade the paper for a single bed that was still standing against the wall. Already all the blankets had disappeared, but I could possibly still live here. For the same motive I was pleased that the coal stove remained behind (the electric model went along with the Greens the first time). The kitchen table and a kitchen chair were saved for me with a few odds and ends which Janny somehow managed to coax into being set aside for me. Janny did her level best to cajole our gentlemen raiders. She became my faithful intercessor. For me it was just too painful a humiliation to ask them for a favour, which is why I did not. But she was willing and able to plead my case, and she did that most successfully.

Broadly speaking, the same situation as before repeated itself over again. I sought out some toilet requisites, but the cake of good bathroom soap that a short while before was on the sink had moments later disappeared, along with Domie's shaving soap.

Suddenly I looked up in surprise. From the empty living room downstairs emanated the most beautiful, melodious sound! Our piano was being played. "Who is doing that?" I asked the removalist.

"One of the Greens, the short one," he replied.

Amazed, I just stood there, listening. I was wondering how such a quiet and reserved man, who just sat there waiting and staring disconsolately at a box, could enlist voluntarily in the *Grüne Polizei*. Finally, after the piano was the last piece of furniture to be loaded into the van, I got my answer.

"It's a French piano," he commented. "A Pleyel. A good quality brand. I also once had one myself."

"Had?"

"Ja, I lost everything in a bombardment."

"Where do you live then?"

"In Duisburg. I was just having leave. War is the greatest pig-sty that ever did exist!"

I asked him bluntly, "Why then did you enlist voluntarily in the *Grüne Polizei?"* And I felt compelled to add, "You are far too human for them."

"I assure you it wasn't by choice," he said. "I was wounded three times in the war and when I was deemed unfit for combat, they shoved me over here."

But his superior was in a hurry because he wanted to resume the hunt that afternoon. At noon they treated themselves to fried eggs, beer and bread with thick slabs of butter from our cellar stores.

The baptismal registers would be transferred into the custody of the mayor, said their leader, together with the house key. He could either withhold it or return it to me at his discretion. What the mayor would actually decide, as soon as the Church Council had provided to the lawyer a written explanation concerning Domie, was not in doubt in my own mind. I definitely expected to get the key back.

My brother had meanwhile arrived, while they were still busy hauling out the remaining booty. He showed his identity card and the notary acts which he had brought with him. I explained to the gentlemen that he was *"mein Brüder.[159]"* He looked around the chaos. Having seen the notarial acts in my brother's hand, the tall Green appeared to feel rather more insecure under that glance. But really – what right did they have to rob me in broad daylight? Reacting from his insecurity, he started yelling with false bravado. He shouted himself hoarse about *"die stinkischen Juden[160]"* whom we had had in the house, just as they had effectively drilled him to do. Stinking Jews that were Lily and Esther, Naomi and Miriam and two modest, older people whom we had certainly had in our home. Good thing we had put a stop to all that then, hè?

But now – now that we were standing out here, he by his vehicle and I by my bike, all his drill training suddenly evaporated and he became a man. "What have I gone and done?" he inquired, looking around at the empty house they had left behind as a ruin, with up-ended empty drawers removed from the desk, dirty pots and pans from their lavish meal, desultory empty bottles and papers scattered all over the floor.

I replied that I didn't know, and asked then, motivated by a sudden impulse, "Why has this happened?"

He did not scold me now, but said simply, "I don't know... but they say that Jews and terrorism... you haven't had anything to do with that though... with terrorism, I mean. For how long has your husband been absent?"

"Almost five months."

"You can reclaim all this at the Scholtenhuis. It has already happened that a wife once received everything back."

---

159 "My brother."
160 "The stinking Jews."

"I wouldn't count on it."

"Sure you can, you have a real chance," he countered. And then, "Do you have any money?"

"Money is useless these days. You know very well that you can't buy anything with it."

He paused and looked thoughtful. "That's true," he said and blipped the accelerator.

"Anyway... I feel no hatred," I said. I could tell him that in all truth, because I meant it. They had been badly enslaved by a cursed regime that was doomed to be overthrown. They had been guilty of a grievous sin: the sin against the first commandment: *Thou shalt have no other gods before Me. Thou shalt not bow down to them nor serve them.*[161] The latter had they certainly done instead of worshipping the God of our fathers and of the ancient Hebrews; they had made themselves gods of race, blood and soil, and even of the man who together with all his 'Führer-sheep' led them to fall into ruin. They had taken our property, but I would never wish to change places with them.

"No hatred."

He stepped on the accelerator again. The vehicle lurched forward and disappeared around the bend.

But at any rate the continuing hunt that afternoon must somehow have boosted his ego, because our own mayor never received the *pastorie* front door key from the Greens. However, we could still get into the house through the *leerkamer,* which of course was officially released back to the church, but would we dare retrieve the empty bottles and the Weck jars from the cellar to fill them with tasty new beans and apple sauce? We risked it. The girls picked the beans in the garden while I selected apples lying under the trees, for there were many ripe ones lying there on the ground that had recently fallen.

---

161 Exodus 20:3-5.

Chapter 64

The weather had changed: from very hot and windy it had suddenly turned cold. The shutters over the uncurtained windows of the empty *pastorie* rattled eerily. Even over the garden lay a great desolation. How were we to ever come back here again – to live and be happy? I could not see into the future, nor even imagine it. There seemed to stand an impenetrable wall before us which blocked all perspective. My brother visited the Scholtenhuis in Groningen, but got absolutely nowhere. He was harshly snubbed. Even his argument that the spinet was a family heirloom more than 200 years old made no impression. *Someone who had done this and that and that... well... therefore, no penalty measures were too much. Please, let us not come back to this matter again, for the sake of Domie's safety. Let him and the whole matter rest; please forget it as soon as possible, and let nothing more be dragged up about it.* Because Domie was still not safe and I could yet be summoned for more questioning.

Involuntarily, I lay at night listening to every car that approached from the distance. Would it stop at our house? No, fortunately, he's just passing through. Family members and friends advised me to go away and leave my dwelling place behind. Off yet again – with my little boy? I felt extremely reluctant for the child's sake, who felt at home here, and also for myself. Yet 'the Lord' had an excellent memory and whoever wanted to know something about our church could contact him. He spiced up his tales with pithy sayings like:

Man! Did you think, then, that I can gasp with flour in my mouth?

or:

Whoever is used to running over cobbles, is hopeless on clods, I always say.

But the loving pressure that was exerted on me became ever stronger, until I finally capitulated. But before our departure they had asked me to speak at the funeral of two young men who were killed in a bombing raid at Emden. So I stayed on for a few days, but when the opportunity presented itself to get away by car, I seized it willingly.

Bare and unwelcoming seemed that familiar land; bleak and utterly lonely. My mood was therefore in like measure. Off we went again, my youngster and I, toward an unknown future. Because the *pastorie*, which had once offered me such hospitality, I no longer knew.

But it would be ungrateful of me to express such thoughts to the Churchwarden's son. We first drove to his daughter's place. Her husband was in the prison camp at Amersfoort and he went to their farm every week to help supervise the work. From there I would go further by bike, with Hansje perched up front in the basket.

While we drove in silence along the straight and level roads of that lonely polderland, I thought about what I had left behind: the church and the *pastorie*, which now presented such a gloomy sight. I had been there only yesterday afternoon, and when I walked for the last time through the empty rooms, with only the flotsam of shards, paper and debris on all the floors, I recalled a question asked about Job:

Is it for nothing that Job serves the Lord?[162]

I too had already been deprived of everything that makes life enjoyable, and of a home too. I had nevertheless also been met by kindness and would encounter it once again in the new *pastorie* where I was going. While I was away, someone would try to fill up the empty

---

162 Job 1:9.

preserving jars with produce and Froukje would help the new housekeeper with that task.

"The *juffrouw* has grown up under the pulpit," 'the Lord' had remarked. "But she lives it, too: every day and every hour."

It's nice when they can say that of you.

Chapter 65

And now a vibrant new life knocks and calls increasingly urgently to me; a triumphant life, beyond all external circumstances. It is something that nobody can take from me, not even the Greens or the Gestapo. It has become my most profound inner possession. It stirs in the silence and solitude of the night as a sweet consolation, which does not only touch me, but also Hansje when he sleeps peacefully. Then the vision sometimes returns, like once when I was outside on a moonlit night, bringing in the washing. In raising my hands to the line, Mother's wedding ring fell off. I searched vainly in the cool grass, for the moonlight was not bright enough. Then a voice inside me said, "Do not worry about that ring, tomorrow you will find it again. That was only a means in order to attract your attention." I stood very still, while the bounds of this earthly existence expanded and the wall that separates us from other worlds became transparent. Iris,[163] dweller in the heavens and proclaimer of new life, came gently down on the shafts of white moonlight and touched my forehead. I knew then that I would soon be the bearer of a new living being.

But where would my baby be born? Mary asked that question too. In Bethlehem they finally found a stable. But this war is still ongoing and I had no home. And in the nights, the long nights, I thought of Domie. Because everything was taking so long! The liberation seemed so close, but the attack on the bridge at Arnhem with British paratroopers failed

---

163 Iris is a bright asteroid, whose orbital path around the sun lies in the belt between Mars and Jupiter, and which was named according to Greek mythology by John Hind in 1847.

through the treachery of a Dutchman. Field-Marshall Montgomery had instructed him to pass on details of the landing zone to the Dutch underground army, but he was a spy and instead gave the message to the Germans. Now we had to face a long, long winter full of hunger and misery and agonising uncertainty.

It's September 25, the anniversary of our wedding day, and early morning finds me pouring out my heart on paper in the light of a small lamp. Would he also be thinking of this day, or would he know neither the date nor the time in that dark prison? And nine years ago, neither did we know what was ahead! "For better or for worse, in prosperity and adversity," *Saevis Tranquillus In Undis.*

Weteringschans, Thursday, Sept. 28

The chances of getting in touch with you are so minimal, that I'll really, really be so glad if you are able to hear from me again and if I can possibly also receive a message from you. And above all I really need that now, because you may have heard how half the men here have been released and you've of course then noticed that I was not among them. You may have asked all kinds of questions and drawn all sorts of conclusions. And so I have a lot of sympathy for you. Especially since I now know that they've emptied our house and you no longer have a home. (I found this out at the station about three and a half weeks ago when we were supposed to go to Vught, but then it all fell through).

I hope so very much that it's still well with you and with the second child that we're expecting. I had for a time hoped that I would be by your side for the birth, but at the moment it does not seem very likely, since inside here we still have a very good perspective on the current news: first the paratroopers routed at Arnhem and Nijmegen, then the battle of Brabant not going favourably. It could be that there's a sudden unexpected reversal in the picture, but at the moment it looks as if there's only a very slim chance of that happening. Our country still seems to be going through a painful, prolonged history. And so I am very happy every time when I get in touch with you again.

To me, the overall picture looks like this: when the Allied paratroopers advanced to Arnhem and Nijmegen the Germans wanted to let us walk free. That's what happened to the plain SD cases here. As for the other ones (of the Feldgendarmerie[164] etc.) they were still waiting for a telephone call. Had the Allies managed to hold fast their positions at Arnhem and Nijmegen, one day later we would have been standing out on the street in freedom. But now they have us firmly in their grasp and will hold us firmly until the need for the gentlemen to leave will be greater, which we indeed hope for with all our hearts. There is no reason for this to make you so worried, unless the war here reaches an impasse, in which case they could well be thinking about transporting us to Germany.

At present they still have no transportation planned, but if they have any further military successes, at any moment the transport process could be resumed. And that's exactly what we do not hope for! What I do not trust about this whole situation is that on the Russian front the battle has stalled. I'm afraid that they might move troops from there to the West. And that could very well change the whole picture to our disadvantage. May God, who has helped us and preserved us thus far, forbid such an outcome.

And how is it going with me? Good. Certainly not emaciated. I'm healthy, and have something to eat here, including what we get from the Red Cross once a fortnight – that's enough. So don't worry about that. Perhaps you were surprised that I sent out so little laundry. That is because I'd rather be dirty than cold. I have a thick hunter's tracksuit and wouldn't willingly exchange that for thinner clothing, because if I ever have to go on a transport in the open air, then I might well have to

---

164 The uniformed German military police units attending to duties in the occupied territories of the *Reich*.

sit for a long time in the middle of winter without thick insulation. I have some dirty, torn pyjamas on, but I'm not parting with them until I have received another pair. Furthermore, I would still really like some laces, a pullover and a thick winter coat for the coming season. At the moment I really have no desire at all for anything more.

But I would very much like to know what's going on with you. I believe that you occasionally bring my laundry here yourself, although I do not understand how that could be with such poor travel connections. I hope that you weren't coming by train. Far too dangerous right now! Perhaps though you weren't, because there are no trains running.

But where are you living? In Zeist? But how can you get from there to here? Or are you in Amsterdam? And where exactly? Surely you're with our son? Do you have any books? What about clothes? And what did you retrieve from the Blasiusstraat? My doctoral thesis? You should know that I've received just one message from you. Only your first letter after you had received mine – but from that point on, nothing more. That it's beyond your control, I understand completely. I hardly need to tell you that, my dear.

That's why, if it may be at all possible, I would like you to write quite extensively. On thin sheets of paper, letters close together, and with pencil. Sharpened to a fine point and pressed firmly.

After the saga of our failed transport to Vught, I have not been questioned any further. And it may never happen again. Also, the weeks of solitude in my cell have come to an end. First up, for 14 days I had with me someone from Haarlem and a former missionary teacher from Zeist. Both of them went home on Saturday. I now have a reformed policeman from Utrecht and a young man from Wassenaar. I'm so glad that the loneliness is over. It had started to press me quite heavily. But anyway, how is the church functioning now that you are gone? My thoughts often turn to them.

That I am still being held here, as indeed are more than 100 others, is probably because mine is a combined case under both the SD and the Feldgendarmerie. I do not believe that much can be done at this stage to get me out. Quite possibly Henny of The Hague would be able to advise on that (Mejuffrouw Henny c/- Mijneer Kloosterman in The Hague). The Dennen family in Rotterdam might be able to reach her. But I do not believe that she could exert the slightest influence on my case. Up to now I have already had reason enough to be grateful to her. I also want to congratulate you too, even if it's belated. A few days ago it was our wedding day: 25th September. Nine years! I was congratulated right here in the cell by my two colleagues. Indeed, we are both still around, despite everything. And it could have been quite different. I am so immensely grateful for that. But we are not out of the woods yet. God has protected us so far and helped us immensely. Yet I'm never quite sure whether He will send me to work again as a pastor and we shall have our family all together again. And in despondent moments (which I have had several times) I would dearly love to receive a crystal clear leading on that point.

Because... Och... to wait is sometimes just so difficult. You would also have experienced that. How disappointed you will be that the war has not gone better for us in our own country. God knows that I wholeheartedly yearn to be back with you and the children again. And again to be a pastor in a world trying to cope with moments of despondency. But I'm struggling myself right now with ever more dispirited moments. It will be exactly the same with you. But I'll keep rising up again and again until I'm on top. I am so happy to have my pocket Bible here. It's already given me so much solace. And right now a song comes again to mind:

The clouds and winds and sky
Point to the way ahead,
And find a path for aye
Where feet may safely tread.

But then again, sometimes it seems so cruel, that God, after having given us so much hope, would seem to back away again. But ja, His ways are different from ours. Yet I remain in good spirits, because my heart is full of love for you and for the work. I still do have a lot to give. And my whole heart goes out to you, my dear brave wife. How I imagine you in the thoughts that often fill my vision is like this: I see you riding your bike through the village, with Hans up front in the basket, that timeless cap on your head, and wearing your fur coat. And I see our youngster, as a small child nestling between us in bed, so touching to the heart, with his blond head as fair and smooth as pure silk.

And when I see such wonders before my eyes, and knowing what yet hides in the secret place of your womb, given that all is well with you up to now, then within me arises a very strong prayer to be allowed to be with you again and to live for you.

I wish this sometimes for a brief moment. But when I think back on what further sufferings abound in the world, at the front and beyond, I recall that God receives all of our prayers and not one hair of our heads will fall except by His will. Then I can take courage. I know that we deserve nothing, but He is gracious and takes care of our prayers. And His eye sees you and me at the same time. And this is also good. But now the dinner bell is ringing downstairs. So writing has become unsafe, and that's why I need to stop now. It's done me infinite good to chat with you once more.

Friday morning

Darling, it is no longer a sure thing that we won't be going to Germany. My enthusiasm for going there is obviously nil. But this I know; that God is with me. Hold fast, my darling. So – naturally I don't know if I will ever see you again. One advantage for me is: I'll be going there in good health and the war has now reached its ultimate stage. I may very well return. But if not, my darling, you must know that till my last hour, I will always be thinking of you and the children with such undying love. Even in a distant land I will continue to pray for you.

As they grow, nourish our children in the belief that for the thinking man many problems have to be faced regarding God, but He is always there when you need Him, proving His eternal existence by the fact that He can't ever leave us in the lurch. Greet my parents and thank them for the wonderful gift of the gospel that they have entrusted to me in my youth. That precious gift alone has made everything right and worthwhile.

And ask forgiveness from all those that I have caused to endure sadness. With much love I think of them and of my sister. Greet A. from me. And of course my relatives on your side: sisters-in-law, brothers-in-law, cousins... Thank them for the love with which they have included me in their precious family, and for all the good that I've received from them. And to whom should you further pass my greetings? Greet, Froukje, Polletje, Elderling, Lisette, the neighbours, the Dennens, and so forth. If I do not return, let it be known in our church I thank them for every token of love that I've encountered in their midst; ask forgiveness of anyone to whom I might have done wrong, or whom I have failed. Let them know of my comings and goings over the last year and give them from me this personal blessing:
"The Lord bless you and keep you..."

Well, I have now actually related all the essentials. If I forgot something, you can easily fill that in, knowing my thoughts as you do.

Thank you my dear wife, for all you've given me. It has been an amazingly massive contribution. Much more than you might guess. It may be that I will come back to you and the children. If so, this letter, which I've written entirely in the tone of a farewell, will do you no harm. If I do come to you once again, we will start afresh. And if not, then I'm glad I have at least shared my inner thoughts in this way. Also, if I do not return, and if the prospect of living in Europe remains as dire as it appears now, go to America. But come what may... God bless you richly. It could be that this letter is premature, because at the moment we're still here. But I don't believe so. And in any case we can't be sure that we'll be granted more hours like these ones.

That is why I'm sending this off now, for I do not know if I will ever get another chance.

Tot ziens;[165] either here on earth or in Heaven above.

---

165 "See you," "Till we meet again," or "Farewell."

Chapter 66

Just as I have with the other letters, I've left certain sections out, but from the weighty content that I have openly shared, which was not intended for me alone, but in part for all of you and for the church, you will have been able to grasp why I suffered such a leaden heaviness in my arms. So heavy, that they seemed to be paralysed, and I could barely lift them for a week. The sun shone on the pretty array of colours of the dahlias in the garden beds of the new *pastorie* where I was a guest – it was nurturing and warm. I did not feel it however, nor see it. An icy hand had clamped around my heart.

For on the outside of the letter was printed:

FROM A DUTCH PRISONER WHO HAS BEEN TRANSPORTED TO GERMANY.

"But that cannot be!" said the lady who brought me the letter. "He was still in jail when he passed the letter on."

But I was so paralysed that I no longer could take any initiative. The *Dominee* where I was staying offered to telephone my family in the province of Holland. They should have been informed of any new developments.

A little while later the *Dominee* returned. It was a false alarm! My special man was still exactly in the same place, the prison on the Weteringschans. His laundry had still been collected that same morning and he was in good spirits, despite passing through a temporary depression, probably because he had been on his own for so long. But he now had company... and had asked after me...

I had once been in a pitch-dark cave. Then suddenly I saw again the faint suffused daylight around a craggy corner of the rock face. I never realised that the light I saw was 'just' common daylight; it was so beautiful. I now received that same sensation and an inexpressible gratitude filled my heart.

That night I dreamed that a car took me to the hospital. I had been passing through a dark valley of searing pain and dismay. But then there came the bliss of motherhood and of Heaven, because I held my baby in my arms and was transported to another world, where I saw people and things that were dear to me on earth. November mists hung low over the meadows and the vast, bare, ploughed farmland. I wanted to return once more to the *pastorie*, to say goodbye to everything. The roosters crowed; it was morning, but not a frigid November morning. Instead the sky radiated red and gold, birds sang in the tender green grass; it was spring.

In a dream anything is possible and a dark November morning can even be transformed into eternal spring. From the ploughed fields before my gaze arose the enchanting scent of rich earth; everywhere the country verdure was springing forth. Wherever my thoughts roamed, there was I also. There stood the old house in the dawn. A blackbird sang in the beech, whose leaves shone with the glow of copper. Behind the house the first spring flowers unfolded to welcome the sun. I unlatched the shutters and nodded. Everything was as it should be; there was the divan bed, the dresser with the baby clothes. Everything was restored to order; the furniture was returned and each piece was back in its customary place. But when I looked over the low-trimmed hedge, I saw men in prison clothing... digging.

They were digging a long straight trench, and one of them, at the head of the row, was Domie. I went to him, bent toward him and kissed his forehead. Then he threw his shovel away: he was free! His grey clothes fell away from his body like a worn, shed cocoon, and made way for the suit he was wearing when he was my bridegroom. He stooped and picked flowers. Right there and then his hands wove a bridal wreath, which he set carefully on my head. Through our garden flowed a broad river. On the other side stood Hansje, crying with his little fists over his eyes. "Mama!" he cried passionately. Then I stretched out my arms to him and the banks of the river moved and closed upon each other, so that I could reach him. Domie watched on attentively, holding our new baby in his arms.

Then life came back to the old house; the lodgers were awake! Froukje was there. She opened the blinds on the inside, but the outside shutters she had left closed. Why did she do that? And Greet was there too. She went to feed the pig, because she was carrying a pail outside into the garden. And Polletje let the sheep loose that had been with Elderling since the Germans had looted the house. When I checked through all the rooms, there they all were – back again! The boys were still asleep, with their window open. As usual. Frits had hung his clothes over the back of a chair and his tie was hanging on the doorknob. Chris' coats were rolled up in a tote bag, fastened by a piece of wire around it in order to facilitate his dive down the hidden corridor in an instant. That was no longer necessary, but the preparation had become second nature to him. I looked at their faces in tenderness. They looked so young in their sleep! Then, as I watched, Frits opened his eyes, smiled at me, turned on his side and fell asleep again.

Up in the attic, in their own room, the Mice lay sleeping. Lily's dark curls caressed her forehead. A book still lay open on Esther's blanket. She had been reading in bed, and had fallen asleep like that. And there were Naomi and Miriam. Miriam held her arm above her head, bent gracefully at the elbow inside the pink silk sleeve of her pyjama top, while Naomi lay skewed across her bed, as always. That's how it had been before and they had all come back, now free, because there was peace.

I turned to go to our bedroom. There, in my own bed, I lay motionless and white. I had died. I understood now: they had all passed over before me. Even the Mole was there; he suddenly popped up out of the tunnel. He always turned up unexpectedly. He also belonged here. He'd come to rouse the people in the house, for he found that they had slept long enough.

I'd had such concern for him, but there he was now... and Wil and Lisette! All cares, all the dark shadows were gone, all that remained was the clear morning light. There was movement upstairs; the folk were getting up. But they did so very softly, because there was a corpse in the house. They sneaked on their toes through the hallway; they slipped down the loft stairs. The treads creaked. Startled, they stopped, and a whispering voice called,

"Sssst! Tante Jo is sleeping!"

Chapter 67

Then I awoke. Rain trickled down onto the balcony, right against the balcony door, then down to the canal below and soaked down through the bales of straw laden onto a canal boat that was slowly being punted forwards. Rain, rain. And everybody is digging. A whole line, from Zwolle to Delfzijl. No one can avoid the rain. In this emergency they'll just have to suffer getting soaked through. From our community the men are away. And then there's that young farmer, at whose home the Mice had once stayed. They took him away to a concentration camp too, which happened after they set a trap for his mother and sister. They're digging now at Zwolle. The Netherlands has become a concentration camp in the cold, wet, everlasting rain, without any prospect of liberation. The Germans have held their positions for five weeks along our great rivers. It's the middle of October. This week the boys wrote a letter, the contents of which amounted to this: "We have been devastated and cut off from you, but we long to return."

And there before me stood Greet, wearing waterproof leggings – on that same morning of rain and homesickness for the life that I had dreamed about the night before. She had a few days off and now was coming over to the Hörn, first to see me at my new address, and then off back to our village of Nieuw Beerta to tidy up the *leerkamer* and set up for the church services there, because she thought it was too cold without a heater. That cheered me up tremendously. How selflessly faithful Greet was!

She also had recruited an army of helpers! Froukje, Janny, Imke; they all went over to the *pastorie* to lend a hand. Everywhere there was scrubbing and mopping. Windows were made to sparkle with a chamois; sofas, chairs, tables and cabinets moved aside, cobwebs swept, the organ polished. Then everything was ready for the service. Even a glass of water for the preacher was not forgotten; nicely covered with a saucer and placed at the improvised lectern.

Once everything was ship-shape, the girls became aware that they felt rather hungry. Greet went down to the cellar and fetched some potatoes. She also found a jar of rancid fat. She peeled the potatoes, and they stoked up the *leerkamer* stove and fried them on top. Then they ate them gratefully. It was an old-fashioned-cosy gathering there, around the hot stove, just like old times. "You must come back again, Greet, so it'll be just as nice as before," said Imke. Janny commented that all it lacked was for our own Domie to preach the Sunday sermon.

They were lonely, those children. The empty *leerkamer* was for them like a life-book's chapter which had closed. They had suffered "lost time with Domie and *Mevrouw*," as they called it; time which could never be recovered. No house-warming, no association meetings, no folk dancing, no singing at the organ, no summer camp days, nothing of their past innocent joy was there and nothing had been there all this summer and autumn. I received letters from them, from whose pages their hearts' desires spoke so clearly.

I had to go back to them; I longed for them with all of my being. By Christmas, the youth must have their spiritual home back again. A fresh beginning also had to be made with the Association for the elderly. This current state of affairs should not go on longer than was strictly necessary. I would just have to make do in that ransacked house, although it would be difficult with a newborn baby.

There was always some hope that although the last stage of the war seemed to have reached a temporary impasse, suddenly a breakthrough would come and Domie would return before Christmas. What more could I desire? Always my thoughts and prayers went out to Esther and Lily. A Polish winter... would Lily survive? How gladly I would have them back under our roof in freedom and compensate them for all the misery they have endured.

And the boys – how were they getting on? This week I handed a birthday letter to Greet to take with her to pass on to one of them. If they could just hang on a bit longer! From Naomi a few months ago I also received a letter. She would already be free, as she was staying in Limburg with the elderly couple who had been our guests. The Tommies' advance units had already passed through there in mid-September. And Miriam surprised me with a whole bunch of her own hand-made baby clothes. I so longed for them all. When they all returned to the *pastorie* there would be no beds for them, but we would sleep in the straw on the ground as princes and princesses!

Little Dikkie was born under the roar of English aircraft and the shouts of German commandos on exercise in the Winschoten Hospital grounds. There still was no peace in the land when my son was born, despite all the favourable predictions to the contrary, and his own father was still languishing in prison. I won't forget that trip to the hospital in the pale, dim light of a November morning. My thoughts were with Domie, as they always were. Occasionally, whenever I was not in too much pain, the doctor and I exchanged a few words en-route in the car.

We had prayed that morning, the *Dominee*, his wife and I. It was only six o'clock. Then I left the *pastorie* in the same direction the car had come from on that fog bound morning. A stretcher had been provided but it had not been necessary. After leaving me at the hospital the doctor returned home. A day's schedule of consultations was waiting for him, with many patients to see.

A young sister showed me the way to my room and then left me alone. The English planes roaring overhead, German commandos outside the windows, and here I would bear a child. Not a peace child. But it would be his father's joy when he came home, this great gift that I could give him. The house would be bare and empty, but standing there in the midst of nothing would be flowers and a crib.

"When I return, we should be happy and festive for one another's sakes," Domie had written. And why shouldn't we be so joyous? Wouldn't it be such a grand party – where we poor folk could gather round each other again, with Hansje there also and a new little baby? And with that thought I gritted my teeth together and endured the pain.

At a quarter past one during the afternoon, Dikkie was born. Exactly at the same time as Hansje, although his birth was in the middle of the night. I called him Dikkie Victor Emmanuel, because this child was the victory over all grief... God with us. When I saw him lying there, naked and crying, I was suffused by the same tender feeling for him that I had experienced with Hansje too, but now there was something more, a sense of endless mercy for your father, dear child. When your brother was born the circumstances were as bright as they are sad now.

But finally grief was overcome by joy, as the sun does eventually break through the tenacious fog. I had absolutely had it with these fierce pains and was now waiting for the stretcher to be taken to the operating room until my turn came to be helped, for I had to undergo a minor post-natal repair. The earlier mists of morning had been wiped out. Large, white fluffy clouds, drifting along in the blue sky; mountain monsters and caves. It made me think of Johan. With him I had also looked up there while I read him a poem by Henriette Roland Holst. About birth and death, the two poles between which this short earthly life moves. Then came my turn. Back pain, excruciating pain... I'd thought I was past all that now.

"... not like that, Sister. Just put her cap on."

All I saw momentarily were the gleaming instruments, white aprons and coats. Then it got dark, and I closed my eyes.

"Count," said the doctor, "...not so fast."

At the count of 50 I felt myself starting to drift off, but continued deliberately on towards 70. I heard myself very slowly mumble 68, 69, 70... then nothing.

Where does the spirit of a human remain during anaesthesia? In dreams? I dreamed very well, or was that just prior to reawakening? I roughly recalled the world in which I lived during my dream. This one was something indescribable, and when I came to, I had no pain. I could hear a metallic clanking sound, like small hammers. It pulsed in my ears.

"I'm awake, you know."

"*Ja* , that's good. You're done."

"I had such a wonderful dream."

"What did you dream about?"

"About our church."

Then a couple of sisters lifted me onto the trolley and pushed me away down the hall to a clean bed. Stillness and bliss. I had a new child. It would later be brought in to me. It weighed nearly eight pounds; it could really take a beating! So it was a boy. I had entertained thoughts of a girl, but it was better this way. Hans had a brother.

There was another bed in the room. The patient lying there turned her head towards me. So she was awake.

"Do you have paper and pencil for me?" Tomorrow was Sunday. Back home they just had to get my news, and so I wrote at once, since the messenger was still able to take my report to be read tomorrow in church. I had been requested to do this, and so wrote my cheery letter whilst lying flat on my back, because I had been given strict orders not to move.

The letter reached its destination in time. I was amazed by the arrival of this frail life into a harsh world, but was everything going to be alright after all? He had been born in the same hospital as his brother, but had he been as well cared for? And later on we'll go back together to our own church. We will have to refurbish and decorate our home when Domie returns, because some day there will have to come an end to this war.

A minor incident arose at the hospital: our marriage certificate had been taken away by the Germans and the surgeon who had helped me was a Jew who did not dare to come before the day arrived to deliver the baby. Instead an Officer of the Civil Registry had to come to the hospital, where the sister acted as witness and I dictated our names.

While still there, I received a letter from my former director from Amsterdam. I had asked him to try to search out Domie on my behalf, but got a message back that he had gone from one prison to the next, but Domie was nowhere to be found. I was not overly worried. Probably he was assigned to dig wells. All the men in the concentration camp at Amersfoort had to do this duty. Edzo as well – the young farmer from our village. But one day that young man returned home unexpectedly, almost running up to their door. Suddenly his sister called, "Look! It's Edzo."

Shouldn't Domie be able to do the same? To his fellow inmates he always said, "I'm aiming to be home by mid-November."

So, wouldn't he then make every possible effort to get here? I caught myself sometimes waiting by the door to watch for his arrival, because waiting for him had absorbed my whole life.

He just had to see our boy and the flowers and I had to tell him how good the people had been to me, and how they'd brought me milk and eggs and cake... so much on one occasion that the sister brought all the parcels in on a trolley.

My former room-mate had improved enough to go home, and her place was taken by a day-patient. Therefore I was left very much alone.

"Oh, my boy, why ever did you leave?" I heard myself say in the silence. I myself knew the answer.

It was to relieve the distress of many, however much difficulty remained for us.

Hansje, who had stayed over at a neighbouring *pastorie*, came over with his uncle and aunt to see his little brother and Mama. The morning I had gone away to hospital he was still asleep, so I had kissed him goodbye softly and on my tiptoes I had sneaked downstairs so as not to wake him.

On that visit he brought a wooden rattle for his little brother along with a pink bow that his aunt had poetically wound around the handle. He first looked around in amazement, but jumped in the air when he discovered me in the white linen bed.

"Mama!" he cried beaming. However, after that one visit he hasn't been back, because since that evening after being put to bed, he has been very sad and constantly crying for Mama. How fine it will be when we're all back together again! But for now we can't. Anyway, first things first... we still have to return to our own community, and for the present I will be taking the children home to Nieuw Beerta to stay at Elderling's house.

Chapter 68

After ten days I have recovered so well that we can manage the trip, and the baby is also doing well. The page has turned and happiness is now my portion. Sunday morning before church a telephone message came in response to my question about where Domie is, whom my ex-director could not locate. I need not at all be concerned about it, read the telephone message. Domie is still in the same section where the low-risk prisoners are housed, whatever the colour code of his laundry cart, and whatever the floor level to which he'd been confined, and has probably already heard yesterday (Saturday) of the birth of his son, because they had made it an urgent priority to get that message through to him.

With joy and thankfulness I walk to church with Elderling. A good healthy son, and with Domie everything seems satisfactory. That is worth a thank offering. In the service the 91st psalm is read.

He that dwelleth in the secret place of the most High shall abide under the shadow of the Almighty.

I will say of the LORD, He is my refuge and my fortress: my God; in him will I trust.

Surely he shall deliver thee from the snare of the fowler, and from the noisome pestilence.

He shall cover thee with his feathers, and under his wings shalt thou trust: his truth shall be thy shield and buckler.

Thou shalt not be afraid for the terror by night; nor for the arrow that flieth by day;

Nor for the pestilence that walketh in darkness; nor for the destruction that wasteth at noonday.

A thousand shall fall at thy side, and ten thousand at thy right hand; but it shall not come nigh thee.

Only with thine eyes shalt thou behold and see the reward of the wicked.

Because thou hast made the LORD, which is my refuge, even the most High, thy habitation;

There shall no evil befall thee, neither shall any plague come nigh thy dwelling.

For he shall give his angels charge over thee, to keep thee in all thy ways.

They shall bear thee up in their hands, lest thou dash thy foot against a stone.

Thou shalt tread upon the lion and adder: the young lion and the dragon shalt thou trample under feet.

Because he hath set his love upon me, therefore will I deliver him: I will set him on high, because he hath known my name.

He shall call upon me, and I will answer him: I will be with him in trouble; I will deliver him, and honour him.

With long life will I satisfy him, and show him my salvation.

That's a fine promise, I reflect:

A thousand shall fall at thy side, and ten thousand at thy right hand; but it shall not come nigh thee.

But whatever has happened since? Is this a long, fearful dream? The earth lies covered with a white cloth. Is that a death shroud? The night before little Dikkie was born a birdie honed his beak on my window; so gentle and unassuming as a bird can only be in the autumn. And now here in my own village I lie in bed and I hear a magpie scratching on one of the tall elms in the front garden.

"Papa is gone," Hansje said this evening, as he sat on Elderling's lap.

When I think of this, I suddenly see Domie very clearly, lying on his prison cot in the dark, because there is no electric light. I now know something of that horrible prison life from the accounts of his fellow prisoners who have already been released. The constant lurking eye at the peephole, so that one of the inmates inside the cell would stand to block its view when Domie wanted to read or write, because all such activities were forbidden; the Red Cross parcels, over which they rejoiced like children, because the prison food is nowhere near nutritious enough; the one litre of water per day, which is all they have to drink, wash and keep their cells clean; the all-consuming longing for home revealed by the intricate description he gave another inmate of what his house looked like. All of that I know.

But I do not know that these feet will never run to me, that his arms will no longer encircle me, because that entire body that I have loved so much lies stiff and cold. The heart is pierced through as is the high forehead behind which lived such good and noble thoughts. It is not the silence of the Amsterdam prison that haunts my space, but the silence of the monotonous rustling of rain on the shroud of fallen leaves. I do not know. Not so much as a single inkling. One could not keep such a secret from me. It is the night of Monday to Tuesday. The tidings will only reach me on Friday.

"You will just have to bear it," says Elderling, after he told me.

Ja, I have to bear it. But I do not believe it. The room is spinning around me. Is this the sick joke of a drunken guard or someone else? For surely it can't be true. It's impossible! I should immediately call them to hear that lie refuted, just like when I got the false message that he was on the transport to Germany.

Dikkie is hungry because it's now noon. Mechanically, I take him out of the crib and lay him at my breast. All the richness and goodness of one's life is decidedly inherent in this act, but in order that the child may drink, my own milk must now taste as bitter as gall. Oh, that I had died at his birth! He is now sixteen days old, and I did my best to recover my stamina quickly. See, I had to be ready for Domie who could be coming home. That was my glorious expectation, every day and every hour.

Hansje is lying in bed. He has the measles. I feed him some porridge, but he refuses it. How can a man still eat, even a very small man, who is unaware of the evil that overshadows him? How can I still provide food and see my children grow up in such a dreadful world? I didn't have that! I never had that! I wish, for the first time, that I would not continue to live any longer. To go where there are no duties which bind me to this odious life. Where there is no small, sick voice that calls, "Mama, will you stay with me?"

If God is not there, then I am free to separate myself from this miserable existence to be with my man in his death. Baucis and Philemon. The enemy had let me share in everything, why not also in his death? That would be a mercy. But no, I must continue alone... and every day brings a new torment. I must sleep, eat, live... because of my children. I have recently endured the pangs of labour, but this is an emotional distress so great that the physical pain fades in comparison. God! Where is God? Impenetrable darkness everywherc...

Thou shalt not be afraid for the terror by night; nor the arrow that flieth by day...

And they had him shot!

But he was not afraid of that. He wrote: *As for me, even as the damp mists swirl around us in the cold, pale dawn, in endless compassion, Thou wilt hide me forever in Thine everlasting arms.*

A thousand shall fall at thy side, and ten thousand at thy right hand;
but it shall not come nigh thee...

What an insult, such a promise! What a lie! Or is he not dead? God, then say something! Just answer me!

For him who is of Thee, and Thine entirely,
Naught is destroyed for truly Death is Life!

Who said that? Whose answer is that? Domie's... Domie says it. But he just can't – he can't set off on a trip to those distant coasts of light! He has to put a baby in his cot. And he says that as well in his letters! He still knows that! He must not leave me here, so helpless and forsaken. Everything, everything I have found before was so good. But this is not. He can't do this to me. To leave me, to never, never come back!

Elderling is like a father who comforts his sick child. He understands it all, and does not say much.

Nevertheless, this has still happened... the terrible, the incomprehensible! How did it happen? Where did it happen? Why did it happen? It is like groping in the dark. A repeated experience of the same things, over and over again...

A brief order, given the previous evening, in Amsterdam:
"Tomorrow line up at seven o'clock..."
And then out through the prison yard, which I had managed to infiltrate once. So I knew it, the pale pink of dawn, the wet mists.... and one night, the night before in fact, in which Domie said goodbye in the spirit to me, to Hans who is "Daddy's close chum" and who whispers in his sleep. Also to the very small child, that he has never seen and will never see, who will play every day and grow up, but Latin themes will not be his greatest companions. Domie's parents, who remain shattered, his church, his friends, his house, the old *pastorie*, upon whose threshold he will never again set foot, the small bathroom, from which

he will never emerge, yearning for closeness, quietly entering our room to sit on the edge of my bed.

His poems speak of eternal peace, above all clamour and strife.

"I was altogether done with it," he wrote, "but a man so quickly gets attached to all kinds of things..."

Later he continued, "God does not want to have me in my death, but to prepare me for life." And in another letter he wrote, "But you can be sure of this, that however and wherever in the world I am destined to die, I shall never be alone, but will always have God by my side." Does this life only get granted an extension after our surrender and willingness, so that it can become even purer?

To me his letters breathe so much goodness and devotion, such love and reverence. If God had granted him back to me now, what a blessing he would have been to us, to his church!

"But God's ways are often different from our ways,[166]" he wrote.

Has there really been a liberation? Certainly a release from prison. After all, Greek philosophy claims that the spirit is trapped in one's body as in a dungeon. Liberation only comes at death.

I am busy wrestling day and night with these thoughts and questions.

For thou, Lord, art my refuge.[167]

I know that God has been Domie's refuge and strength. But... that gloomy courtyard of the Weteringschans!

Assumptions, guesses.

Until one evening the doctor rang. He had received a message by telephone from my brother.

At Veenendaal there was an exclusion zone. A couple of Dutchmen had entered the area that was off limits, and therefore were trespassing. A German shot at them; one of the Dutchmen returned fire and the German was wounded. In reprisal six prisoners were then selected and

166 Isaiah 55:9.
167 Psalm 142:5.

executed. Three from the Weteringschans, Amsterdam, and three from Utrecht. What took place there? When the cell door was opened on that fateful dawn, had they been told why they were being collected?

Although the dread knock troubleth me with fears,
That knock that calls me to my final walk...

One would suspect as much, because he had given them my address and that of his parents. But it is also possible that they all thought they were about to be deported to Germany, because one of the selected men had stuffed some bread in his pocket.

What was really going on in the mind of my husband? What did he imagine? Hansje playing? He had lived through these moments already and was prepared to depart. What else?

But you can be sure of this, that however and wherever in the world I am destined to die, I shall never be alone, but will always have God by my side.

The shouts of German soldiers. *"Heraus!*[168]*"* One last time a hand reached for the straw palliasse where a Bible, a few letters and a hymn book were hidden. The letters were widely read. They were from his parents and me. Two other prisoners were also taken from there that morning. Across the yard and through the gateway they went; through the same gateway, beneath which I had passed one time, yearning to perhaps catch a glimpse of him. And one of those three men, who passed under the gate, stepping into the waiting car, was the most treasured possession that I had. The most? *Ja.* I had two children now to look after, but at the same time, he was entirely there for me. With him I had lived through so much, with him I had suffered so much. With him I had also known such great joy. For him I had sat waiting in suspense night and day. I had wanted to hold onto him at any price and keep him from adversity.

"I must do this," he said, when I brought to his attention our perilous situation.

---

168 "Out of here!" or "Get out!"

"But think of yourself, think of all of us here at home, the people under our roof," I answered.

"I must, because there are so many who are depending on me," he said again.

This created a painful conflict. And now after all that? I had lost!

The church of William the Silent... Psalm 27, where we were married. S.T.I.U. *Saevis, Tranquillis in Undis.*

The door snapped shut, the car drove away. Where now? Domie knew our country so well: the flooded pastures, the river Vecht, which meandered through that November gloom, because it was a grey foggy day. Then the tower of the *Dom*[169] of Utrecht rose above the mist, the city where we had both been students. The car stopped at the prison. Three young lads were escorted from there. He spoke with these desperate boys, calmed them, prayed with them. He was a Minister, a Minister of Christ and was possessed of a great love. Christ had given him an assignment. He had once helped carry someone across the chasm of death. That was Johan. Now these five others and he himself were also to be brought safely across.

"So know then, that until my last hour I shall think of you all with love," he wrote. And on the other side of the chasm stood Christ, who gave His life for Domie. It was between four and five in the afternoon when the car stopped in the forests of Agterberg. The night was already falling. The November twilight faded behind the woodland. The voices of the German soldiers were the only sound that broke the silence. The trees stood motionless, like the pillars of a cathedral. A short, sharp command. Then twelve shots rang out and echoed around the edges of the forest. The mouth that had spoken that last blessing was closed forever.

---

169 Cathedral.

Chapter 69

I've relived this so many times... have seen it and experienced it so often that it is now a relief to finally write it down. He had wanted to come home, had asked for paper and pencil with increasing urgency. He wanted to write to the German authorities as the desire grew stronger. Now the prison doors had been flung wide open. On the 20th November. Liberation!

Liberation? Could it really be true? It seemed so, because the gatekeeper gave him all his papers back and that meant you were free and could go home. Go home? *Ja*, to the Father's House. Set free and with Christ!

The German soldiers had done their work. They were merely henchmen, tools of an infernal machine. *Father, forgive them, for they know not what they do.*[170] They are accountable only in very small measure for this murder.

They departed, leaving their victims in the rain, which dripped mournfully onto the dense carpet of leaves. Nobody knew anything. It was all completely silent and had been carried out in secret. Yet that very same night my sister-in-law had a remarkable dream. She dreamed that she saw a strange funeral procession; a farm cart with a white cloth draped over it. My brother walked behind with a baby of 14 days in his arms. They had strewn flowers over the coffin. They were proceeding down a long hilly road when suddenly they were mortally terrified by rifle shots. "Oh, God," she said softly. "They've killed another one!"

---

170 Luke 23:34.

When she awoke the next morning she related the dream to her daughter Margo who had helped Domie so faithfully in his undercover work. That was on Tuesday morning. On Wednesday morning that dream became reality. Domie was buried in the churchyard in Veenendaal without anyone knowing or coming to pay respects, laid out on a farm cart brought along the very road which she had seen in her dream.

When she cycled along the same route on the following Saturday, after rumours of the terrible fact had penetrated her consciousness and she wanted to gather further information, she affirmed to Margo, "It was this road! This really was the road from my dream!"

And how is it to be explained that during his imprisonment, some friends of Domie in Rotterdam, who had never before played Domie's favourite gramophone recording of Cesar Franck, now did so on that very evening of 20th November?

Two days later, in silence and reverence, some loyal Dutchmen dug in the churchyard at Veenendaal. No one knew who they were, but there were found in Domie's sack a Bible full of notes and a hymn book with my name inside and a few letters. By these Domie could be identified. They therefore made the connection with my family. In the hymn book Domie had put a crease through the last verses of hymn 139:

No sparrow falls on earth without Your will,
And Lord, my heart finds comfort and is still,
Because You watch with care o'er all my ways.

So God my shield and help shall surely be,
Nought do I fear in sky, on earth and sea,
He maketh all things good throughout my days.

Chapter 70

This serves as a tender admonition to us who are left behind. To me, to help me think of all this and yet not get distraught.

And indeed, here I first saw the hand of God behind human arbitrariness. Why Domie? Well, he was completely willing. How many people live their daily lives unprepared for death while being hunted during war? I had not been able to pray for some time. But now I could do so again. The moon shone peacefully above the dark land and the stars were there as an eternal witness to the greatness of God who carries the whole breadth of the universe in His hand, and with it also our small lives.

I had received a letter. In it was described to me how Domie's body had been transferred from Veenendaal to our family grave in Driebergen. "Although we should not have," read the letter, "we have nevertheless seen him." For myself, I wanted to have certainty, because so many people who came with condolences asked, "Do you know for sure?"

In all those past sixteen days, Domie had not changed. A face full of peace and tranquillity, hands outspread, proved that he felt nothing of pain and struggle during his very last moments. Over his underclothing, he was wearing his blue suit and his long-sleeved brown shirt from Palestine.

Domie's hands! How I loved and admired them! What could he not do with them? The hands of an artist, they were; very long and narrow and beautifully formed. With them he conjured up music from the Lochem organ in the church with the high vaults. During a New Year's Eve service he played Cesar Franck and I sat crouched in the glow of the stove in the aisle below and the music filled the whole space. With them he could make music or dig the soil. He would pick up a little boy or tenderly stroke my hair. He constructed a folding ladder, and picked a bunch of marsh marigolds for me with those fine hands, which would also extend in blessing over his congregation. He was my pride and my absolute joy, and I would say to him: "I love you a lot more than I even think I know myself." The days and years would come, in which I would realise that far better and far more deeply.

On that moon-lit night I was in the Spirit, after receiving a letter about the grave site. The letter stated:

"The wreath and the cross which were sent from your church are still lying on the grave. On his birthday we also brought a bouquet of blue spruce, holly and silver birch catkins, so that the whole grave is now completely covered with green foliage, sloe berries, catkins and purple beauty-berries. The wreath which was given by you and your two children is a very fine arrangement of young foliage – fine palm leaf with white cyclamens. The flowers that were on the casket have been placed into the grave."

"God watches over a matter," my father-in-law wrote to me, and it indeed seemed so. Johan and Domie: they now rest side by side.

To Thee belongs my greatest treasure
For Thou hast surely first loved me.
Soul, mind and body for Thy pleasure
I gladly sacrifice to Thee.

His body lies there now, slowly combusting back into earth, because he had voluntarily laid it on God's altar. And I had wanted to wait. For us to continue his work, finish what he had started; that which I had had to leave half-done. To continue our God-assigned work together. And then, after all that, would finally come the great "Goodbye" for both of us.

Once we made a trip to England. I was working then at the editorial office in Amsterdam and had a fortnight's vacation. But Domie had already departed; he had decided to cycle the whole way, both within the Netherlands as far as the coast and then in England after his arrival. We planned to meet up in a small town in Wales with a long name, in which many L's occurred. I sat on the train, dreaming a little while, looking through the window at the scenery of green hills and dales lying beneath the heavens. I did not pay attention very well. The train had already passed through so many tiny stations with large sign boards displaying seemingly unpronounceable names. Until I suddenly saw a tall slim figure with a blond, swaying crest. The joyful surprise I felt then! I could not believe it! It was Domie who had come to fetch me!

Trains have always played a major role in our lives, because it was on a train that we met for the first time. For us there has always been a sense of things foreordained. Thus, we hadn't met simply by chance, but this was a divine plan that from eternity past was already established. It was a miracle, that meeting. Neither of us would have ever thought to contrive such an event. It was a radiant May day, and he joined me in an otherwise empty compartment. Rijpma's history open on my lap provided just the stimulus toward a conversation. The train rolled through a landscape alive with blooms and among that fair display was a forest blackthorn, its blossoms white in the sun. It was clothed with a delicate silver-green haze like a wedding veil. We both gazed at it and then at each other with joyful, radiant eyes, because we realised here was something of a deep mystery that God was trying to reveal to us. We recognised His presence. Yet we knew nothing of each other; just our names were exchanged upon parting. How would we ever find each other again in a big university town without any addresses?

But we were as happy, carefree children who without any preconceptions had allowed one glance to strike deeply within our souls. From this developed the awareness and also the desire, not to lose each other, but to find each other again for forever. What God foreordains for us, happens. We found each other again on that memorable day in the park... and we shall find each other again there with God, where the needs of others will not separate us and where there will be no more tears.

Eye hath not seen, nor ear heard, neither have entered into the heart of man, the things which God hath prepared for them that love him.[171]

God speaks to us in images because they are the shadow of eternal truths, and we with our flawed perceptions can only poorly grasp these matters in such a way.

In Jesus my inheritance lies,
Hidden with God beyond the skies,
He is my place of rest.
I praise and lift my songs on high,
I await His coming by and by,
He's my delight, my best.

---

171 1 Corinthians 2:9.

Chapter 71

First the nights were almost entirely filled with wakefulness. Later came the dreams. In those dreams we were together at the *pastorie* in the midst of our ministry. It was the night of the Women's Fellowship. In the *leerkamer* all was warm, bright and cosy. The women sat around the large, square table. "Would you help me out here with my bike?" asked Domie. He had to go off to the other women's meeting in Oldiek, then he would come back home and I would leave to take his place there. Each week we alternated this sequence. Domie's bike was standing in the corridor. I held the door for him, so he could ride out, but my cheek brushed against the roughness of his coat at the height of his shoulder, because I did not reach any further.

"My kitty," he said tenderly, as this accidental gesture reminded him of a cat that rubs against its owner.

Then to wake up in a strange bed and gradually realise it's not all familiar and so good, but the full stark, reality of loss!

Or in a dream to live together again at the Leidsegracht in Amsterdam, when it was still the wonderful, atmospheric city it used to be, and gradually see the streetlights come on; to see them reflected in the water and illuminate the back of the Schouwburg.[172] To walk beneath the leafy elms planted alongside the canals, where on a sunshiny spring morning a boat laden with flowers from Aalsmeer was being lazily punted forward. Sometimes he accompanied me to my office, or he came to pick me up there on a sultry, scented spring

---

172 *Leidse Schouwburg* – The oldest Dutch theatre in continual use. Built in 1705.

evening. How much I looked forward to those times, and what a sense of pride and happiness it gave me as I spied his lofty stature in the distance, or if suddenly the door of my private office opened and he stood before me in a light-grey flannel suit. Happy times, when we strolled along the rows of shops on Saturday afternoons and urged ourselves to buy an oak bedroom suite in the *Bijenkorf!*[173] How young and carefree we were during that joyful, light time full of dreams and expectations for our future. What a poignant contrast to now, in this dark winter of 1944 - 45.

Yet, in all those years of joyful festivity never had I loved him as much as now, in the darkness of prison and death. Never had I imagined him with such a yearning, consuming desire by night and by day as I do today.

After that first honeymoon period of our marriage, when we cooked our greens in the evenings after office hours, and fetched some potatoes from the cellar of *Oom* Kees[174] or ate them hot in town, towards spring a restlessness came over Domie that I could not fathom.

"What do you need?" I asked him. The strange call of the wild birds appeared to run in his veins. "I need to go away... far away," he said.

"Where then?"

"I don't know. To Czechoslovakia or somewhere like that, but at any rate, far away."

Maps were obtained for the day; new maps were purchased. For whole mornings and sometimes even whole afternoons, he would sit at a desk in the ANWB.[175]

"I want to go to Palestine," he finally declared to me one day.

"How will you get there?"

"By bike." He enthusiastically unfolded to me his plans. I saw half a

---

173 The Beehive, a large Dutch department store in Amsterdam, now a chain of stores.
174 Uncle Kees.
175 *Algemene Nederlandse Wielrijders-Bond*, the Royal Dutch Tourism Association.

year of loneliness for me, but it was indeed wonderful that he dared undertake this adventure – and it would succeed too – though everyone was already saying that it was "a crazy business".

In everyone else's opinions, I thought. But not to him. I believed in him and that faith made him strong.

But the night before his departure, he could feel my body tremble in the small bed. Concerned, he asked what was the matter.

"It is so terrible that you're leaving."

"So you've kept that from me all this time," he said, aghast. "I would gladly stay here at home, but it's just that I have already prepared everything for the journey."

We both felt unhappy that night, he due to indecision, and I, because I knew that I should let him go, but really couldn't bring myself to. "No... you have to go," I said finally, "and I freely grant you that privilege."

And since he was leaving on his bike the next day, a Friday, we agreed that I should follow him on my free Saturday afternoon to Lochem, where on Sunday morning he would play for his last service in six months, because taking such a long vacation would be necessary to accomplish the entire journey. A trainee organist would replace him for the duration.

We spent a wonderful and happy weekend in Lochem together. In the narrow street at the sexton's house, where he had returned the keys of the church, I waved him off for the last time. No tears... please... no tears! After all, that would only spoil for him the journey ahead.

I knew there were dangers associated with such a long trip; cycling alone through isolated mountainous regions and along the fringes of deserts, but my faith and trust in him were so great that I had freely let him go. But nevertheless I'd certainly been feeling the tension. After he passed through and beyond Constantinople, I heard nothing more of him for three weeks, despite the postal connections, including airmail, which for the whole world was so reliable at that time. He had been lying under a tree, debilitated by Typhus, and had later been taken into a Mission Hospital. In a church in Hungary, he was once almost crushed by a roll of copper sheeting that had suddenly fallen from a pulley hoist that had been set up to effect repairs to the roof. In Palestine he found himself a hair's breadth away from becoming an accidental victim of the war between the Jews and the Arabs.

But he always came back to me, my travelling adventurer. After everything, he always found a way back into a safe haven. And so I had waited with high expectations that he would come home safely once more after all these vicissitudes of war.

"But a warrior can only come home after the battle is over," he writes in one of his letters.

He booked his return from Egypt on cargo ships and by train. At Central Station I went to pick him up in a taxi. The festive homecoming was on the 20th November, and the magnificent eleven metre long room had been decorated by a friend. Greet had cooked a wonderful array of food and the painter living upstairs had brushed a welcome greeting on our door.

It was cosy and companionable all that evening, but over the next few days Domie started feeling uncomfortable. For he now had to get used to being grounded and remain in the same place, and there were no more new and exciting things to experience on the immediate horizon. Moreover, upon his return in November, the weather was chilly, foggy and gloomy, after experiencing all those bright, warm countries from which he had returned!

"Who has tasted the water of the Nile, always longs to return," says the proverb. That was also Domie's experience. He had tasted of another world, where other things were possible, but not here. A world that I did not know, and he sometimes longed to return there, and he even made plans for a next time, when we could both go together.

And in these recent dark days before Christmas, whenever I walked along the road in the cold, damp fog to our uninhabited *pastorie*, the house where we were together and later were happy with so many others despite war and persecution, the *pastorie*, which stood now so desolate and abandoned, with its shuttered windows, then a nameless anguish caught me by the throat and I wondered how could he be so happy if he left me so sad and lonely? Or was it that he had forgotten me, with all the new things that he would now experience... all God's wonders that had opened to him?

I recall how it was when he played on the Lochem organ. As he played and drew open the various combinations of stops of this magnificent instrument, he became completely lost in the miracle of glorious sound. He forgot the time and sometimes I thought he forgot my small, insignificant figure hiding down there in the church pew. When I asked him about it, he said, "No, I was playing just for you!"

So then, had he forgotten me now? Did he ever think of us, or was he lost in the contemplation of the majestic wonders of God? It may not be that difficult to give a typically orthodox answer derived from doctrines enshrined in the catechism, but for those who have to deal with the reality of death, seeking answers about the hereafter, and our relationship with the one we love so much, this is a pressing question. But what did I really want? Would I wish to have him back in the ashen-grey of days, back in prison perhaps, in a world of bombs and misery, hunger and war? How much food would the people in the Amsterdam prison get, since the Germans had blocked the receiving of all Christmas parcels from the Red Cross?

I had granted him his Palestine journey. Now I granted him this journey to the The Holy Land from which no one may return: but with that contract there came a secret, strong yearning within me to be able to go there too.

Jo with Domie at the start of his solo trip to Palestine by bicycle.

"Mama, you're not going away, are you?" Hans has become afraid; a consequence of our life of restless wandering.

"No, my darling, I'm sticking with you."

"Always?"

"*Ja* always."

My little boy settles contentedly in my arms. I pull the covers over us. Nothing binds us to life so strongly as the helplessness of an infant.

"Footsie..." the little voice says again.

I take his little foot in my hand. This is after all "bone of his bone." In the crib the baby is breathing audibly. All fits together. Such truth reaches very deeply within me. But the one big boy for whom I have also nurtured a deep maternal love, alongside my other feelings, is now gone from me. Forever. Or at least for the whole of this earthly existence. Or does his love endure, but he can't contact me, nor I him, like when he was in prison? Furthermore, I am also sitting in a cell, limited by my sensory perceptions. But sometimes there suddenly comes a flash of intuitive knowing... that we are not left alone. Occasionally it even extends to a broader spiritual vision that betokens a closer, glorious reality. As when one is dying and heavenly music is often heard in the distance, so sometimes grace is given to get in touch with the invisible world.

Chapter 72

I have received many letters from released prisoners, staff and people who were rescued by Domie. One of his associates in the Resistance wrote:

Now that for the first time a reliable messenger is travelling north, I cannot pass up this opportunity to share the feelings that inspire me on a daily basis, whenever I think of the passing on of your husband. Feelings and thoughts that readily speak for themselves and even though we don't know each other, must also find an echo in your heart.

It was only in 1943 that I first met your husband. I still remember how we were sitting together in a small back room and he said: "What I do is founded on solid Christian principles."

I confess to you that I was rather sceptical when I heard this statement. As a free thinker, one is soon inclined to regard such glib words as just a pat answer. During the year when I had the opportunity and was able to assist him now and then, working for a common ideal which was based on trust, I discovered that the words he spoke at our first interview were the pure and unmitigated truth.

With a passion that I have only rarely seen, he has given everything right up to the last hour of his life for whatever his principles demanded. The last words I heard from him were when he called out to Miens at the station in Amsterdam on the 4th September when he was to be transferred to Vught: "I've never suffered one minute of regret for what I have done. I will not retreat one step!" He remains for me and for so many, a true hero, who fought for his principles right to the bitter end. If anyone ever were for me a pure and shining example, then he is that, and so shall he remain. Now I read over this I see how meagre and inadequate my words seem. I hope to be permitted to pay a visit to you after the war. Until then it is better to write under my pseudonym.

From his fellow prisoners I know that he helped to ease the time of their incarceration by telling them anecdotes from his trip to Palestine – every day a small extract. That he never complained and when they grumbled about the food, responded: "Outside the prison, they might be getting even less than we are." That together they hummed songs from the hymn book whenever the guard's leering eye was not at the peephole and how they sat shielded behind their barricade of mattresses, in order, at the slightest sound, to hide their little Bible or hymn book in the straw. That he, before they went to sleep, prayed aloud with them, and after a sleepless, heavy night, in which he "wrestled with God," the next morning told his most trusted cell-mate that he was now altogether ready and willing to go any way that God wanted him go. And that companion was entrusted to write to me personally about his willingness to face death, if it ever came to that.

Another inmate from Wassenaar paid me a personal visit and confided that Domie said that if he should not return home, it would give him such peace to know that I would continue the work of the church.

And a young Jewish man, Miriam's fiancé, wrote: *When, at that all-critical moment, when we were absolutely desperate, because there was no other prospect for us than the mass graves in East Prussia, in our extremity came Domie, a complete stranger. He came to help us, came to our rescue...*

The man who made the impossible possible.

And then there was Chris, who said Domie never wanted to be a soldier, but that he had in reality become one, not to destroy men's lives, but to save them; and from this you could see that Domie was a true soldier of Christ.

And finally, the letter of a friend from Amsterdam: *On Wednesday morning we heard the terrible news, but we did not have confirmation. That we did get... however, not expressly, but from observing the conduct of official people and circumstances on the following Friday, when we had to fetch his laundry from the Weteringschans. At both the Weteringschans and in Euterpestraat where Jo has been, their evasive responses and terse "no comment" confirmed the truth that something irreparable had occurred.*

This same friend who with his wife has cared so faithfully for Domie's laundry linen, reproached himself severely that on the Saturday, when my letter arrived announcing the birth of our son, he did not go straightaway to the prison that evening to pass it on.

When he did get there the following Monday, it was already too late, because Domie had been escorted out of the prison that same day between eleven and one.

Perhaps it was better this way; the message of the birth would have intensified his strident longing to go home and would have only increased his struggles. The uncertainty in which he then lived also left open the possibility that I would not survive the birth and we would thus meet again in the new life in Heaven. I can only resign myself to God's greater wisdom and trust that in His mercy He had provided a better way.

For some time Domie had not been given various things we sent to him in prison. He walked around in old, dirty and threadbare pyjamas. He never received the new clothes that we sent, including additional warm underwear and socks. He had requested his thick jacket. We also sent that. Did he ever receive it? On his last trip to Veenendaal he was not wearing a jacket. However, curiously enough, he was wearing one of the tan sport shirts in which he had made the journey to Palestine!

At the last *pastorie* I'd stayed at, I had felt really sad that it would soon be the season for *Sinterklaas*, but Domie would still be sitting in a prison cell and I couldn't even send him a single present. What a fine job we used to make of that old traditional Dutch Christmas celebration! Last year we had the members of the Youth Fellowship cooking a big pot of bean soup. Each one of them brought a handful of beans, an onion, a potato and some Maggi stock cubes. In the *leerkamer* we then held a celebration meal all together. And whoever found a raw bean in the soup had to recite something. There were quite a few who found raw beans. These ones then had to act out a charade together: "The Wolf and the Seven Young Kids". And then after the meal Domie appeared on the stage dressed as *Sinterklaas* and accompanied by his servant. He then talked to all his youthful friends before, one by one, giving out the gifts he'd brought with him.

The day after that we held a party for our house-mates, who had already been busy for at least a month with the preparations. The Mole also came together with a friend of Esther's from Amsterdam, and lots of presents. He had painted that picture for us, of the well-known *Magere Brug* over the Amstel. Domie and I had lived on the other side of it, so could easily pass across that bridge during the day. And that we certainly did! When I was working at my office, I myself crossed over at least four times a day. And how often we walked across there together – even more frequently if we went out for an evening stroll. The atmosphere then was so fantastically lovely, with the boats floating silently on the canal, each carrying a single lamp that was reflected on the surface of the shadowy water, and the many, many lights of the city in the distance casting a red glow against the dark sky. And it was so quiet there. The sounds seemed muted to us: a tram which rode over a bridge, a car horn hooting and a vague murmur in the distance; the voices and footsteps of many pedestrians. It was like the sound of blood that the heart of the city caused to stream through her veins.

There, on that narrow double drawbridge over which we were strolling, lost in thought and arm in arm, Domie asked me in earnest whether we shouldn't go to America, to escape the full terrors of war, which he foresaw were inevitably bound to engulf us. He had only recently completed his journey through the countries of Eastern Europe, and in particular through Germany, and what he had witnessed there had fully persuaded him of what was imminent. But I did not take his view with the deadly serious import that he gave it. I had not seen as much as he had, and was more drawn to what we would have to leave behind. I also knew that we would find no peace abroad in a strange land, despite all those terrible things happening to our country, but we would rather bear the imposition or defend ourselves against the threat here among our own folk, with whom we felt we were one. That argument Domie could readily accept. Should we have gone to America, or have we chosen the right way; he to "fight the good fight"[176] and to sacrifice his life... and I then to sacrifice him?

I ask that question of myself this *Sinterklaas* Eve, as I cycle by the empty *pastorie* along the road to the doctor's house. A year ago there was such joyous festivity behind those closed shutters; now I recognise only emptiness and hollowness, with here and there a broken chair, and in the hollow hallways are scattered empty, discarded boxes that were robbed of their contents. Desultory rubbish lying everywhere, in chaotic disarray.

"Here once lived people who opposed the Third *Reich*," you could put up over the front door of this house. Between this year and the previous Christmas two have been taken to their deaths in Poland, a third (the Mole) is in a concentration camp. The man who was head of

---

176 2 Timothy 4:7

this house was shot and his wife is an outcast. And whether the battle is finally over, is a matter of conjecture.

I constantly see, again and again, an image of Domie; even now, when I cycle past his abandoned home. His body lies stretched out, far away, and very still under the ground, and he has a hole in his forehead.

After such thoughts it becomes difficult to find the thread again which binds us safely to God. I'm not someone who simply just fantasises through beautiful dreams and takes flight into an illusory world, but I also see the full gruesome realities of life. However much I saw of those, I would just have to endure. But in my need, I learned to pray again. "Anyone who has once been well able to does not forget how," said Elderling, when I told him I couldn't do it any more. He was right. Groping in the dark at first, I have had to learn to live by God's grace. I have had to learn to surrender a gift to the others who had been in the cell with him and yet came back... but not my own husband. I walk through this ruined house with my ruined life, in barren, bitter desolation.

Chapter 73

The Magere Brug[177]... the prophecy and its fulfilment. The power of the Evil One that seemed almighty in this world. Domie had, in his own words, joined hands "with the doomed". He saw the devastation from day to day that had been wrought in the lives of many. He always tried to turn away the destructive power as much as possible. The ordinary everyday life thus becomes insignificant; you evaluate it now with a different measuring rod; your resistance melts and you are drawn deeper in – you cannot loosen its ties, because that means breaking trust with so many and betrayal of the good cause that you stand for.

On one of those more recent days I was conversing with a kind-hearted lad who is Polletje's brother.

"I started off my Resistance work with small tasks," he said, "but they became more and more, because, you see, I just had to. But if they do arrest me and for this I have to die, I hope that I shall be as courageous as Domie."

One Sunday in the church, Domie spoke on being worthy to suffer for Christ's sake. I stood there feeling rather sceptical. After all, every man or woman fears and shuns suffering. Yet Domie has proved that this text can be fully realised, because he had by virtue of his convictions literally been mocked, maltreated, put in prison and slain,

---

177 Here the author uses the bridge as a metaphor of the narrow way of Christ, the way which Domie also took, following Christ through death, to link a broken world to Heaven.

all because he had *fulfilled the law of Christ,*[178] and with the laying down of his own life he helped and served those who were in distress.

No one, it says in John 15, *has greater love than he that lays down his life for his friends.* What applied to the first Christians was true for Domie. Thank God also for the many Christians throughout history whose profession was, *The love of Christ constraineth us.*[179]

Christmas was fast approaching. In other years I had walked the entire district with the Christmas list. Presents for the children... could you even obtain them now? My heart was not in it, for my baby took up a lot of my time. He was a harmonious child that did not appear to have suffered, despite having been with me in a police cell and having endured many other disasters with me. Later he would prove to be a very sunny and very smiley little chap. Janny, also a member of the Youth Fellowship, unloaded a great burden from my shoulders by promising that she would take on responsibility for all the preparations for Christmas. The others would help her, including Froukje and Petertje. And so, on a certain day in the week before Christmas, they got busy decorating the *leerkamer*. Elder Mulder came with tables and chairs from the Oldiek congregation. Oldiek no longer had any fuel for heating, and so we could make use of their borrowed furniture here in our village during the celebrations.

And then unexpectedly, there appeared some unwelcome visitors. Three party members, an NSB mayor from the neighbouring village (who because of the illness of our own mayor had taken over the local reins), a traitorous innkeeper and a third man. They came to see if there was anything left in the *pastorie* to scavenge, and clumped with their heavy boots throughout the empty house. Then Janny appeared from the passage leading from the *leerkamer*, and noticed the rapacious lords looting a preserving jar, some buckets, some small dishes, some mats,

---

178 Galatians 6:2.
179 2 Corinthians 5:14.

some left-behind brooms and brushes, and some old clothes, which the Germans had discarded from a chest which they found upstairs. They got busy transferring everything to a car which was waiting outside the gate. The old coal stove was also standing right by the front door. They had made a terrible mess by dragging it through the kitchen and hallway, which were littered and smudged with ashes and soot.

"What are you doing?" Janny asked innocently in her mother dialect. They looked at each other, as if trapped. How did that wench appear here so suddenly?

"This stove was released and left behind by Germans for *Mevrouw* to cook on," continued Janny. "They already took away the electric oven."

"How do you know that?"

"Because I was right here in the house when we were preserving beans with the Weck."

"Where is Domie?" one of the uninvited miscreants had the insolence to ask.

Suddenly Janny recovered her mastery of Dutch.

"You don't need to ask me that, as you know very well yourself," she said, her lips trembling.

"*Joa*, right, they know right well."

"He should have been thinking about his own household," said the renegade innkeeper.

The two others nodded. *Joa*, that was so...

"And if he'd only listened to his conscience," judged the mayor.

"Domie was a Christian and he has shown that by word and deed!" said Janny, fiercely.

"But he has hidden Jews and that is not allowed."

"But aren't Jews people like us?"

"No, Jews aren't even human."

Then Janny received a surprising offer.

"If you still want to get married, wench, I have the key of the *pastorie*."

"You have the key? And you would really give me that?"

"If you go and get married, wench. I got the key back from the Scholtenhuis and I can let whoever I want live in the *pastorie*."

"What about *Mevrouw* then?"

"*Mevrouw* no. She won't get the key. And that butter churn I'll be taking as well. The people may not have that."

"They had a permit to use it for goats' milk."

"Doesn't matter. They may not have it."

After this philosophical discussion, they left the house, taking with them the last items that the Germans had previously left behind. But they left the heavy coal stove standing at the front door, ready for an imminent removal. Elder Mulder told the mayor in the *leerkamer* that he should be ashamed of himself. But shame was certainly one of those unaffordable bourgeois notions of the pre-war era. It did not find any place in the conscience of a mayor of the New Order.

I had just finished bathing the baby, when an agitated Petertje rang the doorbell at Elderling's house.

"*Mevrouw*, they're at your house again and now they're taking out the last things."

"Who are in my house again, and what are they taking out?"

"Mayor and them... the stove and whatever."

I was shocked. Would they never leave me alone? And if I ever hoped to go back to the *pastorie*, then at least I'd have a chance to cook. Without the stove, it was not possible. And you couldn't buy a replacement.

"I'll be right there, Petertje. You go ahead."

I searched out Elderling in the stables and found him. Then I described the situation and asked if he would mind coming along. That rapacious mayor was a bankrupt farmer. He would know Elderling and perhaps feel a little embarrassed when confronted face to face by him, and caught in the very act of pilfering the last usable items from the house. But when we reached the *pastorie*, the lords had already departed and only Janny was there to provide a faithful account, during which she broke into tears when she told us of their asinine question, "Where is Domie?"

Mulder shook his head sadly and continued to load his chairs and tables back onto the cart. Elderling walked thoughtfully through the cold, abandoned house that stood there, shivering in its nakedness, seemingly ashamed because such unholy eyes had pried into empty cupboards and discovered the secrets of stairs and hidden corners where persecuted people could hide.

Elderling came back, ripe with indignation. He had already witnessed the mess of soot and ashes in the kitchen and also the stove, which stood by the front door with its half section of flue pipe attached. That evening he wrote a letter to take over to the substitute mayor and on that same afternoon the Consulent,[180] at my request, also visited the fellow to serve notice that his disgraceful deeds had been brought to light. Under German law, items which have been released by the Germans may not be removed by the NSB.

The result? I could retrieve my things, except for the churn, which the mayor had apparently never set eyes on, but which "must have been taken away by others." *Ja* - sure! The Youth Fellowship perhaps? Or maybe the Church Council members? The mayor appeared to have suffered a sudden frightful attack of mercy, where the lords were once more constrained to perform folksy acts of charity.

Therefore, he had had the brilliant idea to take the whole bundle up to the Almshouse. However, the Consulent made him to understand that no one in this community was as poor and destitute as I was at the moment, so that kind of generosity, to put it mildly, seemed misplaced. Furthermore, that he, now in his official capacity as Consulent, came to

180 Minister from another district serving as an advisor and advocate while the
    resident pastor is away.

enquire about the key of the *pastorie*, because he had heard that it was in the mayor's possession. At any rate, it was high time that I had a roof over my head and that my long peregrinations with two small children in tow, including a newborn, should now finally come to an end. To which the mayor replied, "Hard times, hard measures." I wonder whether he will as glibly apply this philosophy to himself should like troubles come his way?

Chapter 74

Christmas! Here they come again! For the first time after a long time they will be together in the *leerkamer* once more to celebrate this festival together. Would I be able to do it? First at the Christmas celebration with the youth, then with the women soon after – all without Domie? But it had to be. He expected it of me. And the older boys and girls, they had helped me so much! They had prepared everything. Here they came now. A hefty fifty of them! They came inside very quietly, these otherwise rambunctious young people, by the light of the oilseed lamps which had to replace the customary candles. Now we were a family again, connected together by a great sorrow: Domie...

He would never cease to speak to them, I told them. Tonight he spoke to all of us, perhaps now more than ever... We sang Christmas carols and read the Christmas Gospel.

Make me free by thy bonds,
Make me live through thy death.

We'd never understood the full meaning and value of these lines as much as on this Christmas. And with the women who came not only from our village but all the way from the farthest corners of Oldiek, it was especially so.

"It was wonderful tonight, *Mevrouw*," two of them said to me as they left with tears in their eyes.

Outside it had been snowing. I was sad, but I was also grateful. The unending white bleakness of the fields stretched out on either side of the road where I cycled back over to Elderling's farm. The stars shone in the sky. They all had their heavenly destinations and I, a lonely woman, had also discovered something tonight; the destination of my own life. It had been so good there in the *leerkamer*. Why should I not be here doing this work? This was my spiritual home. Service... the great law of life. Serve God and thy neighbour. And so, embrace life once more and thereby come close to the one who had done this himself and who had gained my infinite love.

The second of January. One of the older boys of the Youth Fellowship opens the shutters outside the *pastorie* windows. That seems like a symbolic act. The New Year has arrived and the *pastorie* shall be inhabited again. Will this year bring peace? For me the tension has dissolved away, but I also wish that experience for many millions of others. How faithful and true are these grown-up boys and girls. They do not realise how much good that does to me, and I can only falteringly express to them that which I feel. They heave pails of water around the house to wash the windows and scrub the floors. They beat the dust from the runners, move the coal oven from the front door and put it back in its rightful place, drag the portable heater down from the *leerkamer* loft, where the Germans, thanks to the secret folding stepladder, had never been, because their searches had not revealed it. The heater they install back in the study. They cut turves of peat and fill a container full. Now they're lighting the stove. They want it to be the best it's ever been. It is warm and cosy in that room. The study has largely remained as before because of the large bookcase and corner sofa, as the limited furnishings that belonged to the *pastorie* were left where they were. On the walls also have been hung the paintings that were rescued, restored to their rightful places. Even the picture of the *Magere Brug!*

In a corner of the cupboard, I rediscover some of Domie's written sermons. They'd lain in a desk drawer and had been thrown to the floor during the raid. In his time early on as curate of a congregation under the smoky skies of Amsterdam, he had typed these out on the machine. Later, a few notes sufficed, and sometimes just the central Scripture text itself. But I am so happy with his detailed sermon notes! The sun is shining in the room, the stove is burning and I read the words of eternal life and hear again Domie's voice speaking to me. He is nearer to me here than anywhere else. It is therefore good to return to the *pastorie*, however much it resembles a hollow, empty shell. I search respectfully through the contents and arrange them in a reasonable semblance of order. How much of a spiritual inheritance he has left me! Enough to abundantly supply my whole future life. There is an unfinished sermon whose title caught my eye: *He that endureth to the end shall receive a crown of life.*[181]

I read what Domie has written on this topic and I am seized by a great desire to finish the sermon. But I understand that I have to complete it, not with words, but with the fruitful expression of my own life; that it is my task to endure to the end, and to continue what Domie and I had started together.

Our young helpers also felt a kind of nostalgic longing for their Domie. Frequently their thoughts and conversations turned in that direction, but even so, their boisterous youth could not be denied.

After finishing work on an early arriving evening, the boys sat at dusk in the study, while the girls emptied the contents of a box they found on the stage in the *leerkamer.* Inside they discovered masks, which they put on their faces and draped themselves around the head with pieces of green cloth. They looked like prehistoric monsters, and the boys started in to scare and chase them. But things turned out differently than they had intended, because in the hall they bumped into Hansje, who began to scream loudly. After that incident they no longer came into the study.

---

181 Composite text derived from Matthew 24:13 and James 1:12.

But how Domie would have enjoyed their fun and joined in! His own youthful spirit was tireless in inventing pranks. That was one of the reasons why he was so popular with the youngsters.

After about a fortnight of intense labour the ground floor of the house was once again rendered clean and habitable. Hayo, who rode along with the milk wagon every morning and evening, nodded approvingly and said that it was more liveable now that the curtains were up, and the others unanimously agreed with him.

In those days a wonderful surprise came our way via a wagon from a neighbouring church community, where the pastor had put together a few things for me. Stashed on top was a bedroom suite of furniture and safety pins for the baby's nappies. Also crockery, utensils and some linen. Precisely those things without which it is actually impossible to run a household. The preacher had spent three days at the Scholtenhuis. He had crawled through the eye of a needle in the process because he himself had harboured a downed British pilot. Thus he could identify with our plight.

Chapter 75

At last the children would now get back their own roof over their heads. Really our return was quite different than I had imagined, but I had to get through it all anyhow, and consequently, for the sake of the work and of the children, the sooner the better. Teaching the catechismal confession of faith and the work for various associations could now begin again, not at night however, but in the afternoon, because a curfew was still imposed and commenced at eight o'clock. On the first floor, there was a complete void; no signs of occupation anywhere.

I was not going to sleep up there. I would be still listening for that familiar step on the stairs, which never would sound again. Or for the creaking of the bathroom door, which would never be pushed open by Domie. I realise why these things are so; the subconscious mind does not accept truth and it holds on firmly to those familiar, habitual sounds. It awaits them, expectantly, listening intently.

Lily's feather quilt, which the Germans overlooked because it was packed in a box in the attic, now lies on my bed. Whenever I draw the covers back so I can get in, I see her shivering and shaking on her thin straw palliasse in the Polish camp. They took her away in her summer clothes, like they did Esther and Wil. If only Lily could have her quilt back! Those poor, poor captured Mice! Hunger and misery have been your lot! Poor, brave Wil! Sometimes I imagine a transport with Jews going to another camp and I see you there among them on open coal wagons, without nourishment in 20 degrees of frost, or I see a huge column of people plodding through the freezing cold along the icy roads. Every night I think of you, but I'd better pray that you would be freed from your suffering, for to this war comes no end... and in a Polish winter, as Jews in German captivity... I hardly even dare to think...

In the evenings we have oilseed lamps for lighting; the power station no longer supplies current through the mains. Not, at any rate, for the Dutch.

Our footsteps sound hollow throughout the empty house. Their sound seems amplified tenfold. Where last year at this time in January exuberant young voices rang out, there now sound only sinister echoes that really frighten us. Froukje and I have been by ourselves for months in the house, but we've never heard before this sound of boots upstairs over our heads, and boxes being shoved aside.

We listen at the bottom of the stairs and have become convinced that someone is stalking around up there. Someone who fancies that he is alone in the house now that it's become dark, because he doesn't have the slightest concern about needing to walk softly. For the past fourteen days the young people's cleaning squad has always left here for their homes about dusk. And so at that time he has his domain to himself, or so he thinks. He must have occupied the upstairs now as a squatter. Has he come to steal the few blankets and clothes that I have scraped together, or has he been hidden away here, perhaps for months already? Or is he perhaps a deserting German soldier, who has made a shelter for himself? Perhaps in one or another of the deep inbuilt wardrobes.

I considered this final option only after I called the *Veldwachter*[182] and some neighbours. Petertje came over as well with two of his older friends, and Froukje and Janny were there.

The *Veldwachter* even brought his son along. Or so he said. I went to the front door to see if it was true, because that son was an old acquaintance who used to come here often in the past to attend the

---

182 *Veldwachter* – literally "Field watchman" – a constable assigned duties in rural areas of the Netherlands before the war.

Youth Fellowship in the *leerkamer*, and in those days he had benefited a great deal from Domie's friendship and assistance. By the kerb I spotted three shadowy figures, who remained hesitant when they saw my silhouette in the doorway. One of them had boots on, just like the ones the Germans and the NSB wear. Don't they say that a criminal always returns to the scene of the crime?

I turned back inside without a word. The three dark figures must have followed me in and then disappeared upstairs, for I heard later that the little 'Kaiser' himself was now sitting up in the attic and had declared with much bravado that he dared to stay put for the whole night. *Ja*! Why not! That was the attic room of the Mice, whose presence he had betrayed. A bounty had been placed on each head. The more Jews he caught to be sent to be murdered in Poland or Germany, the richer he would become. And so such venal thinking always came back to that one big word, 'Money'.

It was a long time ago when he was last here at the *pastorie*. It was during winter – I forget which year. But it was a time when the Germans were making huge advances; that's when he became a recruit to their New Order. There was a new world coming, he believed, and he would be one of the solid pillars that supported it. He spoke about that to Domie, not about his chances therein, but about the envisaged 'New World' itself. It was on a Sunday evening and they sat around the stove in the study, the same stove that the boys had fetched once more from the loft above the *leerkamer* where it now stands. I had to keep an eye on the party the young people were holding in the *leerkamer*, and could only occasionally get a look into the study. The ongoing conversation did not appeal to me at all. It was about the NSB which this boy was keen to be a member of (or secretly was already?). Domie argued, cajoled, warned... but the oaf who sat cockily in the chair opposite, with a cigarette between his fingers and his knees wide apart, thought he knew better.

Endless, endless was Domie's patience. So endless that I got impatient. "Don't gabble on any longer. You can clearly see he's not going to do anything other than what he wants!"

Domie kept persevering, attempting to appeal to the good that he saw in this boy.

When I came out of the *leerkamer* one time, I overheard the little Kaiser loudly insinuating; "You *Domies* are all the same!" Quivering with indignation, I stormed into the room. "What did you say? Domie should take you by the scruff of the neck and throw you off the *stoep*!"

"You won't get anywhere with that," said Domie. He was right of course, but even he had reached an impasse with his tactic of peaceful dialogue. All his effort rebounded because it came down to the lad's hard-hearted unwillingness. The hours passed. The Youth Fellowship party had broken up and they had already long departed for home. It struck midnight, one o'clock, two o'clock...

I did not go to bed that night. We once had taken a long walk together, Domie and I. It was a lovely evening in the manor park, soon after we had met for the first time on the train. It was May. The blossoms freely gave out their scent, and nightingales sang in the ancient beeches of the forest of Rhijnauwen. Dew hung over the river meadows where cows stood still, dreaming. Suddenly, spontaneously, Domie made me a promise. "I'll protect you," he told me, his hands on my shoulders. He also stood still, and he spoke these words earnestly and solemnly. It sounded rather eccentric, because the world seemed so peaceful and good on that glorious evening in May. But in that still moment, when Domie suddenly spoke so convincingly and fervently, a frisson of impending danger brushed me faintly – as from afar.

I looked up at him solemnly.

"Against what?" I asked.

"I do not know. From everything that will threaten us in life," he said.

"That's what I also will do," I said. "I will also protect you."

And now, here in this study, the indefinable, which had already hung like a shadow over our recently endowed happiness, assumed a tangible form. It became so large and alive and real; it was in the form of the ever gaping mouth of this young man who spoke rapidly and angrily and hissed like an adder. The mouth which would betray. I stayed on then, because I didn't want Domie to be left alone, but desired to shield him from that lurking threat!

The glow of the stove died out and it became cold in the study. But that was not the worst of it. My heart had also turned frigid as I looked deep into an abyss of corruption, from which this boy seemed incapable of being saved, because he was so full of his own importance. He felt he could lecture us on how life was to be lived.

"That you can. But I think, if you really knew, that you would recoil from what you will face one day, if you take that road right to the very end," I said.

Alas! How true did these words come! Persuasiveness did not help convict him, nor bring dark things into the light. Neither did the *passion des ames,*[183] which Domie always inspired as a true pastor. This boy inwardly was being seduced along a path that would lead to his destruction. He was not to be held back. It was half past three when he finally stood up to leave. Domie gave him a book to read, *The Village on the Hill* by John Maarten.[184] Its story concerns the struggle of the German Church against Nazism, and centres on the fictional community of a small village named Lindenkopf, whose pastor is put in a concentration camp from which he never comes back.

When the little Kaiser returned the book with his thanks, he was wearing for the first time the 'Mark of the Beast' - the heraldic *Wolfsangel,*[185] on the lapel of his coat. He had become a fully- fledged member of the NSB. I was told that he behaved deliberately like an

---

183 The brotherly love of a friend.
184 Student Christian Movement Press, London (1940).
185 A heraldic image inspired by the pattern of a historic wolf trap, and adopted by the NSB.

innocuous teenager in order to let down the guard of anyone he talked with. You could certainly achieve more at the Scholtenhuis as a covert NSB member. To his undercover role testified the recordings of many phone conversations with the SD that were found in his house at the liberation. He also travelled extensively. His cover was provided by his job at the aircraft factory just across the German border.

Once Domie crossed paths with him while staying at a hotel in Amsterdam, where many Germans also took rooms. Domie routinely did that intentionally for camouflage. There he caught sight of the little Kaiser, but not vice-versa. It was a narrow escape! But what was the fellow doing there? Could it really be true that he travelled through town and province, all to catch Domie? According to his own words, the boy had only been sent out through the country to source caviar which was needed for a Nazi Party celebration at the aircraft factory, where one of the Party big-shots would be in attendance. But Domie was convinced otherwise; that he was being vigorously and secretly pursued, just as he'd previously been warned by special courier. It seems that the mysterious 500 guilders that were handed over to the little Kaiser on a dusky dim morning at the border railway station could not bear exposure to the light.

On one afternoon much later after all this happened, I rode my bike through the village with Hansje in the basket. A tall, lanky lad, who now looked more like a beaten dog, walked ahead of me leading two goats on a rope, which he tethered to the strip of grass in front of his house. Could it really be true, I thought, that this lout had done everything he could to take away my little boy's father? I suddenly found it all too incredible and impossible to fathom. Hansje pointed his little finger at the goats and babbled something in his childish language.

But right now the little Kaiser was sitting up there in the attic and playing the hero who dared stay there alone in the dark throughout the night. Later he went through the whole house and delved and probed in all the nooks and crannies and secret compartments. He must have felt extremely pleased with himself. Such a chance to take a look through the old *pastorie* from the inside had not earlier presented itself to him, who always preferred to do his murky work behind the scenes.

Our house had a strange, enigmatic history. Every evening, when it was finally quiet and dark inside, the strange sounds returned: the creaking of the loft stairs, the sliding of boxes, the tread of heavy boots. Were they the echoes that found their way to us from far away in Poland, and from the prison camp where the Mole was held? It was all so eerie and unsettling, that I decided to do my utmost to get to the bottom of it all; to trace the source of all these mysterious noises. The *Veldwachter* turned up to explain that in his opinion they were caused by rats. He had no more interest in the affair, and furthermore felt ill at ease in this empty house with all its memories.

But I still had one good friend to turn to. And that was the Chief. He had always avoided our house during the day, because that could spell danger for him. But if I rang him now, over in the neighbouring village... The last time he was here he brought us bad news about the arrest of Wil. That was nine months ago.

The doctor still had a telephone. From his house I called the military police barracks and gave the Chief my account of the strange happenings at home.

"Is it really necessary that I come right away, *Mevrouw*? Today I made a six hour trip on the bike in the wind and the rain, and I've only just arrived home dead tired... Are you sure it's not rats?" I called Eltjo as a witness, who had gone with me to check. "No, they are not rats," he said, "which do make a lot of noise but that is quite another thing. This sounds like the boxes are sliding around and there are heavy footsteps made by solid boots."

So our kind-hearted Chief set out once more, cycling through the wind and darkness. Equipped with a couple of bright torches, he went with his assistant to investigate upstairs and searched the whole house, in all the nooks and crannies and secret places, the entrances to which he was so familiar with. As we listened below the stairs, we heard an overwhelming series of noises, but as we went up, it died and we heard nothing.

"Let's go down again and have a listen in the cellar," said Janny.

"Listen down in the cellar again? Haven't you heard enough already?" said Petertje, rather irately.

"It's rats," said the Chief with generous laughter, when we were all once more gathered in the dining room. "They are rats, hear. Don't get anxious. This home has been empty for so long that they have now fully taken up residence here. When we go up to check with our torches, then they flee from the light and so of course we see nothing."

About Domie and about what had happened here in the last nine months we did not even speak. But we were both thinking about him.

I led him through the dark hallway and thanked him that he had still been so kind to come. *"Glück auf[86]"* I called, when I saw him off through the darkness and the rain. He had regularly come here to the *pastorie* at ungodly hours of the night like this one, often carrying a precious cargo on his bicycle; a real living person, whom he had brought safely home to our door. Yet I would never see him again. Because not long after this last visit, his 'lifeboat' would capsize and be wrecked during the ongoing stormy night of this war.

O, tossing barque 'neath Jesus' care,
His cross-flag high upon the mast,
All those who are in need are there
Within the ark. His power is vast.
Though this sea rolls so deep and high,

---

86 German for "Best of luck!"

And loud the storm that drives us on,
We have our Father's Son aboard,
At His rebuke the waves are calm.

The Chief also personally knew God's eternal security and was not afraid to die. And so to him was thrown the heavenly lifeline so that he arrived, with his life fully preserved, upon the safe strands of that "far coast".

But it was not rats after all. The noises were our own eerie echoes, which now sounded uncannily through the empty rooms and in the hollow cellar below the room where we were living and where the boys had broken a wooden partition, so that there now arose a strange, strong resonance which nobody had discovered, no youth members and no neighbours, no *Veldwachter* and no Chief, but which we, Froukje and I, discovered by chance one day.

Chapter 76

Now it is Sunday once more. The first Sunday at the *pastorie* after our homecoming. The morning sermon is being preached by one *Dominee* listed on the roster of preachers. Then Sunday School. I play the hymns on the organ, Domie's favourite instrument, even if it is only a two-manual pedal harmonium. How it must have cost him to have to relinquish his beloved church organ at Lochem! I still see him coming home that last Sunday when he had had to retire from his curacy appointment in Amsterdam.

That morning there was something strange with his alarm clock. It was supposed to wake him up at half past six, but at half past four, he awoke with a start, for he had dreamed that he had forgotten to wind it. In his dream the time was two minutes after half past six. Not enough time to get ready and make the usual seven o'clock train, which then pulled away without him aboard. Feeling fazed by such a vivid dream, he switched on the lamp beside his bed and looked at the clock. Indeed, it had not been wound. So he made sure of that and fell asleep again – only, with a shock, to actually wake up at six thirty-two, just at the same moment in his dream! So the train would now in reality depart without him. However, his clock actually read six thirty-seven, which showed that his subconscious had even taken account of the five-minutes his clock had been set deliberately ahead. The button, which you firmly press down to switch off the alarm, was in the down position. Therefore, the alarm had not even gone off at half past six.

"And here I thought that I, as a clear-headed Northerner, had no talent for such things," he told me.

"Don't you have subconscious thoughts, you silly boy? Here, eat your porridge up, or you will miss the eight o'clock train as well."

"No, that mustn't happen. Not on this, my last morning there."

Greet produced a packed lunch of fresh sandwiches to take with him. A dash to the corner of the canal, catch the line ten tram to Central Station, second platform, hop aboard the train and off to Lochem, to the church where his pupil had just finished playing the first chorale. Throughout that afternoon, he remained on the organ bench just to extract from this last experience "everything that I can get from it."

He also remained there to play for the evening service. Saddened at the final departure, he finally came home. It was as if he had lost a beloved friend. I comforted him as I would a child, but also felt the tears running down my own cheeks. What precious hours we had lived together there in the time of our first love! I told him that maybe he would someday be called to serve again in that beautiful part of the country, and then the organ would again be waiting there for him.

"*Ja*, but if I am pastor, I can't be an organist at the same time. I have to leave that all behind for good now."

"No, because you can still teach classes in harmony, perhaps even at one of the large organs here in Amsterdam."

Although in his heart this gave him new hope, he was just afraid that he might not be able to carry all that through simultaneously – that life would end up being much too short.

"I have so much to accomplish," he said, "and I'll never be ready."

I often thought that flaws in his character, which only I was privy to, found their cause in a personality gifted with too versatile a range of talents, thus creating an inner dissonance because the most contradictory things were equally represented in him. He had *a great musicality and surprisingly fresh style of improvisation, through a vivid imagination and wealth of chordal structure*, as his successor in Lochem explained when he wrote to me recently.

He also composed, but if he produced something new, he threw it carelessly away, as it usually comprised only a little melody that had begun to surge within him. Only his Christmas cantata, which he composed here for the youth, still exists in written form.

From his earliest childhood the railways had seized his full attention. Several times he had climbed up onto the footplate, and when it became apparent from his conversation with the driver that he was quite knowledgeable, he was allowed to ride on the engine. Once the driver suggested to him, "You are definitely bound for a great career, sir," and when the reply came, "No, I am actually a pastor," the other could scarcely believe it!

Next to his technical prowess was ranked his 'mystical talent,' for which reason, he moved school from the HBS[187] and enrolled in the Gymnasium,[188] because he had finally decided not to train as a railway engineer, but to become a preacher of the gospel. This choice probably catalysed his innate vagabond spirit that drove him away on long solo trips, in contrast to his customary yearning for the bright companionship of a cosy home. For he very much enjoyed the company of others when they were gathered with us in the *leerkamer* or in the living room.

From me he also wanted to have everything done all at the same time. He let me manage his extensive correspondence regarding lectures about Palestine etc., do his paperwork and a large part of the additional social church work within our parish. In addition, I had to always present a 'warm and happy' disposition. I found I could not always meet such expectations.

---

187 *Hogere Burgerschool* – Dutch Secondary School.
188 Grammar School for students intending to proceed to higher studies, such as University.

"You're asking for a sheep with five legs," I said, in jest. "But really, you know, I've got only four."

A richly rewarding marriage is not always an easy marriage. But how worthwhile it has all been!

To that substantial Groningen predilection for austerity he matched a sensitivity to the Heavenly realm. Last year he shared an example of this after our Christmas dinner, when we had all the extended family together in the study. In a small hamlet in Hungary, he had attended a church service. He himself spoke there through an interpreter. At the end of the service he had a strong conviction that he had to part with the last of his cash and place it all in the church collection as a gift to God. But that was a very risky venture; he had nothing left. It was towards the end of the month, so in a couple of days I could telegraph part of my salary, but where would he live for those two days? Yet he had done it because he was convinced that it was the right thing to do. That afternoon he saw a small party of Hungarians coming toward him: two girls and a boy, who helped him push his heavily loaded bike up the mountainside. Along the way they naturally fell into a conversation. When they had reached the top, the young people told him,

"In our country we have a tradition that when we meet a stranger who we find is friendly toward us, we give him one of the coins we have in our purse, as a kind of lucky coin. No, you must not refuse to take it, because it's one of the good traditions of this country that you are passing through."

And a moment later he had several coins in his hand, which, when he afterward calculated their value, represented exactly double the amount that he had previously given in the church. He stood there for a moment, stunned at the outcome. He had dared to risk living by God's faith. He had also dared to risk dying by God's faith. In that last act too he had given up all that he missed the most. And I am convinced that this final journey has been the greatest adventure of his life, which is why he came through it undaunted.

From the ends of the earth to the feast stream through
O ye countless heroes who are faithful and true.
...sing the children round the organ.

Now a big lump forms in my throat. His hands will never again touch these keys. They lie still, outspread.

Well done, thou good and faithful servant: thou hast been faithful over a few things, I will make thee ruler over many things: enter thou into the joy of thy Lord.[189]

I speak of the parable of the talents. When I am absorbed in my work, in his work, then everything is fine. But when I am alone with the children on that first Sunday afternoon back home in the *pastorie*, I am seized by a sudden panic attack. I can hardly stand the jabbering of Hansje. "Mama, I'm de baker. Will you buy a li'l loaf?" And I see through the window the white snow blanketed garden with the hill that Domie made during the excavation of the bomb-shelter. Through the back door, I visualise his tall figure entering the kitchen with his hat on, which still hangs in the hallway. I've just taken a look at that hat. The impressions of his fingers are still there; I can see the slight indentations. Outside, children are skating; gliding along on the ice of the neighbours' canal. His children... from the Sunday School and the catechism classes. When they grow up, they will forget Domie.

"Well you mustn't cry," said Hans. "Papa is coming back soon. He's coming to play with me, with de train. Dere is Papa al'eady." And he points out the side window. Really, the tall man on the bike does bear a striking resemblance to Papa. When Hans sees the alarm clock again, the one that went on the long journey to Palestine and also into hiding with Domie in Amsterdam, he comments, "Dat mus' go by Papa's bed."

---

189 Matthew 25:21.

And if he comes across to our spare bedroom, he says, "Here's where Papa sleeps..." and points to the spot where six months ago Domie's bed still stood. A wooden desk that Domie had constructed at my flat in Amsterdam during our engagement had been left behind up in the loft by the Germans. The youth carried it down for me and put it in the study, in place of the old one. When Hansje comes into the study, he says, "Papa al'ays sits dere, hè? Behin' de desk."

I am grateful that he remembers it all so well and I press him again to my heart. That other big boy for whom I have an all-consuming passion will never come back, but he has left me these two little boys. They may never fully make up for my loss. There will always be a longing in my heart to hear his footsteps, to be close to his figure, within the circle of his loving, embracing arms. The desire for our reunion will never be extinguished, and I will also nurture that in my own children. In Hansje, who knew him and considered him as his best playmate. "Close chums," he stammered, half asleep, when he saw his father on one of the last nights they were together. And then for little Dikkie, who still smiles in blissful ignorance. But this book will tell him of his father.

Dear Jesus, make me worship thee,
That I in Heaven come to be.
...Hansje prays at night in his bed.

And the youth sing in their afternoon meeting:

Blest are those who die in Christ,
The ones who inherit Heaven.
For whom He has prepared a home
After nights of grief and pain.
For them doth rise th' eternal dawn,
Immortal life is now their own.
They rest in peace,

Set free from strife,
Hallelujah!
Before the throne, where stands His Son,
Their glorious reward is given.

Blessed are the righteous ones that sleep,
Too soon before full ripening,
But who at God's appointed hour
The end of His last days,
The Father's house do enter in,
Like ripe fruit to their harvest home.
They live by Him,
And sin no more,
Hallelujah!
It's finished and the night is o'er,
God's Kingdom reigns in might and power.

Thanks, worship, praise and glory sound
To thee, O Prince of life!
An anthem sung by Thy redeemed;
Blessed to have overcome.
Let praise arise unto the King!
The lamb for us was slain!
For us, He stepped into the grave.
His goodness wipes away
Our flowing tears.
He led the way through death's dark vale,
On Heaven's path we follow.

For the youth that is their Domie, who has marked a luminous trail to Heaven by which they can follow. Domie has always joked that his parishioners were so slow in following their shepherd. "But they will come," he said. "Even if you do not expect them to, they will still come," for in the end, a Groninger always exceeds one's expectations.

And he would say to me, "I have the feeling that I shall never leave here, but shall remain as *Dominee* until my dying day." And the Mice once commented, laughing, when I went upstairs to see them, "Domie's hair will turn grey here."

Grey, he never became, but he certainly remained here until his death, and in truth he also never departed from this, his first and only congregation.

Chapter 77

To this nightmare that we call war, an end has finally come. A very unreal and anticlimactic end.

On a May morning back in 1940, at the dawn of the day, we were startled by the roar of German airborne divisions flying overhead. The first German ground troops invaded our border shortly after that; a few scouting outriders on their bikes, everywhere spying for the soldiers who themselves arrived armed to the teeth, and carrying a grenade in each hand, ready to throw them. We had got dressed and were standing on the *stoep* in front of our house.

Wo ist die Schule?[190] they shouted to us, whereupon we turned our backs and retreated inside. A feeling of nameless dread kept me feeling trapped.

And so it had begun.

Now, it is 16 April, 1945. I am standing again on the *stoep*, but this time I am standing there alone. There was some exchange of fire, short but intense. Then the fast Canadian tanks rumbled past. And it became quiet once more. We have been liberated. People came out of their hiding places and looked rather surprised in the broad light of day. This is an April afternoon lit by a hazy sun. The tower clock has stopped at five minutes past two; the moment when it was shot to pieces.

Now it has to come, even for me. The whole atmosphere already spoke of expectation and for days in advance hundreds of people have

---

190 "Where is the school?"

been passing through here already, all of whom have come back over the border, heading for home. Now it was really all over. Now Domie would also come home!

To wait... by day and by night. The call of spring is irresistible and always fills us with an indescribable longing. The silence of the night envelops me. I lie and listen for the familiar footsteps on the stairs. Am I awake or dreaming? Surely he has to come now! Or is he busy with his sermon? It is the night of Saturday through to Sunday morning. Could he have fallen asleep downstairs over his sermon notes? I once found him with his head slumped on the hood of the typewriter. Could that have happened now? I must go to him, but something holds me back. I lie, still waiting... There is a pulsating silence around me. Finally I overcome the invisible restraint that keeps me here, and I slip gently into the darkness and down the stairs.

I listen at the study door. Not a sound. My heart is bursting. Would he be there – behind that door? I gently turn the door handle and slip inside. The reading lamp is lit and Domie is sitting behind the desk. A feeling of inexpressible happiness seizes me, but he puts a forefinger to his lips. That's why we must whisper, as Hansje is sleeping directly above, because it's a quarter past one. I approach him, but there is something, just as in those few moments ago, that holds me back.

"I thought you had fallen asleep over your sermon," I say. I stand beside the desk, illuminated by the desk lamp. The corners of the room are hidden in shadow.

"I must tell you something," he says. "I can't stay with you for long."

I sigh... it's the same old story. I have to yield him up once again.

The last few times I met up with him, it was almost always at night and then he had to be away before the dawn overtook us.

"When will we be together? At last... and forever?" I ask. "Peace has now truly come."

He shakes his head. "Here on earth there is never peace," he says.

"You're still right in the midst of the earthly battle. But you must be brave and persevere. I'm counting on you."

"You always respond that way when we have to say goodbye."

"Ja, you've always done those things that I did not manage to get to... and now there remains so very much more to await fulfilment, so much unfinished, but for all that I'm counting on you again."

"But we can't live without you – the children and I can't and neither can our church."

At my words, he smiled. "I'm not really leaving you," he said. "Did Stephen ever really depart from the first Christian church? The blood of the martyrs is indeed the seed of the Church. What my life could never achieve, God now will perhaps do through my death and so I will not have died for nothing."

"For nothing! Think of all the lives you've saved! Sometimes people ask me if it was worth the price."

"Whoever is constrained by the love of Christ, does not count the cost," he said. "Someone once hung on a cross. He was a Jew. He hung there for us, for Aryans, for you and for me. Were we worth it? That Jesus died for us?"

I lay back down in my bed. In the silence of the night I heard soft music. The music of Handel. *He that endures to the end, shall receive the crown of life.* Again and again I hear that music, when life looks so bleak and the road seems endlessly long and arduous.

And midst the battle strife, and suff'ring long,
Sounds from afar the victor's joyful song,
Gives to the heart its courage ever strong,
Hallelujah!

Hail company of saints in joy and pain!
We now in weakness robed in brightness reign,
And heart to heart we're bound with His love's chain,
Hallelujah!

Lightning Source UK Ltd.
Milton Keynes UK
UKHW012141191121
394209UK00001B/20

9 781911 473763